SANZAR
Saga

BOB HOWITT

Harper*Sports*
An imprint of HarperCollins*Publishers*

National Library of New Zealand Cataloguing-in-Publication Data

Howitt, Bob, 1941–
SANZAR saga : ten years of Super 12 and Tri-Nations rugby /
Bob Howitt.
ISBN 1-86950-566-2
1. Super 12 (Competition)—History. 2. Tri-Nations (Competition)—History.
3. Rugby Union football—Tournaments—History. I. Title.
796.33365—dc 22

Harper*Sports*
An imprint of HarperCollins*Publishers*

First published 2005
HarperCollins*Publishers (New Zealand) Limited*
P.O. Box 1, Auckland

ISBN 1 86950 566 2

Cover design by Darren Holt, HarperCollins Design Studio
Cover photographs by Fotopress
Internal text typesetting by Island Bridge

Printed by Griffin Press, Australia, on 79 gsm Bulky Paperback

Contents

Acknowledgements

SANZAR SAGA was completed right on the final whistle thanks to the input and co-operation of several champion individuals.

I am hugely indebted to Sydney journalist and author Peter FitzSimons, who granted me unrestricted access to his wonderfully enlightening book published by HarperCollins in 1996, *The Rugby War*, without which the introductory chapter would have been a monumental undertaking.

Campbell Burnes, the talented features editor of *Rugby News*, kindly assisted with the compilation of Tri-nations match descriptions, in the process proving that he, too, is skilled at meeting tight deadlines, while Dianne Haworth, my co-author of *Rugby Nomads*, *All Black Magic* and *1905 Originals*, came up with glowing portraits of several of the Tri-nations personalities.

The book would certainly have not been as accurate or as enlightening without the invaluable contribution from NZRU statistician Geoff Miller, who, amazingly, provides the answer to every rugby question you throw at him. And I threw more questions at him to field than Byron Kelleher throws passes in a training session. The fascinating facts associated with each Super 12 season were all supplied by the walking encyclopaedia that is Geoff.

Margaret Mitchell, managing director of Rugby Press International, kindly granted me unrestricted access to the back files of *Rugby News*, while Gerhard Burger and Paul Dobson in South Africa and Barry Ross and Brumbies media manager David Pembroke in Australia answered all the curly questions that were posed them regarding the Springboks and the Wallabies. New Zealand's first Super 12 commissioner, Peter Thorburn, was a valuable source of information also. All the photos that appear in the book are from the files of Fotopress whose gifted principal photographer Ross Land has been on the international rugby trail for at least three decades.

Bob Howitt
Auckland, September 2005

Introduction

FOR RUGBY ENTHUSIASTS in New Zealand, Australia and South Africa, it's hard to imagine a Friday evening from the tailend of February until late May without at least one cracking game of Super 12 being beamed into your lounge. And that's not all, of course, because exotic contests — part of the same competition — feature on the screen every Saturday and Sunday morning throughout that same time frame.

Tens of thousands of dedicated rugby enthusiasts in the three countries design their whole weekends in March, April and May around Super 12 matches. It's the thing to do. And in July and August the rugby world is focused on the Tri-nations championship as the All Blacks, the Springboks and the Wallabies strive for Southern Hemisphere (and, many would claim, therefore, world) supremacy.

It didn't used to be like this. March and April used to be pretty desolate months for rugby addicts in the Southern Hemisphere. If it was live footie action you were after in Australasia, you had to focus on the league's Winfield Cup, the biff-and-bash game that ruled the roost in most Australian cities outside Melbourne. No wonder so many Kiwi kids were running around in Canberra Raiders and Brisbane Broncos jerseys.

Rugby administrators Down Under became anxious when they realised how many footie followers were hooking into league ahead of their own game. It wasn't hard to understand why: for about the first three months of each winter season, league was serving up exciting live contests on television, and rugby wasn't.

Rugby tried to counter with a Super 10 competition that pitted the champion provincial teams of New Zealand, Australia and South Africa against each other, but, although it gave the sport's fanatics something to focus on through April and May, television didn't get too enthused over the competition and league continued to flourish.

Then in 1995 came the revolution, after which neither code would be quite the same again. Rupert Murdoch's News Corporation was entirely responsible for the most profound changes in both codes. On league's side, much to the chagrin of previous backer Kerry Packer, the Winfield Cup was supplanted by the NRL, with players' salaries tripled and quadrupled. That was remarkable enough, but not as earth-shattering as the transformation that rugby underwent. Virtually overnight, the game metamorphosed from amateur to professional. Players, who had previously haggled for travel expenses and survived on a modest daily allowance while sacrificing wages, were now suddenly being awarded salaries in excess of $150,000 and $200,000.

News Corporation's massive investment — US$550 million over 10 years — spawned the Super 12 and Tri-nations competitions. No longer would rugby administrators puzzle over how to attract the public's attention through the balmy summer months of March and April and on into the thick of the rugby season. Now they had not one, but two, competitions that would quickly become the envy of the sporting world.

SANZAR Saga vividly recounts the drama and subterfuge that was played out before the three-nation entity that is SANZAR was formed, and captures the excitement, heroism and sensations of a complete decade of Super 12 and Tri-nations action. All the leading personalities from the three nations are profiled, every Tri-nations game is featured along with the Super 12 semi-finals and finals, and there is a wealth of statistics. With Super 12 about to become Super 14, *SANZAR Saga* provides a timely and appropriate chronicle of an epic chapter in rugby's evolution.

How SANZAR was born

THE HUNDREDS OF THOUSANDS of New Zealanders who dragged themselves from their warm beds in the middle of the night in June 1995 to watch the All Blacks crush England in the World Cup semifinal at Cape Town would have recognised long before the final whistle that they were witnessing a true sporting phenomenon: Jonah Lomu.

What they wouldn't have realised, couldn't have realised, was that his remarkable performance would have a profound effect upon their beloved game, in a manner none of them could have ever imagined. For beyond the fields of action in South Africa, where the game's greatest showpiece was being played out, a cloak-and-dagger struggle was unfolding for the right to administer, on an international scale, the great game of rugby.

Lomu's heroics at Cape Town would help save the game for the establishment. If that sounds exaggerated, know that among the millions watching the game around the globe was Rupert Murdoch, the boss of News Corporation in Sydney, whose company was considering a proposal jointly presented by rugby administrators from Australia, New Zealand and South Africa, calling themselves SANZAR, to fund two new southern hemisphere competitions (that would become the Super 12 and the Tri-nations).

Negotiations had stalled somewhat over the amount of money News Corporation was prepared to put up. The SANZAR group, advised by Ian Frykberg, the chief executive of Communications Services International, a London-based international brokerage house for television rights, had valued their product at US$650 million for 10 years, a figure at which Sam Chisholm, the head of Murdoch's global television empire outside the USA, had baulked. The two parties were plainly still some distance apart at the time Jonah the Giant made try scoring look as easy as pulling on a jersey. Within hours of the completion of the game at Cape Town, Murdoch telephoned Chisholm.

'That was amazing,' said Murdoch. 'We've got to have that guy.'

'I agree,' replied Chisholm. 'That was the most electrifying thing I have ever seen in sport.'

Chisholm promptly contacted Louis Luyt, whom the SANZAR group had appointed as their chairman, and suggested Luyt get himself from Johannesburg to London pronto, because he was ready to approve News Corporation's funding. The amount he offered, and which Luyt accepted, was US$550 million for a decade of exclusive worldwide television and radio rights.

It was a breathtaking amount of money being committed to a sport that at that precise moment in time was still amateur. But the winds of change were building to gale force in rugby. Professionalism was inevitable if the game was to survive as an élite sport internationally. The major southern hemisphere nations, if not all their northern hemisphere counterparts, recognised this.

Rugby had been under assault on two fronts — from Super League, which on a scale of 10 probably presented a threat equalling about 3, and from a Sydney-based group calling themselves World Rugby Corporation (WRC), who threatened to not only contract most of the world's leading players but to literally hijack the game. Fronted by former prominent Sydney businessman and former Wallaby Ross Turnbull, WRC, if successful in their objectives, would usurp the power of the International Rugby Board (IRB). On a scale of 10, their level of threat extended to about 12!

So precisely how did all this come about?
Super League started it all in 1995. Well, more accurately, News Corporation, eager for the television broadcasting rights for league that belonged to Kerry Packer's company, started it all by launching Super League, winning over all the leading (league) players by offering them four times what they were previously earning. Rugby recognised the ominous implications. The New Zealand Rugby Union (NZRU) had yielded the occasional player to league down the years — as had South Africa — but it had never been a source of concern. They knew the All Black jersey was the greatest dissuader for anyone contemplating playing for money. But if league scouts were to come offering salaries of $300,000 and beyond, that put an entirely different complexion on matters.

NZRU's chairman in 1995, Richie Guy, realised that his union had to offer the All Blacks a realistic income. A working committee had concluded $5 million was necessary if the union was to contract up to 150 players. 'The problem,' said Guy, 'was where that money was going to come from.'

Across in Sydney, Wallaby icon Simon Poidevin, who also identified the danger signs for his beloved game, contacted a colleague of his at the BSkyB offices in London, Sam Chisholm, inquiring if News Corporation might be interested in buying into rugby as well. 'Just because we've signed with league doesn't preclude us dealing with other sports,' he told Poidevin. Chisholm's door was obviously open.

Around this time, Guy spoke to the All Blacks, indicating that rugby was advancing quite rapidly towards professionalism and inquired what size salaries the players considered realistic. The answer was in the region of $100,000 to $150,000.

When leading officials from Australia and New Zealand met in April to discuss how to combat Super League — blissfully unaware at that stage that WRC, a far more ominous threat, had been formed — they agreed rugby needed a competition with international appeal.

New Zealand promoted a Sky TV proposal pitting the leading six provincial teams in New Zealand against the two best teams in Australia. The Australians weren't particularly enthusiastic, arguing it would not generate enough funds to pay the players. Any worthwhile southern hemisphere competition, they felt, had to involve South Africa. It was agreed that both nations would work towards the Perfect Rugby Product (PRP), involving Australia, New Zealand and South Africa, which once formulated would be offered to News Corporation. Both bodies also agreed to work towards an announcement that amateurism as a concept for rugby was outmoded.

That PRP was hatched during a brainstorming session in Brisbane involving Queensland CEO Terry Doyle, New South Wales CEO David Moffett and Australian Rugby Union CEO Bruce Hayman. They devised a competition embracing five teams from New Zealand, four from South Africa and three from Australia to run from March to May, to be known as the Super 12. After the three nations then played their inbound international fixtures, in June–July, they would confront each other annually, on a home-and-away basis, a Tri-nations event. The desirability of this PRP was that it allowed the NPC in New Zealand and the Currie Cup in South Africa to continue in existing form with only minor overlapping.

In New Zealand, David Galvin, Richie Guy and Rob Fisher came up with a similar concept, except that their three-nation provincial competition involved 16 teams.

The South Africans were kept informed of developments but not pressured for input because they were hosting the third World Cup, scheduled to kick off in late May, and had quite enough to worry about.

About the same time that the All Blacks and the Wallabies were flying to South Africa — on the same plane, funnily enough — to commence their World Cup preparations, a delegation of officials from Australia and New Zealand headed to the UK to talk with Chisholm. Representing New Zealand were Richie Guy and Rob Fisher and alongside them were Dick McGruther and David Moffett from Australia. Ian Frykberg also attended the meeting.

Their concept was well received by Chisholm, who suggested they should come back to him once the competition was formulated. He felt they should work towards wrapping up a deal by the end of the World Cup. In the meantime, they should keep quiet about it. In case they didn't fully understand that, he said that if he read one word about it, the whole deal was off.

Around this time, while the leading southern hemisphere nations were advancing post haste towards professionalism, knowing it was the only way to preserve the game, the secretary of the RFU, Dudley Wood, issued this statement in London: 'We believe we are running a sport as a recreation for players to play in their spare time. I think money is a corrosive influence.' Plainly, Dudley didn't have a clue about the imminent threats to his game.

The biggest threat of all, hazy details of which were just beginning to filter through to the rugby bosses in New Zealand, Australia and South Africa, came from WRC, the organisation spawned in Sydney

It was a lawyer working for the business advisory firm of Wentworth Associates, Geoff Levy, who while considering options that might allow Kerry Packer to fight back against Rupert Murdoch's audacious new Super League competition, first conceived a professional worldwide rugby competition. Levy felt that because rugby was truly international, whereas league had status in only a handful of countries, there was enormous potential to develop the game.

He approached Ross Turnbull, the former test prop, former Wallaby manager and former chairman of the New South Wales Rugby Union, outlining his concept, and asking if Turnbull might be interested in getting involved. Would he what! Turnbull was totally enthused, declaring Levy's idea for an international professional rugby competition to be his destiny. He threw himself into the project wholeheartedly and in double-quick time came up with a plan to create three professional rugby 'conferences' that would operate from March to October each year, involving all the major rugby nations of the world. Turnbull believed he could structure it in such a way that the existing amateur unions would become part-owners of the competition.

To level out the playing strengths, each country would be restricted to a squad of 30 players. The surplus would be divvied up among the minnow nations. So you could have, say, half a dozen high-quality New Zealanders despatched to play for Japan or the United States. Turnbull perceived their competition would effectively produce a World Cup winner annually. He wanted the players to have a greater input than they did under the existing amateur structure. And he was confident that with the massive salaries on offer, they would have no problems contracting players from around the globe.

Of course, there was the matter of financing the project, but Levy and Turnbull were optimistic that the Packer organisation, desperate for a product that would allow them to strike back at Murdoch's News Corporation, would buy into it. Turnbull's initial planning suggested it would cost US$229 million to set up, but the first year would return US$209 from marketing and merchandising rights, ticket sales and, most importantly, television rights.

Packer's organisation considered it, liked it, but said they didn't want to get directly involved until such time as Levy and Turnbull's new professional organisation, which was about to register itself as the WRC, had won over the necessary players.

The NZRU chairman, Richie Guy, was never going to the World Cup. A farmer at Waipu, north of Auckland, he had commitments back home. But the whole developing rugby issue was so important and urgent that Moffett convinced him that, following their meeting with Chisholm in the UK, he should accompany him to Cape Town. There they met with Louis Luyt and Leo Williams, agreeing to form a company with two directors from each of the participating nations, Australia, New Zealand and South Africa. Luyt was appointed chairman and Moffett made CEO. On the recommendation of Frykberg, they agreed the deal they would offer News Corporation should be for 10 years, not five.

Whereupon, Moffett and Luyt flew back to see Chisholm in the UK. They proudly presented their concept for the Super 12 and Tri-nations competitions. The asking price, they said, was US$650,000. Chisholm loved the concept, not the price. They would renew their negotiations at a later date.

Just what price Chisholm would have countered with had the World Cup progressed unspectacularly, with the New Zealand–England game a boring kick-fest (like the play-off for third between England and France), will never be known. But thanks to Jonah the Giant, who stampeded over, round and through Englishmen with spectacular effect in the semifinal at Newlands in Cape Town, becoming the talk of the sporting world, the men of SANZAR now had a marvellously marketable product.

So thanks to Jonah's impeccably timed performance, Chisholm agreed to a 10-year deal worth US$555 million, incremental payments as follows: 1996, $32 million; 1997, $43 million; 1998, $46 million; 1999, $48 million; 2000, $52 million; 2001, $57 million; 2002, $61 million; 2003, $66 million; 2004, $72 million; 2005, $78 million.

One significant clause in the contract gave News Corporation considerable powers. It read: 'SANZAR shall . . . ensure that all matches are convened and scheduled to maximise the value of televisions rights. Without limiting the generality of the foregoing, News shall have the right of veto over schedulings and match timings although such right shall not be exercised unreasonably or capriciously.'

After Chisholm and Luyt had signed the contract and shaken hands, Chisholm introduced a note of urgency. 'Make sure you get all those players signed up . . . immediately.' At that precise moment, Luyt didn't anticipate too many difficulties in doing so.

The formation of SANZAR and the declaration of two marvellous new competitions, Super 12 and Tri-nations, to be funded by News Corporation for a cool US$550 million, were revealed at a press conference in the trophy room at Ellis Park on the eve of the World Cup final.

The media were so stunned by what Louis Luyt had just announced that none of them noticed that down below on the stadium surface, about 28 hours before kick-off in the World Cup final, ashen-faced All Blacks were taking their traditional stroll around the match venue, several of them so weakened by food poisoning they could scarcely summon the energy to remain upright. A couple of the players actually threw up.

Australia, New Zealand and South Africa were receiving US$5.7 million, collectively, for television rights in 1995. That would soar to $32 million in 1996, a staggering amount for a game that was ostensibly still amateur. Luyt blissfully assured the media gathering that the money would be used for rugby development but, following the formal announcement, other officials from SANZAR nations speculated that this would undoubtedly hasten rugby's advancement towards professionalism. And how!

If the officials who had been involved in putting together the SANZAR deal thought its announcement would blow WRC out of the water, they were wrong. Levy and Turnbull would claim they were, in fact, buoyed by the developments, for now they could show prospective investors that rugby really was a powerful international product in which it was worth investing vast amounts of money.

In the weeks before the World Cup final — won in the most dramatic fashion, in extra time, by host nation South Africa — and in the days immediately following, WRC's agents were busily signing up players all around the globe. Pretty soon, they had the bulk of the World Cup squads of South Africa, Australia, New Zealand, France and Samoa committed to their cause.

It was a monumental coup for Turnbull and co to secure signatures (of intent) from the world champion Springboks, along with the All Blacks, the Wallabies and the French, arguably the four strongest teams in the world at that moment. What the players found appealing about the WRC concept, besides the massive salaries being talked, was that the players would be involved in running the competitions.

WRC had maintained great secrecy as they had gone about signing up players throughout the rugby world. Turnbull believed once he could reveal the mass commitment of players from the major nations, rugby administrators would have no alternative but to buy into their product.

Back in New Zealand, the All Blacks were entertained at a parliamentary reception, after which they were ushered back to NZRU headquarters where chairman Guy addressed them and said that as a consequence of the SANZAR deal he could guarantee them $150,000 a year for three years with individuals possibly able to negotiate higher amounts. To his dismay, the All Blacks appeared totally underwhelmed. And no wonder, for WRC was talking salaries of four times that amount. Sean Fitzpatrick would later say, 'It was a bit of a laugh.'

The first official confirmation that WRC was making rapid progress and represented a major threat came when former Wallaby Michael O'Connor, representing Murdoch, lobbed into South Africa hoping to sign a few Springboks for Super League. The players he approached declined with thanks because, one said, they had more tempting offers in front of them. Initially, O'Connor thought he'd been beaten to the punch by Australian Rugby League, until one Springbok spilled the beans. A rebel rugby organisation, headed by Ross Turnbull, and backed by Kerry Packer, was offering players massive contracts to participate in a new professional rugby competition.

When O'Connor reported his findings to his bosses back in Sydney there was obvious concern, and these concerns deepened when Ian Frykberg advised that from his inquiries it was obvious WRC was making major inroads into the three SANZAR nations particularly. And that put the new competitions in jeopardy.

Richie Guy knew things were getting serious when, with News Corporation's encouragement, he offered the All Blacks, through their captain Sean Fitzpatrick, NZ$300,000 a year for three years, and Fitzpatrick turned it down. 'I couldn't believe it,' said Guy, 'and still can't.' Fitzpatrick was quoted by Peter FitzSimons in his book *The Rugby Wars* as saying that the All Blacks were committed to the WRC concepts for reasons other than the financial bottom line.

Following the Bledisloe Cup contest in Auckland, Mike Brewer, the All Black loose forward, in conversation with Rob Fisher, intimated that the players were committed to 'another organisation'. Fisher asked why they couldn't wait until the IRB meeting at the end of August when drastic changes to the amateurism regulations would be made. 'Fish,' said Brewer, 'I hope you enjoy the last meeting of the International Rugby Board.'

As news of WRC's progress was relayed to Chisholm at News Corporation's headquarters, he accused the national rugby unions of Australia, South Africa and New Zealand of 'going to sleep at the wheel'. Plainly they had not heeded his warning to get all the players signed quickly. He summoned to his house in Sydney the three chairmen of the SANZAR countries plus David Moffett (from the New South Wales Rugby Union), Ian Frykberg and Jim Fitzmaurice (both from Communications Services International) and Bruce McWilliam (Chisholm's lawyer) and told them they had to get 'their arses into gear'. They had to start offering the players a fair dollar. 'By offering them the money you have been, you're jeopardising this whole deal. We did a deal and you have not delivered what you promised.'

From the establishment's vantage point, the plot worsened when, in late July, the Packer Organisation PBL agreed to come 'on board' with WRC for an initial outlay of A$4 million. It gave PBL an option to acquire majority ownership of WRC. The deal was structured so PBL could feed in money progressively and take a greater control each time. The money provided credibility for WRC and much-needed capital (although the company had always been telling the players they'd signed that 22 November was when they would have the funding in place to get the whole show up and running).

The NZRU heeded the warnings and staged an emergency board meeting in Sydney on the morning of the second Bledisloe Cup test. Jock Hobbs chaired the meeting. 'Unless we take action immediately,' he said, 'this may well be the last time this body meets as a significant force of New Zealand rugby.'

The board gave Hobbs and his fellow negotiators, Brian Lochore and Rob Fisher, authority to launch an immediate counterattack. It would start with a letter addressed to each All Black personally, that Lochore, one of the most admired and respected rugby individuals on the globe, would personally deliver to the players after that day's game.

The test was won handsomely by the All Blacks with Jonah Lomu again a commanding individual. At the cup presentation following the game, ARU president Phil Harry concluded his comments with these words: 'This is the end of the season and in many ways is the end of an era. Let me say this . . . that sort of spectacular, passionate game between two nations is something that money can't buy.'

When Phil Kearns then spoke, as Australian captain, he wound up his words with, 'And whatever happens in the future we hope you and the union support us.'

En route to the test dinner that evening, the All Black players insisted their bus stop at the Vaucluse home of Kerry Packer's managing director Brian Powers. All Black manager Colin Meads, who was most uncomfortable about the whole thing, and coach Laurie Mains remained in the bus while the players were presented with contracts that would legally commit them to WRC from that moment. Only four players, including Jonah Lomu, declined to sign.

Through the early days of August, the fate of rugby hung in the balance. Would the establishment, which plainly had public sentiment behind it, retain its grip on the game, or would it yield to WRC?

In South Africa, Louis Luyt confronted the Springboks. A powerful individual, in all senses, he assured the players that neither the South African Rugby Union nor the Transvaal Rugby Union would ever do a deal with WRC. So if they thought by signing with WRC they would ever play on Ellis Park again, they were wrong. If it meant fielding Transvaal's C team, he would do it. Plainly, he made an impression on the younger players, who realised a commitment to WRC meant they could never be Springboks again.

In Australia, Phil Harry and Ian Ferrier confronted the Wallabies individually, doing their best to discredit WRC while tempting the players with offers of around A\$250,000 for a full season. And each player was asked whether there was anything they had signed that prevented them from signing a contract with the ARU.

In New Zealand the negotiating team of Hobbs, Lochore and Fisher, plus the CEO of the All Blacks Club, Iain Abercrombie, were hurrying about the country desperately seeking to sign up provincial players. They weren't giving up on the All Blacks — who were Abercrombie's specific target — but they were grimly determined to retain the rank-and-file player.

As the Springboks were the recently crowned world champions, there was a feeling that whoever won the battle to sign them would ultimately win the war. No Springbok was feeling the heat more than Francois Pienaar, who was obviously torn between the two causes and who, because of all the pressure, was looking terrible, not at all like the beaming Bok captain who had held the World Cup aloft at Ellis Park back in June.

WRC sensed that the South African players were in danger of reneging on their signings under pressure from Louis Luyt, so they decided to hold a video link-up involving several leading players from each country so they could all reassure themselves that what they were doing was the right thing. Back at WRC headquarters in Sydney, Geoff Levy was so confident that everything would come together, he was working on a press release. The release would embody glowing comments from Francois Pienaar, Phil Kearns and Sean Fitzpatrick, the three SANZAR captains. Levy was counting on a satisfactory discussion via the video link-up and also on WRC receiving substantial financial backing the following day from South African television channel M-Net.

The press release never got past Levy's desk. Sometimes rugby teams lose from seemingly impregnable positions when events go seriously awry. And that was about to happen to WRC.

Unbeknown to Turnbull, who organised the video link-up, Pienaar had fielded a call from Sam Chisholm. Speaking from the UK, Chisholm convinced Pienaar that attending the video hook-up that day would be entirely the wrong thing for him and his country. He emphasised that WRC, for all their mighty planning and bravado, had no money. They were still negotiating for it. Chisholm convinced Pienaar that he had to do the right thing for rugby because the rugby world was counting on him. The video link-up would represent a pivotal moment in the whole professional rugby war. Everyone who should be there was there . . . except for Pienaar, to the dismay of Turnbull.

The show went on. Sean Fitzpatrick and several other All Blacks were in a studio in Auckland, Phil Kearns and a cluster of Wallabies were in a studio in Sydney, and a bunch of Springboks were in a studio in Johannesburg. But not Pienaar. The All Blacks and the Wallabies spoke positively of WRC. Sixty-four New Zealanders were signed up, including 23 World Cup squad members, and 60 Australian players were committed. The Australian number would soon swell to 90.

So now the focus swung to Johannesburg. To the surprise of those viewing in Auckland and Sydney, Hennie le Roux was speaking on behalf of the Springbok players. He apologised for Pienaar's absence, saying he had been under immense pressure.

Le Roux didn't match Fitzpatrick and Kearns' positivity. All he said was that they were putting in their best endeavours and he was certain the best contract on the table would win the day. Then Tiaan Strauss spoke up. He said they needed a little more time to sort out the contracts coming from SARU and from 'the other people'. He said they wanted to ensure they made the best deal for the players.

Very obviously the South Africans were not as committed as the Australians and the New Zealanders, leaving a lot of people annoyed and concerned. Fitzpatrick was extremely angry, although not as angry as Ross Turnbull, who'd been sitting in the background of the studio in Johannesburg, fuming from the moment he realised Pienaar wasn't going to front. He would tell Peter FitzSimons for his book *The Rugby War* that it was 'the most bloody pathetic performance by a group of sportsmen I'd seen'.

If that was a setback, so was M-Net's failure to front for the business meeting at which they were going to commit themselves to a business arrangement with WRC for a substantial amount of money, in the order of US$18 million. They never got back to WRC. If M-Net had come up with that funding, even allowing for the Springbok players' prevaricating, it's almost certain WRC would have gone ahead. It seems, however, that Sam Chisholm had been on the phone again!

Friday, 4 August, was D-day for the world-champion Springboks. The contracts, worth US$250,000 a year for three years, being offered by the South African Rugby Union expired at 5 p.m. *Either you sign now, guys, or your contract will be torn up*. SARU officials said they appreciated that the players had signed contracts with WRC, but very obviously WRC hadn't fronted with any money, and those contracts were still in the possession of Francois Pienaar. *They're in his car outside. The condition on which SARU will engage you is that you must first hand in your WRC contract.*

Before midday all the Springboks, with a couple of odd exceptions, had signed, allowing the union's CEO Edward Griffiths to announce to the press the following day that, 'The threat to rugby in this country has been thwarted. We have faced the rape of rugby in this country and withstood it.'

Turnbull refused to accept defeat; instead, he came out with all guns blazing. At a press conference, he said he expected the WRC contracts to be honoured. 'I think the atmosphere within the administration of rugby in South Africa is surrounded by threats, intimidation and misinformation. Rugby should be above that. Rugby players around the world have generously embraced the vision of WRC and have made commitments accordingly.' Although he didn't announce it at the time, Turnbull intended to take SARU to court for breaching the WRC contracts.

Meanwhile, back in Australia the experienced Wallaby No 8 Tim Gavin had signed with the ARU, the first current international to break ranks.

Around this time a letter was published in the *Sydney Morning Herald* signed by 13 former Wallaby captains, including such legendary figures as Nick Farr-Jones, Ken Catchpole, Mark Loane, John Hipwell, John Thornett, Tony Shaw, Mark Ella and Simon Poidevin.

It was a long letter, but in essence it implored the current Wallabies to reconsider their decision to sign with WRC. 'We older players beseech you not to be swayed,' they wrote. 'We who are retired realise more than ever what a precious honour it was to play for the Wallabies. We believe the traditional game will continue and it would be a tragedy if all of us were deprived of your unquestionable talent and guts and the pride you have engendered in us all.'

Turnbull won a minor battle back in Cape Town where he presented to the court a 40-page affidavit claiming Francois Pienaar was promised $300,000 once he handed over the Springboks' contracts and that SARU had brought enormous pressure to bear on the Springboks to return to the establishment. The judge granted an interim injunction to WRC, forbidding SARU from having contact with any players in South Africa already contracted to WRC until the following Thursday, when he would examine the issue more fully. The ruling allowed Turnbull to talk to anyone he wanted to, while SARU was rendered powerless for five days.

Back in New Zealand the establishment was about to make a major breakthrough. Jock Hobbs and his hearty assistants had won over the provincial rugby players of Auckland, Counties, Waikato, Wellington and Otago. Representatives of each of those teams were on their way to Wellington Airport where Hobbs was convening a press conference to let the country know that the establishment was fighting back. By chance, the entire Otago team would be present, en route to Te Kuiti for an NPC game against King Country. Hobbs knew that two vital members of that Otago team, Jeff Wilson and Josh Kronfeld, were considering signing with the NZRU.

The Otago players were each handed NZRU contracts before they departed Dunedin, to read and digest on the flight. They all signed, except for Wilson and Kronfeld. Waiting at Wellington Airport was sports lawyer David Howman, acting for the NZRU. He took the contracts as the players handed them across. Then came the two All Black stars and for 20 minutes they chatted. Howman told them they would be national heroes if they signed and that they would be helping to save New Zealand rugby. Finally, they too signed the contracts.

Hobbs' press conference went ahead. It wasn't just good news he was about to deliver. It was bloody fantastic news . . . Jeff Wilson and Josh Kronfeld had committed themselves to the New Zealand Rugby Union. Hip, hip, hooray!

Daggers had been plunged into the WRC heart in South Africa and New Zealand. And almost simultaneously in Australia another dagger would deliver the ultimately fatal blow. It would be delivered, ironically, by James Erskine, head of IMG Australia, the company that had a powerful business relationship with the Australian Rugby Union. Erskine had been invited along by Phil Kearns to present an alternative viewpoint to those players who had signed contracts with WRC. Before committing themselves finally, Kearns, for one, felt it was important to hear arguments both for and against. Geoff Levy would present the case for, Erskine the case against.

Erskine did such a demolition job on WRC, there were almost no pieces left for Levy to pick up. Having studied WRC's proposals, he estimated they would lose US$80 million the first year, probably $40 million the second year and something between break-even and $30 million the third year. Packer wasn't prepared to put up that sort of money, and WRC itself was worth $2. After Erskine and Levy had finished, the players decided to form a seven-man committee to analyse both arguments and report back within a fortnight.

In Cape Town, after a typically aggressive attack upon WRC by Luyt, and following an adjournment, the judge lifted the injunction against SARU and ruled that the matter 'be struck from the roll'. Another major setback for WRC.

The indefatigable Turnbull battled on in South Africa, signing up provincial players and continuing to pursue the funding that was needed for his 'destiny' to materialise. That funding would never be forthcoming.

Once Wilson and Kronfeld committed themselves to the NZRU, others followed. Because Fitzpatrick and co, who genuinely believed WRC's set-up was for the greater good of rugby and the players, had always said it was a case of all or nothing, they were not prepared to commit themselves to the NZRU.

And so it came to pass on a Monday morning in Wellington, not at NZRU headquarters but at the Airport Travelodge, that all the would-be revolutionaries, overseen by Jock Hobbs, contracted themselves to the NZRU. They were given assurances that there would be no recriminations against them for their involvement with WRC and that the Players Committee would be re-formed.

Hobbs and Fitzpatrick then appeared on television to confirm to the nation that normality was about to return to rugby. Well, as normal as the grand old amateur game could be with all its national heroes now contracted for upwards of $200,000. Which, of course, raised a delicate point . . . rugby was still an amateur game.

With the Springboks and the All Blacks abandoning the WRC concept, suddenly there was little future in the rebel organisation for the Wallabies. They too signed with the establishment, but where New Zealand and Australia rigidly declined to acknowledge WRC's involvement, in Australia the players' signing was presented as a compromise situation between ARU and WRC.

Before the tumultuous month of August was ended, the International Rugby Board would declare the game professional. After more than a century of stringent amateurism, where a player could be banned for accepting royalties or pocketing unreasonable expenses, players could now make a living from the game. It was the only realistic decision the IRB could make.

To the immense relief of Sam Chisholm and News Corporation, the show could go on. The red carpet could be rolled out at the start of the 1996 season, ushering in two fantastic new competitions, the Super 12 and the Tri-nations.

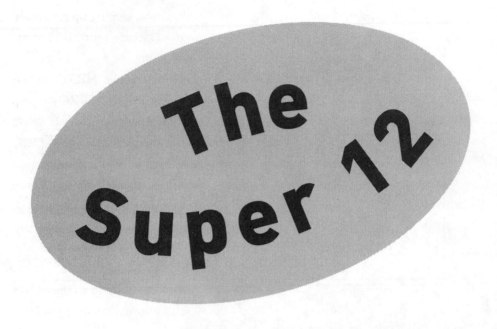

IN AUGUST 1995 THE INTERNATIONAL RUGBY BOARD
declared the game professional. After more than
a century of stringent amateurism, where a player
could be banned for accepting royalties or pocketing
unreasonable expenses, players could now make
a living from the game.

1996

THE SUPER 12, FUNDED BY NEWS CORP boss Rupert Murdoch's mega millions, was daringly innovative when it was launched in 1996, for suddenly the premier rugby players of New Zealand, Australia and South African were professionals.

The competition was completely different to anything that had functioned within rugby before, and each country went about preparing for it their own way. South Africa simply decided the four premier teams in its Currie Cup provincial competition would represent it in Super 12; Australia not unnaturally gave its three slots to the strongest rugby states, those based in Sydney, Brisbane and Canberra; while the New Zealand Rugby Union (NZRU) set about establishing five franchises.

Four were obvious, going to the major metropolitan cities of Auckland, Wellington, Christchurch and Dunedin, but the fifth somewhat controversially went to Hamilton. Because All Black test teams of the time were dominated by players from Auckland and North Harbour, which operated on either side of the Auckland Harbour Bridge, the NZRU decided to separate the two, even though they were, metaphorically speaking, joined at the hip.

And so while Auckland was paired off with its southern neighbour Counties Manukau, North Harbour found itself lumped in with Bay of Plenty, King Country, Northland, Thames Valley and Waikato. It was an 'arranged marriage' that, inevitably a few years down the line, would end in divorce.

If the NZRU had left it to the individual franchises to select their original squads, civil war could have broken out; instead, it intelligently appointed a Super 12 commissioner, former All Black selector Peter Thorburn, to ensure an equitable distribution of talent.

With input from each franchise, he compiled an initial list of more than 250 players which he distributed to the leading selector/coaches of the time — Laurie Mains, Earle Kirton, Ross Cooper and John Hart — inviting them to independently rate the players in each position. From those rankings the inaugural pool of 125 players, who became contracted to the NZRU, was established.

Delighted Blues players congratulate Charles Riechelmann after his try in the final against Natal.

Fotopress

The competition kicked off with lots of razzmatazz at the unlikely venue of Palmerston North where the Wellington Hurricanes, with the home advantage, made all the play, only to be swamped in the dramatic final few moments by the Auckland Blues who, a dozen outings further on, would take out the inaugural event in style.

Graham Henry's men had something of a roller-coaster ride before exerting their authority at the business end of the competition. They remarkably rebounded from a 51–13 hammering from the Queensland Reds in Brisbane and losses in Canberra and Johannesburg to score an epic victory over the Ian McIntosh-coached Natal in Durban, which secured them an all-important home semifinal.

The home advantage was most significant throughout the initial Super 12, underlining the enormity of the Blues' achievement in winning in Durban.

John Connolly's Queensland Reds, featuring such international superstars as John Eales, Ben Tune, Tim Horan and Jason Little, had also beaten Natal in Durban and by qualifying top were in the luxurious situation of having home advantage for the semifinals and, most anticipated, for the final. But Connolly's team were spectacularly derailed in Brisbane by Natal, which unexpectedly handed the Blues the home advantage for the final.

Coached by Vance Stewart and captained by Richard Loe, the Canterbury Crusaders, who would go on become one of the dominating sides of the Super 12, had an appalling debut year. They lost eight of their 11 matches and conceded 50 points to the Reds, Transvaal and Natal, eventually finishing a humiliating last.

THE STARS

JOELI VIDIRI (Auckland Blues)

With a name like Joeli Vidiridirinatabua Nalewavada he was bound to make an impact when he forsook Fiji and began playing rugby in New Zealand.

But neither Joeli Vidiri, which he adopted as a stage name, nor the Counties Manukau administrators who persuaded him to display his talents in New Zealand, could ever have imagined he would begin destroying opponents and wowing audiences as emphatically as he did.

With dazzling pace that belied his muscular build, Vidiri began running in truckloads of tries, initially for Counties Manukau in the NPC and then in 1996, when the Super 12 kicked off, spectacularly for the Auckland Blues.

The Vidiri magic that would produce 10 tries in 10 outings and consistently challenge opposition defences would lead to him being named the first New Zealand Super 12 Player of the Year.

From a tiny village in the Fijian highland area of Nausori, Vidiri had first caught the attention of New Zealand rugby judges when he toured with the Fijian team in 1994. Just a few months later he was playing for the Counties Manukau NPC team, on the opposite wing to another emerging superstar, Jonah Lomu. Within a year he had become a vital member of the New Zealand sevens team and in 1996 he was in the right place at the right time when the Auckland Blues were contracting players for Super 12.

While the inaugural Blues squad was dominated by players from the champion Auckland NPC team, Graham Henry and co were delighted to welcome into the fold the two fliers from Counties Manukau. Vidiri and Lomu became instant crowd-pleasers.

ANDRÉ JOUBERT (Natal)

England coach Jack Rowell once famously branded André Joubert the 'Rolls-Royce of fullbacks'. It was an appropriate description, for through the World Cup of 1995 and the Super 12 of 1996, when Joubert was at the peak of his powers, there was no more complete fullback on the international stage.

That Graham Henry's Auckland Blues were forced to devise special tactics for the 1996 Super 12 final to 'close him down' is testimony to Joubert's greatness. He arrived at Eden Park boasting 11 tries and 102 points for the series, and although the Blues contained him pretty effectively he still managed to run in another try.

A glance at Joubert's scoring achievements for 1996 reveal that he amassed 30 points in his team's thrashing of the Waikato Chiefs and scored tries in eight of Natal's 13 outings, including two each against the Otago Highlanders and Queensland Reds. He aggregated 107 points for the series.

Chester Williams, in his biography, would write of Joubert that he was one of the most natural athletes that he had ever seen on a football field. 'He always had time when fielding the ball,' said Williams, 'which is the trademark of a good player. His vision on the field was without comparison, his left boot was among the best in the game, and he had a presence on attack. One of his greatest strengths was that he could counterattack effectively with the boot. The manner in which he used to mix up his grubber kicks with his counterattacking always meant the opposition was in two minds when kicking the ball to him.'

Fotopress

That Natal scored 47 tries in round-robin play had much to do with the impetus Joubert provided from fullback. Not insignificantly, Natal's three-quarters James Small, Cabous van der Westhuizen and Joos Joubert collectively accounted for 22 of those tries. Of the season's 56 tries, Joubert accounted for 30: an outstanding statistic.

A mature 32 in 1996, Joubert grew up in the Free State, initially preferred cricket to rugby and only began to take rugby seriously while studying at Free State University.

THE FACTS

The first Super 12 game was between the Wellington Hurricanes and the Auckland Blues at the Showgrounds Oval, Palmerston North, on 1 March 1996. It was refereed by Paddy O'Brien.

The first try was scored by Alama Ieremia of the Hurricanes; the first conversion and the first penalty goal were kicked by Jamie Cameron of the Hurricanes; the first dropped goal went to Andy Miller of the Canterbury Crusaders; and the first penalty try was credited to the Auckland Blues against the Crusaders.

Travelling across the Indian Ocean proved a major challenge for teams in the first Super 12. New Zealand and Australian teams played 16 matches in South Africa for five wins and 11 losses, while in their 16 matches in Australasia, South African teams fared even worse, registering just three wins and a draw against 12 losses.

The Waikato Chiefs squad included five players who had locked an All Black scrum — Mark Cooksley, Steve Gordon, Ian Jones, Blair Larsen and Glenn Taylor. A further three players who had played lock for Waikato were drafted to other franchises.

The 39 points Jannie Kruger scored for Northern Transvaal against the Otago Highlanders at Pretoria was the most any player from any country had scored against any New Zealand team in first-class rugby.

All Black Ian Jones scored three tries for the Waikato Chiefs against the New South Wales Waratahs. This was the first time a New Zealand lock had achieved a hat trick of tries since Alan Sutherland did it for the All Blacks against ACT at Canberra in 1968.

James Small of Natal was the leading try scorer in the inaugural Super 12 with 13, a figure that was beaten only by the anonymous 'penalty try', there being 14 of them.

THE FIRST SEMIFINAL
NATAL 43, QUEENSLAND REDS 25
AT BALLYMORE, BRISBANE, 18 MAY

With New Zealand-born halfback Kevin Putt the star, Natal pulled off an upset of monumental proportions in overwhelming the top-qualifying Queensland Reds at Ballymore. Unbeaten at home throughout the series and having downed Natal 21–20 in Durban a fortnight earlier, John Connolly's Reds were hot favourites to advance to the final. But fleet-footed individuals like Putt, fullback André Joubert and wingers Cabous van der Westhuizen and James Small never let the Reds into the game.

The Reds fans were stunned into near silence. Only briefly during the second half, when Queensland pulled up from 8–29 to 18–29, did the crowd become vocal. But the Natalians finished the stronger, scoring two late, spectacular tries to secure a most emphatic victory.

Queensland coach Connolly admitted to being 'shell-shocked' at the way the game unfolded. 'We made too many mistakes, which you cannot afford against a team of Natal's calibre.' The result was a shattering blow both to Connolly and the Queensland officials, who were anticipating a bonanza from staging the final a week later. Chock-full of Wallabies, the Reds had taken out the Super 10 finals in 1994 and 1995 and it was almost taken for granted they would advance to the final, given the not inconsiderable advantage of playing in tropical Brisbane.

In one of the more unusual happenings in 1996, Transvaal underwent a change of coach. World Cup hero Kitch Christie started out as the team's mentor, but after a disastrous, winless sequence of matches in New Zealand and Australia, and with his health failing, South African rugby boss Luis Luyt forced him to resign. His surprise replacement was Alex Wyllie, who had enjoyed success with the Eastern Province Currie Cup team. Under 'Grizz', Transvaal scored three notable victories at Ellis Park against his ex-countrymen Waikato Chiefs, Canterbury Crusaders and Auckland Blues.

But it wasn't to be. Putt, who was approaching his 31st birthday and whose provincial debut (for Otago) dated back to 1984, was too much for the Queenslanders to handle as he consistently probed the blindside. His crisp passing, pinpoint kicking and quick thinking caused the Queenslanders no end of trouble.

Throughout the match Natal made clever use of the blindside from scrums and rucks, and it was Putt who invariably instigated these raids. It was an inspired decision by Natal coach Ian McIntosh to replace winger Joos Joubert at the last minute with Cabous van der Westhuizen, the speedster racing in for three tries.

The Queenslanders plainly missed midfielder Jason Little, who was injured. But few would have expected the team to be 24–3 down approaching half-time after having first use of a fresh breeze. A try by Queensland hooker Michael Foley right on half-time that made the score 8–24 gave his team a glimmer of hope, but that was instantly cancelled out upon the resumption when André Joubert scored for Natal.

FOR NATAL: Tries by Cabous van der Westhuizen 3, André Joubert 2, Jeremy Thomson and Wickus van Heerden; conversions by Joubert 2 and Henri Honiball 2.

FOR QUEENSLAND REDS: Tries by Tim Horan and Michael Foley; penalty try; 2 conversions and 2 penalty goals by John Eales.

NATAL: André Joubert, James Small, Jeremy Thomson, Dick Muir, Cabous van der Westhuizen, Henry Honiball, Kevin Putt, Gary Teichmann (captain), Wickus van Heerden (replaced by Dieter Kriese), Wayne Fyvie, Steve Atherton, Mark Andrews, Adrian Garvey, John Allan, Ollie le Roux.

QUEENSLAND REDS: Tyron Mandrusiak, Ben Tune, Daniel Herbert, Tim Horan (captain), Paul Carozza, Elton Flatley, Brett Johnstone, Mark Connors, David Wilson, Toutai Kefu, John Eales, Garrick Morgan, Tony Daly, Michael Foley, Dan Crowley.

REFEREE: Paddy O'Brien (New Zealand)

CROWD: 23,000

The unlikely kicker of the first conversion for the champion Auckland Blues team was Zinzan Brooke in the inaugural game at Palmerston North. Less than impressed with his team's goal kicking, he finally demonstrated how to do it. It was the only place kick he landed in a long and distinguished first-class career.

THE SECOND SEMIFINAL
AUCKLAND BLUES 48, NORTHERN TRANSVAAL 11

AT EDEN PARK, AUCKLAND, 19 MAY

If evidence was needed of the awesome regard in which opponents held Jonah Lomu, who was at the peak of his powers in 1996, Northern Transvaal provided it by placing crack halfback Joost van der Westhuizen on the wing to mark him in this semifinal. The strategy predictably failed — there was scarcely a player in the world in 1996 who could contain Jonah the Giant — and van der Westhuizen at half-time was switched to halfback, where he should have been all along. By then, his team was out of contention against a super-slick opponent that was decisively superior in all aspects of play.

Lomu, who hadn't seen a lot of action in previous matches, used his fabulous attacking skills to score two tries, a tally that should have been matched by fellow wing Joeli Vidiri. But in a bizarre act, not appreciated by his coach Graham Henry, Vidiri gifted a try to team-mate Robin Brooke with a daring in-goal pass. Vidiri was about to touch down near the corner flag when he looked across and saw Brooke pointing to the goalposts. 'Because a Northern Transvaal player was advancing towards me,' he said, 'I didn't feel I could get there, so I threw the pass and said, "Score it yourself!"'

Brooke accepted the bonus five-pointer, which was converted by Adrian Cashmore and said to Vidiri, 'Thank you, bro.' Henry wasn't so complimentary. He later described Vidiri's pass as 'absolutely bloody ridiculous, quite frankly'. Asked if the move had a code name, Henry said, 'Yes — stupidity.' Vidiri preferred to describe the move as 'a little Fijian magic'.

Jonah Lomu heads for the goalline at Eden Park. Fotopress

Notwithstanding that moment of rashness, Vidiri managed one try, taking his 1996 haul to 10 from just eight outings.

The Blues produced scintillating rugby (an adjective used by Henry after the match) to demoralise the Northern Transvaal players, who had extended the Blues to 26–30 on their earlier visit to Eden Park.

'We were outplayed from the start,' admitted Northern's classy skipper Ruben Kruger. The tempo at which the Blues operated overwhelmed the South Africans, who couldn't assemble their defenders rapidly enough as Zinzan Brooke's men came at them in droves.

Given a flying start by their forwards, the Blues backs were in sensational mood, tackling hard and running incisively, repeatedly ripping open the Northern Transvaal defence.

FOR AUCKLAND BLUES: Tries by Jonah Lomu 2, Joeli Vidiri, Adrian Cashmore, John Ngauamo, Junior Tonu'u, Robin Brooke and Sean Fitzpatrick; 4 conversions by Cashmore.

FOR NORTHERN TRANSVAAL: Try by Conrad Breytenbach; 2 penalty goals by Jannie Kruger.

AUCKLAND BLUES: Adrian Cashmore, Joeli Vidiri, Eroni Clarke, John Ngauamo, Jonah Lomu, Lee Stensness, Junior Tonu'u, Zinzan Brooke (captain), Andrew Blowers, Dylan Mika, Charles Riechelmann, Robin Brooke, Olo Brown, Sean Fitzpatrick, Craig Dowd.

NORTHERN TRANSVAAL: Theo van Rensburg, Joost van der Westhuizen, Jannie Claassens, Danie van Schalkwyk (replaced by Braam van Straaten, replaced by Dawie du Toit), Hannes Venter, Jannie Kruger (replaced by Robbie Rein), Conrad Breytenbach, Adriaan Richter, Schutte Bekker, Ruben Kruger (captain), Krynauw Otto, Johan Ackermann, Marius Hurter, Andries Truscott, Frikkie Bosman.

REFEREE: Wayne Erickson (Australia)

CROWD: 42,000

Tim Horan, who achieved international renown as an inside centre, captained the Queensland Reds in their two matches in New Zealand, at Dunedin and Wellington, from fullback. Preferred in the midfield were Jason Little and Daniel Herbert.

THE FINAL

AUCKLAND BLUES 45, NATAL 21

AT EDEN PARK, AUCKLAND, 25 MAY

Auckland Blues coach Graham Henry pinpointed the planning and execution of events against Natal in the round-robin fixture at Durban a fortnight earlier as the key to his team's triumph in the inaugural Super 12 final.

'If we hadn't won at Durban,' said Henry, 'we would have been playing our semifinal back there seven days later, and I don't believe we would have won the title in those circumstances.' The 30–23 win in Durban was a masterpiece of strategic planning, which carried over into the final at Eden Park.

Henry had identified line-out specialists Mark Andrews and Steve Atherton, running flyhalf Henry Honiball and multi-talented fullback André Joubert as the greatest threats to his team. So he devised special tactics to neutralise them. The Blues forwards didn't jump on Natal's line-out throws (commonplace now, but revolutionary in 1996), stopping Natal's powerful forward drives. And Michael Jones was deployed to close down Honiball.

The tactics worked stunningly in Durban and, while modified for Eden Park, ensured Ian McIntosh's high-flying Natalians, a team chock-full of Springboks, never got a sniff of victory. Only late in the first spell, when Natal bounded back from 3–20 to a half-time score of 16–20, were the Natalians genuinely competitive. But two Blues tries immediately after half-time soon had Henry's men in charge again.

An analysis of the statistics would never lead one to believe the Blues won this game by six tries to two. Through the mighty leaping of Andrews and Atherton, Natal claimed the line-outs 18–7, while the penalty count favoured the visitors 18–10.

So how did the Natalians finish so far adrift? Answer: because of the attacking genius of players like Jonah Lomu and Carlos Spencer, the ferocious

Twenty-four of the 29 players who made appearances for the Auckland Blues in 1996 scored points for their team.

defence of 'Iceman' Jones, the inventiveness of Henry's side and the alarming number of turnovers made by Natal.

The Blues' originality was never better exemplified than in the creation of their first try, one sweetly finished off by Andrew Blowers. When Lomu was moved into the line-out, it was obvious where the ball would be thrown. Well, that's what the Natalians thought. But Sean Fitzpatrick caught them napping by throwing short to halfback Junior Tonu'u. He flicked the ball back to Fitzpatrick, who burst along the sideline and set up the try for Blowers.

The Blues' aggressive defence stung Natal. Jones, Blowers and Zinzan Brooke, regularly working in pairs, halted many of Natal's budding attacks. It was vintage Jones, a performance to rank with some of his mightiest displays of the 1980s, and it won him the man of the match award.

The superstar of the backline was Lomu, who blitzed Joubert in scoring his try and caused the visitors endless problems throughout.

FOR AUCKLAND BLUES: Tries by Andrew Blowers 2, Jonah Lomu, Eroni Clarke, Carlos Spencer and Charles Riechelmann; 3 conversions and 3 penalty goals by Adrian Cashmore.

FOR NATAL: Tries by André Joubert and James Small; conversion and 3 penalty goals by Henry Honiball.

AUCKLAND BLUES: Adrian Cashmore, Joeli Vidiri, Eroni Clarke, John Ngauamo, Jonah Lomu, Carlos Spencer, Junior Tonu'u, Zinzan Brooke (captain), Andrew Blowers, Michael Jones, Charles Riechelmann (replaced by Jason Chandler), Robin Brooke, Olo Brown, Sean Fitzpatrick, Craig Dowd.

NATAL: André Joubert, James Small (replaced by Joost Joubert), Jeremy Thomson, Dick Muir, Cabous van der Westhuizen, Henry Honiball, Kevin Putt (replaced by Robert du Preez), Gary Teichmann (captain), Wickus van Heerden (replaced by Dieter Kriese), Wayne Fyvie, Steve Atherton, Mark Andrews, Adrian Garvey, John Allan, Ollie le Roux.

REFEREE: Wayne Erickson (Australia)

CROWD: 46,000

Three South African teams, Western Province, Transvaal and Northern Transvaal, had the dubious distinction of landing more penalty goals than they managed tries in the first season of Super 12. The only other team to finish in the negative was bottom-placed Canterbury Crusaders.

THE RESULTS

QUEENSLAND REDS
(coach John Connolly)

lost to	Otago Highlanders at Dunedin	17–57
beat	Waikato Chiefs at Brisbane	26–22
beat	Canterbury Crusaders at Brisbane	52–16
beat	Wellington Hurricanes at Wellington	32–25
beat	Northern Transvaal at Brisbane	25–18
beat	Western Province at Brisbane	36–26
beat	New South Wales Waratahs at Brisbane	15–13
lost to	ACT Brumbies at Canberra	20–21
beat	Auckland Blues at Brisbane	51–13
beat	Natal at Durban	21–20
beat	Transvaal at Johannesburg	25–16

Won 9, lost 2; placing: 1st
Tries scored: 35

Semifinal: lost to Natal at Brisbane 25–43

Most tries: Ben Tune 8, Tim Horan 5, Garrick Morgan 5
Most points: John Eales 155, Ben Tune 40

NORTHERN TRANSVAAL
(coach John Williams)

beat	Natal at Pretoria	30–8
beat	New South Wales Waratahs at Pretoria	32–29
beat	Otago Highlanders at Pretoria	59–29
lost to	Queensland Reds at Brisbane	18–25
beat	Canterbury Crusaders at Christchurch	34–18
lost to	Auckland Blues at Auckland	26–30
lost to	Waikato Chiefs at Hamilton	9–17
beat	Transvaal at Pretoria	25–15
beat	Wellington Hurricanes at Pretoria	38–20
beat	ACT Brumbies at Pretoria	23–10
beat	Western Province at Cape Town	35–7

Won 8, lost 3; placing: 3rd
Tries scored: 31

Semifinal: lost to Auckland Blues at Auckland 11–48

Most tries: Adriaan Richter 4, Theo van Rensburg 4
Most points: Jannie Kruger 142, Lance Sherrell 45

AUCKLAND BLUES
(coach Graham Henry)

beat	Wellington Hurricanes at Palmerston North	36–28
beat	Canterbury Crusaders at Christchurch	49–18
lost to	ACT Brumbies at Canberra	34–40
beat	Western Province at Auckland	48–30
beat	Otago Highlanders at Pukekohe	51–29
beat	Northern Transvaal at Auckland	30–26
beat	Waikato Chiefs at Auckland	39–31
lost to	Queensland Reds at Brisbane	13–51
beat	New South Wales Waratahs at Auckland	56–44
lost to	Transvaal at Johannesburg	22–34
beat	Natal at Durban	30–23

Won 8, lost 3; placing: 2nd
Tries scored: 56

Semifinal: beat Northern Transvaal at Auckland 48–11

Final: beat Natal at Auckland 45–21

Most tries: Joeli Vidiri 10, Andrew Blowers 8,
Jonah Lomu 8, Eroni Clarke 7
Most points: Carlos Spencer 84, Adrian Cashmore 79,
Joeli Vidiri 50

NATAL
(coach Ian McIntosh)

beat	Western Province at Durban	28–22
lost to	Northern Transvaal at Pretoria	8–30
beat	Waikato Chiefs at Durban	63–25
lost to	ACT Brumbies at Canberra	31–44
beat	New South Wales Waratahs at Sydney	34–6
beat	Wellington Hurricanes at Wellington	43–27
lost to	Otago Highlanders at Dunedin	32–33
beat	Canterbury Crusaders at Durban	58–26
beat	Transvaal at Durban	49–13
lost to	Queensland Reds at Durban	20–21
lost to	Auckland Blues at Durban	23–30

Won 6, lost 5; placing: 4th
Tries scored: 47

Semifinal: beat Queensland Reds at Brisbane 43–25

Final: lost to Auckland Blues at Auckland 21–45

Most tries: James Small 13, André Joubert 12, Jeremy
Thompson 7, Cabous van der Westhuizen 5
Most points: Henry Honiball 138, André Joubert 107,
James Small 68

ACT BRUMBIES
(coach Rod Macqueen)

beat	Transvaal at Canberra	13–9
beat	Wellington Hurricanes at Canberra	35–28
beat	Auckland Blues at Canberra	40–34
lost to	New South Wales Waratahs at Sydney	10–44
beat	Natal at Canberra	44–31
lost to	Waikato Chiefs at Whangarei	18–26
beat	Canterbury Crusaders at Christchurch	29–7
beat	Queensland Reds at Canberra	21–20
lost to	Western Province at Cape Town	16–25
lost to	Northern Transvaal at Pretoria	10–23
beat	Otago Highlanders at Canberra	70–26

Won 7, lost 4; placing: 5th
Tries scored: 37

Most tries: Joe Roff 7, Mitch Hardy 6, Ipolito Fenukitau 6
Most points: Adam Friend 66, David Knox 50, Joe Roff 42

NEW SOUTH WALES WARATAHS
(coach Chris Hawkins)

beat	Transvaal at Sydney	32–11
beat	Western Province at Cape Town	30–22
lost to	Northern Transvaal at Pretoria	29–32
beat	ACT Brumbies at Sydney	44–10
lost to	Canterbury Crusaders at Christchurch	16–21
lost to	Natal at Sydney	6–34
lost to	Queensland Reds at Brisbane	13–15
beat	Otago Highlanders at Sydney	29–25
lost to	Waikato Chiefs at Hamilton	17–39
lost to	Auckland Blues at Auckland	44–56
beat	Wellington Hurricanes at Sydney	52–25

Won 5, lost 6; placing: 7th
Tries scored: 36

Most tries: Alistair Murdoch 8, Matt Burke 5,
Jason Madz 4, David Campese 4
Most points: Matt Burke 157, Alistair Murdoch 40

WAIKATO CHIEFS
(coach Brad Meurant)

beat	Canterbury Crusaders at Hamilton	27–26
lost to	Queensland Reds at Brisbane	22–26
lost to	Natal at Durban	25–63
lost to	Transvaal at Johannesburg	23–26
beat	Western Province at Hamilton	44–17
beat	ACT Brumbies at Whangarei	26–18
beat	Northern Transvaal at Hamilton	17–9
beat	Otago Highlanders at Invercargill	22–5
lost to	Auckland Blues at Auckland	31–39
beat	New South Wales Waratahs at Hamilton	39–17
lost to	Wellington Hurricanes at Rotorua	15–23

Won 6, lost 5; placing: 6th
Tries scored: 32

Most tries: Glen Osborne 4, Eric Rush 4
Most points: Ian Foster 95, Warren Burton 47

OTAGO HIGHLANDERS
(coach Gordon Hunter)

beat	Queensland Reds at Dunedin	57–17
beat	Transvaal at Dunedin	29–15
beat	Western Province at Cape Town	52–25
lost to	Northern Transvaal at Pretoria	29–59
lost to	Wellington Hurricanes at Dunedin	15–44
lost to	Auckland Blues at Pukekohe	29–51
beat	Natal at Dunedin	33–32
lost to	Waikato Chiefs at Invercargill	5–22
lost to	New South Wales Waratahs at Sydney	25–29
beat	Canterbury Crusaders at Christchurch	29–27
lost to	ACT Brumbies at Canberra	26–70

Won 5, lost 6; placing: 8th
Tries scored: 39

Most tries: Jeff Wilson 6, Brian Lima 6, Matt Cooper 4,
To'o Vaega 4
Most points: Matt Cooper 86, Jeff Wilson 70

The Otago Highlanders' come-from-behind win against Natal in Dunedin, when they got up from 13–32 to win 33–32, brought to mind another famous comeback win against a South African opponent. Andy Leslie's 1976 All Blacks had come from 9–31 down to defeat the Quagga-Barbarians at Ellis Park 32–31. And who was the skipper when the Highlanders repeated the feat? None other than Andy's son John!

WELLINGTON HURRICANES
(coach Frank Oliver)

lost to	Auckland Blues at Palmerston North	28–36
lost to	ACT Brumbies at Canberra	28–35
beat	Transvaal at Napier	32–16
lost to	Queensland Reds at Wellington	25–32
beat	Otago Highlanders at Dunedin	44–15
lost to	Natal at Wellington	27–43
lost to	Canterbury Crusaders at New Plymouth	13–36
lost to	Western Province at Cape Town	25–35
lost to	Northern Transvaal at Pretoria	20–38
beat	Waikato Chiefs at Rotorua	23–15
lost to	New South Wales Waratahs at Sydney	25–52

Won 3, lost 8; placing: 9th
Tries scored: 31

Most tries: Christian Cullen 7, Tana Umaga 4
Most points: Jamie Cameron 91, Christian Cullen 35

WESTERN PROVINCE
(coach Alan Zondagh)

lost to	Natal at Durban	22–28
lost to	New South Wales Waratahs at Cape Town	22–30
lost to	Otago Highlanders at Cape Town	25–52
drew with	Canterbury Crusaders at Christchurch	16–16
lost to	Auckland Blues at Auckland	30–48
lost to	Waikato Chiefs at Hamilton	44–17
lost to	Queensland Reds at Brisbane	26–36
beat	Transvaal at Johannesburg	26–23
beat	Wellington Hurricanes at Cape Town	35–25
beat	ACT Brumbies at Cape Town	25–16
lost to	Northern Transvaal at Cape Town	7–35

Won 3, lost 7, drew 1; placing: 11th
Tries scored: 24

Most tries: Justin Swart 8, Johan Kapp 3,
Joggie Viljoen 3
Most points: Joel Stransky 117, Justin Swart 40

TRANSVAAL
(coach Kitch Christie, replaced by Alex Wyllie)

lost to	New South Wales Waratahs at Sydney	11–32
lost to	ACT Brumbies at Canberra	9–13
lost to	Otago Highlanders at Dunedin	15–29
lost to	Wellington Hurricanes at Napier	16–32
beat	Waikato Chiefs at Johannesburg	26–23
lost to	Western Province at Johannesburg	23–26
lost to	Northern Transvaal at Pretoria	15–25
beat	Canterbury Crusaders at Johannesburg	50–23
lost to	Natal at Durban	13–49
beat	Auckland Blues at Johannesburg	34–22
lost to	Queensland Reds at Johannesburg	16–25

Won 3, lost 8; placing: 10th
Tries scored: 24

Most tries: Gavin Lawless 4, Pieter Hendricks 3,
Johan Roux 3
Most points: Gavin Lawless 111

CANTERBURY CRUSADERS
(coach Vance Stewart)

lost to	Waikato Chiefs at Hamilton	26–27
lost to	Auckland Blues at Christchurch	18–49
lost to	Queensland Reds at Brisbane	16–52
drew with	Western Province at Christchurch	16–16
beat	New South Wales Waratahs at Christchurch	21–16
lost to	Northern Transvaal at Christchurch	18–34
lost to	ACT Brumbies at Christchurch	7–29
beat	Wellington Hurricanes at New Plymouth	36–13
lost to	Transvaal at Johannesburg	23–50
lost to	Natal at Durban	26–58
lost to	Otago Highlanders at Christchurch	27–29

Won 2, lost 8, drew 1; placing: 12th
Tries scored: 24

Most tries: Damon Kaui 3, Adrian Tukaki 3,
Justin Marshall 3
Most points: Andy Miller 77, Greg Coffey 21

In only six of the 69 matches did a team fail to score a try. This compared more than favourably with the 1996 Five Nations championship, when in 20 matches 10 teams failed to register a try.

1997

ONCE AGAIN THE ARDUOUS TREK across the Indian Ocean proved an almost insurmountable barrier for teams competing in the Super 12 in 1997. Of the 16 matches Australasian teams played in South Africa, a mere three were won (and one drawn) while South African teams, incredibly, fared even worse on the road, registering just two wins (and a draw) in their 16 outings in Australia and New Zealand.

The one team that broke the trend was the mighty Auckland Blues, the playing-through champions. They escaped from the Republic with an amazing 40-all draw against Northern Transvaal and a 24–15 victory against Free State Cheetahs. Fortified by these results, Graham Henry's men took a stranglehold on the competition, going through undefeated, without the services of Jonah Lomu, who had been knocked flat with a rare kidney disease.

The Blues triumphed in style, averaging 40 points and five tries a game. There were a couple of close calls. They just managed to hold out the Crusaders 29–28 at Pukekohe and stayed ahead of the Wellington Hurricanes, 45–42, in an absolute thriller at Eden Park. They were the class side of the competition, as they proved in smashing Ian McIntosh's Natalians in the semifinals and Rod Macqueen's Brumbies in a rain-spoiled final.

The Brumbies proved that their spirited showing in the inaugural series in 1996 was no flash in the pan. Not only were they the highest-ranking Australian side again, invincible at Bruce Stadium in Canberra, but they powered their way through to the final. To get there they had to overcome a dynamic Wellington Hurricanes team, which played to full stadiums everywhere, such was its crowd appeal. With flyers like Christian Cullen and Tana Umaga running in the tries and Jon Preston banging over the goals, the Hurricanes seemed capable of going all the way . . . until they ran into the cool, calculating Brumbies.

There were some amazing individual achievements in 1997, the gold medal effort being Gavin Lawless's incredible 50-point haul for the Natal Sharks in their 75–43 win over the Otago Highlanders. Lawless, not surprisingly, finished up as the most prolific scorer in the competition. Joe Roff also entered the record book, as a try scorer, touching down 15 times in the Brumbies' campaign. It's a record that wasn't equalled until 2005.

In a competition in which big scoring was the norm, Tana Umaga scored 12 tries, Christian Cullen, the standout player of the series, picked up 11, and Joeli Vidiri scored 10.

Disappointingly for New Zealand fans, the Otago Highlanders and the Waikato Chiefs brought up the rear, the Highlanders taking over the wooden spoon from the Canterbury Crusaders. Weakened by injuries, the Highlanders drafted in an 18-year-old winger for their final outing at Taupo. His name was Doug Howlett and he repaid their faith by scoring a hat trick of tries.

The competition featured a new team in 1997, Free State Cheetahs, who had come in at the expense of Western Province (as a consequence of Currie Cup standings). The other South African teams underwent names changes: Northern Transvaal became Northern Transvaal Blue Bulls, Transvaal metamorphosed into the Gauteng Lions and Natal lengthened out to Natal Sharks.

Charles Riechelmann and Carlos Spencer show off the Super 12 Trophy. Fotopress

THE STARS

CHRISTIAN CULLEN (Wellington Hurricanes)

It's rare for a sportsman's chief rival to extol his exceptional qualities. But Springbok André Joubert, to many the most complete fullback in world rugby at the time, didn't hesitate when interviewed in 1997.

'Cullen is a superstar,' he said. 'He is one of the great entertainers. I don't think there's any doubt he's the best fullback in the world. He has the ability to create space for himself as well as his team-mates.'

Cullen was at the peak of his powers in 1997, a try-scoring machine. He grabbed 11 tries for the Hurricanes in 10 outings, went on to score nine for the All Blacks in eight mid-winter internationals, and emerged as top try scorer with seven from five tests on New Zealand's tour of Wales, Ireland and England — an aggregate of 26 for the year. No wonder they dubbed him the Paekakariki Express.

His blistering pace from fullback was a major contributing factor in the Hurricanes emerging as a title contender in the Super 12. The Hurricanes not only galvanised the cluster of mostly second and third division unions that made up the franchise (Cullen's home province in 1997 was Manawatu) but their daring approach also won over the hearts of all New Zealanders.

They scored 52 tries in round-robin play, only four fewer than the all-conquering Auckland Blues achieved. The Hurricanes' nemesis proved to be the ACT Brumbies, who after first denying them a home semifinal eliminated them at the semifinal stage.

This was no fault of Cullen's, though. He single-handedly almost got his team through to the final, scoring a brace of spectacular tries in each clash with Rod Macqueen's men.

And if his electrifying running from fullback wasn't enough, he even helped out with the goal kicking, landing six conversions and a penalty goal against the Highlanders and another two conversions against the Waratahs when Jon Preston was sidelined.

Fotopress

JOE ROFF (ACT Brumbies)

When the Wallabies played the All Blacks in two Bledisloe Cup encounters following the World Cup in 1995, the solitary Australian Capital Territories player involved was 19-year-old winger Joe Roff. ACT players in those days were known as Kookaburras.

When the same two nations clashed in Melbourne two years later, thanks to the advent of the Super 12 championship, the Australian squad included no fewer than eight Canberra-based representatives. By then, the Kookaburras had metamorphosed into the Brumbies.

No centre prospered more from the introduction of the Super 12 than ACT. It had stumbled along as the poor cousin to New South Wales and Queensland, helpless to prevent emerging stars like David Campese from moving away.

Joe Roff, born in Victoria but educated at Marist College in Canberra, and talented enough to represent his country at schools, under-19 and colts level and in sevens, must have been contemplating a transfer to Sydney or Brisbane when Super 12 brought rugby's greatest showcase to his back doorstep.

He didn't waste the opportunity. In the Brumbies' debut season, 1996, he scored seven tries as the team punched above its weight. In 1997, he was truly sensational, using his long stride, pace and strength to score a remarkable 15 tries.

Roff scored in 10 of the Brumbies' 13 matches, which included a hat trick against Northern Transvaal and braces against Free State, the Waratahs and the Chiefs. Put in the clear, he almost invariably scored, getting around almost every fullback in the competition at some stage. Like Christian Cullen, he also played a bit part in 1997 as a goal kicker, but, unlike Cullen, he would go on to become his team's specialist in this role.

Fotopress

THE FACTS

Several notable firsts were recorded when the Chiefs defeated the Hurricanes in the opening encounter of the 1997 series in Palmerston North. Frank Bunce became the first player to receive a yellow card in first-class rugby, Dallas Seymour became the first official tactical substitute when he replaced Filo Tiatia, and the first 10-minute half-time break was taken during this game.

The 50 points Gavin Lawless scored for the Natal Sharks against the Highlanders at Durban, a total comprising four tries, nine conversions and four penalty goals, was a record for any player in any first-class match from a SANZAR country. Lawless notched up a century of points in his first four outings. During the season he scored 94 points against the four New Zealand teams he opposed.

The 118 points scored in the Natal Sharks–Otago Highlanders game in which Lawless achieved his half-century remains the highest for any Super 12 fixture. The final score was 75–43 to the Sharks.

The 40-all draw between the Auckland Blues and Northern Transvaal at Pretoria was the highest-scoring drawn match involving a New Zealand team in first-class rugby.

By the middle of the second Super 12 season, the three highest individual scores recorded — Jannie Kruger's 39 points for Northern Transvaal in 1996, Gavin Lawless' 50 points for Natal Sharks in 1997 and Gavin Johnson's 32 points for Gauteng Lions in 1997 — had all been against the Highlanders in South Africa.

Another unenviable record for the Highlanders came when Free State gave them a 49–18 hiding in Invercargill (seven converted tries against six penalty goals!), when 'away' wins were unfashionable. This remains the highest score by a South African Super 12 team overseas.

THE FIRST SEMIFINAL

AUCKLAND BLUES 55, NATAL SHARKS 36

AT EDEN PARK, AUCKLAND, 24 MAY

WHEN BLUES SKIPPER ZINZAN BROOKE exited the field, queasy of stomach, in the 48th minute, his team was rollicking along at 38–5 against their great rivals from Durban. Either his players relaxed upon his departure or he wielded a greater influence upon matches than most imagined, because in the remaining 32 minutes Natal ran in five tries!

Such was the extent of Natal's revival that at 45–22 Sean Fitzpatrick, who'd taken over the Blues' captaincy, ordered a penalty kick at goal, the Blues' first of the match, to settle things down.

The Blues eventually won by eight tries to six, their fourth victory over Ian McIntosh's enterprising side in a little over 12 months, but the fact they

Mark Carter challenged by Henry Honiball in the Eden Park semifinal in 1997. Fotopress

conceded 31 points in the final 25 minutes gave coach Graham Henry plenty to work on for the final.

McIntosh branded the outcome 'cruel', but acknowledged his team had been punished by the best counterattacking team in the world. 'We had worked hard all week at eliminating turnovers,' he said, 'but out there we kept giving them the ball . . . it was cruel.'

Natal had the satisfaction of scoring the opening try, 90 seconds into the game, but a sensational 90-metre effort by Joeli Vidiri kick-started the Blues into action and by half-time they were cruising at 33–5.

Auckland's back three of Vidiri, Brian Lima and Adrian Cashmore, had huge games, Cashmore being awarded the player of the match award.

FOR AUCKLAND BLUES: Tries by Joeli Vidiri 2, Eroni Clarke 2, Zinzan Brooke, Mark Carter, Carlos Spencer and Adrian Cashmore; 6 conversions and a penalty goal by Cashmore.

FOR NATAL SHARKS: Tries by Shaun Payne 2, Joos Joubert 2, Henry Honiball and Errol Stuart; 3 conversions by Honiball.

AUCKLAND BLUES: Adrian Cashmore, Brian Lima, Eroni Clarke, Lee Stensness, Joeli Vidiri (replaced by Jeremy Stanley), Carlos Spencer, Junior Tonu'u (replaced by Michael Scott), Zinzan Brooke (captain, replaced by Dylan Mika), Mark Carter, Michael Jones, Leo Lafaiali'i (replaced by Charles Riechelmann), Robin Brooke, Olo Brown (replaced by Paul Thomson), Sean Fitzpatrick (replaced by Andrew Roose), Craig Dowd.

NATAL SHARKS: André Joubert, Joos Joubert (replaced by Errol Stuart), Jeremy Thomson, Pieter Muller, Shaun Payne, Henry Honiball, Kevin Putt, Gary Teichmann (captain), Wayne Fyvie, Wickus van Heerden (replaced by Dieter Kriese), Wayne Boardman (replaced by Rob Strudwick), John Slade, Rob Kempson (replaced by André-Henri le Roux), John Allan, Adrian Garvey.

REFEREE: Wayne Erickson (Australia)

CROWD: 32,000

✎ Before coming on as a replacement against the Canterbury Crusaders, Blues hooker Andrew Roose had been a reserve for 16 consecutive Super 12 matches, in all of which the indefatigable Sean Fitzpatrick wore the No 2 jersey. By chance, it was Roose's 100th first-class appearance.

THE SECOND SEMIFINAL

ACT BRUMBIES 33, WELLINGTON HURRICANES 20

AT BRUCE STADIUM, CANBERRA, 24 MAY

THE ONE PLACE A New Zealand team didn't want to be playing a semifinal at during the first two seasons of the Super 12 was Bruce Stadium in Canberra. By the time the Hurricanes fronted up there in May 1997, full of optimism, the Brumbies' home record was 11 victories from 11 outings with an average winning score of 42.

Although Frank Oliver's Hurricanes collectively, and fullback Christian Cullen in particular, threw everything at them, there was an inevitability about the outcome. Even when it was 13-all early in the second half, it seemed only a matter of time before the Brumbies applied the blowtorch. And the player who broke the Hurricanes' hearts was flyhalf David Knox. In rapid succession, the masterful No 10 created tries for centre James Holbeck and winger Mitch Hardy. Suddenly it was 25–13 and the Brumbies were on their way to Eden Park for the final.

The slick inside back trio of George Gregan, David Knox and Pat Howard repeatedly had the alarm bells ringing among the Hurricanes' defence, as they had at Athletic Park in Wellington a week earlier (when the Brumbies won 35–29).

The individual brilliance of Cullen, who scored two cracking tries (as he had at Athletic Park in their round-robin clash a week earlier), wasn't enough to get the Hurricanes through to the final. Cullen threatened to win the game on his own, but the Brumbies simply exerted too much pressure.

And they had champion finishers in Joe Roff, whose first-half try pushed his aggregate for the series to 14, and James Holbeck.

> The first 28 tries scored against the Highlanders in 1997 were, remarkably, all converted. Not until their seventh match, when George Gregan notched up the 29th try against them, did a conversion attempt go astray.

The Hurricanes, whose franchise extended from East Coast and Poverty Bay in the east and Taranaki in the west to Wellington, had headed to Canberra following a series of explosive performances in mid season, genuinely believing they could overcome the Bruce Stadium bogey and make it though to the final.

But coach Oliver was left lamenting, afterwards expressing disappointment that his team never fired and never recreated the dynamism that saw them crush opponents such as Northern Transvaal (64–32), Queensland Reds (47–29), Otago Highlanders (60–34) and run the Auckland Blues to 42–45 on Eden Park in the season's most memorable game.

FOR ACT BRUMBIES: Tries by James Holbeck 2, George Gregan, Joe Roff and Mitch Hardy; conversion and 2 penalty goals by David Knox.

FOR WELLINGTON HURRICANES: Tries by Christian Cullen 2; 2 conversions and 2 penalty goals by Jon Preston.

ACT BRUMBIES: Stephen Larkham, Joe Roff, James Holbeck, Pat Howard, Mitch Hardy, David Knox, George Gregan, Troy Coker (replaced by Ipolito Fenukitau), Brett Robinson (captain), David Giffin (replaced by Justin Harrison), John Langford, Owen Finegan, Patricio Noriega, Marco Caputo, Ewen McKenzie.

WELLINGTON HURRICANES: Christian Cullen, Roger Randle, Mark Ranby, Jason O'Halloran, Tana Umaga, Stephen Bachop, Jon Preston, Filo Tiatia, Martin Leslie (replaced by Finau Maka), Kevin Barrett, Mike Russell (replaced by Dion Waller), Mark Cooksley, Mark Allen (captain), Norm Hewitt, Phil Coffin (replaced by Bill Cavubati).

REFEREE: André Watson (South Africa)

CROWD: 23,730

In the Hurricanes' eighth match, Christian Cullen was given the goal-kicking responsibilities for the first time. He landed six conversions against the Highlanders, a record that was not equalled for the Hurricanes until Jimmy Gopperth popped over six conversions in 2005.

John Eales had a successful penalty kick disallowed in the Reds–Highlanders game because the referee had not whistled 'time on' following an injury stoppage. The retaken kick was unsuccessful, and his only miss of the day.

THE FINAL

AUCKLAND BLUES 23, ACT BRUMBIES 7

AT EDEN PARK, AUCKLAND, 31 MAY

A 32-YEAR-OLD IN HIS 12TH SEASON of top-level rugby, and one of Eden Park's favourite sons, provided the winning edge for the Auckland Blues in the 1997 final. Michael Jones, The Iceman as he was known, wielded a massive influence on this contest between the two giants of the competition. Not only did he, in combination with his fellow loosies Mark Carter and Zinzan Brooke, defuse the potency of the Brumbies' lethal inside backs, but he effectively plunged a dagger into their hearts with a freakish intercept try in the 56th minute.

'Michael's try was the turning point,' conceded Brumbies coach Rod Macqueen afterwards. 'We were only ten points adrift at the time, but his converted try was a heartbreaker.'

Jones, who had been consistently knocking down the most dangerous attacking players behind the advantage line, was lurking in midfield outside the Brumbies 22 when they launched into a counterattack. Suddenly, the ball was tantalisingly in front of him. And the wily veteran didn't need any second invitations. He leapt forward, grasped the ball and, with every defender wrong-footed, ambled across to plant the ball behind the goalposts.

Maintaining relentless pressure against a now frustrated opponent, the Blues extended the scoreline to 23–nil before the Brumbies picked up a late consolation try, almost inevitably scored by Joe Roff.

The Auckland climate worked against the Brumbies, who had fashioned a spectacular record throughout the competition and who were obviously programmed to run the ball at every opportunity. Unfortunately for Macqueen's men, two hours of heavy rain prior to kick-off saturated the ground and made the ball greasy. The Brumbies preferred not to notice the deluge and adhered faithfully to their dry-weather game plan. Against an opponent with a more fragile defence, the Brumbies would probably have prospered, but against Jones, Brooke and Carter, in the slightly sticky conditions, the Brumbies repeatedly broke down under pressure. Blues coach Graham Henry had identified George

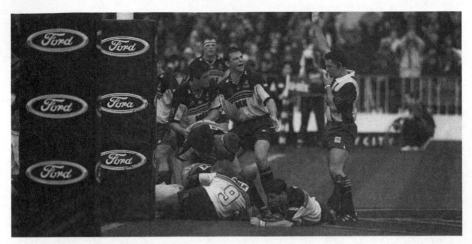

Craig Dowd scores the Blues' first try in the 1997 final. Fotopress

Gregan, David Knox and Pat Howard as the Brumbies' danger trio and had devised a strategy to neutralise them.

Macqueen lamented the lack of attacking opportunities that came to his backline. 'We came to win,' he said, 'we were confident we could, so we have to be disappointed, but Auckland is a great team.'

The final was marred by a fearful collision between celebrated players Gregan and Zinzan Brooke which put both of them out of the game. Brooke walked off, albeit groggily, while Gregan exited on a stretcher. Both were concussed. The accident cost Brooke a test appearance against Fiji and participation in the All Black trial.

FOR AUCKLAND BLUES: Tries by Craig Dowd and Michael Jones; 2 conversions and 3 penalty goals by Adrian Cashmore.

FOR ACT BRUMBIES: Try by Joe Roff; conversion by Roff.

AUCKLAND BLUES: Adrian Cashmore, Brian Lima, Eroni Clarke, Lee Stensness, Joeli Vidiri, Carlos Spencer, Junior Tonu'u, Zinzan Brooke (captain, replaced by Dylan Mika), Mark Carter, Michael Jones, Robin Brooke, Leo Lafaiali'i (replaced by Charles Riechelmann), Olo Brown, Sean Fitzpatrick, Craig Dowd.

ACT BRUMBIES: Stephen Larkham, Joe Roff, James Holbeck, Pat Howard (temporarily replaced by Geoff Logan), Mitch Hardy, David Knox, George Gregan (replaced by Rod Kafer), Troy Coker, Brett Robinson (captain), Owen Finegan (temporarily replaced by Ipolito Fenukitau), David Giffin, John Langford, Patricio Noriega, Marco Caputo, Ewen McKenzie.

REFEREE: Tappe Henning (South Africa)

CROWD: 41,000

THE RESULTS

AUCKLAND BLUES
(coach Graham Henry)

drew with	Northern Transvaal Blue Bulls at Pretoria	40–40
beat	Free State Cheetahs at Bloemfontein	24–15
beat	Waikato Chiefs at Albany	26–16
beat	Queensland Reds at Auckland	49–26
beat	Canterbury Crusaders at Pukekohe	29–28
beat	ACT Brumbies at Pukekohe	41–29
beat	Gauteng Lions at Auckland	63–22
beat	Natal Sharks at Auckland	39–17
beat	Otago Highlanders at Dunedin	45–28
beat	Wellington Hurricanes at Auckland	45–42
beat	New South Wales Waratahs at Sydney	34–20

Won 10, lost 0, drew 1; placing: 1st
Tries scored: 56

Semifinal: beat Natal Sharks at Auckland   55–36

Final: beat ACT Brumbies at Auckland   23–7

Most tries: Joeli Vidiri 10, Brian Lima 7, Carlos Spencer 7, Zinzan Brooke 6, Junior Tonu'u 5
Most points: Adrian Cashmore 142, Carlos Spencer 91, Joeli Vidiri 50

WELLINGTON HURRICANES
(coach Frank Oliver)

lost to	Waikato Chiefs at Palmerston North	18–23
lost to	Canterbury Crusaders at Christchurch	17–19
beat	Nth Transvaal Blue Bulls at New Plymouth	64–32
beat	Gauteng Lions at Johannesburg	37–35
lost to	Natal Sharks at Durban	24–29
beat	Queensland Reds at Brisbane	47–29
beat	Free State Cheetahs at Wellington	59–30
beat	Otago Highlanders at Wellington	60–34
beat	New South Wales Waratahs at Napier	19–3
lost to	Auckland Blues at Auckland	42–45
lost to	ACT Brumbies at Wellington	29–35

Won 6, lost 5; placing: 3rd
Tries scored: 52

Semifinal: lost to ACT Brumbies at Canberra   20–33

Most tries: Tana Umaga 12, Christian Cullen 11, Jason O'Halloran 6
Most points: Jon Preston 155, Christian Cullen 74, Tana Umaga 60

ACT BRUMBIES
(coach Rod Macqueen)

beat	Queensland Reds at Brisbane	24–19
lost to	Gauteng Lions at Johannesburg	36–44
lost to	Natal Sharks at Durban	26–35
beat	Canterbury Crusaders at Canberra	49–29
beat	Northern Transvaal Blue Bulls at Canberra	38–19
beat	Free State Cheetahs at Canberra	50–23
lost to	Auckland Blues at Pukekohe	29–41
beat	Otago Highlanders at Invercargill	15–9
beat	New South Wales Waratahs at Canberra	56–9
beat	Waikato Chiefs at Canberra	48–34
beat	Wellington Hurricanes at Wellington	35–29

Won 8, lost 3; placing: 2nd
Tries scored: 56

Semifinal: beat Wellington Hurricanes at Canberra   33–20

Final: lost to Auckland Blues at Auckland   7–23

Most tries: Joe Roff 15, Mitch Hardy 9, Stephen Larkham 7, George Gregan 7, Ipolito Fenukitau 4, James Holbeck 4
Most points: David Knox 134, Joe Roff 85, Mitch Hardy 45

NATAL SHARKS
(coach Ian McIntosh)

beat	Otago Highlanders at Durban	75–43
beat	ACT Brumbies at Durban	35–26
lost to	Free State Cheetahs at Bloemfontein	40–45
beat	New South Wales Waratahs at Durban	28–23
beat	Wellington Hurricanes at Durban	29–24
beat	Waikato Chiefs at Albany	33–15
drew with	Canterbury Crusaders at Christchurch	26–26
lost to	Auckland Blues at Auckland	17–39
lost to	Queensland Reds at Brisbane	3–40
drew with	Northern Transvaal Blue Bulls at Durban	27–27
lost to	Gauteng Lions at Johannesburg	8–42

Won 5, lost 4, drew 2; placing: 4th
Tries scored: 35

Semifinal: lost to Auckland Blues at Auckland   36–55

Most tries: Joos Joubert 7, Gavin Lawless 6
Most points: Gavin Lawless 170, Joos Joobert 35

GAUTENG LIONS
(coach Ray Mordt)

beat	Free State Cheetahs at Bloemfontein	24–20
beat	ACT Brumbies at Johannesburg	44–36
beat	Otago Highlanders at Johannesburg	47–29
beat	NS Wales Waratahs at Johannesburg	36–27
lost to	Wellington Hurricanes at Johannesburg	35–37
drew with	Northern Transvaal Blue Bulls at Johannesburg	16–16
lost to	Auckland Blues at Auckland	22–63
lost to	Canterbury Crusaders at Christchurch	0–23
lost to	Waikato Chiefs at Hamilton	9–47
lost to	Queensland Reds at Brisbane	27–40
beat	Natal Sharks at Johannesburg	42–8

Won 5, lost 5, drew I; placing: 5th
Tries scored: 32

Most tries: Gavin Johnson 4
Most points: Gavin Johnson 114, Johan Roux 39

FREE STATE CHEETAHS
(coach Peet Kleynhans)

lost to	Gauteng Lions at Bloemfontein	20–24
lost to	Auckland Blues at Bloemfontein	15–24
beat	Queensland Reds at Bloemfontein	35–24
beat	Natal Sharks at Bloemfontein	45–40
beat	Otago Highlanders at Invercargill	49–18
lost to	ACT Brumbies at Canberra	23–50
lost to	New South Wales Waratahs at Sydney	11–36
lost to	Wellington Hurricanes at Wellington	30–59
beat	Waikato Chiefs at Bloemfontein	27–13
lost to	Canterbury Crusaders at Bloemfontein	11–16
beat	Nth Transvaal Blue Bulls at Bloemfontein	35–23

Won 5, lost 6; placing: 7th
Tries scored: 32

Most tries: Chris Badenhorst 5, Stephen Brink 4, Braam Els 4
Most points: Jannie de Beer 83, M J Smith 43

CANTERBURY CRUSADERS
(coach Wayne Smith)

beat	Wellington Hurricanes at Christchurch	19–17
lost to	New South Wales Waratahs at Sydney	8–25
lost to	ACT Brumbies at Canberra	29–49
beat	Waikato Chiefs at Timaru	24–15
lost to	Auckland Blues at Pukekohe	28–29
lost to	Otago Highlanders at Dunedin	29–37
drew with	Natal Sharks at Christchurch	26–26
beat	Gauteng Lions at Christchurch	23–0
lost to	Northern Transvaal Blue Bulls at Pretoria	22–23
beat	Free State Cheetahs at Bloemfontein	16–11
beat	Queensland Reds at Christchurch	48–3

Won 5, lost 5, drew I; placing: 6th
Tries scored: 29

Most tries: Daryl Lilley 4, Daryl Gibson 3, Mark Mayerhofler 3, Afato So'oalo 3
Most points: Andrew Mehrtens 94, Daryl Lilley 54

NORTHERN TRANSVAAL BLUE BULLS
(coach Kitch Christie)

drew with	Auckland Blues at Pretoria	40–40
beat	Queensland Reds at Pretoria	14–3
lost to	Wellington Hurricanes at New Plymouth	32–64
lost to	Otago Highlanders at Dunedin	7–27
lost to	ACT Brumbies at Canberra	19–38
lost to	New South Wales Waratahs at Sydney	29–43
drew with	Gauteng Lions at Johannesburg	16–16
beat	Waikato Chiefs at Pretoria	34–27
beat	Canterbury Crusaders at Pretoria	23–22
drew with	Natal Sharks at Durban	27–27
lost to	Free State Cheetahs at Bloemfontein	23–35

Won 3, lost 5, drew 3; placing: 8th
Tries scored: 33

Most tries: Jacques Olivier 5
Most points: Casper Steyn 50, Theo van Rensburg 30

Northern Transvaal drew three of its 11 matches: 40-all against the Auckland Blues at Pretoria, 16-all against Gauteng at Johannesburg and 27-all against Natal at Durban. It also registered a one-point win against the Canterbury Crusaders at Pretoria.

NEW SOUTH WALES WARATAHS
(coach Matt Williams)

lost to	Waikato Chiefs at Sydney	26–33
beat	Canterbury Crusaders at Sydney	25–8
lost to	Gauteng Lions at Johannesburg	27–36
lost to	Natal Sharks at Durban	23–28
beat	Northern Transvaal Blue Bulls at Sydney	43–29
beat	Free State Cheetahs at Sydney	36–11
lost to	Queensland Reds at Sydney	16–26
lost to	ACT Brumbies at Canberra	9–56
lost to	Wellington Hurricanes at Napier	3–19
beat	Otago Highlanders at Dunedin	27–16
lost to	Auckland Blues at Sydney	20–34

Won 4, lost 7; placing: 9th
Tries scored: 25

Most tries: Alistair Murdoch 5, Matt Burke 4
Most points: Matt Burke 130

WAIKATO CHIEFS
(coach Brad Meurant)

beat	Wellington Hurricanes at Palmerston North	23–18
beat	New South Wales Waratahs at Sydney	33–26
lost to	Auckland Blues at Albany	16–26
beat	Queensland Reds at Hamilton	31–16
lost to	Canterbury Crusaders at Timaru	15–24
lost to	Natal Sharks at Albany	15–33
lost to	Northern Transvaal Blue Bulls at Pretoria	27–34
lost to	Free State Cheetahs at Bloemfontein	13–27
beat	Gauteng Lions at Hamilton	47–9
lost to	ACT Brumbies at Canberra	34–48
lost to	Otago Highlanders at Taupo	18–34

Won 4, lost 7; placing: 11th
Tries scored: 28

Most tries: Eric Rush 6, Glen Osborne 3, Caleb Ralph 3
Most points: Matthew Cooper 108, Eric Rush 30

QUEENSLAND REDS
(coach John Connolly)

lost to	ACT Brumbies at Brisbane	19–24
lost to	Northern Transvaal Blue Bulls at Pretoria	3–14
lost to	Free State Cheetahs at Bloemfontein	24–35
lost to	Waikato Chiefs at Hamilton	16–31
lost to	Auckland Blues at Auckland	26–49
beat	Otago Highlanders at Brisbane	37–24
lost to	Wellington Hurricanes at Brisbane	29–47
beat	New South Wales Waratahs at Sydney	26–16
beat	Natal Sharks at Brisbane	40–3
beat	Gauteng Lions at Brisbane	40–27
lost to	Canterbury Crusaders at Christchurch	3–48

Won 4, lost 7; placing 10th
Tries scored: 29

Most tries: Jason Little 5, Tim Horan 4, Ben Tune 4
Most points: John Eales 120

OTAGO HIGHLANDERS
(coach Glenn Ross)

lost to	Natal Sharks at Durban	43–75
lost to	Gauteng Lions at Johannesburg	29–47
beat	Northern Transvaal Blue Bulls at Dunedin	27–7
lost to	Free State Cheetahs at Invercargill	18–49
lost to	Queensland Reds at Brisbane	24–37
beat	Canterbury Crusaders at Dunedin	37–29
lost to	ACT Brumbies at Invercargill	9–15
lost to	Wellington Hurricanes at Wellington	34–60
lost to	Auckland Blues at Dunedin	28–45
lost to	New South Wales Waratahs at Dunedin	16–27
beat	Waikato Chiefs at Taupo	34–18

Won 3, lost 8; placing: 12th
Tries scored: 31

Most tries: Jeff Wilson 4, Manasa Bari 4, Doug Howlett 3,
              Romi Ropati 3
Most points: Tony Brown 75, Simon Culhane 71

✏ The first try awarded at the new North Harbour Stadium was a penalty try, credited by referee Paddy O'Brien to the Auckland Blues. The first individual to claim a five-pointer at this venue was Blues No 8 Zinzan Brooke. In 1996, the Chiefs had not allocated any matches to North Harbour when its headquarters were still at Onewa Domain, Takapuna.

1998

JUST WHEN RUGBY FANS in the SANZAR territories were claiming that the Super 12 was becoming an Auckland Blues benefit, the competition underwent a dramatic transformation.

Until about 30 minutes from the conclusion of the final at Eden Park, the 1998 series had followed a predictable pattern: the Blues under Graham Henry, with Joeli Vidiri scoring another bucketload of tries, had once again emerged not only as New Zealand's premier side but as the top qualifier, notwithstanding a couple of reversals at Durban and Brisbane.

The Blues had then withstood a spirited challenge from Tony Gilbert's revitalised Otago Highlanders in the semifinals and were on the brink of a memorable third straight triumph, 10–3 ahead of the Canterbury Crusaders, with their scrum awesomely in control and time running out. Anything bar a Blues victory appeared inconceivable. But Crusaders coach Wayne Smith didn't buy into that. He felt that with a little tweaking, his team could rescue this contest. After all, hadn't Canterbury ended Auckland's domination of the NPC just seven months earlier?

A few subtle substitutions, a change in strategy and — whammo — suddenly the Crusaders had the lead, and the trophy. As Auckland Blues fans sat stunned, wondering how on earth such a pleasant afternoon had become so rudely contorted, it was Crusaders captain Todd Blackadder, not their own beloved Michael Jones, who went forward to receive the trophy.

A Crusaders triumph had appeared as unlikely as a Christmas Day snowfall in Christchurch when the team languished in last position at the end of March, after early losses to the Chiefs, the Reds and the Blues. However, they'd hauled themselves up to fifth by the end of April, and just kept on winning. Their stunning defeat of Henry's men in the final represented their ninth victory in succession. The Crusaders' individual hero was undoubtedly Andrew Mehrtens, the darling of Lancaster Park. In converting James Kerr's late try to complete the demise of the Blues, he brought his aggregate of points for the series to a staggering 206.

If New Zealanders thought their teams' domination of the series automatically translated into Tri-nations greatness for the All Blacks (the Crusaders, the Blues and the Highlanders all qualified for the semifinals), that theory would be destroyed three months later. It was the South Africans, whose teams, with the solitary exception of the Coastal Sharks, performed abysmally in the Super 12, who came through at test level.

It was a disappointing Super 12 for Australia. The ACT Brumbies, with Eddie Jones succeeding Rod Macqueen as coach, plunged from runner-up in 1997 to tenth, which included three rare defeats at Bruce Stadium in Canberra. One home game they did win was their final outing against the Queensland Reds, which cost John Connolly's men a place in the play-offs.

South Africa selected regional teams for the first time, while a New Zealand referee, Paddy O'Brien, controlled the all-New Zealand final.

South Africa abandoned its qualifying process for Super 12 in 1998, instead falling into line with New Zealand and Australia by creating four franchises. These were based in Pretoria (Northern Bulls), Johannesburg (Golden Cats), Cape Town (Western Stormers) and Durban (Coastal Sharks).

To appease North Harbour supporters, the fifth New Zealand franchise changed its name from Waikato Chiefs to Chiefs.

Crusaders coach Wayne Smith and captain Todd Blackadder share a moment after the upset win over the Auckland Blues in the 1998 final. Fotopress

THE STARS

ANDREW MEHRTENS (Canterbury Crusaders)

He was born in South Africa, boasts a grandfather who was an All Black and a father who represented New Zealand Juniors and Natal, and has a brain so sharp he won a scholarship for calculus while at college.

He's Andrew Mehrtens, one of Canterbury rugby's favourite sons, a talented entertainer on and off the field, who in 1998 amassed 206 points during the Crusaders' campaign, a Super 12 record that still stood when the series came to its conclusion in 2005.

Mehrtens' grandfather George played three matches for the All Blacks as a fullback in 1928, while his father, a five-eighth, made a handful of appearances for Canterbury. Mehrtens came to be born in Durban because early in 1970 his father Terry and his mother Sandra, who was born in Kaiapoi, headed for South Africa to visit the game reserves. A couple of schoolteachers, they were planning to spend 12 months in the Republic, mostly sightseeing, but they finished up staying almost four years. Terry represented Natal, appearing at fullback against the 1970 All Blacks, and they didn't return to New Zealand until after the birth of Andrew in 1973.

Their son soon demonstrated that he had inherited the family rugby genes. He emerged as a clever reader of the game and, notwithstanding his slight build, as an outstanding punter of the ball and goal kicker. As a 20-year-old, he was selected for Canterbury in 1993, scoring an amazing 45 points in his first two outings. His career as a prolific scorer of points was under way. Within two years he was an All Black, marking his debut with a then world-record 28-point haul against Canada on Eden Park. After that, he was off to the World Cup, where he instantly stamped himself a player of true world class.

Coach Laurie Mains would recall in his biography that, 'If we'd set down on paper, after the frustrations of 1994, all the qualities we sought in the ideal first-five, we could not have improved on Andrew.'

Fotopress

GARY TEICHMANN (Coastal Sharks)

For someone who, in 1998, was reckoned by many to be the best player in the world, Gary Teichmann's rugby career took a long time to develop. He was 24 when he first donned the Natal jersey and just 18 months short of his 30th birthday before he registered his test debut. That was against Wales in late 1995, after the Springboks had achieved greatness at the World Cup.

When he missed selection for that World Cup squad, at the age of 28, it appeared his chance of starring on the world stage had come and gone. But one individual who recognised Teichmann's special qualities was Natal and Coastal Sharks coach Ian McIntosh, who installed him as Natal captain as early as 1996. 'I knew the players had a huge respect for him,' said McIntosh. 'He was a late developer. I know he believed he could have played for Natal and South Africa earlier than he did, but I had a gut feeling he was going to come through late in his career. On his performances in late 1995 and in 1996, I knew we had a giant with us.'

Teichmann, who was born in Gweru, Zimbabwe, and moved to South Africa when he was 12, schooling at the unfashionable Hilton College, assumed the captaincy of the Springboks quite unexpectedly in 1996. That was after Francois Pienaar, the hero of the World Cup campaign, was severely concussed in the Cape Town international against the All Blacks.

Although he made an uncomfortable number of losing speeches in his first two seasons as skipper, Teichmann went on to become one of the Springboks' most successful leaders. Under Nick Mallett, he led the side to a world record-equalling 17 straight test victories and set a South African record of 39 consecutive appearances as test captain.

Fotopress

He was distinctively different to the man he succeeded, Pienaar. 'No way was I going to imitate Francois,' he said. 'He was a one-in-a-million captain, good speaker, good motivator and great captain. My style was different. I believe in a total team game and allow the team to express themselves.'

THE FACTS

Although the Chiefs failed to qualify for the play-offs at their first three attempts, in 1998 they became the only team in the entire competition to start each of the first three seasons with a victory. Two of their first-up wins were over the Crusaders and one at the expense of the Hurricanes.

Meanwhile, the Highlanders became the first New Zealand team to defeat all four South African teams in the one season, downing the Coastal Sharks and the Golden Cats in Dunedin and winning, on the road, at Cape Town and Pretoria.

Andrew Mehrtens, whose career is liberally dotted with occasions on which he has shattered point-scoring records, created a Super 12 milestone in 1998 that has never been bettered. He amassed 206 points, comprising five tries, 23 conversions, 41 penalty goals and four dropped goals.

Occasionally, teams change jerseys at half-time, usually to a drier set. However, in the Highlanders–Stormers match at Cape Town, because of a clash of colours that was confusing the players, the home team changed colours at half-time.

Although they could finish no better than eighth, the Hurricanes became the first team to come away from South Africa with the maximum 10 points, winning at Cape Town and Pretoria. They also became the first New Zealand team to defeat the Brumbies in Canberra.

In their first two home games of 1998, the Golden Cats were comfortably ahead with time running out, only to be outsprinted by teams from New Zealand. They went down 37–38 to the Chiefs and 35–36 to the Blues.

John Eales became the first player to register a century of points in each of the first three seasons of Super 12. Meanwhile, Blues flyer Joeli Vidiri distinguished himself by scoring 10 tries in each of the first three Super 12 campaigns.

THE FIRST SEMIFINAL

AUCKLAND BLUES 37,
OTAGO HIGHLANDERS 31

AT EDEN PARK, AUCKLAND, 23 MAY

IT'S AMAZING HOW FORTUNES can turn around in sport in 12 months, especially when a new coach is involved. Under the inspirational tutelage of Tony Gilbert, the Otago Highlanders rebounded from a dismal 1997 campaign, when they finished an embarrassing last, to qualify for the play-offs a year later.

And against the all-conquering Auckland Blues at Eden Park they almost pulled off an upset of monumental proportions in this breathtaking contest. Six points in arrears with two minutes to play, the Highlanders launched one final assault, and had lock Brendon Timmins been able to hold Jeremy Stanley's pass with the goalline wide open, a famous victory could have been recorded. But alas for the Highlanders, the pass was spilled.

Fullback Adrian Cashmore was the superstar as the Blues qualified for their third consecutive final, personally accounting for 27 of the team's 37 points, a haul that included two tries. His second try was extremely controversial and was still being talked about long after the event, for it provided the Blues with their winning advantage. Cashmore was the innocent party, simply pouncing onto a loose ball and sprinting 45 metres for the touchdown. Television replays — over which the southerners screamed blue murder — showed that Joeli Vidiri none too subtlely shunted Jeremy Stanley, the Highlanders winger, out across the touchline without the ball, creating the try-scoring opportunity for Cashmore. Plainly, a penalty should have been awarded to the Highlanders. It wasn't, and the Blues prospered by seven points instead.

Powerful in the scrum, dynamic in the loose and full of enterprise and daring, the Highlanders had 60 per cent of the territory and possession but made critical mistakes, which the Blues punished.

Coach Gilbert's decision to use Isitolo Maka as an impact player paid huge dividends. He was a commanding individual during the final 30 minutes, brilliantly complementing the Highlanders' standout player, Josh Kronfeld.

Inevitably featuring among the Highlanders try scorers was Jeff Wilson, whose touchdown gave him 10 tries (equal top in the competition) from just nine outings.

Blues halfback Junior Tonu'u was sinbinned for 10 minutes for swearing at a touch judge over what he deemed a bad call. In his absence, the Highlanders scored 10 points.

Tony Gilbert's success as a coach continued in spectacular fashion in the NPC later in 1998, his Otago team averaging 62 points a game during the final six weeks of the competition.

FOR AUCKLAND BLUES: Tries by Adrian Cashmore 2, Joeli Vidiri and Lee Stensness; 4 conversions and 3 penalty goals by Cashmore.

FOR OTAGO HIGHLANDERS: Tries by Taine Randell, Jeff Wilson and Isitolo Maka; conversion and 3 penalty goals by Simon Culhane; conversion and penalty goal by Tony Brown.

AUCKLAND BLUES: Adrian Cashmore, Jonah Lomu, Eroni Clarke, Lee Stensness, Joeli Vidiri, Carlos Spencer, Junior Tonu'u, Xavier Rush, Mark Carter, Michael Jones (captain, replaced by Andrew Blowers), Royce Willis, Robin Brooke, Craig Dowd, Andrew Roose, Olo Brown.

OTAGO HIGHLANDERS: Brendan Laney, Jeremy Stanley (replaced by Pailate Fili), Pita Alatini, John Leslie, Jeff Wilson, Simon Culhane (replaced by Tony Brown), Rhys Duggan, Taine Randell (captain), Josh Kronfeld, Kelvin Middleton (replaced by Isitolo Maka), John Blaikie, Brendon Timmins, Carl Hoeft, Anton Oliver (replaced by Davin Heaps), Kees Meeuws.

REFEREE: Colin Hawke (New Zealand)

CROWD: 38,000

💬 For the first few years of the Super 12, Crusaders hookers Mark Hammett and Matt Sexton job-shared, as they had done for Canterbury in the NPC. However, against the Northern Bulls this job-sharing became quite intricate. Hammett started the game, to be replaced by Sexton early in the second half. When Sexton was sinbinned Hammett came back on to the field. After 10 minutes, Hammett exited and Sexton returned to action. But an injury to Sexton saw him replaced by Hammett, yet again, for the final 15 minutes!

THE SECOND SEMIFINAL

CANTERBURY CRUSADERS 36, COASTAL SHARKS 32

AT LANCASTER PARK, CHRISTCHURCH, 24 MAY

THE TURNING POINT in this unforgettable Sunday semifinal, which had the crowd in a frenzy for most of the second half, came when Coastal Sharks flyhalf Boeta Wessels was sinbinned for a professional foul. At the time that Wessels, deputising for injured Springbok Henry Honiball, was 'potted' by a touch judge for preventing the ball coming back at a ruck, the Sharks were ahead 32–26 and on course for an astonishing victory.

Astonishing because they had been 20–nil down after 15 minutes, but adopting a never-say-die attitude, imbued in them by cagey coach Ian McIntosh, they scored five tries and positioned themselves for a famous victory.

However, with Wessels off the field, the Crusaders assumed an advantage they weren't about to ignore. And it was that man Andrew Mehrtens, at the peak of his powers in 1998, who broke the Sharks' hearts. From a tap penalty his wizardry put replacement fullback Daryl Lilley across for a try that Mehrtens coolly converted to give his team a 33–32 lead. The tension was almost unbearable through the closing minutes as both teams, with players almost out on their feet, strove for the score that would secure a place in the final.

Daryl Gibson scores in the semifinal thriller against the Sharks in 1998. Fotopress

The Sharks, after winning an attacking line-out, surprisingly declined the drop-kick option, opting instead for a kick-and-chase ploy that the Crusaders snuffed out.

Finally, Mehrtens sealed the game with a 42-metre penalty goal, leaving Sharks coach McIntosh seething. 'It's outrageous,' he said. 'The referees decide who wins these matches by their interpretation of the tackle ball law.'

Sharks captain Gary Teichmann conceded that Wessels' departure cost his team the game. 'We defended brilliantly well,' he said, 'but it was simply a question of numbers, and the Crusaders had that extra man.'

Although the Crusaders won, by virtue of their explosive start and Mehrtens' genius, the game's two individual stars were Sharks players, prop Ollie le Roux, who claimed two mighty tries, and halfback Kevin Putt, who, in Honiball's absence, masterminded the team's magnificent comeback

FOR CANTERBURY CRUSADERS: Tries by Norman Berryman 2, Daryl Gibson and Daryl Lilley; 2 conversions and 4 penalty goals by Andrew Mehrtens.

FOR COASTAL SHARKS: Tries by Ollie le Roux 2, Shaun Payne, Stefan Terblanche and Kevin Putt; 2 conversions and a penalty goal by André Joubert.

CANTERBURY CRUSADERS: Daryl Gibson (replaced by Daryl Lilley), Norman Berryman, Tabai Matson (replaced by Tony Marsh), Mark Mayerhofler, James Kerr, Andrew Mehrtens, Aaron Flynn, Steve Surridge, Angus Gardiner (replaced by Scott Robertson), Todd Blackadder (captain), Norm Maxwell, Reuben Thorne, Kevin Nepia, Mark Hammett, Stu Loe.

COASTAL SHARKS: André Joubert, Stefan Terblanche, Jeremy Thomson, Joe Gillingham (replaced by Russell Bennett), Shaun Payne, Boeta Wessels, Kevin Putt, Gary Teichmann (captain), Warren Brosnihan (replaced by Walter Minaar), Dieter Kriese, Mark Andrews, Steve Atherton (replaced by John Slade), Ollie le Roux (replaced by Adrian Garvey), Chris Rossouw (replaced by Morne Visser), Rob Kempson.

REFEREE: Peter Marshall (Australia)

CROWD: 34,000

In scoring all 26 points (from a try and seven penalty goals) against the Reds, Simon Culhane set a record for the Highlanders that was to stand until 2005. Culhane also distinguished himself by scoring 35 consecutive points for the Highlanders in the matches against the Reds and the Brumbies.

THE FINAL

CANTERBURY CRUSADERS 20, AUCKLAND BLUES 13

AT EDEN PARK, AUCKLAND, 30 MAY

FROM LAST IN 1996 to sixth in 1997 to champions in 1998. That was the handsome progress of the Canterbury Crusaders who, under Wayne Smith's guidance, brought a finish to the Auckland Blues' stranglehold on the Super 12 in a pulsating final at Eden Park.

Despite the Crusaders' vastly improved form in the competition, few rated them much chance of downing Graham Henry's rampant Blues at Fortress Eden Park. And even the super-optimists had virtually given up hope when the red and blacks trailed 10–3 into the second half, with their scrum under severe pressure.

One who never abandoned hope was coach Smith, although he knew a mix of daring and inventiveness was necessary if victory was to be achieved. The daring came with a succession of tactical substitutions, five in total, that re-ignited his team in the critical final quarter as Graham Henry resolutely clung to his starting fifteen.

Had the match involved 20 minutes of extra time, as seemed likely when it was 13-all, Henry would have had seven fresh players to bring on. But it didn't get that far, because of the inventiveness Smith demanded of his players. 'Start putting the ball in behind the Blues' was the message he conveyed to his team with about 15 minutes remaining.

'It was obvious the Blues' players' legs had gone,' he said later. 'I knew if we could turn them around, they would be in trouble.'

Todd Blackadder with the Super 12 Trophy.
Fotopress

Twice in the final quarter the Crusaders did as instructed, coming up with seven-pointers both times. Multi-talented Norm Maxwell claimed the first, locking the game up at 13-all, and James Kerr, an Auckland-based winger who was contracted to the Crusaders out of the draft, sensationally secured the matchwinner less than two minutes from time.

After a desperately tense first spell that was the rugby equivalent of arm wrestling, and which produced a solitary penalty goal to Andrew Mehrtens, the Blues appeared in command at 10–3 after new hooker James Christian had scored a try.

The turning point came when the Crusaders somehow managed to survive seven or eight five-metre scrums. Blues fans later argued a penalty try was justified as the Crusaders scrum kept collapsing. But the Crusaders were given the benefit of the doubt, hung in courageously and came away to achieve an unlikely but gallant victory.

Mehrtens' 10 points took his aggregate for the series to 206, a tally that included five tries and four dropped goals. He appeared in all 13 matches. Todd Blackadder, the Crusaders' captain, endeared himself to the team's supporters by acknowledging all the participating unions in his victory speech. 'We're a regional selection,' he said, 'and it's important to remember that, besides Canterbury, we also represent Nelson Bays, Marlborough, Buller, West Coast, Mid-Canterbury and South Canterbury.'

FOR CANTERBURY CRUSADERS: Tries by Norman Maxwell and James Kerr; 2 conversions and 2 penalty goals by Andrew Mehrtens.

FOR AUCKLAND BLUES: Try by James Christian; conversion, penalty goal and dropped goal by Adrian Cashmore.

CANTERBURY CRUSADERS: Daryl Gibson, Norm Berryman (replaced by Daryl Lilley), Tabai Matson (replaced by Tony Marsh), Mark Mayerhofler (replaced by Blair Feeney), James Kerr, Andrew Mehrtens, Aaron Flynn, Steve Surridge, Scott Robertson (replaced by Angus Gardiner), Todd Blackadder (captain), Norm Maxwell, Reuben Thorne, Kevin Nepia (replaced by Greg Feek), Mark Hammett, Stu Loe.

AUCKLAND BLUES: Adrian Cashmore, Caleb Ralph, Eroni Clarke, Lee Stensness, Joeli Vidiri, Carlos Spencer, Junior Tonu'u, Xavier Rush, Mark Carter, Michael Jones (captain), Royce Willis, Robin Brooke, Olo Brown, James Christian, Craig Dowd.

REFEREE: Paddy O'Brien (New Zealand)

CROWD: 46,000

THE RESULTS

AUCKLAND BLUES
(coach Graham Henry)

lost to	Coastal Sharks at Durban	8–24
beat	Golden Cats at Johannesburg	38–37
beat	Otago Highlanders at Auckland	41–22
beat	Chiefs at Auckland	25–23
beat	Canterbury Crusaders at Christchurch	31–24
lost to	Queensland Reds at Brisbane	18–33
beat	New South Wales Waratahs at Auckland	47–25
beat	Northern Bulls at Pukekohe	34–24
beat	Western Stormers at Auckland	74–28
beat	ACT Brumbies at Canberra	27–24
beat	Wellington Hurricanes at Wellington	45–34

Won 9, lost 2; placing: 1st
Tries scored: 49

Semifinal: beat Otago Highlanders at Auckland   37–31

Final: lost to Canterbury Crusaders at Auckland   13–20

Most tries: Joeli Vidiri 10, Jonah Lomu 5,
              Adrian Cashmore 5
Most points: Adrian Cashmore 180, Joeli Vidiri 50

CANTERBURY CRUSADERS
(coach Wayne Smith)

lost to	Chiefs at Albany	23–25
beat	New South Wales Waratahs at Christchurch	33–12
lost to	Queensland Reds at Brisbane	9–35
lost to	Auckland Blues at Christchurch	24–31
beat	Northern Bulls at Christchurch	31–20
beat	ACT Brumbies at Timaru	38–26
beat	Western Stormers at Christchurch	37–25
beat	Otago Highlanders at Christchurch	40–24
beat	Wellington Hurricanes at Napier	39–17
beat	Golden Cats at Bloemfontein	34–25
beat	Coastal Sharks at Durban	32–20

Won 8, lost 3; placing: 2nd
Tries scored: 37

Semifinal: beat Coastal Sharks at Christchurch   36–32

Final: beat Auckland Blues at Auckland   20–13

Most tries: Norm Berryman 9, Andrew Mehrtens 5,
              Mark Mayerhofler 4, Tabai Matson 4,
              Daryl Lilley 4, Daryl Gibson 4
Most points: Andrew Mehrtens 206, Norm Berryman 45

COASTAL SHARKS
(coach Ian McIntosh)

beat	Auckland Blues at Durban	24–8
beat	Western Stormers at Durban	32–17
beat	ACT Brumbies at Canberra	41–23
lost to	Otago Highlanders at Dunedin	35–41
beat	Wellington Hurricanes at Palmerston North	39–23
lost to	New South Wales Waratahs at Sydney	18–51
beat	Golden Cats at Durban	30–18
beat	Chiefs at Port Elizabeth	52–18
lost to	Northern Bulls at Pretoria	8–12
beat	Queensland Reds at Durban	30–20
lost to	Canterbury Crusaders at Durban	20–32

Won 7, lost 4; placing: 3rd
Tries scored: 44

Semifinal: lost to Canterbury Crusaders
    at Christchurch   32–36

Most tries: Stefan Terblanche 10, Gary Teichman 7,
              André Joubert 5, Ollie le Roux 5
Most points: Henry Honiball 97, André Joubert 55,
              Stefan Terblanche 50

OTAGO HIGHLANDERS
(coach Tony Gilbert)

beat	Queensland Reds at Dunedin	26–19
lost to	ACT Brumbies at Canberra	26–34
lost to	Auckland Blues at Auckland	22–41
beat	Coastal Sharks at Dunedin	41–35
beat	Golden Cats at Invercargill	57–27
beat	Chiefs at Dunedin	29–11
beat	Wellington Hurricanes at Dunedin	29–8
lost to	Canterbury Crusaders at Christchurch	24–40
lost to	New South Wales Waratahs at Sydney	22–23
beat	Western Stormers at Cape Town	36–15
beat	Northern Bulls at Pretoria	31–26

Won 7, lost 4; placing: 4th
Tries scored: 37

Semifinal: lost to Auckland Blues at Auckland   31–37

Most tries: Jeff Wilson 10, Isitolo Maka 6, Pita Alatini 4,
              John Leslie 4, Jeremy Stanley 4
Most points: Simon Culhane 91, Tony Brown 90,
              Jeff Wilson 50

QUEENSLAND REDS
(coach John Connolly)

lost to	Otago Highlanders at Dunedin	19–26
lost to	Chiefs at Brisbane	25–28
beat	Canterbury Crusaders at Brisbane	35–9
beat	Wellington Hurricanes at Wellington	41–33
beat	Auckland Blues at Brisbane	33–18
beat	Western Stormers at Brisbane	19–14
Drew with	New South Wales Waratahs at Brisbane	17–17
beat	Northern Bulls at Brisbane	28–15
beat	Golden Cats at Johannesburg	20–16
lost to	Coastal Sharks at Durban	20–30
lost to	ACT Brumbies at Canberra	16–23

Won 6, lost 4, drew 1; placing: 5th
Tries scored: 29

Most tries: Tim Horan 6, Shane Drahm 6, Damian Smith 4,
Ben Tune 4
Most points: John Eales 109, Shane Drahm 49

CHIEFS
(coach Ross Cooper)

beat	Canterbury Crusaders at Albany	25–23
beat	Queensland Reds at Brisbane	28–25
lost to	Wellington Hurricanes at Hamilton	19–22
lost to	Auckland Blues at Auckland	23–25
lost to	Otago Highlanders at Dunedin	11–29
beat	Northern Bulls at Hamilton	37–25
beat	Golden Cats at Bloemfontein	36–35
lost to	Coastal Sharks at Port Elizabeth	18–52
beat	Western Stormers at Rotorua	26–7
beat	ACT Brumbies at Hamilton	35–15
lost to	New South Wales Waratahs at Albany	21–33

Won 6, lost 4; placing 7th
Tries scored: 30

Most tries: Roger Randle 6, Scott McLeod 4
Most points: Ian Foster 59, Matthew Cooper 55

NEW SOUTH WALES WARATAHS
(coach Matt Williams)

beat	ACT Brumbies at Sydney	32–7
lost to	Canterbury Crusaders at Christchurch	12–33
beat	Golden Cats at Sydney	25–10
lost to	Northern Bulls at Witbank	19–34
lost to	Western Stormers at Wellington (SA)	33–35
beat	Coastal Sharks at Sydney	51–18
Drew with	Queensland Reds at Brisbane	17–17
lost to	Auckland Blues at Auckland	25–47
beat	Otago Highlanders at Sydney	23–22
beat	Wellington Hurricanes at Sydney	36–32
beat	Chiefs at Albany	33–21

Won 6, lost 4, drew 1; placing: 6th
Tries scored: 31

Most tries: Semi Taupeaffe 5, Matt Burke 4,
Michael Brial 4
Most points: Manuel Edmonds 94, Matt Burke 80

WELLINGTON HURRICANES
(coach Frank Oliver)

beat	Western Stormers at Cape Town	45–31
beat	Northern Bulls at Pretoria	37–19
beat	Chiefs at Hamilton	22–19
lost to	Queensland Reds at Wellington	33–41
lost to	Coastal Sharks at Palmerston North	23–39
beat	Golden Cats at New Plymouth	30–15
lost to	Otago Highlanders at Dunedin	8–29
beat	ACT Brumbies at Canberra	32–29
lost to	Canterbury Crusaders at Napier	17–39
lost to	New South Wales Waratahs at Sydney	32–36
lost to	Auckland Blues at Wellington	34–45

Won 5, lost 6; placing 8th
Tries scored: 34

Most tries: Alex Telea 6, Christian Cullen 6,
Jason O'Halloran 5, Tana Umaga 4
Most points: Jon Preston 112, Christian Cullen 36

Brothers in opposing teams occur from time to time, but rarely are there two sets of brothers in opposing teams, as happened when the Chiefs played the Crusaders at Albany. Jason Barrell propped the Chiefs' scrum and his brother Con propped the Crusaders' scrum; Glenn Marsh was a flanker for the Chiefs and his brother Tony appeared in the midfield for the Crusaders as a replacement. The Marsh brothers are twins.

WESTERN STORMERS
(coach Harry Viljoen)

lost to	Wellington Hurricanes at Cape Town	31–45
lost to	Coastal Sharks at Durban	17–32
beat	Northern Bulls at Cape Town	35–18
beat	NS Wales Waratahs at Wellington (SA)	35–33
beat	ACT Brumbies at Cape Town	34–3
lost to	Queensland Reds at Brisbane	14–19
lost to	Canterbury Crusaders at Christchurch	25–37
lost to	Auckland Blues at Auckland	28–74
lost to	Chiefs at Rotorua	7–26
lost to	Otago Highlanders at Cape Town	15–36
lost to	Golden Cats at Johannesburg	7–41

Won 3, lost 8; placing: 9th
Tries scored: 33

Most tries: Bobby Skinstad 5, Percy Montgomery 5, Robbie Fleck 4
Most points: Louis Koen 77, Percy Montgomery 41

NORTHERN BULLS
(coach Eugene van Wyk)

lost to	Golden Cats at Pretoria	32–39
lost to	Wellington Hurricanes at Pretoria	19–37
lost to	Western Stormers at Cape Town	18–35
beat	New South Wales Waratahs at Witbank	34–19
beat	ACT Brumbies at Brakpan	24–7
lost to	Canterbury Crusaders at Christchurch	20–31
lost to	Chiefs at Hamilton	25–37
lost to	Auckland Blues at Pukekohe	24–34
lost to	Queensland Reds at Brisbane	15–28
beat	Coastal Sharks at Pretoria	12–8
lost to	Otago Highlanders at Pretoria	26–31

Won 3, lost 8; placing: 11th
Tries scored: 28

Most tries: Casper Steyn 5, Marius Goosen 4
Most points: Franoc Smith 65, Braam van Straaten 62

ACT BRUMBIES
(coach Eddie Jones)

lost to	New South Wales Waratahs at Sydney	7–32
beat	Otago Highlanders at Canberra	34–26
lost to	Coastal Sharks at Canberra	23–41
beat	Golden Cats at Canberra	37–3
lost to	Northern Bulls at Brakpan	7–24
lost to	Western Stormers at Cape Town	3–34
lost to	Canterbury Crusaders at Timaru	26–38
lost to	Wellington Hurricanes at Canberra	29–32
lost to	Auckland Blues at Canberra	24–27
lost to	Chiefs at Hamilton	15–35
beat	Queensland Reds at Canberra	23–16

Won 3, lost 8; placing: 10th
Tries scored: 29

Most tries: Stephen Larkham 8, Stirling Mortlock 5
Most points: Stephen Larkham 62, David Knox 58

GOLDEN CATS
(coach Peet Kleynhans)

beat	Northern Bulls at Pretoria	39–32
lost to	Auckland Blues at Johannesburg	37–38
lost to	New South Wales Waratahs at Sydney	10–25
lost to	ACT Brumbies at Canberra	3–37
lost to	Otago Highlanders at Invercargill	27–57
lost to	Wellington Hurricanes at New Plymouth	15–30
lost to	Coastal Sharks at Durban	18–30
lost to	Chiefs at Bloemfontein	35–36
lost to	Queensland Reds at Johannesburg	16–20
lost to	Canterbury Crusaders at Bloemfontein	25–34
beat	Western Stormers at Johannesburg	41–7

Won 2, lost 9; placing: 12th
Tries scored: 31

Most tries: Jamie van der Walt 9, André Venter 4
Most points: Jannie de Beer 72, Jamie van der Walt 45, M J Smith 32

The Reds rather remarkably scored 35 points into the wind against the Hurricanes at Wellington, in a game they won 41–33. Perhaps even more unbelievably, they did not concede a single penalty against the Western Stormers at Brisbane, a match refereed by New Zealander Colin Hawke.

1999

A DROPPED GOAL THAT SECURED a sensational victory mid-competition, the reaction to which caused an uproar, made possible a second consecutive Super 12 triumph for the Canterbury Crusaders in 1999.

The droppie was landed by Andrew Mehrtens in the final minutes of game against wooden-spooner Northern Bulls at Loftus Versfeld in Pretoria when his team appeared headed for a third consecutive defeat. A loss in that game would have left the Crusaders disspirited and surely out of the reckoning for the play-offs. But Mehrtens' sweet dropped goal provided his team with a 30–28 victory and the boost it needed for the run-in to the semifinals.

'Andrew's dropped goal at Pretoria threw us a lifeline,' confessed Crusaders captain Todd Blackadder after they had won the final against the Otago Highlanders at Dunedin at the end of May. 'If we'd lost to the Northern Bulls we'd probably have been sunk. That was the turning point.'

Mehrtens' reaction to the goal got him into hot water, because he turned to the crowd who, minutes before, had booed him when he was attempting a penalty kick and gave them a defiant two-finger salute.

'I regretted reacting in that way,' he said later. 'I don't normally do stuff like

Justin Marshall and Todd
Blackadder after the 1999
finals victory at Dunedin.
Fotopress

that. I went a bit overboard, but I was annoyed at the crowd's booing when I was kicking for goal.'

Mehrtens soon put the sensations of Pretoria behind him, starring as the Crusaders completed a sequence of dramatic comeback victories leading up to their defeat of the Highlanders in the final. At Nelson they came from 6–31 down to defeat the Cats 58–38, at Christchurch they bounced back from 6–22 to beat the Sharks 34–29 and at Sydney they rebounded from 10–17 to down the Waratahs 38–22.

Despite the Crusaders' great late run, they qualified only fourth, the home semifinals being claimed by the Queensland Reds and the Stormers. It was naturally expected, therefore, that the final would be in either Brisbane or Cape Town. But the Crusaders, who travelled to Brisbane, and the Highlanders, who faced a more exhausting journey through to Cape Town, weren't having any of that. They disregarded home advantage to pull off stunning victories, making for an all-New Zealand final.

The long journey back from South Africa obviously impacted on the Highlanders, who were outmuscled in the final, the Crusaders claiming their second successive title.

Equally as sensational as the Crusaders' success, after they appeared to be down and out, was the demise of the Auckland Blues following Graham Henry's departure as coach. After competing in the first three finals, and winning two, this time they went down like the *Titanic*, finishing an ignominious ninth while scoring just 15 tries (compared to try tallies of 70, 66 and 54 the previous three years). Coach Jed Rowlands was not invited back.

The Stormers–Highlanders game represents the only occasion a Super 12 semifinal has been staged in South Africa.

The Queensland Reds finished top in round-robin play for the second time but, as in 1996, failed to win their home semifinal.

The Chiefs tailed the competition after losing their first five matches, but recovered to finish sixth after winning five of their remaining six games.

The competition embraced the new IRB regulation permitting tactical substitutions. Previously replacements were allowed only when players were injured.

Three of the South African franchises shortened their names in 1999. Golden Cats became Cats, Western Stormers changed to Stormers and Coastal Sharks settled for Sharks.

THE STARS

BYRON KELLEHER (Otago Highlanders)

When you're named after Lord Byron, it's entirely appropriate that your finest accomplishments in rugby should be labelled poetry in motion. Byron Kelleher smiled when one rugby correspondent applied that phrase to one of his performances because, yes, his father Kirk, something of a poet himself, did indeed name his son after the renowned British poet. Probably more pertinently, Kirk Kelleher also had a passion for rugby and was still participating in the lighthearted Golden Oldies version of the game when he enrolled his son, at the age of six, with the Kaikorai club. Young Kelleher never looked back, showing rugby skills above average from a young age. One who instantly recognised his talent was the principal of the Tahuna Intermediate School he attended, Tony Gilbert. By the time Kelleher had captained the Otago Boys High First XV and was slotting into the Dunedin senior club scene, Gilbert had become Otago coach. Almost before you could say 'Lord Byron's a poet', Kelleher was pulling on the representative No 9 jersey, aged 20. He was an instant success.

Ever ambitious, Kelleher thought he might claim the Otago Highlanders halfback slot in 1998, but coach Glenn Ross preferred his old Waikato colleague Rhys Duggan. A few months later Kelleher was a sensation in a sensational team, Otago demolishing every side in the land in taking out the NPC, the team averaging over 60 points a game for the final six weeks of the competition.

When Gilbert took over the Highlanders in 1998, Kelleher was instantly installed at halfback, and has been an automatic Super 12 selection since, forsaking Otago and the Highlanders in 2004 when he moved to the Waikato.

His All Black debut came at the 1999 World Cup and, while there have been several standout performances, the test appearances by the bullet-passing Kelleher were limited because of the presence of the incredibly resilient and talented Justin Marshall.

Fotopress

TIM HORAN (Queensland Reds)

You've got to admire Wallaby coach Bob Dwyer's courage back in 1989 after his team had been humbled by the British Lions. While others were conducting prolonged post-mortems, he set about reconstructing his national side. When the Australians next took the field, against the All Blacks at Eden Park, not only were there three brand-new personalities in the line-up, two of them hadn't even represented their state sides. One was hooker Phil Kearns, the other centre Tim Horan, just 19 at the time (the third newcomer was prop Tony Daly).

All three would go on to achieve greatness, which included sharing in Australia's World Cup triumph at Twickenham in 1991 when Horan ranked close behind David Campese as player of the tournament. Horan would eventually rack up 67 test appearances, 32 of them in partnership with his great mate Jason Little. They formed a lethal midfield combination, one that had an epic battle with New Zealand's great midfield combo of the time, Frank Bunce and Walter Little, in the 1992 Bledisloe Cup series.

Horan, whose father was a Queensland MP, first played league while attending Toowoomba State School, taking up rugby when he moved to Downlands College. He was an instant success in the 15-a-side code. He was an incisive runner and a great chaser of high kicks, while his deadly tackling — in his biography, All Black Ian Jones referred to him as a 'bootlace tackler'

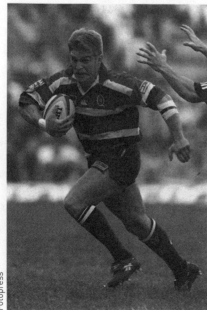

Fotopress

— made him an opponent to be feared.

The Super 12 was ready-made for Horan and the Queensland Reds. They'd already proven themselves the classiest Australasian side in the Super 10 (involving the premier provincial teams of Australia, New Zealand and South Africa), winning the finals in 1994 (in Durban) and 1995 (in Johannesburg).

Horan was captain and fullback as the Reds stormed through the Super 12 in 1996, qualifying top. Many thought that with the home advantage they were a shot's eye for the title . . . until Natal knocked them over in the semifinals.

THE FACTS

At the start of 1999, the Crusaders had not recorded a single Super 12 victory in Australia. By the conclusion of that year's competition, however, they had become the first team to defeat all three Australian teams in Australia in one season, downing the Waratahs in Sydney and the Brumbies in Canberra in round-robin play and outgunning the Reds in Brisbane in the semifinals.

Boundary changes meant Jonah Lomu represented the Chiefs in 1999, having previously participated in the Super 12 as an Auckland Blues player. Largely because of disharmony between the Waikato and North Harbour unions, the NZRU decided to pair off Auckland with North Harbour and Northland in the Blues franchise and put Counties Manukau in with Waikato (and Bay of Plenty, King Country and Thames Valley). Lomu managed just two tries for his new team.

The first tryless game since the Super 12 began was the 12-all draw between the Auckland Blues and the Queensland Reds, at Eden Park. It was four penalty goals by Adrian Cashmore against four penalty goals by Nathan Spooner, the game ranking as one of the dullest Super 12 games on record. Frustratingly for Eden Park fans, there was another tryless game a month later, when the Sharks beat the Blues 12–6, four penalty goals (by Henry Honiball) to two (by Cashmore).

Warwick Waugh became the first player to represent all three Australian teams in Super 12 when he turned out for the Queensland Reds. He'd been with the New South Wales Waratahs in 1996 and the ACT Brumbies in 1998.

When ACT Brumbies fullback Joe Roff dotted down at Eden Park it meant he had scored a try in each of his five outings against the Auckland Blues.

THE FIRST SEMIFINAL

CANTERBURY CRUSADERS 28, QUEENSLAND REDS 22

AT BALLYMORE, BRISBANE, 22 MAY

FOR SOMEONE WITH NO 10 ON HIS JERSEY, Andrew Mehrtens spent an awful lot of time at fullback in this much-hyped semifinal at Ballymore. It wasn't a case of Mehrts being rebellious. He was simply applying strategies the team had devised specifically for this encounter following the Reds' telling victory over them at Jade Stadium in round-robin play.

The Reds put the ball in behind the Crusaders' defence consistently in Christchurch. However, when they attempted it at Ballymore, Mehrtens, who regularly alternated positions with Leon MacDonald, was there to field their kicks and return them with interest. Mehrtens, for the umpteenth time in his celebrated career, was the commanding individual as the Crusaders pulled off a stunning, four-tries-to-one victory against the competition's top qualifier.

Thanks to Mehrtens' mastery, the Crusaders, who in previous seasons had been criticised for being too defence-orientated, completely outdazzled John Connolly's men on this occasion. The highlight was a 95-metre counterattacking try scored right on half-time. The opportunity came when Reuben Thorne tackled Reds halfback Jacob Rauluni so heavily as the Reds advanced towards the goalline that the ball was jolted free. Justin Marshall pounced on it and nine passes later, and notwithstanding Daryl Gibson having to retrieve the ball

*The Sharks became the first team to keep two opponents tryless in the same year, defeating the Northern Bulls 29–nil at Durban and restricting the Auckland Blues to two penalty goals at Eden Park.

*After scoring bucketloads of tries throughout the first three years of the competition, when Graham Henry was in charge, the Auckland Blues came embarrassingly back to earth in 1999, managing just 15 tries in their 11 games, the worst in the competition's history.

after Norman Berryman overran it, Caleb Ralph dotted down for a fabulous five-pointer.

Mehrtens was beaming afterwards. 'Our decision-making was the best all season,' he said. 'While it was a tactic to kick the ball back to them, and pressure them, we were prepared to run turnover ball from anywhere on the field. It paid off.'

The Reds were outsmarted on the night and appeared not to have a Plan B in reserve. They operated without vision and seemingly without confidence. The Crusaders scrum held up strongly against Queensland's Wallaby-embossed pack, while the loose trio of Steve Surridge, Angus Gardiner and Reuben Thorne had the better of Toutai Kefu, Matt Cockbain and Mark Murray.

FOR CANTERBURY CRUSADERS: Tries by Greg Feek, Caleb Ralph, Leon MacDonald and Scott Robertson; conversion and 2 penalty goals by Andrew Mehrtens.

FOR QUEENSLAND REDS: Try by Tim Horan; conversion and 5 penalty goals by Nathan Spooner.

CANTERBURY CRUSADERS: Leon MacDonald, Afato So'oalo, Norm Berryman, Daryl Gibson, Caleb Ralph, Andrew Mehrtens, Justin Marshall, Steve Surridge, Angus Gardiner, Reuben Thorne, Todd Blackadder, Norm Maxwell, Greg Somerville, Mark Hammett, Greg Feek.
Replacements: Scott Robertson, Con Barrell, Matt Sexton.

QUEENSLAND REDS: Chris Latham, Damian Smith, Daniel Herbert, Tim Horan, Ben Tune, Nathan Spooner, Paulo Rauluni, Toutai Kefu, Matt Cockbain, Mark Murray, Mark Connors, Warwick Waugh, Glenn Panoho, Michael Foley, Dan Crowley.
Replacement: Nathan Williams.

REFEREE: André Watson (South Africa)

CROWD: 17,116

🏉 The ACT Brumbies managed to keep Christian Cullen tryless in 1999, no mean achievement. The All Black fullback had helped himself to six tries in his four previous outings against the men from Canberra.

🏉 When Doug Howlett dotted down for the Auckland Blues against the Wellington Hurricanes, he became the first player to score a try for three different Super 12 teams. He'd previously played two games for the Otago Highlanders (and scored three tries) in 1997 and five games for the Hurricanes (when he scored one try) in 1998.

THE SECOND SEMIFINAL

OTAGO HIGHLANDERS 33, STORMERS 18

AT NORWICH STADIUM, CAPE TOWN, 22 MAY

STORMERS COACH ALAN SOLOMONS had literally caused a storm when he rested a dozen of his top-line players for the round-robin fixture against the Highlanders at Carisbrook in only the third match of the campaign. Solomons justified his attitude by claiming it was important to give game time to every member of his squad. The Otago players and fans, and New Zealanders generally, scoffed as the Stormers' alternative fifteen was demolished 46–14. It was a peculiar way of operating, but final judgement would be reserved until the end of the competition, when Solomons' wisdom would be assessed.

Well, post-Carisbrook, the Stormers won six matches out of eight and qualified second, a point ahead of the Highlanders. Solomons was not so stupid after all. No doubt Tony Gilbert and his Highlanders mused on this during the long, wearying flight through from New Zealand to Cape Town. One thing they could be sure of: Solomons would be fielding his finest fifteen on this occasion.

Robbie Fleck in action against the Highlanders at Cape Town. Fotopress

Given their home advantage, with 50,000 fans urging them on, and the inevitable weariness that must have impacted on the Highlanders, the Stormers should have won, more so when they led 11–nil, but it wasn't to be. From 11–nil, it was a downward spiral for the Stormers, arrested only when Jeff Wilson missed touch just before half-time, allowing the ever dangerous Breyton Paulse to launch into a dazzling counterattack that produced a converted try. That made the half-time score 18–22, but amazingly the Stormers never scored again. They were outmuscled and outplayed.

Playing out of their skins and superbly led by Taine Randell, Gilbert's men pressured the Stormers relentlessly and thoroughly deserved their four-tries-to-two victory which, following the Reds' loss in Brisbane, gave them the bonus of a home final.

Corne Krige, who had taken over the Stormers captaincy a month earlier when Bobby Skinstad was injured, acknowledged the Highlanders' superiority. 'They played really well and put us under tremendous pressure,' he said. 'They had the composure at the right times and we didn't.'

Each team operated for 10 minutes with a player in the sin bin. While Andy Marinos cooled off for causing obstruction to Pita Alatini, the Highlanders scored 10 points; while Kees Meeuws was serving his 10-minute penalty, the Highlanders kept the Stormers scoreless.

FOR OTAGO HIGHLANDERS: Tries by Brian Lima, Byron Kelleher, Romi Ropati and Taine Randell; 2 conversions and 3 penalty goals by Tony Brown.

FOR STORMERS: Tries by Breyton Paulse and Charl Marais; conversion and 2 penalty goals by Braam van Straaten.

OTAGO HIGHLANDERS: Jeff Wilson, Brendan Laney, Romi Ropati, Pita Alatini, Brian Lima, Tony Brown, Byron Kelleher, Isitolo Maka (temporarily replaced by Joe McDonnell), Josh Kronfeld, Taine Randell (captain), Brendon Timmins (replaced by Simon Maling), John Blaikie, Kees Meeuws, Anton Oliver, Carl Hoeft.

STORMERS: Percy Montgomery, Breyton Paulse, Robbie Fleck, Andy Marinos, Pieter Rossouw, Braam van Straaten, Dan van Zyl, Anton Leonard, Corne Krige (captain), Rob Brink, Selborne Boome (replaced by Marius Bosman), Johnny Trytsman (replaced by Chean Roux), Cobus Visagie, Charl Marais, Robbie Kempson (replaced by Toks van der Linde).

REFEREE: Peter Marshall (Australia)

CROWD: 50,000

Athletic Park was used as the Wellington Hurricanes' headquarters for the last time in 1999. It scarcely provided home ground advantage, the Hurricanes winning only three of the 10 Super 12 matches played there over four seasons.

THE FINAL

CANTERBURY CRUSADERS 24, OTAGO HIGHLANDERS 19

AT CARISBROOK, DUNEDIN, 30 MAY

FRANK OLIVER'S WELLINGTON HURRICANES endured a forlorn Super 12 series in 1999, but they wielded a massive influence on the outcome of the competition. And that was because they won their final outing, to the dismay of rugby fans in the deep south, against the Otago Highlanders at Athletic Park.

Oh, how that reverse cost the Highlanders. It meant, instead of a cozy semifinal at Carisbrook in front of tens of thousands of admiring fans, an arduous trek across the Indian Ocean to tackle the Stormers at Cape Town. Defying the odds, Tony Gilbert's men pulled off a cracking victory. But they were immediately back on the plane, retracing their flight path back to New Zealand.

The joyous news that the final was to be in Dunedin, thanks to the Crusaders knocking over the top-qualifying Reds, was tempered with concerns about how much the double-whammy across the Indian Ocean had taken out of the players. Without detracting from the Crusaders' mighty performance, it was patently obvious the Highlanders' energy levels were down. They would have had to be a team of supermen to win the final after all that travelling.

The Crusaders retained their crown largely because they possessed two gifted game-breakers in Andrew Mehrtens and Samoan winger Afato So'oalo. Between them, they either set up or scored all 24 of the Crusaders' points. The inimitable Mehrtens created a sweet try for Daryl Gibson, banged over five goals to bring his aggregate for the 1999 campaign to 192 points and consistently turned the Highlanders around with his deadly accurate punting.

So'oalo, who was contracted to Canterbury in 1997 sight unseen on the recommendation of Samoan coach Bryan Williams, uncorked a try any winger would have been proud of. From about 60 metres out, he sidestepped his Samoan team-mate Brian Lima, hurtled away down the touchline and not only judged his kick ahead to perfection but had the audacity to outsprint Jeff Wilson for the touchdown.

The Crusaders show their delight at the final whistle. Fotopress

When Mehrtens landed a penalty goal soon after So'oalo scored, the Crusaders were out to a 24–14 advantage, which appeared an insurmountable lead. But that didn't stop the Highlanders, jetlagged or not, from turning on a barnstorming finish, that yielded a try to powerful No 8 Isitolo Maka. Unfortunately for the Highlanders, time ran out before they could manage another.

The occasion was a glorious celebration for South Island rugby, some enthusiasts rating it the finest provincial encounter ever in New Zealand.

FOR CANTERBURY CRUSADERS: Tries by Daryl Gibson and Afato So'oalo; conversion, dropped goal and 3 penalty goals by Andrew Mehrtens.

FOR OTAGO HIGHLANDERS: Tries by Brian Lima and Isitolo Maka; 2 penalty goals by Tony Brown; dropped goal by Brendan Laney.

CANTERBURY CRUSADERS: Leon MacDonald, Afato So'oalo, Norm Berryman, Daryl Gibson, Caleb Ralph, Andrew Mehrtens, Justin Marshall, Steve Surridge, Angus Gardiner, Reuben Thorne, Norm Maxwell, Todd Blackadder (captain), Greg Somerville, Mark Hammett, Greg Feek.
Replacements: Daryl Lilley, Nathan Mauger, Aaron Flynn, Scott Robertson, Steve Lancaster, Con Barrell.

OTAGO HIGHLANDERS: Jeff Wilson, Brian Lima, Romi Ropati, Pita Alatini, Brendan Laney, Tony Brown, Byron Kelleher, Isitolo Maka, Josh Kronfeld, Taine Randell (captain), John Blaikie, Brendon Timmins, Kees Meeuws, Anton Oliver, Carl Hoeft.
Replacement: Simon Maling.

REFEREE: André Watson (South Africa)

CROWD: 42,000

THE RESULTS

QUEENSLAND REDS
(coach John Connolly)

beat	Wellington Hurricanes at Brisbane	11-0
beat	Chiefs at Hamilton	19-17
beat	ACT Brumbies at Brisbane	19-18
drew with	Auckland Blues at Albany	12-12
beat	Canterbury Crusaders at Christchurch	36-23
lost to	Stormers at Cape Town	14-35
beat	Northern Bulls at Brakpan	17-7
lost to	Otago Highlanders at Brisbane	19-20
beat	New South Wales Waratahs at Sydney	30-13
beat	Cats at Brisbane	22-12
beat	Sharks at Brisbane	34-13

Won 8, lost 2, drew 1; placing: 1st
Tries scored: 20

Semifinal: lost to Canterbury Crusaders
at Brisbane   22-28

Most tries: Daniel Herbert 5, Damian Smith 4,
              Chris Latham 3
Most points: Nathan Spooner 148, Daniel Herbert 25

STORMERS
(coach Alan Solomons)

beat	Northern Bulls at Pretoria	42-19
beat	Wellington Hurricanes at Wellington	24-22
lost to	Otago Highlanders at Dunedin	14-46
lost to	ACT Brumbies at Canberra	15-37
beat	New South Wales Waratahs at Sydney	28-18
beat	Queensland Reds at Cape Town	35-14
beat	Sharks at Cape Town	35-19
beat	Canterbury Crusaders at Cape Town	28-19
beat	Auckland Blues at Cape Town	37-23
beat	Chiefs at Cape Town	16-9
lost to	Cats at Cape Town	16-18

Won 8, lost 3; placing: 2nd
Tries scored: 29

Semifinal: lost to Otago Highlanders at Cape Town 18-33

Most tries: Pieter Rossouw 7, Breyton Paulse 5,
              Robbie Fleck 4
Most points: Braam van Straaten 152, Pieter Rossouw 35

OTAGO HIGHLANDERS
(coach Tony Gilbert)

beat	Auckland Blues at Dunedin	19-13
beat	Northern Bulls at Invercargill	65-23
beat	Stormers at Dunedin	46-14
beat	Cats at Johannesburg	29-28
lost to	Sharks at Durban	8-32
beat	Chiefs at Rotorua	27-16
beat	Canterbury Crusaders at Dunedin	23-6
beat	Queensland Reds at Brisbane	20-19
lost to	New South Wales Waratahs at Dunedin	15-23
beat	ACT Brumbies at Dunedin	9-8
lost to	Wellington Hurricanes at Wellington	19-21

Won 8, lost 3; placing: 3rd
Tries scored: 32

Semifinal: beat Stormers at Cape Town   33-18

Final: lost to Canterbury Crusaders at Dunedin 19-24

Most tries: Brian Lima 7, Romi Ropati 6, Byron Kelleher 6,
              Isitolo Maka 6
Most points: Tony Brown 108, Brian Lima 35

CANTERBURY CRUSADERS
(coach Wayne Smith)

beat	Chiefs at Christchurch	48-3
beat	Auckland Blues at Auckland	22-16
drew with	Wellington Hurricanes	18-18
lost to	Queensland Reds at Christchurch	23-36
beat	ACT Brumbies at Canberra	28-21
lost to	Otago Highlanders at Dunedin	6-23
lost to	Stormers at Cape Town	19-28
beat	Northern Bulls at Pretoria	30-28
beat	Cats at Nelson	58-38
beat	Sharks at Christchurch	34-29
beat	New South Wales Waratahs at Sydney	38-22

Won 7, lost 3, drew 1; placing: 4th
Tries scored: 30

Semifinal: beat Queensland Reds at Brisbane   28-22

Final: beat Otago Highlanders at Dunedin   24-19

Most tries: Afato So'oalo 8, Caleb Ralph 5,
              Norm Berryman 5
Most points: Andrew Mehrtens 192, Afato So'oalo 40

ACT BRUMBIES
(coach Eddie Jones)

lost to	Cats at Johannesburg	22–33
lost to	Sharks at Port Elizabeth	16–21
lost to	Queensland Reds at Brisbane	18–19
beat	Stormers at Canberra	37–15
beat	Northern Bulls at Canberra	73–9
lost to	Canterbury Crusaders at Canberra	21–28
lost to	Chiefs at Canberra	13–16
beat	New South Wales Waratahs at Canberra	27–16
beat	Wellington Hurricanes at Wellington	21–13
lost to	Otago Highlanders at Dunedin	8–9
beat	Auckland Blues at Auckland	22–16

Won 5, lost 6; placing: 5th
Tries scored: 35

Most tries: Joe Roff 8, George Gregan 5
Most points: Stirling Mortlock 77, Joe Roff 68

SHARKS
(coach Ian McIntosh)

drew with	New South Wales Waratahs at Durban	13–13
beat	ACT Brumbies at Port Elizabeth	21–16
beat	Cats at Johannesburg	36–20
beat	Otago Highlanders at Durban	32–8
lost to	Wellington Hurricanes at East London	18–34
lost to	Stormers at Cape Town	19–35
beat	Northern Bulls at Durban	29–0
beat	Auckland Blues at Auckland	12–6
lost to	Chiefs at Hamilton	19–32
lost to	Canterbury Crusaders at Christchurch	29–34
lost to	Queensland Reds at Brisbane	13–34

Won 5, lost 5, drew 1; placing: 7th
Tries scored: 26

Most tries: Stefan Terblanche 4
Most points: Henry Honiball 94, Stefan Terblanche 20

CHIEFS
(coach Ross Cooper)

lost to	Canterbury Crusaders at Christchurch	3–48
lost to	Queensland Reds at Hamilton	17–19
lost to	New South Wales Waratahs at Sydney	30–36
lost to	Auckland Blues at Hamilton	18–29
lost to	Otago Highlanders at Rotorua	16–27
beat	ACT Brumbies at Canberra	16–13
beat	Wellington Hurricanes at New Plymouth	24–21
beat	Cats at Pukekohe	44–42
beat	Sharks at Hamilton	32–19
lost to	Stormers at Cape Town	9–16
beat	Northern Bulls at Pretoria	39–31

Won 5, lost 6; placing: 6th
Tries scored: 26

Most tries: Roger Randle 5, Bruce Reihana 4,
              Rhys Duggan 3, Glenn Marsh 3, Dylan Mika 3
Most points: Glenn Jackson 68, Matthew Cooper 52

NEW SOUTH WALES WARATAHS
(coach Matt Williams)

drew with	Sharks at Durban	13–13
beat	Cats at Bloemfontein	39–10
beat	Chiefs at Sydney	36–30
beat	Northern Bulls at Sydney	39–23
lost to	Stormers at Sydney	18–28
lost to	Auckland Blues at Sydney	20–21
lost to	ACT Brumbies at Canberra	16–27
beat	Otago Highlanders at Dunedin	23–15
lost to	Queensland Reds at Sydney	13–30
lost to	Wellington Hurricanes at Napier	7–13
lost to	Canterbury Crusaders at Sydney	22–38

Won 4, lost 6, drew 1; placing: 8th
Tries scored: 32

Most tries: Matt Dowling 6, Duncan McRae 4,
              Nathan Grey 4, Scott Staniforth 3,
              Tom Bowman 3, Christian Warner 3
Most points: Matt Dowling 56, Christian Warner 36,
              Manuel Edmonds 36

Apart from three unrelated Venters, there were three pairs of brothers involved in the Cats–Northern Bulls game at Johannesburg. Jorrie and Chris Kruger appeared in the backs for the Cats, Nicky and Dan van der Walt were in the Bulls pack, while Conrad Stoltz, a Cats back, and Thys Stoltz, a Bulls forward, opposed each other.

AUCKLAND BLUES
(coach Jed Rowlands)

lost to	Otago Highlanders at Dunedin	13–19
lost to	Canterbury Crusaders at Auckland	16–22
drew with	Queensland Reds at Albany	12–12
beat	Chiefs at Hamilton	29–18
beat	New South Wales Waratahs at Sydney	21–20
beat	Wellington Hurricanes at Auckland	23–7
beat	Cats at Auckland	24–11
lost to	Sharks at Auckland	6–12
lost to	Stormers at Cape Town	23–37
lost to	Northern Bulls at Witbank	19–21
lost to	ACT Brumbies at Auckland	16–22

Won 4, lost 6, drew 1; placing: 9th
Tries scored: 15

Most tries: Joeli Vidiri 4
Most points: Adrian Cashmore 118

CATS
(coach André Markgraaf)

beat	ACT Brumbies at Johannesburg	33–22
lost to	New South Wales Waratahs at Bloemfontein	10–39
lost to	Sharks at Johannesburg	20–36
lost to	Otago Highlanders at Johannesburg	28–29
beat	Wellington Hurricanes at Johannesburg	43–27
beat	Northern Bulls at Johannesburg	57–24
lost to	Auckland Blues at Auckland	11–24
lost to	Chiefs at Pukekohe	42–44
lost to	Canterbury Crusaders at Nelson	38–58
lost to	Queensland Reds at Brisbane	12–22
beat	Stormers at Cape Town	18–16

Won 4, lost 7; placing: 11th
Tries scored: 37

Most tries: Conrad Stoltz 8, Jannie van der Walt 3,
André Venter 3, Johan Erasmus 3,
Naka Drotske 3, Chris Kruger 3
Most points: Pieter O'Neill 65, Conrad Stoltz 40,
Kobus Engelbrecht 28

WELLINGTON HURRICANES
(coach Frank Oliver)

lost to	Queensland Reds at Brisbane	0–11
lost to	Stormers at Wellington	22–24
beat	Northern Bulls at Palmerston North	37–18
drew with	Canterbury Crusaders at Christchurch	18–18
lost to	Cats at Johannesburg	27–43
beat	Sharks at East London	34–18
lost to	Auckland Blues at Auckland	7–23
lost to	Chiefs at New Plymouth	21–24
lost to	ACT Brumbies at Wellington	13–21
beat	New South Wales Waratahs at Napier	13–7
beat	Otago Highlanders at Wellington	21–19

Won 4, lost 6, drew 1; placing: 10th
Tries scored: 24

Most tries: Christian Cullen 5, Tana Umaga 3, Filo Tiatia 3
Most points: David Holwell 79, Mal Arnold 31

NORTHERN BULLS
(coach Eugene van Wyk)

lost to	Stormers at Pretoria	19–42
lost to	Otago Highlanders at Invercargill	23–65
lost to	Wellington Hurricanes at Palmerston North	18–37
lost to	New South Wales Waratahs at Sydney	23–39
lost to	ACT Brumbies at Canberra	9–73
lost to	Cats at Johannesburg	24–57
lost to	Queensland Reds at Brakpan	7–17
lost to	Sharks at Durban	0–29
lost to	Canterbury Crusaders at Pretoria	28–30
beat	Auckland Blues at Witbank	21–19
lost to	Chiefs at Pretoria	31–39

Won 1, lost 10; placing 12th
Tries scored: 21

Most tries: Deon de Kock 2, Schutte Bekker 2,
Wium Basson 2
Most points: Franco Smith 59, Casper Steyn 35

From the believe-it-or-not category, the Crusaders, in winning their last four round-robin matches by scores of 30–28, 58–38, 34–29 and 38–22, actually conceded as many tries as they scored: 17. The winning advantage came from the golden boot of Andrew Mehrtens, who kicked 68 points in those four games.

2000

TWO TEAMS TOWERED OVER their rivals in the 2000 Super 12, the Brumbies and the Crusaders, the title being decided in a shoot-out at an icy Bruce Stadium in Canberra.

The Brumbies were raging hot favourites to win, claiming home advantage, a win over the Crusaders in Christchurch, an awesome record of 48 tries for and 12 against, a swag of Wallabies and virtual invincibility in Canberra. But despite these seemingly insurmountable odds, and the fact the Brumbies controlled possession for four-fifths of the game, the gallant Crusaders somehow finished a point in front, 20–19, thanks to a last-gasp penalty goal from their many-times hero Andrew Mehrtens.

While the outcome left the Brumbies players and fans and coach Eddie Jones stunned, it completed a remarkable hat trick of successes for the Crusaders and coach Wayne Smith; remarkable, because all three finals were won away from home — in 1998 at Auckland, 1999 at Dunedin and finally 2000 at Canberra.

The Crusaders made an uncharacteristically strong start in 2000, winning their first four matches, but when they conceded 54 points to the Cats in Johannesburg, then stumbled against the Brumbies at home, it seemed this would not be their year. But they proved once again they were a team for the big occasion, overcoming massive odds to take out the final.

While it was essentially a team effort that got them home, standout individuals were winger Marika Vunibaka, who scored 11 tries, and the irrepressible Mehrtens, who scored another 160 points, extending his Super 12 aggregate to 652.

Until the Crusaders spoiled their party, it was the Brumbies who'd commanded most of the headlines, although not all of them were complimentary. Five Brumbies players, Joe Roff, Owen Finegan, Rod Kafer, Bill Young and Peter Ryan, had been involved in an unsavoury incident in Cape Town following their match against the Stormers. A taxi driver alleged they refused to pay him and trashed his vehicle, including ripping the fare meter from the dashboard. The players were also allegedly obnoxious at a local restaurant. The ACT Rugby Union conducted an inquiry into the incident and found three of the players guilty, fining them and applying a two-match deferred suspension. The other two escaped with a warning.

On the field, the Brumbies were awesomely efficient. They won in South Africa for the first time and conceded just 12 tries in round-robin play, a record for the competition. Their individual superstars were Stirling Mortlock, who amassed 194 points, and fullback Andrew Walker, who scored 13 tries, two short of Roff's record.

The big improvers were Laurie Mains' Cats, who bounded from 11th to the semifinals, while the Sharks, who'd three times made the play-offs, embarrassingly finished up with the wooden spoon, managing just one win (a difficult one, against the Waratahs in Sydney). The Cats once again lost all four matches in New Zealand and Australia but made it into the top four by winning seven out of seven in South Africa. Meanwhile, the Blues, striving to recapture their glory days, missed out on the semifinals when they stumbled against the Reds in Brisbane in their final game.

Daryl Gibson and Justin Marshall celebrate the Crusaders' 2000 success in Canberra. Fotopress

All the Australian and New Zealand franchises opted to dispense with the geographical identities in their names in 2000. Thus, it was Blues for Auckland, Hurricanes for Wellington Hurricanes, Crusaders for Canterbury Crusaders, Highlanders for Otago Highlanders, Reds for Queensland Reds, Waratahs for New South Wales Waratahs and Brumbies for ACT Brumbies. Even the team from Pretoria got into the act, the Northern Bulls becoming simply the Bulls.

THE STARS

SCOTT ROBERTSON (Crusaders)

Scott Robertson, who won the New Zealand Super 12 Player of the Year award in 2000, could claim the unique experience with the Canterbury Crusaders of sharing in a glorious hat trick of victories at the top end and the wooden spoon at the bottom.

Given their dominance of New Zealand rugby, it's easy to forget that in the inaugural season of Super 12, 1996, the Canterbury Crusaders finished a lonely, and embarrassing, last, astern of Western Province and Transvaal.

As a 21-year-old, fresh out of Mt Maunganui, Robertson was a part of that less than illustrious side coached by Vance Stewart. He observed the first three matches from the reserves bench. When they were all lost, he displaced Dean Coleman on the side of the scrum and secured a regular spot for the remainder of the series.

Robertson has no doubts that the experiences of 1996 counted heavily in the Crusaders' subsequent successes. 'The way we learned from them is one of the main reasons why, in the following seasons, we did so well. A core of our players were there in 1996 and again in 1997 when the turnaround started.'

The player who would acquire the nickname of Razor, for his lethal tackling, came to the rugby public's attention through 1995 and 1996 for a couple of reasons — his aggressive play for Bay of Plenty, New Zealand Colts and the Crusaders, and because of an uncanny resemblance to the man who led the Springboks to World Cup glory, Francois Pienaar. Tall, at 1.92 metres, and blond, Robertson cut a dashing figure on the rugby field. His specialty was scything down opponents and at 100 kg he was difficult to stop when in possession.

Until he was drafted into the Crusaders in 1996, Robertson was very much a man of the Mount. Having been educated at Mt Maunganui College

Fotopress

he enjoyed nothing more, outside the rugby season, than surfing the waves rolling in from the Pacific Ocean.

But once summoned to Christchurch, that became his base for the remainder of his (New Zealand) rugby career. He progressed steadily from New Zealand Colts (being part of an awesomely strong side in 1995, captained by Taine Randell and including no fewer than 16 players who would go on to become All Blacks) to the New Zealand Rugby Academy in 1997 and on to the All Blacks in 1998.

Understudy to the great Josh Kronfeld, he finally claimed the prized All Black No 7 jersey ahead of the incumbent in 2000, after another fabulous campaign with the Crusaders.

Robertson was, remarkably, one of six forwards who appeared in all 13 of the Crusaders' matches in 2000, the others being Ron Cribb, Reuben Thorne, captain Todd Blackadder, Greg Somerville and Mark Hammett. It was the tackling of Robertson and his colleagues that enabled the Crusaders to win the final, in almost unbelievable circumstances, against the Brumbies in Canberra.

TOUTAI KEFU (Reds)

When Tonga toured Australia in 1973 and pulled off an upset of monumental proportions, defeating the Wallabies 16–11 at Brisbane, one of the fullbacks in the touring party was Fatai Kefu. He was so impressed with what Queensland had to offer that two years later he emigrated to Brisbane with his wife Neomai and one-year-old son Toutai, never imagining that within 25 years his boy would not only be representing Australia but would be lauded as a hero of his country's World Cup success.

Kefu endured some anxious moments before sharing in the World Cup glory after being ordered off in a pool match at Lansdowne Road for trying to reshape Irishman Trevor Brennan's face. It was out-of-character behaviour for Kefu, but it earned him a two-match suspension, forcing him to sit out the quarter-final against Wales at the Millennium Stadium.

'It was the low point of my career,' he declared later. 'I felt terribly guilty. Had we lost to Wales with me in the stand I would have felt I'd let the whole team down.' Such was Kefu's status, he received staunch support from his captain John Eales and other senior team members, who considered the two-week ban excessive.

Kefu rounded out a perfectly equipped loose forward trio with David Wilson and Matt Cockbain. They'd helped the Queensland Reds qualify top in the Super 12 in 1999 and went on to contribute

Fotopress

massively to Australia's triumphant progress at the World Cup. This was the second World Cup won by Australia, and each time a player of Tongan heritage starred in the No 8 jersey. In 1991, it was Willie Ofahengaue, who'd been a huge inspiration to Kefu. Now it was Kefu's turn.

Kefu had almost quit Australia a couple of years earlier because of frustration at having to share game time with his major rival Tiaan Strauss. Kefu wanted to contribute an 80-minute effort, but he was regularly subbed after 45 or 50 minutes, sometimes even at half-time. When word spread that he was thinking of abandoning Australia, offers flooded in from clubs in England, Japan, France and Wales. But after a lot of soul-searching, Kefu decided to stay, to the everlasting relief of Australian fans.

When Rod Macqueen took over as Australian coach, he identified Kefu as the ideal player to pack down at the back of his scrum. In the two years leading up to the World Cup Kefu played in all 20 Wallaby tests. The King of Tonga, King Taufa'ahau Tupou IV, presented Kefu with a silver medal while the Tongan Rugby Union recognised his achievements by presenting him with a certificate of merit.

THE FACTS

In achieving their third straight Super 12 title, the Crusaders made it three finals victories away from home. In 1998, they'd beaten the Blues at Eden Park, in 1999 they overcame the Highlanders at Carisbrook, and in 2000 they edged out the Brumbies in Canberra.

The Sharks' burly prop Ollie le Roux became the first player to register 50 appearances in Super 12. Remarkably, by the conclusion of the fifth series he was the only South African player to have attained that milestone whereas 14 New Zealanders and 12 Australians had notched up their 50th appearance. The busiest Super 12 player by the end of 2000 was Todd Blackadder (Crusaders) with 60 games, followed by le Roux, 58, Anton Oliver (Highlanders), 57, Joeli Vidiri (Blues), 56, Daryl Gibson (Crusaders), 56, Norm Hewitt (Hurricanes), 55, Daniel Herbert (Reds), 55, and Ipolito Fenukitau (Brumbies), 55.

Brumbies midfielder Stirling Mortlock finished the season with 194 points, the most by an Australian player in a Super 12 campaign. In all, he converted 75 per cent of the Brumbies' tries, but in the final against the Crusaders he missed four penalty kicks at goal, which was more than any other kicker in any other Super 12 match in 2000.

The Brumbies kept four teams — the Stormers, the Cats, the Highlanders and the Crusaders — tryless in round-robin play in 2000. Such was the quality of their defence, they conceded only 12 tries in their 11 matches, 14 fewer than any other team.

When Cats winger Jannie van der Walt dotted down in the semifinal against the Brumbies in Canberra, it was the first try he'd scored outside South Africa, notable considering it was his 16th Super 12 try.

Former All Black greats and contemporaries, Bryan Williams and Grant Batty, featured as assistant coaches in 2000: 'Beegee' with the Hurricanes and 'Bats' with the Reds.

When the Blues first played the Chiefs at Albany it was a home game for the Blues. When they last played at Albany, in 1997, it was a home game for the Chiefs.

Although Todd Blackadder represented Nelson Bays in 1990, he had to wait until 2000 and the Crusaders–Stormers game before he registered his first try on Nelson's Trafalgar Park.

For the second time, the Hurricanes halted the Crusaders' winning streak of 11 games. They'd done it in 1999 by holding the Crusaders to an 18-all draw in Christchurch and in 2000 they gave the red and blacks a 28–22 beating in Wellington.

The Stormers, coached by Alan Solomons, became the first South African team to win consecutive matches in New Zealand when they downed the Chiefs 28–25 at Pukekohe and the Blues 39–18 at Auckland. Winger Breyton Paulse not only scored two tries in each game, he also scored two tries in each of the Stormers' next two matches, against the Reds at Brisbane and the Highlanders at Cape Town.

Coming on as a replacement for Elton Flatley against the Cats at Bloemfontein (in a match lost 32–36), Reds five-eighth Shane Drahm kicked eight goals from eight attempts, including four penalty goals within eight minutes. He finished with 22 points, repeating the feat in the next game against the Brumbies at Canberra, when the Reds lost again, 32–38.

Jannie de Beer, who had demoralised England with five dropped goals in the World Cup quarter-final in Paris the year previously, landed four dropped goals for the Northern Bulls in 2000, a Super 12 record (since surpassed by Louis Koen). They didn't help his team much, the Bulls finishing a humble 11th, ahead of only the Sharks.

THE FIRST SEMIFINAL
CRUSADERS 37,
HIGHLANDERS 15

AT JADE STADIUM, CHRISTCHURCH, 20 MAY

IT WAS A PECULIARITY OF Peter Sloane's term coaching the Otago Highlanders that, while they were near invincible at Carisbrook, away from home they couldn't win to save themselves. In round-robin play in 2000, they disposed of the Reds, the Sharks, the Hurricanes, the Cats and the Chiefs at the House of Pain, but stumbled at Christchurch, Canberra, Auckland, Cape Town and Sydney, breaking the sequence only against the lowly Bulls at Pretoria. (Things would not change in 2001, Sloane's men winning all six matches at home and losing all five on the road.)

So there were no great expectations upon the Highlanders when, as the third qualifier, they ventured to Jade Stadium to tackle the Crusaders, the second qualifier, in the opening semifinal of 2000. Even the absence of key Crusaders Justin Marshall and Norm Maxwell, along with Leon MacDonald spending 10 minutes in the sin bin, couldn't level the playing field. The Highlanders were steamrollered out of the game, pressured relentlessly by the Crusaders' mighty forwards, who set up another vintage evening for Andrew Mehrtens. Fresh back from injury, Mehrtens ran the show, helping create tries while kicking 22 points in a near impeccable display.

The Highlanders were unlucky to lose their playmaker Tony Brown, who limped out of the game with a thigh injury four minutes into the second half. Sloane switched Marc Ellis into first-five, introducing Brendan Laney on the wing. The changes proved unsettling. The men from the deep south hung in grittily, but two late tries by Marika Vunibaka took the Crusaders from 25–15 to 37–15, and gave a realistic appearance to the scoreboard.

Sloane heaped praise on the Crusaders at the finish. 'They are a class act,' he said. 'When Norm Berryman can't make the starting fifteen, it shows the team's strength. Their outstanding tackling pressured us into mistakes and turnovers.'

Sloane didn't offer it as an excuse, but said it hadn't helped his team that they'd been on the road for six of the last seven weeks.

Next to Mehrtens, the Crusaders' best player was prop Greg Somerville, who recorded a remarkably high tackle count.

FOR CRUSADERS: Tries by Marika Vunibaka 2 and Ron Cribb; 2 conversions and 6 penalty goals by Andrew Mehrtens.

FOR HIGHLANDERS: Tries by Byron Kelleher and Simon Maling; conversion by Brendon Laney; penalty goal by Tony Brown.

CRUSADERS: Leon MacDonald, Marika Vunibaka, Mark Robinson, Daryl Gibson, Caleb Ralph, Andrew Mehrtens, Ben Hurst, Ron Cribb, Scott Robertson, Reuben Thorne, Chris Jack, Todd Blackadder (captain), Greg Somerville, Mark Hammett, Greg Feek.
Replacements: Mark Mayerhofler, Aaron Mauger, Billy Fulton, Dallas Seymour, Steve Lancaster, Slade McFarland, Con Barrell.

HIGHLANDERS: Jeff Wilson, Rua Tipoki, Romi Ropati, Pita Alatini, Marc Ellis, Tony Brown, Byron Kelleher, Taine Randell (captain), Josh Kronfeld, Kelvin Middleton, John Blaikie, Simon Maling, Carl Hoeft, Anton Oliver, Joe McDonnell.
Replacements: Brendon Laney, Brendon Timmins, Paul Miller, Carl Hayman.

REFEREE: Wayne Erickson (Australia)

CROWD: 30,000

THE SECOND SEMIFINAL

BRUMBIES 28, CATS 5

AT BRUCE STADIUM, CANBERRA, 20 MAY

GIVEN THAT LAURIE MAINS' CATS had endured a fearful 64–nil pasting from the Brumbies at the same venue seven weeks earlier, it was little short of a miracle that with 52 minutes played they were still in the game at 5–6.

But they'd given so much of themselves, against a tenacious defence that had denied them at least two tries, that it was understandable that their resistance should crumble right at the end. The two late converted tries the Brumbies scored gave an unrealistic appearance to the scoreline. Certainly, Eddie Jones' men deserved to win, but they had had to withstand an explosive opening from the Cats.

Jones admitted afterwards that he had prepared his players for the Cats' opening onslaught. 'I knew they'd throw everything at us,' he said. 'Semifinals rugby is not always about being showy. It's about being patient and grinding out your victory.'

The gutsiest of the Cats' defenders, centre Japie Mulder, who'd been an inspiration throughout the first half, misjudged a tackle on Stirling Mortlock

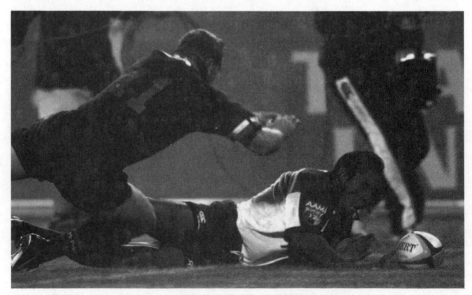

Andrew Walker scores the opening try against the Cats in 2000. Fotopress

five minutes into the second half and damaged his neck muscles, forcing him to retire. With his departure the Cats' defensive patterns became less effective and were eventually exploited by the Brumbies, who were delighted to qualify for the final for the second time.

Mains, chuffed that the Cats had qualified for the play-offs for the first time, lamented that his team had missed a couple of golden try-scoring opportunities. And who was the player responsible for stopping them? None other than little George Gregan, the 80 kg scrumhalf who fought above his weight in every contest.

'Had we scored even one of those tries,' said Mains, 'it would have been a different game. When the Brumbies had the opportunities at the other end, they took them.'

The Cats' loosies, André Venter, André Vos and Johan Erasmus, were a complete unit and they all had big games. It says much for the Brumbies players that they withstood everything the South Africans threw at them before finishing over the top of them. New Zealand referee Paddy O'Brien admitted afterwards that the contest had the intensity of a test match. 'The Brumbies showed what a great team they are by waiting, waiting and waiting,' he said. 'They were outstanding, to be honest.'

FOR BRUMBIES: Tries by Andrew Walker, Mitch Hardy and Joe Roff; 2 conversions and 3 penalty goals by Stirling Mortlock.

FOR CATS: Try by Jannie van der Walt.

BRUMBIES: Andrew Walker, Mark Bartholomeusz, Stirling Mortlock, Rod Kafer, Joe Roff, Stephen Larkham, George Gregan (captain), Jim Williams, George Smith, Ipolito Fenukitau, David Giffin, Justin Harrison, Patricio Noriega, Jeremy Paul, Bill Young. Replacements: Mitch Hardy, James Holbeck, Travis Hall, Peter Ryan, Troy Jacques, Ben Darwin, Tom Murphy.

CATS: Tinus Delport, Chester Williams, Grant Esterhuizen, Japier Mulder, Jannie van der Walt, Louis Koen, Werner Swanepoel, André Vos, André Venter, Johan Erasmus (captain), Jannes Labuschagne, Johan Ackerman, Willie Meyer, Leon Boshoff, Marius Mostert. Replacements: Dean Hall, Jimmy Powell, Adrian Garvey, Delarey du Preez.

REFEREE: Paddy O'Brien (New Zealand)

CROWD: 25,126

THE FINAL

CRUSADERS 20, BRUMBIES 19

AT BRUCE STADIUM, CANBERRA, 22 MAY

BRUMBIES FANS ARE STILL shaking their heads at how their team managed to lose the 2000 final in the frigid conditions of Bruce Stadium. After all, their team did win the rucks and mauls 165–34 and launch wave after wave of attack at the New Zealanders. But Robbie Deans' men were incredibly resolute, holding firm where a lesser side would have been submerged. And just when the Brumbies were getting ready to celebrate a famous victory, Andrew Mehrtens, despite struggling with cramp, landed a superb penalty goal from 40 metres to complete a hat trick of successes for the Crusaders.

It really was the impossible victory. Everything pointed to a Brumbies win. They'd been the standout team in the competition, arriving at the final with 48 tries to their credit while conceding just 12, along the way managing to defeat the Crusaders at Jade Stadium, a rare achievement indeed.

And with the amount of possession they generated, they should have swamped the challengers from across the Tasman. However, on a night when the temperature began at 3°C and kept dropping, with light snow falling at one stage, a surreal event unfolded out in the middle.

The Crusaders' fanatical fear of losing obviously played a big part in the outcome, and so did the team's tactical planning, for Deans and his assistant Steve Hansen had come up with a counter for every Brumbies ploy. They were fortunate that the conditions militated against the Brumbies' wide-ranging game.

The Brumbies won the second-half ruck and maul count 99–11, but found progress difficult against the Crusaders' superbly organised fan defence. For all their possession, the Brumbies squeezed through for just one try, achieved when replacement loosie George Smith burst between Mehrtens and Scott Robertson to score under the bar. That brought the Brumbies up to 13–17 and when Stirling Mortlock added two penalty goals to put them ahead 19–17, the locals obviously thought justice was about to be done.

But the Crusaders weren't having any of that. They chased the restart enthusiastically and when a Brumbies player was penalised for failing to release,

Crusaders reserves try to keep warm during the final in icy Canberra. Fotopress

Mehrtens, notwithstanding cramping which had almost taken him out of the game, was up to landing the matchwinner.

The Crusaders' try was a masterpiece of improvisation from No 8 Ron Cribb. After taking an inside pass from Mehrtens, he smashed through Jeremy Paul's tackle, and placed a deft grubber kick through that he regathered on the goalline.

Jones, who defended his team's tactics — saying they were the same tactics that had got them to the final — expressed understandable disappointment. 'We've played good rugby throughout, but things just didn't roll our way in the final.'

FOR CRUSADERS: Try by Ron Cribb; 5 penalty goals by Andrew Mehrtens.

FOR BRUMBIES: Try by George Smith; conversion and 4 penalty goals by Stirling Mortlock.

BRUMBIES: Andrew Walker, Mark Bartholomeusz, Stirling Mortlock, Rod Kafer, Joe Roff, Stephen Larkham, George Gregan, Jim Williams, Brett Robinson (captain), Ipolito Fenukitau, Justin Harrison, David Giffin, Patricio Noriega, Jeremy Paul, Bill Young. Replacements: George Smith, Troy Jacques.

CRUSADERS: Leon MacDonald, Marika Vunibaka, Mark Robinson, Daryl Gibson, Caleb Ralph, Andrew Mehrtens, Ben Hurst, Ron Cribb, Scott Robertson, Reuben Thorne, Norm Maxwell, Todd Blackadder (captain), Greg Somerville, Mark Hammett, Greg Feek. Replacements: Mark Mayerhofler, Aaron Mauger, Dallas Seymour, Con Barrell, Chris Jack.

REFEREE: André Watson (South Africa)

CROWD: 27,489

THE RESULTS

BRUMBIES
(coach Eddie Jones)

lost to	Blues at Canberra	15–18
beat	Sharks at Canberra	51–10
beat	Stormers at Cape Town	29–15
beat	Bulls at Pretoria	28–19
beat	Cats at Canberra	64–0
beat	Highlanders at Canberra	34–15
lost to	Waratahs at Sydney	25–30
beat	Hurricanes at Canberra	47–28
beat	Chiefs at Hamilton	45–17
beat	Reds at Canberra	38–32
beat	Crusaders at Christchurch	17–12

Won 9, lost 2; placing: 1st
Tries scored: 48

Semifinal: beat Cats at Canberra — 28–5

Final: lost to Crusaders at Canberra — 19–20

Most tries: Andrew Walker 13, Mark Bartholomeusz 7, Joe Roff 5, Owen Finegan 5, Stirling Mortlock 4

Most points: Stirling Mortlock 194, Andrew Walker 68

HIGHLANDERS
(coach Peter Sloane)

beat	Reds at Dunedin	50–13
beat	Sharks at Dunedin	27–20
beat	Hurricanes at Dunedin	35–19
beat	Cats at Dunedin	33–31
lost to	Crusaders at Christchurch	36–42
lost to	Brumbies at Canberra	15–34
lost to	Blues at Auckland	16–26
beat	Chiefs at Dunedin	38–6
lost to	Stormers at Cape Town	13–27
beat	Bulls at Pretoria	42–40
lost to	Waratahs at Sydney	15–22

Won 6, lost 5; placing: 3rd
Tries scored: 32

Semifinal: lost to Crusaders at Christchurch — 15–37

Most tries: Jeff Wilson 5, Byron Kelleher 5, Romi Ropati 4, Pita Alatini 4

Most points: Tony Brown 150, Jeff Wilson 30

CRUSADERS
(coach Robbie Deans)

beat	Chiefs at Hamilton	27–24
beat	Blues at Christchurch	32–20
beat	Reds at Brisbane	27–19
beat	Stormers at Nelson	47–31
beat	Highlanders at Christchurch	42–36
lost to	Hurricanes at Wellington	22–28
beat	Sharks at Durban	32–24
lost to	Cats at Johannesburg	31–54
beat	Bulls at Christchurch	75–27
beat	Waratahs at Christchurch	22–13
lost to	Brumbies at Christchurch	12–17

Won 8, lost 3; placing: 2nd
Tries scored: 43

Semifinal: beat Highlanders at Christchurch — 37–15

Final: beat Brumbies at Canberra — 20–19

Most tries: Marika Vunibaka 11, Caleb Ralph 8, Ron Cribb 7, Leon MacDonald 5, Justin Marshall 5

Most points: Andrew Mehrtens 160, Marika Vunibaka 55, Leon MacDonald 41

CATS
(coach Laurie Mains)

beat	Bulls at Pretoria	23–19
beat	Stormers at Johannesburg	22–18
lost to	Waratahs at Sydney	16–51
lost to	Highlanders at Dunedin	31–33
lost to	Hurricanes at Palmerston North	23–29
lost to	Brumbies at Canberra	0–64
beat	Sharks at Durban	28–27
beat	Crusaders at Johannesburg	54–31
beat	Reds at Bloemfontein	36–32
beat	Blues at Johannesburg	34–27
beat	Chiefs at Bloemfontein	53–3

Won 6, lost 5; placing: 4th
Tries scored: 32

Semifinal: lost to Brumbies at Canberra — 5–28

Most tries: Chester Williams 5, Tinus Delport 4, Jannie van der Walt 4, André Venter 4

Most points: Louis Koen 135, Chester Williams 25

STORMERS
(coach Alan Solomons)

beat	Waratahs at Cape Town	22–15
lost to	Cats at Johannesburg	18–22
drew with	Bulls at Cape Town	19–19
lost to	Brumbies at Cape Town	15–29
lost to	Crusaders at Nelson	31–47
beat	Chiefs at Pukekohe	28–25
beat	Blues at Auckland	39–18
lost to	Reds at Brisbane	24–37
beat	Highlanders at Cape Town	27–13
beat	Hurricanes at Cape Town	43–23
beat	Sharks at Durban	32–28

Won 6, lost 4, drew 1; placing: 5th
Tries scored: 28

Most tries: Breyton Paulse 10, Pieter Rossouw 4
Most points: Braam van Straaten 129, Breyton Paulse 50,
Percy Montgomery 39

REDS
(coach John Connolly)

lost to	Highlanders at Dunedin	13–50
lost to	Hurricanes at New Plymouth	25–43
lost to	Crusaders at Brisbane	19–27
beat	Chiefs at Brisbane	37–17
beat	Waratahs at Brisbane	31–16
beat	Bulls at Brisbane	34–15
beat	Stormers at Brisbane	37–24
beat	Sharks at Durban	24–13
lost to	Cats at Bloemfontein	32–36
lost to	Brumbies at Canberra	32–38
beat	Blues at Brisbane	33–26

Won 6, lost 5; placing: 7th
Tries scored: 31

Most tries: Chris Latham 7, Elton Flatley 3,
Matt Cockbain 3, Damian Smith 3,
Sam Cordingley 3
Most points: Shane Drahm 91, Elton Flatley 86,
Chris Latham 35

BLUES
(coach Gordon Hunter)

beat	Brumbies at Canberra	18–15
lost to	Chiefs at Albany	25–32
lost to	Crusaders at Christchurch	20–32
beat	Waratahs at Auckland	31–17
beat	Hurricanes at Wellington	25–14
lost to	Stormers at Auckland	18–39
beat	Highlanders at Auckland	26–16
beat	Bulls at Auckland	54–11
beat	Sharks at Durban	30–19
lost to	Cats at Johannesburg	27–34
lost to	Reds at Brisbane	26–33

Won 6, lost 5; placing: 6th
Tries scored: 37

Most tries: Joeli Vidiri 6, Troy Flavell 4, Craig Dowd 4
Most points: Adrian Cashmore 98, Joeli Vidiri 30,
Hayden Taylor 25

HURRICANES
(coach Graham Mourie)

beat	Sharks at Wellington	40–23
beat	Reds at New Plymouth	43–25
lost to	Highlanders at Dunedin	19–35
beat	Chiefs at Hamilton	24–19
beat	Cats at Palmerston North	29–23
lost to	Blues at Wellington	14–25
beat	Crusaders at Wellington	28–22
lost to	Brumbies at Canberra	28–47
beat	Waratahs at Sydney	27–20
lost to	Stormers at Cape Town	23–43
lost to	Bulls at Pretoria	33–47

Won 6, lost 5; placing 8th
Tries scored: 37

Most tries: Christian Cullen 10, Jonah Lomu 6,
Tana Umaga 5, Brad Fleming 4
Most points: David Holwell 105, Christian Cullen 50,
Daryl Lilley 43

WARATAHS
(coach Ian Kennedy)

lost to	Stormers at Cape Town	15–22
beat	Bulls at Pretoria	33–13
beat	Cats at Sydney	51–16
lost to	Sharks at Sydney	19–26
lost to	Blues at Auckland	17–31
lost to	Reds at Brisbane	16–31
beat	Chiefs at Hamilton	37–30
beat	Brumbies at Sydney	30–25
lost to	Hurricanes at Sydney	20–27
lost to	Crusaders at Christchurch	13–22
beat	Highlanders at Sydney	22–15

Won 5, lost 6; placing: 9th
Tries scored: 24

Most tries: Scott Staniforth 6, Matt Burke 3
Most points: Matt Burke 158, Scott Staniforth 30

BULLS
(coach Heyneke Meyer)

lost to	Cats at Pretoria	19–23
lost to	Waratahs at Pretoria	13–33
drew with	Stormers at Cape Town	19–19
lost to	Brumbies at Pretoria	19–28
drew with	Sharks at Pretoria	14–14
lost to	Reds at Brisbane	15–34
lost to	Chiefs at Rotorua	7–40
lost to	Blues at Auckland	11–54
lost to	Crusaders at Christchurch	27–75
lost to	Highlanders at Pretoria	40–42
beat	Hurricanes at Pretoria	47–33

Won 1, lost 8, drew 2; placing: 11th
Tries scored: 19

Most tries: Deon de Koch 3
Most points: Jannie de Beer 123,
              Jaco van der Westhuysen 18

CHIEFS
(coach Ross Cooper)

lost to	Crusaders at Hamilton	24–27
beat	Blues at Albany	32–25
lost to	Hurricanes at Hamilton	19–24
lost to	Reds at Brisbane	17–37
lost to	Stormers at Pukekohe	25–28
lost to	Waratahs at Hamilton	30–37
beat	Bulls at Rotorua	40–7
lost to	Highlanders at Dunedin	6–38
lost to	Brumbies at Hamilton	17–45
beat	Sharks at Durban	44–31
lost to	Cats at Bloemfontein	3–53

Won 3, lost 8; placing: 10th
Tries scored: 27

Most tries: Roger Randle 4, Bruce Reihana 4
Most points: Glenn Jackson 81, Loki Crichton 56

SHARKS
(coach Hugh Reece-Edwards)

lost to	Hurricanes at Wellington	23–40
lost to	Highlanders at Dunedin	20–27
lost to	Brumbies at Canberra	10–51
beat	Waratahs at Sydney	26–19
drew with	Bulls at Pretoria	14–14
lost to	Cats at Durban	27–28
lost to	Crusaders at Durban	24–32
lost to	Reds at Durban	13–24
lost to	Blues at Durban	19–30
lost to	Chiefs at Durban	31–44
lost to	Stormers at Durban	28–32

Won 1, lost 9, drew 1; placing: 12th
Tries scored: 25

Most tries: Clinton van Rensburg 3, Pieter Muller 3,
              Stefan Terblanche 3
Most points: Gaffie du Toit 91, Clinton van Rensburg 34

2001

IT TOOK SIX YEARS, but finally the Super 12 crown was wrenched away from New Zealand, moving across the Tasman Sea to Australia to join the World Cup, the Tri-nations Trophy and the Bledisloe Cup. Yes, the Aussies boasted a full set of silverware after the Brumbies, well coached by Eddie Jones, comprehensively disposed of South Africa's best team, the Sharks, in the Super 12 final in Canberra. Not only didn't a New Zealand team win the competition — the Blues and the Crusaders having shared the first five titles — none of the five Kiwi teams even qualified for the semifinals. Midway between the fourth and fifth World Cups, it was a worrying sign for New Zealand rugby.

But all the glory was with the Brumbies, who qualified top for the second year in succession and hosted the final for the second year in a row. The difference was: this time they won it! And won it in style, providing a fitting send-off for the team's ace try scorer Joe Roff, who was heading to France.

Justin Harrison and David Giffin celebrate the Brumbies' 2001 win against the Crusaders. Fotopress

Ever since their anguishing loss to the Crusaders in 2000, the Brumbies had been focused on reaching the final again, and this time winning. In 2001 they struck trouble ahead of the final, when they lost two of their outstanding campaigners, Stirling Mortlock to injury and Owen Finegan to suspension.

Such were the quality of their back-up players, however, they crushed the Sharks 30–nil in the second half of the final to stamp themselves the champion side of the SANZAR nations.

With the Kiwis reduced to TV viewers, the semifinals were fought out between two Australia teams (the Brumbies and the Reds) and two South African teams (the Sharks and the Cats). The Sharks' achievement in qualifying for the final was truly outstanding, given that they had taken out the wooden spoon in 2000. New coach Rudolf Straueli transformed the side from chumps to near champs in double-quick time.

While the Sharks were the greatest movers in 2001, two New Zealand franchises were responsible for the most serious slumps. The Crusaders plummeted from first to 10th and the Blues from sixth to 11th. Former All Black coach Laurie Mains got his Cats team through to the play-offs for the second year running and helped them make a famous breakthrough — they won two matches in New Zealand, their first ever. Cats flyhalf Louis Koen had the distinction of scoring the most points in the competition, 157, closely followed by Braam von Straaten (Stormers) on 153 and Mortlock on 144. Andrew Walker (Brumbies) and Aisea Tuilevu (Highlanders) were the leading try scorers, with eight each.

THE STARS

STEPHEN LARKHAM (Brumbies)

Two nicknames that Stephen Larkham has acquired during his rugby career provide a vivid illustration of his character and effectiveness. As a youngster growing up on a sheep station at Yass near Canberra, he was tagged The Phantom by his team-mates for the manner in which he kept bobbing up where least expected. Many years later, on his first Wallaby tour, his perpetual silences in social situations led to him being named Bernie, a nickname that has stuck. It comes from the movie *Weekend at Bernie's* in which a deceased character named Bernie is carted around by his mates because they don't want anyone to know he's dead.

Joost van der Westhuizen expresses Northern Transvaal's despair as the Auckland Blues score yet another try in their 48–11 semifinal win at Eden Park in 1996. Fotopress

An elated James Kerr scores the matchwinner for Canterbury Crusaders against Auckland Blues in the 1998 final. Fotopress

Tryscorer Afato So'oalo celebrates Canterbury Crusaders' finals win over Otago Highlanders at Carisbrook in 1999. Fotopress

Joe Roff all smiles after the Brumbies' breakthrough win in Canberra in 2001. Fotopress

Double tryscorer Charl van Rensburg earns a hug from Sharks team-mates in the 2001 semifinal against the Cats in Durban. Fotopress

New Zealand Player of the Year in 2002, Chris Jack, in rampaging mood. Fotopress

Stormers midfielder De Wet Barry scores in the semifinal against the Crusaders in 2004. Fotopress

Mark Bartholomeusz wins George Gregan's approval after setting up a try in the 2004 final against the Crusaders. Fotopress

Ettienne Botha attacks for the Bulls against the Waratahs in the 2005 semifinal. Fotopress

Crusaders' leading try scorer Rico Gear on attack in the final at Jade Stadium. Fotopress

Fotopress

The taciturn Larkham lets his on-field exploits do the talking for him. He has been a revelation in international rugby since 1998, when Rod Macqueen transformed him from a fullback and sometimes wing into a flyhalf. The All Blacks of that year were among the first opponents to appreciate how dangerously effective Larkham could be operating outside George Gregan. He was sensationally effective in Australia's 24–16 win at the MCG, as a kicker, passer and runner who was extremely busy around the field.

When the Wallabies then dropped the next Tri-nations encounter to South Africa, 14–13 in Perth, he was quizzed by Macqueen about why he hadn't considered a dropped goal as his team attacked in the desperate final moments.

'I guess,' he replied to Macqueen, 'because the last time I even attempted a dropped goal was when I was in the under-9s!'

Macqueen ordered him to start practising drop-kicking, which he mastered so effectively that in November 1999 he broke the deadlock in the World Cup semifinal against the Springboks — when the teams were locked together at 21-all — with a booming drop-kick from 45 metres.

By the completion of the 2001 season, Larkham, firmly established as one of world rugby's most accomplished performers, had shared in almost every major prize the game had to offer: the World Cup, the Tri-nations Trophy, the Super 12 Trophy and the Bledisloe Cup.

Larkham's father Geoff, who played more than 300 matches in the Canberra competition for the Western Districts club, was president of the ACT Brumbies in 2005, at the conclusion of which season his only son had chalked up 98 appearances in Super 12 and scored 30 tries.

MARK ANDREWS (Sharks)

Probably the greatest tribute New Zealanders could pay to Mark Andrews is to say that they would have loved to have had him as one of their own. He embodied everything Kiwis looked for in a lock: he had a commanding presence at the line-out, he effortlessly gathered restarts, he was as resilient as Sean Fitzpatrick — his career spanning eight years and 77 Springbok tests — and he possessed leadership qualities. The toughness probably came from the season he spent with the Aurillac club in France when he was just 19, getting the position when he kidded them he was 21. He claims only a handful of the matches he played there did not turn into mass brawls.

Andrews was always destined to make an impact in rugby. His father and two brothers had all played for the Selborne College First XV in East London, as did his cousin Keith, who would go on to represent South Africa as a prop. Andrews had put his studies at Stellenbosch University on hold to play in France, but upon his return to South Africa he opted to spend time in Durban where he was soon 'spotted'.

He was rushed into Ian McIntosh's Natal team in 1993 as a 21-year-old, and before the year was out, following McIntosh's unexpected promotion to Springbok coach, he found himself touring Argentina as a loose forward. His test debut, at lock, came in 1994 against England at Cape Town. It marked the commencement of a celebrated international career. After he'd starred on the Bok tour of New Zealand that year, McIntosh said, 'He's got the ability to become one of the great players.'

Fotopress

How perceptive was McIntosh. Andrews became a permanent fixture in the Springbok side. In his eight years as a Springbok he would play under six different coaches and lock the scrum with eight different partners. And he would score 12 tries, the most by a Springbok forward. He would also play 122 matches for Natal. He helped the Sharks reach the Super 12 semifinals in 1996, 1997, 1998 and 2001, he was in two Currie Cup winning sides and, most treasured of all, he was a member of South Africa's World Cup winning side of 1995.

THE FACTS

Scoring his 20th Super 12 try in the semifinal against the Reds at Canberra, Brumbies flanker Owen Finegan became the first forward in the competition to bring up a century of points from tries alone. Finegan also became the first forward to score a hat trick of tries in a Super 12 match on two occasions when he dotted down three times against the Crusaders in Canberra. He'd previously achieved the feat against the Cats in 2000.

The champion Brumbies did not concede a try in the final three matches of the 2001 season, allowing the Chiefs, the Reds (in the semifinal) and the Sharks (in the final) to score just six points each. While the Brumbies were accumulating 12 tries, their opponents garnered just six penalty goals.

When he missed the Sharks–Hurricanes game, prop Ollie le Roux ended a record run of 61 consecutive games for the Sharks. That record was surpassed by Highlanders hooker Anton Oliver, whose new mark stopped at 65 when he missed the game against the Brumbies.

When the Highlanders defeated the Waratahs 39–20, it was, astonishingly, the first time since 1901 that a Dunedin-based team had defeated a Sydney-based team in Dunedin.

The Chiefs recorded their third cliff-hanger victory against the Cats. In 1998, they won 36–35; in 1999, they sneaked home 44–22; and in 2001, they hung on to win 22–18. On all three occasions, the referee was Australia's Stu Dickinson.

After 21 consecutive defeats, the Cats, coached in 2001 by Laurie Mains, finally broke through for their first victory outside South Africa, defeating the Blues 26–23 at Whangarei. They obviously enjoyed the experience, because nine days later they nosed out the Crusaders 32–31 at Nelson.

THE FIRST SEMIFINAL

BRUMBIES 30, REDS 6

AT BRUCE STADIUM, CANBERRA, 19 MAY

BRUMBIES HOOKER JEREMY PAUL'S SMILE said it all at the final whistle after the Reds had been comfortably despatched at Bruce Stadium, where the Brumbies hadn't lost since the final of 2000.

'We started planning for this day immediately following our disappointing loss to the Crusaders in last year's final,' he said. 'Our whole campaign has been aimed at qualifying for the final again so we could avenge what happened last time.'

It was Paul who provided the trimmings with his last-minute five-pointer that made the victory look a little more comfortable than it actually was. The Reds had still been hanging in grimly 6–7 at half-time.

But John Eales' team simply couldn't find a way through the Brumbies' steel-chain defence. They didn't manage a try against the Brumbies in round-robin action at Brisbane and they missed out again here. The Reds international centre Daniel Herbert afterwards paid a glowing tribute to the Brumbies' defence. 'They're regularly praised for their attacking skills,' he said, 'but rarely for their defence. We found it impossible to get through.'

Paul was the only one of the Brumbies' three try scorers to survive the match. Stirling Mortlock — who'd aggregated 139 points in the series — dislocated his shoulder while slithering across for the team's first five-pointer; flanker Owen Finegan, who dotted down in the second half, incurred a suspension the instant referee Jonathan Kaplan showed him a yellow card. Three yellow cards, which Finegan acquired during the Super 12 campaign, equate to a red card.

So while there was general delight in the Brumbies camp that they had qualified for another final, there was also an element of apprehension knowing that two of their most experienced players would be on the sideline.

When the Hurricanes defeated the Highlanders 35–33 in Napier, David Holwell became the first New Zealand player to score 30 points in a Super 12 match. His tally came from seven penalty goals, two conversions and a try.

The Matt McBain-coached Reds, who had done amazingly well to qualify for the play-offs after losing five of their first six encounters, had their opportunities in the opening quarter when they were all over the home team. But after Joe Roff pulled off a magnificent try-saving tackle, the Reds never looked like getting over the line. They conceded the second half 23–nil.

Brumbies lock David Giffin won the man-of-the-match award for a great 80-minute effort. He helped build a strong defensive wall around the rucks and mauls and helped close down the Reds' dangerous line-out. The Reds had the misfortune to lose flyhalf Elton Flatley, who was knocked out tackling Stephen Larkham and had to be stretchered from the field.

FOR BRUMBIES: Tries by Stirling Mortlock, Owen Finegan and Jeremy Paul; 3 conversions and 2 penalty goals by Andrew Walker; dropped goal by Stephen Larkham.

FOR REDS: Penalty goals by Elton Flatley and Shane Drahm.

BRUMBIES: Andrew Walker, Graeme Bond, Stirling Mortlock, Rod Kafer, Joe Roff, Stephen Larkham, George Gregan (captain), Jim Williams, George Smith, Owen Finegan, David Giffin, Justin Harrison, Ben Darwin, Jeremy Paul, Bill Young.
Replacements: Mark Bartholomeusz, James Holbeck, Travis Hall, Peter Ryan, David Pusey, Matt Weaver, Tom Murphy.

REDS: Chris Latham, Junior Pelesasa, Daniel Herbert, Steve Kefu, Ricky Nalatu, Elton Flatley, Jacob Rauluni, Toutai Kefu, David Croft, Matt Cockbain, John Eales (captain), Nathan Sharpe, Glenn Panoho, Michael Foley, Nick Stiles.
Replacements: Nathan Williams, Shane Drahm, Sam Cordingley, John Roe, Mark Connors, Fletcher Dyson, Sean Hardman.

REFEREE: Jonathan Kaplan (South Africa)

CROWD: 25,273

Both replacement hookers in the Crusaders–Sharks match at Christchurch scored a try — Mark Hammett for the home team and Lukas van Biljon for the visitors.

When Hurricanes fullback Christian Cullen dotted down twice against the Crusaders at Christchurch, it was the third consecutive occasion he had registered a pair of tries against this opponent. No other player in Super 12 had achieved this feat.

THE SECOND SEMIFINAL

SHARKS 30, CATS 12

AT KING'S PARK, DURBAN, 19 MAY

ONE OF THE TRUE MIRACLES of the first decade of the Super 12 belonged to the Sharks, who qualified for the final in 2001, a year after finishing stone cold last in the competition.

Rudolf Straueli inherited from Hugh Reece-Edwards a bedraggled team that had finished the 2000 season with the humiliating record (humiliating for a franchise that had three times qualified for the semifinals) of one win, one draw and nine defeats. The team had rounded out its 2000 campaign with six straight losses at King's Park, Durban, previously regarded, along with Auckland's Eden Park, Christchurch's Jade Stadium, Brisbane's Ballymore and Johannesburg's Ellis Park, as a rugby fortress.

What a difference a new coach can make. Straueli, operating with essentially the same players, plus a couple of exciting newcomers, transformed the Sharks instantly into a winning combination. This time, the team's six home matches were all won!

So when the Cats journeyed down to Durban for the first all-South African Super 12 semifinal, the advantage was very definitely with the Sharks. Laurie Mains, coach of the Cats, had anticipated a home semifinal but, in the season's biggest upset, that prospect disintegrated when his team inexplicably went down to the wooden spooners, the Bulls, at Ellis Park, in the final qualifying game. Mains would reveal later that the relationship between himself and his captain Johan 'Rassie' Erasmus had seriously deteriorated by the time the team returned from its Australasian sojourn and, unfortunately for the team, this impacted on the onfield performance.

So the Cats team that journeyed down from Johannesburg to Durban wasn't perhaps as razor sharp as it had been earlier in the season.

Butch James, one of Straueli's newcomers, demoralised the Cats with a magical performance. He was personally responsible for three Sharks tries in the 15 minutes before half-time, after the Cats had led 6–3.

Down 6–20 at the break, the Cats dominated the first 30 minutes of the second half, but the best they could manage was two penalty goals, whereupon

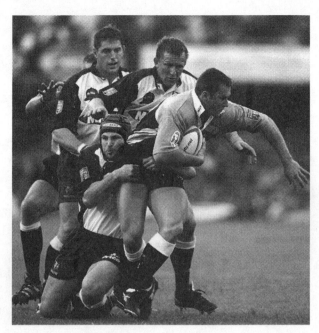

Sharks midfielder Trevor Halstead ambushed during the Durban semifinal. Fotopress

James finished them off. He regathered his own grubber kick, on a rare attacking foray, to set up try number two for van Rensburg. James said he'd decided he wouldn't attempt chip kicks in this game because they had only been turning over possession.

Mains said the Sharks deserved their victory. 'They took their chances professionally. We had opportunities in the second half but didn't take them.'

FOR SHARKS: **Tries by Charl van Rensburg 2, Stefan Terblanche, Trevor Halstead and Warren Britz; conversion and penalty goal by Butch James.**

FOR CATS: **4 penalty goals by Louis Koen.**

SHARKS: **Richard Loubscher, Stefan Terblanche, Deon Kayser, Trevor Halstead, Justin Swart, Butch James, Craig Davidson, A J Venter, Charl van Rensburg, Warren Britz, Mark Andrews (captain), Albert van den Berg, Etienne Fynn, John Smit, Ollie le Roux. Replacements: André Snyman, Gaffie du Toit, Hentie Martens, Brad MacLeod-Henderson, Shawn Sowerby, Brent Moyle, Lukas van Biljon.**

CATS: **Tinus Delport, Wylie Human, Grant Esterhuizen, Eugene Meyer, Dean Hall, Louis Koen, Werner Swanepoel, André Vos, André Venter, Johan Erasmus (captain), Jannes Labuschagne, John Ackerman, Baksteen Nel, Leon Boshoff, Marius Mostert. Replacements: Conrad Jantjes, Clinton van Rensburg, Chad Alcock, Piet Krause, André van Niekerk, Kleinjan Tromp, Pietman van Niekerk.**

REFEREE: **Stu Dickinson (Australia)**

CROWD: **52,750**

THE FINAL

BRUMBIES 36, SHARKS 6

AT BRUCE STADIUM, CANBERRA, 26 MAY

JOE ROFF, ONE OF THE BRUMBIES' great achievers, was off for a year's sabbatical to France following this game and dearly wanted to exit in style. He did, scoring two tries to help his team sweep aside Rudolf Straueli's Sharks. While his touchdowns promoted him to equal top Super 12 try scorer, on 44 with Christian Cullen, his personal accomplishment was thoroughly overshadowed by the Brumbies' momentous breakthrough victory.

They'd come close in both 1997, against the Blues, and 2000, when the Crusaders burgled a victory in Canberra, and now finally they'd broken the New Zealand stranglehold on the Super 12 trophy. It represented a remarkable achievement for a team that had started out in 1996 as Australia's 'spare parts' franchise, a fascinating mix of local hopefuls and rejects from New South Wales and Queensland.

Still 'bleeding' from the 2000 final against the Crusaders that they won everywhere but on the scoreboard, the Brumbies weren't going to let this one get away. Maintaining composure, they absorbed the Shark's early pressure before waltzing away with the game in the second half.

An elated Brumbies captain after the big win over the Sharks. Fotopress

When it was 6-all at half-time, many of the Brumbies' fans, recalling how Andrew Mehrtens had denied them glory with a late penalty goal in 2000, were apprehensive, but not coach Eddie Jones. 'The game unfolded exactly as we expected,' he said. 'We knew they'd come out hard and even try and intimidate us. Our research had shown they scored most of their points in the first half.'

So when the Brumbies restricted them to two Butch James penalty goals in the opening 40 minutes, they knew their game plan was working. The Brumbies won the second half 30–nil. Roff was at his devastating best in the second half, slicing through for two great tries, the team's other five-pointer going to lock David Giffin, who took out the man-of-the-match award. The balance of the points were provided by Andrew Walker, who landed eight goals from eight attempts.

The Brumbies had received a stirring pre-match team talk from their former skipper Brett Robinson, who flew in especially for the game from Oxford University where he was studying. He reminded the players of the pain of the 2000 final.

Delighted to be sharing in the victory was former Broncos league star Peter Ryan, who was in the starting fifteen for the first time after 17 appearances as a substitute. He got his chance when Owen Finegan was suspended.

Sharks coach Straueli said he was proud of his team if disappointed in the outcome. 'We are a young team and the players will learn from this experience. We missed opportunities to score tries in the first half, and you can't afford that in a Super 12 final.'

FOR BRUMBIES: Tries by Joe Roff 2 and David Giffin; 3 conversions and 5 penalty goals by Andrew Walker.

FOR SHARKS: 2 penalty goals by Butch James.

BRUMBIES: Andrew Walker, Graeme Bond, James Holbeck, Rod Kafer, Joe Roff, Stephen Larkham, George Gregan (captain), Jim Williams, George Smith, Peter Ryan, David Giffin, Justin Harrison, Ben Darwin, Jeremy Paul, Bill Young.
Replacements: Mark Bartholomeusz, Matt Weaver.

SHARKS: Ricardo Loubscher, Stefan Terblanche, Deon Kayser, Trevor Halstead, Justin Swart, Butch James, Craig Davidson, A J Venter, Charl van Rensburg, Warren Britz, Mark Andrews (captain), Albert van den Berg, Etienne Fynn, John Smit, Ollie le Roux.
Replacements: Gaffie du Toit, Hentie Martens, Shaun Sowerby, Brad MacLeod-Henderson, Lukas van Biljon, Brent Moyle.

REFEREE: Paddy O'Brien

CROWD: 26,271

In 1996, Zinzan Brooke, the captain, kicked the only conversion of his career as he guided the Blues to a win over the Hurricanes in the very first Super 12 contest. Five years later, his brother Robin Brooke, also the captain, landed the only conversion of his career to help the Blues finish off the Hurricanes 36–17 at Eden Park. It was only the Blues' fourth win in a dismal campaign.

THE RESULTS

BRUMBIES
(coach Eddie Jones)

beat	Crusaders at Canberra	51–16
lost to	Sharks at Durban	16–17
beat	Cats at Johannesburg	19–17
beat	Bulls at Canberra	39–30
beat	Stormers at Canberra	40–25
beat	Reds at Brisbane	23–15
lost to	Hurricanes at Wellington	19–34
beat	Waratahs at Canberra	48–21
lost to	Highlanders at Dunedin	9–16
beat	Blues at Auckland	35–7
beat	Chiefs at Canberra	49–6

Won 8, lost 3; placing 1st
Tries scored: 39

Semifinal: beat Reds at Canberra	30–6
Final: beat Sharks at Canberra	36–6

Most tries: Andrew Walker 8, Owen Finegan 7,
Joe Roff 6, Jeremy Paul 5, Graeme Bond 4
Most points: Stirling Mortlock 144, Andrew Walker 75,
Joe Roff 35, Owen Finegan 3

CATS
(coach Laurie Mains)

beat	Stormers at Cape Town	29–24
beat	Highlanders at Johannesburg	56–21
lost to	Brumbies at Johannesburg	17–19
beat	Waratahs at Bloemfontein	28–21
beat	Hurricanes at Bloemfontein	18–15
beat	Sharks at Bloemfontein	26–25
lost to	Chiefs at Tauranga	18–22
beat	Blues at Whangarei	26–23
beat	Crusaders at Nelson	32–31
lost to	Reds at Brisbane	16–22
lost to	Bulls at Johannesburg	19–21

Won 7, lost 4; placing: 3rd
Tries scored: 27

Semifinal: lost to Sharks at Durban	12–30

Most tries: Wylie Human 5, Japie Mulder 4
Most points: Louis Koen 157, Wylie Human 25

SHARKS
(coach Rudolf Straueli)

beat	Bulls at Durban	30–17
beat	Brumbies at Durban	17–16
beat	Highlanders at Durban	30–29
beat	Hurricanes at Durban	39–21
beat	Waratahs at Durban	42–17
lost to	Cats at Bloemfontein	25–26
beat	Blues at Auckland	41–27
beat	Chiefs at Taupo	24–8
lost to	Reds at Brisbane	27–32
lost to	Crusaders at Christchurch	24–34
beat	Stormers at Cape Town	23–19

Won 8, lost 3; placing: 2nd
Tries scored: 34

Semifinal: beat Cats at Durban	30–12
Final: lost to Brumbies at Canberra	6–36

Most tries: Deon Kayser 6, Justin Swart 5,
Charl van Rensburg 5, Trevor Halstead 4,
Stefan Terblanche 4
Most points: Butch James 117, Gaffie du Toit 44,
Deon Kayser 30

REDS
(coach Mark McBain)

beat	Hurricanes at Brisbane	27–18
lost to	Chiefs at Rotorua	29–32
lost to	Blues at Albany	35–39
lost to	Crusaders at Christchurch	26–32
lost to	Brumbies at Brisbane	15–23
lost to	Stormers at George	27–29
beat	Bulls at Pretoria	29–19
beat	Sharks at Brisbane	32–27
beat	Cats at Brisbane	22–16
beat	Highlanders at Brisbane	33–22
beat	Waratahs at Sydney	25–20

Won 6, lost 5; placing: 4th
Tries scored: 29

Semifinal: lost to Brumbies at Canberra	6–30

Most tries: Chris Latham 7, Junior Pelasasa 3,
Nathan Williams 3
Most points: Elton Flatley 112, Nathan Spooner 55,
Chris Latham 35

HIGHLANDERS
(coach Peter Sloane)

beat	Blues at Dunedin	23–8
lost to	Cats at Johannesburg	21–56
lost to	Sharks at Durban	29–30
beat	Stormers at Dunedin	24–23
beat	Bulls at Dunedin	32–10
lost to	Chiefs at Rotorua	19–50
beat	Waratahs at Dunedin	39–20
lost to	Hurricanes at Napier	33–35
beat	Brumbies at Dunedin	16–9
lost to	Reds at Brisbane	22–33
beat	Crusaders at Dunedin	26–21

Won 6, lost 5; placing: 5th
Tries scored: 30

Most tries: Aisea Tuilevu 8, Romi Ropati 4
Most points: Tony Brown 122, Aisea Tuilevu 40,
Brendan Laney 27

STORMERS
(coach Alan Solomons)

lost to	Cats at Cape Town	24–29
lost to	Waratahs at Sydney	7–35
beat	Hurricanes at Wellington	27–15
lost to	Highlanders at Dunedin	23–24
lost to	Brumbies at Canberra	25–40
beat	Reds at George	29–27
beat	Canterbury Crusaders at Cape Town	49–28
lost to	Blues at Cape Town	12–26
beat	Chiefs at Cape Town	29–15
beat	Bulls at Pretoria	34–23
lost to	Sharks at Cape Town	19–23

Won 5, lost 6; placing: 7th
Tries scored: 26

Most tries: Breyton Paulse 7, Pieter Rossouw 3
Most points: Braam van Straaten 153, Breyton Paulse 35

CHIEFS
(coach John Mitchell)

lost to	Waratahs at Sydney	23–42
beat	Reds at Rotorua	32–29
lost to	Crusaders at Christchurch	11–40
beat	Blues at Rotorua	34–16
beat	Otago Highlanders at Rotorua	50–19
beat	Cats at Tauranga	22–18
lost to	Sharks at Taupo	8–24
beat	Bulls at Pretoria	49–37
lost to	Stormers at Cape Town	15–29
beat	Hurricanes at Wellington	51–27
lost to	Brumbies at Canberra	6–49

Won 6, lost 5; placing: 6th
Tries scored: 31

Most tries: Bruce Reihana 5, Keith Lowen 4,
Roger Randle 4
Most points: Glenn Jackson 128, David Hill 28

WARATAHS
(coach Bob Dwyer)

beat	Chiefs at Sydney	42–23
beat	Stormers at Sydney	35–7
beat	Bulls at Sydney	53–7
lost to	Cats at Bloemfontein	21–28
lost to	Sharks at Durban	17–42
beat	Blues at Sydney	35–19
lost to	Highlanders at Dunedin	20–39
lost to	Brumbies at Canberra	21–48
lost to	Hurricanes at New Plymouth	17–42
beat	Crusaders at Sydney	25–22
lost to	Reds at Sydney	20–25

Won 5, lost 6; placing: 8th
Tries scored: 33

Most tries: Luke Inman 5, Sam Payne 4
Most points: Matt Burke 129, Sam Payne 28,
Manuel Edmonds 26

🏉 Stormers lock Quinton Davids was subbed off before half-time in each of his five appearances in 2001. In the final match, against the Sharks, his coach allowed him to stay involved beyond half-time, and he rewarded him by scoring a try four minutes into the second half.

HURRICANES
(coach Graham Mourie)

lost to	Reds at Brisbane	18–27
beat	Bulls at Wellington	26–20
lost to	Stormers at Wellington	15–27
lost to	Sharks at Durban	21–39
lost to	Cats at Bloemfontein	15–18
beat	Crusaders at Christchurch	41–29
beat	Brumbies at Wellington	34–19
beat	Highlanders at Napier	35–33
beat	Waratahs at New Plymouth	42–17
lost to	Chiefs at Wellington	27–51
lost to	Blues at Auckland	17–36

Won 5, lost 6; placing: 9th
Tries scored: 30

Most tries: Christian Cullen 5, Jonah Lomu 4,
Daryl Lilley 4
Most points: David Holwell 126, Daryl Lilley 43,
Christian Cullen 25

BLUES
(coach Frank Oliver)

lost to	Highlanders at Dunedin	8–23
beat	Crusaders at Auckland	17–12
beat	Reds at Albany	39–35
lost to	Chiefs at Rotorua	16–34
lost to	Waratahs at Sydney	19–35
lost to	Sharks at Auckland	27–41
lost to	Cats at Whangarei	23–26
beat	Stormers at Cape Town	26–12
lost to	Bulls at Pretoria	25–28
lost to	Brumbies at Auckland	7–35
beat	Hurricanes at Auckland	36–17

Won 4, lost 7; placing: 11th
Tries scored: 27

Most tries: Doug Howlett 6, Ron Cribb 4, Joeli Vidiri 3,
Mils Muliaina 3, Mark Robinson 3
Most points: James Arlidge 70, Carlos Spencer 34,
Doug Howlett 30

CRUSADERS
(coach Robbie Deans)

lost to	Brumbies at Canberra	16–51
lost to	Blues at Auckland	12–17
beat	Chiefs at Christchurch	40–11
beat	Reds at Christchurch	32–26
lost to	Hurricanes at Christchurch	29–41
beat	Bulls at Pretoria	42–29
lost to	Stormers at Cape Town	28–49
lost to	Cats at Nelson	31–32
beat	Sharks at Christchurch	34–24
lost to	Waratahs at Sydney	22–25
lost to	Highlanders at Dunedin	21–26

Won 4, lost 7; placing: 10th
Tries scored: 29

Most tries: Afato So'oalo 5, Leon MacDonald 4,
Justin Marshall 3
Most points: Ben Blair 113, Andrew Mehrtens 49

BULLS
(coach Phil Pretorius)

lost to	Sharks at Durban	17–30
lost to	Hurricanes at Wellington	20–26
lost to	Waratahs at Sydney	7–53
lost to	Brumbies at Canberra	30–39
lost to	Highlanders at Dunedin	10–32
lost to	Crusaders at Pretoria	29–42
lost to	Reds at Pretoria	19–29
lost to	Chiefs at Pretoria	37–49
beat	Blues at Pretoria	28–25
lost to	Stormers at Pretoria	23–34
beat	Cats at Johannesburg	21–19

Won 2, lost 9; placing: 12th
Tries scored: 26

Most tries: Adrian Jacobs 4, Friedrich Lombard 4,
Frikkie Welsh 4
Most points: Casper Steyn 94

> 🏉 Bulls lock Victor Matfield scored his first try in his third season of Super 12 play when he dotted down against the Waratahs at Sydney. His team lost the game 7–53.

2002

IN WINNING THEIR FOURTH Super 12 title in seven seasons, the Crusaders lifted the bar. They became the first team to win all 13 matches, they destroyed fellow semifinalist the Waratahs 96–19, and they scored a record number of points.

Under the guidance again of modest Robbie Deans (who had an NZRU exemption to double as the All Blacks' assistant coach), the Crusaders restored their country's credibility after New Zealand had failed to get a team into the semifinals in 2001 (and been bundled out of the World Cup at the semifinal stage). This time, with Andrew Mehrtens again in prolific point-scoring form, the Crusaders overcame an improved Highlanders team in the semifinals before roaring away from the Brumbies in the closing stages of the final. The success manifested itself in a powerful representation in the national team, no fewer than 15 Crusaders being included in the All Black Tri-nations squad.

The Crusaders celebrate another Super 12 success — and an undefeated season. Fotopress

The Crusaders had a couple of close calls in round-robin play — 30–28 against the Highlanders, 33–32 against the Brumbies and 37–34 against the Sharks in Durban — but always had enough in reserve to win, and finished a whopping 12 points ahead of the Waratahs, who qualified for the semifinals for the first time in seven years.

The Brumbies, coached again by David Nucifora, strove hard to retain their title. A sensational 51–10 semifinal defeat of the Waratahs, representing their first win in Sydney, gave their fans hope, and a typically audacious intercept try by Andrew Walker in the final in Christchurch brought them within a point of the Crusaders inside the last quarter. But when it mattered most, the Crusaders powered away like the champion team they were.

After two seasons coaching the Johannesburg-based Cats, and getting them into the semifinals both times, Laurie Mains was back in New Zealand preparing the Highlanders. They, too, qualified for the play-offs before stumbling against the mighty Crusaders. The South Africa franchises could have done with Mains' coaching talent, for it was a dismal competition for them. The Sharks (finalists in 2001), Cats and Bulls occupied the three bottom positions, with the Stormers faring marginally better, coming home in seventh spot.

Mehrtens emerged as the leading point scorer for the third occasion, aggregating 182 points. But for missing two matches mid-competition he could have threatened his record of 206 (set in 1998). He finished well clear of Elton Flatley (Reds), 148, Matt Burke (Waratahs), 143, and Tony Brown (Highlanders), 138. Wingers Roger Randle (Chiefs) and Pieter Rossouw (Stormers) were the top try scorers, with a dozen touchdowns each.

THE STARS

CHRIS JACK (Crusaders)

It's rare for a lock to be named New Zealand's rugby player of the year. Colin 'Pinetree' Meads managed it way back in the 1970s and Andy Haden gave the title a nudge in the 1980s, but normally the annual award goes to one of the glamour boys of the backline or a dashing loose forward. So for Chris Jack to walk off with the title at the conclusion of the 2002 season — a season in which the All Blacks won the Tri-nations and the Crusaders were supreme in the Super 12 — represented a truly phenomenal achievement, especially as he was just 23.

No less an authority than England's Paul Ackford, a mighty accomplished lock himself in his day, declared Jack the best second rower in the world. 'He roams all over the paddock as a loose forward,' declared Ackford. 'He wins more than his fair share of loose ball and shows an uncompromising presence on the field.'

Rugby was coursing through Chris Jack's veins from an early age. Two uncles had represented Southland, his father had played for Taranaki and older brother Graham, also a lock, made 21 appearances for Canterbury, his career winding down just as lanky Chris was entering the first-class arena. Graham fulfilled a valuable role as Chris's mentor from the moment he first pulled on the black jersey, which was in 1997 as a member of the New Zealand Under-19 team that scored a handsome win over their Australian counterparts at the Melbourne Cricket Ground (in a curtainraiser to the Tri-nations game).

'That was the year that counted,' says Jack. 'The game had become professional and I was lucky to be coming in at that stage. Graham was playing for Canterbury at the time and he and I studied videos of games and he discussed elements of my play and what I needed to work on.'

Jack first wore the Canterbury jersey in 1999, featuring five times as a substitute before getting a start against Otago when Todd Blackadder was moved to the blindside flank. By 2000, acknowledged as a star of the future, he toured France, Wales and Romania with New Zealand A as the back-up boy to Royce Willis and Dion Waller, getting a start against Wales A. The next season, aged just 22, he bounded into the All Blacks. Coaches Wayne Smith and Tony Gilbert started with Norm Maxwell and Troy Flavell at lock, but after the shock loss to Australia at Carisbrook they introduced the lanky lad from Canterbury. And he's been a first-choice test selection ever since.

His focus is total. Rugby is his job and that means doing his homework. He considers his key zones to be line-outs, restarts, ruck clean-outs and tackling. 'I always try to achieve physical dominance,' he says.

MATT BURKE (Waratahs)

When it comes to prolific scoring, there are few better at it than Matt Burke, who thrives on pressure situations. His performances at the 1999 World Cup proved that. In the semifinal against the Springboks, which the Aussies just won 27–21, he banged over eight penalty goals. A week later, in the final against France, he goaled another seven penalties and two conversions.

He once scored 39 points in a test against Canada, the Wallaby record by some distance, and it took Andrew Mehrtens, in his ninth year of involvement, some considerable effort in 2005 to finally wrench the Super 12 point-scoring record away from Burke. They each finished within sight of 1000 points.

To participate in the 1999 World Cup at all Burke had to triumph over adversity after suffering a fearful injury playing against the All Blacks in the 1998 Tri-nations match in Sydney. Landing awkwardly while scoring a try, he suffered a severe dislocation of his right shoulder. His arm was in a sling for two months, to allow a graft to heal, and it was 10 months before he could play sport again. But you can't keep a good man down and Burke, who had been Australia's first-choice fullback since 1995, was back in the No 15 jersey for the 1999 Tri-nations campaign.

A product of St Josephs College in Sydney, a top rugby nursery, Burke had all the skills to go to the top. In 1992, as a 19-year-old, he represented Australia at the Hong Kong sevens, the following year participating in the

Fotopress

World Cup sevens in Scotland. By then, Wallaby coach Bob Dwyer had him firmly in his sights and introduced him to the national squad for the 1993 series against the Springboks. He then went on the end-of-year tour of North America and France, playing in the first test at Bordeaux.

That Burke almost beat Mehrtens to the thousand-point mark in Super 12 is true testimony to his amazing capacity to accumulate points, for it wasn't until 2002 that the Waratahs qualified for the semifinals.

THE FACTS

In crushing the Waratahs 96–19 at Jade Stadium, the Crusaders created a number of Super 12 records: highest score (96), biggest winning margin (77), most tries in a match (14), most conversions in a match (13) and most points in 40 minutes (63). Remarkably, there was no attempt at a penalty goal by either side in the game.

In each of the four years the Crusaders have won the Super 12, Andrew Mehrtens has scored 160 points or more, viz: 1998 — 206; 1999 — 192; 2000 — 160; 2002 — 182. At the end of the 2002 campaign Mehrtens had scored 117 points in Super 12 play-off matches, 55 of them in finals alone.

The Crusaders did not score less than 30 points in any of their 13 matches. At the end of round-robin play they had registered a record 51 championship points and scored a record 469 points. They became and remain the only team to win all 13 matches in a Super 12 campaign.

At the opposite end of the scale to the Crusaders, the hapless Bulls conceded a record 67 tries and 500 points during the season, and conceded a try-scoring bonus point in each of their first nine matches.

Famous for his match-winning dropped goal against the Springboks in the World Cup semifinals of 2001, a happening that was described at the time as a rarity, Stephen Larkham in 2002 landed a 'droppie' against the Reds for the third consecutive time.

When the Highlanders defeated the Blues 20–13, it represented the first time a Dunedin-based team had won a first-class fixture on Eden Park since Otago defeated Auckland in the first year of the NPC, 1976, a span of 26 years.

When the Brumbies defeated the Waratahs 51–10 in the 2002 semifinal, it was their first Super 12 win in Sydney. They'd lost 10–44 in 1996, 7–32 in 1998, 25–30 in 2000 and 11–19 earlier in 2002.

THE FIRST SEMIFINAL

CRUSADERS 34, HIGHLANDERS 24

AT JADE STADIUM, CHRISTCHURCH, 18 MAY

OTAGO FANS HAD TWO REASONS to feel morose at the final whistle of this hard-fought semifinal at Jade Stadium — the fact the Crusaders had once again eliminated them from the competition and because it was Jeff Wilson's farewell to big-time rugby. At 28, Wilson, or 'Goldie' as his adoring fans knew him, had decided to pull the pin on rugby. He'd missed selection on the 2001 All Black tour to Ireland, Scotland and Argentina, and had decided that following the Super 12 he would refocus his sporting attentions on cricket again.

Fittingly, 'Goldie' scored a try in this encounter, his 35th for the Highlanders (to go with the then record 44 he'd scored for the All Blacks), and once again demonstrated his wonderfully instinctive qualities. But, sadly, it wasn't enough to get the Highlanders through to the final against Robbie Deans' awesomely efficient Crusaders.

Even though the Highlanders exited, their achievement in qualifying for the play-offs was testimony to the exceptional coaching talents of Laurie Mains, who'd returned to his homeland in 2001. Prior to Mains taking over the Johannesburg-based Cats they had finished 12th and 11th in the Super 12. Under Mains, they made the semifinals two years running. Upon his exit, they dropped back to 11th! Similarly, the Highlanders had missed the play-offs in 2001 (as had the other four New Zealand franchises) when coached by Peter Sloane but now, with Mains in charge, they finished among the top four through beating the Brumbies in Canberra and the Blues in Auckland.

Because Deans and Mains knew each other's games, this semifinal became a real dogfight. Deans described it as 'not pretty' and said he was content 'just to get the job done'.

> ☕ The 34 championship points achieved by the Queensland Reds weren't enough to qualify them for the semifinals. Thirty-four points would have put them into the play-offs in any other season, 1996 through 2005!

Lock Chris Jack turned in a man-of-the-match performance and it was his crunching tackle in the 25th minute that set up the Crusaders' first try, by centre Mark Robinson. Ten minutes later Robinson was in again after Andrew Mehrtens and Leon MacDonald worked the blindside.

The Crusaders led 18–6 at half-time and seemed to be cruising at 21–6, but a penalty goal and Wilson's try brought the Highlanders up to 16–21, at which point the Crusaders went into overdrive. A magnificent 20-metre rolling maul set up a try for Richie McCaw, after which the Crusaders maintained relentless pressure till the final whistle.

FOR CRUSADERS: Tries by Mark Robinson 2 and Richie McCaw; 2 conversions, 3 penalty goals and a dropped goal by Andrew Mehrtens; dropped goal by Aaron Mauger.

FOR HIGHLANDERS: Tries by Jeff Wilson and Willie Walker; 2 conversions and 3 penalty goals by Walker.

CRUSADERS: Leon MacDonald, Marika Vunibaka, Mark Robinson, Aaron Mauger, Caleb Ralph, Andrew Mehrtens, Justin Marshall, Scott Robertson, Richie McCaw, Reuben Thorne (captain), Norm Maxwell, Chris Jack, Greg Somerville, Mark Hammett, Greg Feek.
Replacements: Ben Blair, Daryl Gibson, Ben Hurst, Johnny Leo'o, Sam Broomhall, Corey Flynn, David Hewett.

HIGHLANDERS: Jeff Wilson, Aisea Tuilevu, Ryan Nicholas, Paul Steinmetz, Romi Ropati, Willie Walker, Byron Kelleher, Kelvin Middleton, Craig Newby, Taine Randell (captain), Simon Maling, Filipo Levi, Carl Hayman, Tom Willis, Carl Hoeft.
Replacements: David Gibson, Sam Harding, Peter Bowden, Joe McDonnell.

REFEREE: Stu Dickinson (Australia)

CROWD: 36,000

The Chiefs defeated the Hurricanes in Hamilton to reverse a six-year tradition of the visiting team always winning. The Chiefs had previously won in Palmerston North (1997), New Plymouth (1999) and Wellington (2001), while the Hurricanes had been successful at Rotorua (1996) and Hamilton (1998 and 2000).

Sharks lock Phillip Smit had to wait 39 Super 12 games for his first try, but only a further three games for his second.

THE SECOND SEMIFINAL
BRUMBIES 51, WARATAHS 10
AT STADIUM AUSTRALIA, SYDNEY, 18 MAY

The Waratahs, the traditional underachievers of the Super 12 competition, had been going along swimmingly in 2002, until journeying to Christchurch to take on the Crusaders in their final round-robin fixture. They had already qualified for the semifinals but the blitzkrieg they experienced at Jade Stadium so devastated them it was inconceivable they could regroup within a week to seriously challenge the Brumbies, for the Crusaders had put 14 tries on them in winning 96–19, an astonishing outcome. It was a result that left the normally garrulous Bob Dwyer, the Waratahs coach, almost speechless.

It was in the Waratahs' favour that the Brumbies had never won in Sydney, but the Brumbies hadn't missed the events in Christchurch. They'd seen how the Crusaders had ruthlessly exposed defensive deficiencies in the Waratahs, and they'd taken notes. And at Stadium Australia the floodgates opened once again, to the dismay of Dwyer and the Waratah fans. The Brumbies piled on 41 unanswered points in the final 35 minutes to crack the half-century mark.

Justin Harrison rejoices in a rare try-scoring moment. Fotopress

When the Brumbies scored their sixth try, it meant the Waratahs had conceded 20 tries in two outings, a woeful statistic. Two of the tries were from intercepts of passes thrown by flyhalf Duncan McRae, who had a shocker. One of his wayward passes presented a rare five-pointer to lock Justin Harrison.

On a night when the Waratahs needed to eliminate errors, they erred badly. In addition to the intercept passes, they botched six of their own line-out throws. Notwithstanding all this, they were still hanging in at 10–13 five minutes into the second half, but from that moment on there was only one team in it.

The game's leading point scorer, Julian Huxley, started the evening on the reserves bench, joining the action when fullback Mark Bartholomeusz retired injured at half-time. Huxley, who had been excelling for the Australian sevens team, instantly made his mark and landed seven goals from seven attempts. The Brumbies' man of the match was winger Graeme Bond, whose two five-pointers established him as the team's leading try scorer for the series. He was in dynamic form, while Stephen Larkham comprehensively outplayed the luckless McRae.

Dwyer had accused the Brumbies in general and George Gregan in particular of arrogance in the lead-up to the game. After it, Brumbies coach David Nucifora said he thought Gregan's captaincy and leadership were outstanding and he, personally, thought Dwyer's comments reeked of arrogance.

FOR BRUMBIES: Tries by Graeme Bond 2, Jeremy Paul, Owen Finegan, Justin Harrison and Pat Howard; conversions by Julian Huxley 5 and Andrew Walker.

FOR WARATAHS: Try by Scott Staniforth; conversion and penalty goal by Matt Burke.

WARATAHS: Mat Rogers, Scott Staniforth, Matt Burke (captain), Sam Harris, Marc Stcherbina, Duncan McRae, Chris Whitaker, David Lyons, Phil Waugh, Des Tuiavi'i, Van Humphries, Tom Bowman, Rod Moore, Brendan Cannon, Patricio Noriega. Replacements: Manny Edmonds, Francis Cullimore, Tim Clark, Huia Edmonds, Jone Tawake, Steve Talbot, Matt Dunning, Matt Bowman.

BRUMBIES: Mark Bartholomeusz, Graeme Bond, Stirling Mortlock, Pat Howard, Andrew Walker, Stephen Larkham, George Gregan (captain), Scott Fava, George Smith, Owen Finegan, Dan Vickerman, Justin Harrison, Ben Darwin, Jeremy Paul, Bill Young. Replacements: Julian Huxley, Joel Wilson, Travis Hall, Tamaiti Horua, David Pusey, Angus Scott, Damian Flynn.

REFEREE: Paddy O'Brien (New Zealand)

CROWD: 36,146

🖊 Matt Burke's favourite opponent was obviously the Pretoria-based Bulls (who featured also as Northern Transvaal and Northern Bulls). In five outings against them he scored 119 points from hauls of 19, 33, 23, 23 and 21.

🖊 The six penalty goals kicked by Julian Huxley on debut, as a replacement against the Highlanders, represented a Brumbies match record.

THE FINAL

CRUSADERS 31, BRUMBIES 13

AT JADE STADIUM, CHRISTCHURCH, 25 MAY

IT WAS ENTIRELY APPROPRIATE that winger Caleb Ralph should be the leading try scorer as the Crusaders celebrated their fourth Tri-nations triumph by defeating 2001 champions the Brumbies in freezing conditions at Jade Stadium. Overshadowed by many of the team's 'glamour' players, Ralph could claim a remarkable record, one that illustrated his exceptional fitness and durability. Since his debut at the commencement of the 1999 season, he was the only Crusaders player to appear in all 50 matches over four seasons. What's more, in 2002, he was off the field for only five minutes during the entire campaign, and that while being treated in the blood bin. The fittest of all the Crusaders — a fact annually confirmed in pre-season testing — Ralph's two tries in the 2002 final brought his aggregate in all Super 12 matches to 31, sixth best among a celebrated group headed by Christian Cullen, Joe Roff and Joeli Vidiri.

Though it's as a Crusader that Ralph made his mark, he broke into the Super 12 in 1997 as a 19-year-old with the Chiefs and then had a season with the Blues before heading south. Auckland and the Blues were reluctant to release him, but Ralph was emphatic he wanted to play out of Christchurch and eventually got his way.

Ralph's two late tries gave the Crusaders the advantage they deserved after a sensational intercept try from a Justin Marshall pass in the 72nd minute by Andrew Walker gave the red and blacks a huge fright. Suddenly, 6–14 became 13–14 and a Brumbies team that had been comprehensively outplayed was in with a sniff.

That's when the Crusaders demonstrated their greatness, upping the tempo to a degree that the Brumbies were ruthlessly swept aside. An Andrew Mehrtens dropped goal was followed in double-quick fashion by Ralph's two tries, both converted, and before George Gregan's men knew what had hit them, that one-point deficit had become 17.

Giant lock Chris Jack was named man of the match after a mighty performance. Besides demonstrating great athleticism, he consistently upset the Brumbies line-out.

Crusaders captain Reuben Thorne takes the game to the Brumbies. Fotopress

Brumbies coach David Nucifora paid a glowing tribute to the Crusaders. 'They were outstanding in all facets of the game,' he said. 'They've taken the game to a new level and set the standard for all others to aspire to.'

His team was unlucky to lose star flyhalf Stephen Larkham with an elbow injury in the 30th minute that was to put him out of rugby for a month. It was initially thought the elbow was broken.

The Crusaders could reflect on a season of exceptional achievement. Not only did they win all 13 matches, they scored better than 30 points in every one of them. The 534 points they accumulated was a new Super 12 record.

FOR CRUSADERS: Tries by Caleb Ralph 2 and Marika Vunibaka; 2 conversions, 3 penalty goals and a dropped goal by Andrew Mehrtens.

FOR BRUMBIES: Try, conversion and 2 penalty goals by Andrew Walker.

CRUSADERS: Leon MacDonald, Marika Vunibaka, Mark Robinson, Aaron Mauger, Caleb Ralph, Andrew Mehrtens, Justin Marshall, Scott Robertson, Richie McCaw, Reuben Thorne (captain), Norm Maxwell, Chris Jack, Greg Somerville, Mark Hammett, Greg Feek.
Replacements; Daryl Gibson, Sam Broomhall, David Hewett.

BRUMBIES: Mark Bartholomeusz, Graeme Bond, Stirling Mortlock, Pat Howard, Andrew Walker, Stephen Larkham, George Gregan (captain), Scott Fava, George Smith, Owen Finegan, Dan Vickerman, Justin Harrison, Ben Darwin, Jeremy Paul, Bill Young.
Replacements: Julian Huxley, Peter Ryan, David Pusey.

REFEREE: André Watson (South Africa)

CROWD: 36,500

THE RESULTS

CRUSADERS
(coach Robbie Deans)

beat	Highlanders at Christchurch	30–28
beat	Chiefs at Hamilton	34–27
beat	Blues at Christchurch	30–11
beat	Reds at Brisbane	34–27
beat	Brumbies at Christchurch	33–32
beat	Bulls at Christchurch	49–15
beat	Stormers at Christchurch	41–21
beat	Sharks at Durban	37–34
beat	Cats at Johannesburg	37–30
beat	Hurricanes at Wellington	48–20
beat	Waratahs at Christchurch	96–19

Won 11, lost 0; placing: 1st
Tries scored: 56

Semifinal: beat Highlanders at Christchurch 34–23

Final: beat Brumbies at Christchurch 31–13

Most tries: Caleb Ralph 10, Marika Vunibaka 9,
Leon MacDonald 8, Aaron Mauger 4,
Scott Robertson 4
Most points: Andrew Mehrtens 182, Leon MacDonald 62,
Caleb Ralph 50, Marika Vunibaka 45,
Ben Blair 31

BRUMBIES
(coach David Nucifore)

beat	Reds at Canberra	29–19
beat	Cats at Canberra	64–16
beat	Sharks at Canberra	38–8
beat	Bulls at Pretoria	45–35
beat	Stormers at Cape Town	36–15
lost to	Crusaders at Christchurch	32–33
lost to	Hurricanes at Canberra	13–20
lost to	Waratahs at Sydney	11–19
lost to	Highlanders at Canberra	18–25
beat	Chiefs at Rotorua	42–15
beat	Blues at Canberra	46–25

Won 7, lost 4; placing: 3rd
Tries scored: 45

Semifinal: beat Waratahs at Sydney 51–10

Final: lost to Crusaders at Christchurch 13–31

Most tries: Graeme Bond 9, Stirling Mortlock 8,
Stephen Larkham 5, Jeremy Paul 5,
Mark Bartholomeusz 5, Owen Finegan 4
Most points: Stirling Mortlock 121, Andrew Walker 68,
Graeme Bond 45, Julian Huxley 36,
Stephen Larkham 33

WARATAHS
(coach Bob Dwyer)

beat	Chiefs at Rotorua	42–25
beat	Stormers at Cape Town	26–25
beat	Bulls at Pretoria	51–19
beat	Cats at Sydney	44–21
beat	Sharks at Sydney	42–8
lost to	Blues at Albany	20–22
beat	Highlanders at Sydney	31–13
beat	Brumbies at Sydney	19–11
beat	Hurricanes at Sydney	19–13
lost to	Reds at Brisbane	24–31
lost to	Crusaders at Christchurch	19–96

Won 8, lost 3; placing: 2nd
Tries scored: 41

Semifinal: lost to Brumbies at Sydney 10–51

Most tries: Scott Staniforth 9, Marc Stcherbina 6,
Duncan McRae 4, Nathan Grey 4,
Mat Rogers 4
Most points: Matt Burke 143, Scott Staniforth 45

HIGHLANDERS
(coach Peter Sloane)

lost to	Crusaders at Christchurch	28–30
beat	Sharks at Dunedin	45–5
beat	Cats at Dunedin	40–8
beat	Stormers at Cape Town	21–20
beat	Bulls at Pretoria	54–17
lost to	Chiefs at Invercargill	24–29
beat	Hurricanes at Dunedin	19–10
lost to	Waratahs at Sydney	13–31
beat	Brumbies at Canberra	25–18
beat	Blues at Auckland	20–13
beat	Reds at Dunedin	40–26

Won 8, lost 3; placing: 4th
Tries scored: 34 tries

Semifinal: lost to Crusaders at Christchurch 23–34

Most tries: Ryan Nicholas 7, Jeff Wilson 6,
Willie Walker 5, Paul Steinmetz 5
Most points: Tony Brown 141, Willie Walker 61

REDS
(coach Mark McBain)

lost to	Brumbies at Canberra	19-29
beat	Blues at Brisbane	34-23
beat	Chiefs at Brisbane	27-13
lost to	Crusaders at Brisbane	27-34
lost to	Hurricanes at Palmerston North	18-22
beat	Stormers at Brisbane	49-46
beat	Bulls at Brisbane	48-12
beat	Cats at Johannesburg	27-15
beat	Sharks at Durban	30-29
beat	Waratahs at Brisbane	31-24
lost to	Highlanders at Dunedin	26-40

Won 7, lost 4; placing: 5th
Tries scored: 36

Most tries: Chris Latham 10, Ben Tune 5
Most points: Elton Flatley 148, Chris Latham 50

STORMERS
(coach Alan Solomons)

beat	Sharks at Durban	25-18
lost to	Waratahs at Cape Town	25-26
beat	Hurricanes at Cape Town	40-13
lost to	Highlanders at Cape Town	20-21
lost to	Brumbies at Cape Town	15-36
lost to	Reds at Brisbane	46-49
lost to	Crusaders at Christchurch	21-41
beat	Chiefs at Hamilton	45-33
lost to	Blues at Auckland	6-25
beat	Cats at Johannesburg	36-25
beat	Bulls at Cape Town	31-27

Won 5, lost 6; placing: 7th
Tries scored: 34

Most tries: Pieter Rossouw 12, Marius Joubert 5,
              Werner Greeff 4
Most points: Percy Montgomery 120, Pieter Rossouw 60

BLUES
(coach Peter Sloane)

beat	Hurricanes at Wellington	60-7
lost to	Reds at Brisbane	23-34
lost to	Crusaders at Christchurch	11-30
beat	Chiefs at Auckland	37-30
beat	Waratahs at Albany	22-20
lost to	Sharks at Durban	13-20
beat	Cats at Bloemfontein	24-12
beat	Bulls at Auckland	65-24
beat	Stormers at Auckland	25-6
lost to	Highlanders at Auckland	13-20
lost to	Brumbies at Canberra	25-46

Won 6, lost 5; placing: 6th
Tries scored: 37

Most tries: Doug Howlett 10, Rico Gear 4,
              Mils Muliaina 4
Most points: Carlos Spencer 101, Doug Howlett 50,
             James Arlidge 37

CHIEFS
(coach John Mitchell)

lost to	Waratahs at Rotorua	25-42
lost to	Crusaders at Hamilton	27-34
lost to	Reds at Brisbane	13-27
lost to	Blues at Auckland	30-37
beat	Highlanders at Invercargill	29-24
beat	Cats at Bloemfontein	36-25
lost to	Sharks at Durban	18-21
lost to	Stormers at Hamilton	33-45
beat	Bulls at Hamilton	53-24
lost to	Brumbies at Rotorua	15-42
beat	Hurricanes at Hamilton	44-20

Won 4, lost 7; placing: 8th
Tries scored: 39

Most tries: Roger Randle 12, Bruce Reihana 6,
              Glenn Jackson 4, Nicky Collins 4
Most points: David Hill 77, Glenn Jackson 76,
             Roger Randle 60

🏉 Northlander Glenn Taylor became the first individual to captain two different Super 12 teams — the Chiefs in 2000 and the Blues in 2002.

🏉 The 46 points scored by the Stormers in losing to the Queensland Reds represented the highest losing score to date in the Super 12.

HURRICANES
(coach Graham Mourie)

lost to	Blues at Wellington	7–60
beat	Bulls at Pretoria	37–18
lost to	Stormers at Cape Town	13–40
beat	Sharks at Wellington	40–17
beat	Cats at Wellington	30–21
beat	Reds at Palmerston North	22–18
lost to	Highlanders at Dunedin	10–19
beat	Brumbies at Canberra	20–13
lost to	Waratahs at Sydney	13–19
lost to	Crusaders at Wellington	20–48
lost to	Chiefs at Hamilton	20–44

Won 5, lost 6; placing: 9th
Tries scored: 24

Most tries: Christian Cullen 4, Pita Alatini 4
Most points: David Holwell 90, Christian Cullen 20, Pita Alatini 20

CATS
(coach Laurie Mains)

beat	Bulls at Pretoria	44–31
lost to	Brumbies at Canberra	16–64
lost to	Highlanders at Dunedin	8–40
lost to	Waratahs at Sydney	21–44
lost to	Hurricanes at Wellington	21–30
lost to	Chiefs at Bloemfontein	25–36
lost to	Blues at Bloemfontein	12–24
lost to	Reds at Johannesburg	15–27
lost to	Crusaders at Johannesburg	30–37
lost to	Stormers at Johannesburg	25–36
lost to	Sharks at Durban	11–38

Won 1, lost 10; placing: 11th
Tries scored: 23

Most tries: Gcobani Bobo 4, John Daniels 4, André Pretorius 4
Most points: André Pretorius 95, Louis Koen 38

SHARKS
(coach Rudolf Straueli)

lost to	Stormers at Durban	18–25
lost to	Highlanders at Dunedin	5–45
lost to	Brumbies at Canberra	8–38
lost to	Hurricanes at Wellington	17–40
lost to	Waratahs at Sydney	8–42
beat	Blues at Durban	20–13
beat	Chiefs at Durban	21–18
lost to	Crusaders at Durban	34–37
lost to	Reds at Durban	29–30
beat	Bulls at Pretoria	23–10
beat	Cats at Durban	38–11

Won 4, lost 7; placing: 10th
Tries scored: 25

Most tries: Stefan Terblanche 7
Most points: Gaffie du Toit 69, Stefan Terblanche 35, Herkie Kruger 27

BULLS
(coach Phil Pretorius)

lost to	Cats at Pretoria	31–44
lost to	Hurricanes at Pretoria	18–37
lost to	Waratahs at Pretoria	19–51
lost to	Brumbies at Pretoria	35–45
lost to	Highlanders at Pretoria	17–54
lost to	Crusaders at Christchurch	15–49
lost to	Reds at Brisbane	12–48
lost to	Blues at Auckland	24–65
lost to	Chiefs at Hamilton	24–53
lost to	Sharks at Pretoria	10–23
lost to	Stormers at Cape Town	27–31

Won 0, lost 11; placing: 12th
Tries scored: 31

Most tries: Adrian Jacobs 5, Wylie Human 5, Giscard Pieters 4
Most points: Boeta Wessels 29, Adrian Jacobs 25, Wylie Human 25, Leon van der Heever 21

Former league star Wendell Sailor's switch to rugby was accompanied by a vast amount of publicity. But it took him seven matches before he finally scored a try for the Reds, against the Bulls. He dotted down twice, his only tries in 11 outings.

2003

AFTER FIVE YEARS OUT OF THE FRAME, the Blues were back, recapturing much of the razzle-dazzle and glory of the halcyon seasons of 1996 and 1997, when Graham Henry's originals were almost unstoppable, sweeping through to defeat four-time winners, the Crusaders, in the 2003 final at Eden Park. Carlos Spencer was the solitary link with the champion side of 1997 that had featured such potent performers as Zinzan Brooke, Michael Jones, Sean Fitzpatrick, Olo Brown, Robin Brooke and Joeli Vidiri. Vidiri had been the try-scoring hero of 1997 with 10 touchdowns, a total bettered in 2003 by Doug Howlett, who ran in a dozen tries, including a vital one in the final that the Blues took out 21–17.

Spencer was only the back-up goal kicker in 1997 behind Adrian Cashmore, but, helped by seven tries, still accumulated 91 points. This time he handled all the goal-kicking duties and amassed 143 points, the first time a Blues player had topped the Super 12 point-scoring list.

The Blues' success was a triumph for former Highlanders coach Peter Sloane, who had been introduced after a disastrous 2001 campaign when the team finished an embarrassing 11th and managed just four victories. To the delight

Blues captain Xavier Rush after his team's triumph at Eden Park in 2003. Fotopress

of the Eden Park faithful, the Blues adopted a policy of all-out attack that produced spectacular, winning rugby and tries aplenty for speedsters Howlett, Joe Rokocoko and Rupeni Caucaunibuca. Indeed, the Blues' haul of 61 tries was only nine short of the 1997 team's record of 70.

The 2003 competition was dominated by the New Zealand franchises, with the Blues, the Crusaders and the Hurricanes occupying the top three qualifying positions, the ever-powerful Brumbies claiming the fourth play-off spot on countback from the Waratahs, who, competitive as ever, missed out on the play-offs for the seventh time in eight years.

When the All Blacks went on to win the Tri-nations championship decisively, New Zealand fans were on good terms with themselves, but if they thought all this SANZAR success would automatically translate into World Cup glory they were to be hugely disappointed come November. The title would go to the Wallabies, who would finish a distant second in the Tri-nations and whose teams came home fourth, fifth and eighth in the Super 12.

Once again, the South African teams failed to fire. By winning their last four matches, the Bulls finished a creditable sixth (helped by Louis Koen's seven dropped goals) but the Stormers, the Sharks and the Cats occupied three of the bottom four positions.

Next behind Spencer in point scoring came Willie Walker (Highlanders) on 142, followed by Koen (Bulls) 139 and Roff (Brumbies) 133. Howlett was out on his own as a try scorer with 12. Three players managed eight tries — Caleb Ralph (Crusaders), Christian Cullen (Hurricanes) and Rupeni Caucaunibuca (Blues).

THE STARS

JOE ROKOCOKO (Blues)

New Zealand's sevens supremo Gordon Tietjens knows exactly why Joe Rokocoko is a try-scoring machine — because he's so fast. Tietjens unhesitatingly labels him the quickest player he's dealt with in his crack national squad. And given that Jonah Lomu, Christian Cullen, Joeli Vidiri, Glen Osborne, Mils Muliaina, Rico Gear, Bruce Reihana, Brad Fleming and Roger Randle have all passed that way, that's really saying something.

'When he came into the All Blacks in 2003 he was most certainly the quickest player in the land,' said Tietjens. 'I would have loved to have had him in the sevens for another year. As a Fijian, he was a natural at the game. He had size, strength, tremendous pace and the ability to beat opponents one on one and turn them inside out.'

No wonder opponents were blown away when he slotted in on the end of the All Black backline in 2003. There has never been an introduction to test rugby like Joe's, as his try-scoring achievements in his first dozen internationals illustrate: 0, 2, 3, 2, 3, 1, 0, 1, 3, 1, 2, 0. Eighteen tries from 12 tests against opponents as challenging as England, Wales, France, Australia, South Africa, Argentina and the Pacific Islands.

Fotopress

Without having played for Auckland, but with a background of spectacular achievement for New Zealand schools and in sevens, Rokocoko first alerted the rugby world to his marvellous talents in the 2003 Super 12 when he completed a lethal back three for the Blues, who won the title. In combination with fellow Fijian Rupeni Caucaunibuca and Doug Howlett, Rokocoko prospered in a team committed to all-out attack. Collectively, the trio ran in 26 of the team's 61 tries, Rokocoko dotting down twice in the semifinal win over the Brumbies.

Rokocoko came to New Zealand with his family when he was four. Counties Manukau officials saw him as an exciting asset while he was attending James Cook High School in Manurewa, but when St Kentigern College lured him to Auckland, he became Auckland's (hot) property. From St Kentigern, he gained a place in the New Zealand schools side, starring in the 33–7 defeat of England schools in the Bledisloe Cup curtainraiser at Carisbrook in 2000, scoring a hat trick of tries.

Having been born in Fiji, Rokocoko was eligible to play international rugby for that country, but from the age of 16 committed himself to New Zealand. His family still own land near Nadi and he enjoys his not infrequent visits there.

DE WET BARRY (Stormers)

One South African pen portrait of De Wet Barry describes him as a 'brutal defender', which pretty much sums up this strong-running, hard-tackling midfielder who has had a mortgage on the Springbok and Stormers No 12 jerseys since 2000.

When Stormers coach Gert Smal appointed him captain of his Super 12 team during the 2005 campaign, he likened him to Corne Krige because of his never-say-die attitude and the manner in which he leads from the front. Others have compared him to the great Springbok midfielder of the 1970s, Joggie Jansen, because of his fearlessness and ability to influence the course of matches with his aggressive defence.

The onfield aggressor is hard to recognise in a social setting, Barry being an extremely quiet, reserved individual. Interviewed after his promotion to the Stormers captaincy, he said, modestly, 'I'm not much of a talker — I prefer to lead by example. Obviously, I'll have to make decisions, but it will be a case of collective responsibility.'

He has formed a lethal midfield combination with fellow Stormer Marius Joubert. They were both nominees for the South African Super 12 player of the year in 2004, with the award going to Barry, after his team had made it through to the semifinals (where they gave the Crusaders plenty of hurry-up in Christchurch). Barry and Joubert continued their good work for the Springboks, contributing mightily to the team's Tri-nations success.

Born at Ceres, Barry was educated at Paarl Gymnasium, first making his mark for the South African Under-21 team in 1998, scoring a vital try to help

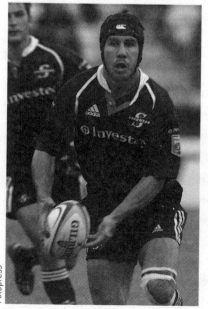

defeat New Zealand in the final of the southern hemisphere Colts tournament in Buenos Aires in 1999. The following year he graduated to the Springboks and has been an almost automatic selection since, except in 2001, when he suffered both a broken cheekbone and a broken bone in his hand. Current Springbok coach Jake White says of him that he is a 'calming influence' on the team and the players at the back.

Born in 1978, he is single and has the nickname of Page. His hobbies are diving for crayfish and fishing. Prior to becoming a professional rugby player he studied small business management in Cape Town.

Fotopress

THE FACTS

THE 143 POINTS CARLOS SPENCER scored in the 2003 Super 12 represented the first time a Blues player had emerged as the leading point scorer, surprising considering this was the fourth time the Blues had won the competition.

The conversion landed by Andrew Mehrtens in the final was the only successful kick at goal by a Crusaders player in two matches against the Blues in 2003. The Crusaders' points in these two encounters — lost 5–39 and 17–21 — otherwise comprised tries.

The differential between points scored and points conceded by the Blues, 233, is a new Super 12 record and the first time any team has scored twice as many points as they have conceded (456 against 223).

When the Blues defeated the Crusaders in the final, it represented the first occasion a team had won the final scoring fewer tries than its opponent.

Bobby Skinstad became the first forward to drop-kick a goal in Super 12, landing one for the Cats, of which he was captain, against the Highlanders at Johannesburg. He was joined later in the season by Jonno Gibbes of the Chiefs and Matt Dunning of the Waratahs.

Hurricanes goal kicker David Holwell landed 16 conversions before he was successful with a penalty goal (against the Chiefs). It was the eighth round and their 24th try before the Hurricanes goal kickers (Holwell and Riki Flutey) finally missed a conversion.

The Bulls' 11-match losing streak came to an end with the 34–26 defeat of the Cats, surprisingly away from home. Cats reject Louis Koen accounted for 29 of the Bulls' points, including three dropped goals. After just two games, Koen had equalled Andrew Mehrtens' Super 12 record of four dropped goals in a season. Koen went on to finish with seven.

THE FIRST SEMIFINAL
CRUSADERS 39, HURRICANES 16

AT JADE STADIUM, CHRISTCHURCH, 16 MAY

THIS GAME IS PROBABLY MOST FAMOUS for Hurricanes captain Tana Umaga's quip to Australian referee Peter Marshall that the players were not there 'to play tiddlywinks'. Umaga had become frustrated because Marshall and his touch judges had issued a number of warnings and even a couple of yellow cards for high tackles that didn't, in Umaga's considered opinion, fall into the category of dangerous. Umaga silently accepted most of the rulings before deciding it was time he reminded referee Marshall that rugby is, after all, a physical contact sport played by mature men. Marshall's response, if there was one, is not recorded.

The Hurricanes' dynamic loose forward trio dominated much of the publicity in the build-up to this semifinal at Jade Stadium, but it was their Crusaders counterparts who stole the show, scoring a try each to guide their team through to the Super 12 final for the fifth time. While the backs, who had scored 31 tries in round-robin play, looked on, Sam Broomhall, Scott Robertson and man-of-the-match Richie McCaw dotted down, to extend the Crusaders' winning sequence at Jade Stadium to 15.

It was McCaw who broke the hearts of the Hurricanes fans, for until he secured his try well into the second half the visitors had a sniff of a famous victory. They'd rebounded from 6–19 at half-time to 16–22, their try a freakish effort when a Justin Marshall grubber kick rebounded into Ma'a Nonu's hands, enabling him to send Brent Ward racing for the goalline. Suddenly only six points in arrears, the Hurricanes, desperate to progress to the final, threw everything

Ma'a Nonu in action for the Hurricanes. Fotopress

at the home side, but coach Robbie Deans' team was equal to the challenge and gradually regained the initiative.

McCaw, who'd already scored six tries during the 2003 campaign, struck the telling blow. Back from the blood bin, he picked up from an attacking scrum and was driven across the goalline by his eager team-mates. Dan Carter's wide-angle conversion made it 29–16 and the Hurricanes challenge was effectively repulsed. There was time for another try, a farewell gift to the Christchurch fans from Robertson, who following the Super 12 was off to join the Perpignan club in France.

Norm Maxwell, wanting to impress the All Black selectors, got a start at lock ahead of Brad Thorn, but came to grief in the sixth minute with a ruptured cruciate ligament.

The Hurricanes' loose trio of Rodney So'oialo, Jerry Collins and Kupu Vanisi had their moments, but failed to make the impact of McCaw and co.

FOR CRUSADERS: Tries by Sam Broomhall, Richie McCaw and Scott Robertson; 3 conversions and 5 penalty goals by Dan Carter; dropped goal by Aaron Mauger.

FOR HURRICANES: Try by Brent Ward; conversion and 3 penalty goals by David Holwell.

CRUSADERS: Leon MacDonald, Marika Vunibaka, Caleb Ralph, Dan Carter, Joe Maddock, Aaron Mauger, Justin Marshall, Sam Broomhall, Richie McCaw, Reuben Thorne (captain), Norm Maxwell, Chris Jack, Greg Somerville, Mark Hammett, Dave Hewett.
Replacements: Brad Thorn, Scott Robertson, Andrew Mehrtens, Greg Feek, Ben Hurst, Scott Hamilton, Slade McFarland.

HURRICANES: Christian Cullen, Brent Ward, Ma'a Nonu, Tana Umaga (captain), Lome Fa'atau, David Holwell, Jason Spice, Rodney So'oialo, Kupu Vanisi, Jerry Collins, Paul Tito, Kristian Ormsby, Tim Fairbrother, Daniel Smith, Tony Penn.
Replacements: Riki Flutey, Brendan Haami, Brent Thompson, Neil Brew, Ross Kennedy, Joe Ward, Tama Tuirirangi.

REFEREE: Peter Marshall (Australia)

CROWD: 35,000

For the first time, the Chiefs lost all four games against New Zealand opponents, going down to the Highlanders and Blues in Hamilton, the Crusaders in Christchurch and the Hurricanes in Wellington.

THE SECOND SEMIFINAL
BLUES 42, BRUMBIES 21

AT EDEN PARK, AUCKLAND, 17 MAY

THE BRUMBIES LIMPED INTO TOWN for this semifinal still counting the casualties from their physical clash with the Crusaders the weekend before. Left behind, wounded, were three of the team's superstars — winger Andrew Walker, midfielder Matt Giteau and, most tellingly of all, flyhalf Stephen Larkham. Already crocked was the team's captain, Stirling Mortlock, which meant that for this all-important contest against the most electrifying team in the competition, the Brumbies had to field a completely reshaped backline. Winger Mark Bartholomeusz became a makeshift flyhalf, regular reserve Pat Howard slotted in at second-five and Damian McInally, who'd only started in a Super 12 game once since 1999, was on the wing.

Not surprisingly the patched-up Brumbies were painfully exposed by the Blues' super-slick backs and found themselves 22–nil behind at half-time, a situation from which they never recovered, although they managed three second-half tries. Given the circumstances, it was not a surprise to find Brumbies captain George Gregan shattered after the loss. He attended the press conference in body alone, leaving most of the comments to coach David Nucifora, who conceded 'the new backline combinations struggled out there'.

'We fought bravely to the finish,' he said, 'but it's a tough ask when you're coming from 22 points down.'

The home town fans weren't bothered whether the Brumbies were operating below full strength — they were just thrilled to have their team back in the limelight for the first time since Graham Henry headed for Wales. He'd guided the side to greatness in 1996 and 1997 and into the final again in 1998. In the

---

The Crusaders ended the Highlanders' sequence of 16 consecutive victories at Carisbrook with a 17–16 win. Before the competition was over, the Highlanders would also lose at home to the Waratahs, a result that would cost Laurie Mains' team its place in the play-offs.

interim, the Blues had finished ninth, sixth, eleventh and sixth, pretty humbling stuff for a once-great franchise.

The Blues had been setting the pace throughout 2003 and it's doubtful whether even a full-strength Brumbies combination would have barred their path to the final. They ruthlessly probed openings in the Brumbies' defence, with Steve Devine, Kees Meeuws and Joe Rokocoko scoring tries within the space of 12 minutes in the first half. The Brumbies hit back briefly after half-time before Mils Muliaina, Doug Howlett and Rokocoko again joined in the the try-scoring spree.

Although the backs did most of the try scoring, it was the performance of the forwards that most delighted Blues coach Peter Sloane. 'We've copped some flak over our forwards,' he said, 'but we've worked hard on the scrum and it's paid off. I thought the pack generally was in blockbusting form tonight.'

FOR BLUES: Tries by Joe Rokocoko 2, Steve Devine, Kees Meeuws, Mils Muliaina and Doug Howlett; 3 conversions and 2 penalty goals by Carlos Spencer.

FOR BRUMBIES: Tries by Joel Wilson, Owen Finegan and Mark Bartholomeusz; 3 conversions by Joe Roff.

BLUES: Doug Howlett, Rico Gear, Mils Muliaina, Sam Tuitupou, Joe Rokocoko, Carlos Spencer, Steve Devine, Xavier Rush (captain), Daniel Braid, Justin Collins, Angus Macdonald, Ali Williams, Kees Meeuws, Keven Mealamu, Deacon Manu.
Replacements: Lee Stensness, David Gibson, Mose Tuiali'i, Brad Mika, Tony Woodcock, Derren Witcombe.

BRUMBIES: Joe Roff, Damian McInally, Joel Wilson, Pat Howard, Mark Gerrard, Mark Bartholomeusz, George Gregan (captain), Scott Fava, George Smith, Tamaiti Horua, Dan Vickerman, David Giffin, Ben Darwin, Jeremy Paul, Bill Young.
Replacements: Lenny Beckett, Owen Finegan, Justin Harrison, Digby Beaumont, David Fitter.

REFEREE: Jonathan Kaplan (South Africa)

CROWD: 40,000

The five conversions kicked by Willie Walker in the Highlanders' 45–19 win over the Brumbies at Carisbrook equalled the total number of conversions the Highlanders had managed in this encounter in the previous seven seasons.

THE FINAL

BLUES 21, CRUSADERS 17

AT EDEN PARK, AUCKLAND, 24 MAY

FROM ELEVENTH TO SIXTH TO FIRST in three years. That was the glowing success story of the Blues who, in capturing the Super 12 crown for 2003, spectacularly demonstrated that winning rugby can also be entertaining, crowd-pleasing rugby. When Peter Sloane took over the once-proud franchise after the woeful 2001 season, things couldn't have been much bleaker. Not only were the All Black selectors ignoring the team — Doug Howlett was the solitary Blues representative in the national squad of 2001 — but the fans were staying away in droves.

'It's fair to say the players' fitness in 2001 wasn't that crash-hot,' said Sloane. 'It quickly became apparent that a lot of hard work lay ahead if the Blues were going to recapture the glory days.'

It took only two seasons for Sloane, initially assisted by Grant Fox and then in 2003 by Bruce Robertson and Graham Henry (back from Wales), to not only rediscover those 'glory days' but to spark a thrilling new era in New Zealand rugby. By investing in youth, upgrading fitness levels several octaves and committing to a bold attacking policy, the Blues electrified the competition and, in the process, seduced the New Zealand selectors. From one lone ranger in 2001, the Blues could claim nine All Blacks after an astonishing campaign in which they scored most tries (61, compared with 27 in 2001), conceded fewest and dropped just the one match, to the Highlanders at Carisbrook.

The team that flopped in 2001 had an average age of 26; the team that triumphed in 2003 averaged just 23, surely the youngest Super 12 team fielded by any franchise in the history of the event. The investment in youth paid handsome dividends and the quality the young dashers brought to the team that most excited Sloane was speed. 'There's no substitute for pace,' he said.

First it was Rupeni Caucaunibuca who dazzled opponents, scoring eight tries in six outings. When he was injured, the spotlight focused on 20-year-old Joe Rokocoko and the team's No 1 'hunk' Doug Howlett. Between them, they scored 18 tries. The other unexpected star of the final was halfback David Gibson, deputising for Steve Devine, who was stretchered off in the semifinal.

Gibson delivered an impeccable service to Carlos Spencer — 'King' Carlos as he was in 2003 — and three times ripped open the Crusaders' defence with his incisive running.

A rare Spencer blunder — dropping a pass inside his 22 — conceded a second try to livewire hooker Mark Hammett and the half-time lead. But by persisting with their attacking policy, the Blues regained the lead in the second half and held it, defiantly, until the finish. The Crusaders, seeking a fifth title, were as competitive as ever, but surprisingly fell down in the goal-kicking department. Dan Carter couldn't find the

Doug Howlett hugged by Sam Tuitupou after scoring in the 2003 final. Fotopress

uprights and it was left to Andrew Mehrtens, on as a replacement, to land the solitary conversion.

FOR BLUES: Tries by Doug Howlett and Daniel Braid; conversion and 3 penalty goals by Carlos Spencer.

FOR CRUSADERS: Tries by Mark Hammett 2 and Caleb Ralph; conversion by Andrew Mehrtens.

BLUES: Doug Howlett, Rico Gear, Mils Muliaina, Sam Tuitupou, Joe Rokocoko, Carlos Spencer, David Gibson, Xavier Rush (captain), Daniel Braid, Justin Collins, Ali Williams, Angus Macdonald, Kees Meeuws, Keven Mealamu, Deacon Manu. Replacements: Derren Witcombe, Brad Mika, Tony Woodcock.

CRUSADERS: Leon MacDonald, Marika Vunibaka, Caleb Ralph, Dan Carter, Joe Maddock, Aaron Mauger, Justin Marshall, Scott Robertson, Richie McCaw, Reuben Thorne (captain), Chris Jack, Brad Thorn, Greg Somerville, Mark Hammett, David Hewett. Replacements: Scott Hamilton, Andrew Mehrtens, Sam Broomhall, Johnny Leo'o.

REFEREE: André Watson (South Africa)

CROWD: 46,000

THE RESULTS

BLUES
(coach Peter Sloane)

beat	Waratahs at Sydney	31–18
beat	Chiefs at Hamilton	30–27
beat	Crusaders at Albany	39–5
beat	Reds at Whangarei	62–20
beat	Brumbies at Auckland	41–15
lost to	Highlanders at Dunedin	11–22
beat	Bulls at Pretoria	56–28
beat	Stormers at Cape Town	36–8
beat	Sharks at Auckland	25–16
beat	Cats at Auckland	33–9
beat	Hurricanes at Auckland	29–17

Won 10, lost 1; placing: 1st
Tries scored: 53

Semifinal: beat Brumbies at Auckland   42–21

Final: beat Crusaders at Auckland   21–17

Most tries: Doug Howlett 12, Rupeni Caucaunibuca 8,
Joe Rokocoko 6, Sam Tuitupou 4
Most points: Carlos Spencer 143, Doug Howlett 60,
Rupeni Caucaunibuca 40, Orene Ai'i 36

HURRICANES
(coach Colin Cooper)

lost to	Crusaders at Christchurch	21–37
lost to	Bulls at Napier	34–46
beat	Stormers at Wellington	33–18
beat	Sharks at Durban	35–20
beat	Cats at Bloemfontein	28–21
beat	Chiefs at Wellington	24–14
beat	Reds at Brisbane	26–23
beat	Waratahs at Wellington	42–26
beat	Highlanders at New Plymouth	37–15
lost to	Brumbies at Wellington	27–35
lost to	Blues at Auckland	17–29

Won 7, lost 4; placing: 3rd
Tries scored: 41

Semifinal: lost to Crusaders at Christchurch   16–39

Most tries: Christian Cullen 8, Ma'a Nonu 6,
Lome Fa'atau 5, Tana Umaga 5, Brent Ward 5
Most points: David Holwell 89, Riki Flutey 46

CRUSADERS
(coach Robbie Deans)

beat	Hurricanes at Christchurch	37–21
beat	Reds at Christchurch	34–6
lost to	Blues at Albany	5–39
beat	Chiefs at Christchurch	36–29
beat	Highlanders at Dunedin	17–16
lost to	Waratahs at Sydney	31–34
beat	Cats at Christchurch	65–34
beat	Sharks at Christchurch	23–18
lost to	Bulls at Pretoria	31–32
beat	Stormers at Cape Town	51–13
beat	Brumbies at Canberra	28–21

Won 8, lost 3; placing: 2nd
Tries scored: 45

Semifinal: beat Hurricanes at Christchurch   39–16

Final: lost to Blues at Auckland   17–21

Most tries: Caleb Ralph 8, Richie McCaw 7,
Marika Vunibaka 7, Leon MacDonald 4
Most points: Dan Carter 102, Leon MacDonald 49,
Andrew Mehrtens 43

BRUMBIES
(coach David Nucifora)

beat	Reds at Brisbane	22–19
lost to	Sharks at Durban	17–25
lost to	Cats at Johannesburg	32–34
beat	Stormers at Canberra	37–22
beat	Bulls at Canberra	64–26
lost to	Blues at Auckland	15–41
beat	Chiefs at Canberra	55–31
beat	Waratahs at Canberra	41–15
lost to	Highlanders at Dunedin	19–45
beat	Hurricanes at Wellington	35–27
lost to	Crusaders at Canberra	21–28

Won 6, lost 5; placing: 4th
Tries scored: 45

Semifinal: lost to Blues at Auckland   21–42

Most tries: Andrew Walker 7, Joe Roff 6, Mark Gerrard 5,
Joel Wilson 5, Matt Giteau 4, George Gregan 4,
Tamaiti Horua 4, George Smith 4
Most points: Joe Roff 136, Stirling Mortlock 36

WARATAHS
(coach Bob Dwyer)

lost to	Blues at Sydney	18–31
beat	Cats at Bloemfontein	48–36
beat	Sharks at Durban	49–36
beat	Bulls at Sydney	26–16
lost to	Stormers at Sydney	29–39
lost to	Reds at Sydney	23–35
beat	Crusaders at Sydney	34–31
lost to	Hurricanes at Wellington	26–42
lost to	Brumbies at Canberra	15–41
beat	Highlanders at Dunedin	27–23
beat	Chiefs at Sydney	25–14

Won 6, lost 5; placing 5th
Tries scored: 42

Most tries: Lote Tuqiri 5, Morgan Turinui 4
Most points: Matt Burke 80, Mat Rogers 38, Lote Tuqiri 25,
             Shaun Berne 24

HIGHLANDERS
(coach Laurie Mains)

beat	Chiefs at Hamilton	29–16
beat	Stormers at Dunedin	41–17
beat	Bulls at Invercargill	29–22
lost to	Cats at Johannesburg	21–33
beat	Sharks at Durban	23–19
lost to	Crusaders at Dunedin	16–17
beat	Blues at Dunedin	22–11
lost to	Hurricanes at New Plymouth	15–37
beat	Brumbies at Dunedin	45–19
lost to	Waratahs at Dunedin	23–27
lost to	Reds at Brisbane	23–28

Won 6, lost 5; placing 7th
Tries scored: 27

Most tries: Aisea Tuilevu 4, Brad Fleming 3, Seru
              Rabeni 3, Paul Steinmetz 3, Iliesa Tanivula 3
Most points: Willie Walker 142, Aisea Tuilevu 20,
             Tony Brown 18

BULLS
(coach Rudy Joubert)

beat	Cats at Bloemfontein	34–26
beat	Hurricanes at Napier	46–34
lost to	Highlanders at Invercargill	22–29
lost to	Waratahs at Sydney	16–26
lost to	Brumbies at Canberra	26–64
lost to	Stormers at Pretoria	24–27
lost to	Blues at Pretoria	28–56
beat	Reds at Pretoria	39–19
beat	Crusaders at Pretoria	32–31
beat	Chiefs at Pretoria	29–26
beat	Sharks at Durban	24–16

Won 6, lost 5; placing 6th
Tries scored: 31

Most tries: Frikkie Welsh 5, Jaco van der Westhuyzen 4,
              Fabian Jones 3
Most points: Louis Koen 139, Derrick Hougaard 26

REDS
(coach Andrew Slack)

lost to	Brumbies at Brisbane	19–22
lost to	Crusaders at Christchurch	6–34
lost to	Chiefs at Hamilton	27–43
lost to	Blues at Whangarei	20–62
beat	Waratahs at Sydney	35–23
lost to	Hurricanes at Brisbane	23–26
beat	Stormers at Cape Town	41–20
lost to	Bulls at Pretoria	19–39
beat	Cats at Brisbane	41–13
beat	Sharks at Brisbane	22–13
beat	Highlanders at Brisbane	28–23

Won 5, lost 6; placing 8th
Tries scored: 30

Most tries: Wendell Sailor 4, Julian Huxley 3,
              Toutai Kefu 3, Chris Latham 3
Most points: Elton Flatley 125, Julian Huxley 31

When Joe Roff scored against the Reds, it gave him a clean sweep of tries against all the other Super 12 franchises. He also scored a hat trick of tries against the Stormers for the second time, but notwithstanding his try-scoring exploits, the Brumbies returned from South Africa winless for the fifth time in eight seasons.

STORMERS
(coach Gert Smal)

beat	Sharks at Cape Town	40–18
lost to	Highlanders at Dunedin	17–41
lost to	Hurricanes at Wellington	18–33
lost to	Brumbies at Canberra	22–37
beat	Waratahs at Sydney	39–29
beat	Bulls at Pretoria	27–24
lost to	Reds at Cape Town	20–41
lost to	Blues at Cape Town	8–36
beat	Chiefs at Cape Town	24–23
lost to	Crusaders at Cape Town	13–51
beat	Cats at Cape Town	27–21

Won 5, lost 6; placing: 9th
Tries scored: 31

Most tries: Robbie Fleck 4, Selborne Boome 3, Quinton Davids 3, Pieter Rossouw 3, Gus Theron 3
Most points: Leon van der Heever 73, Robbie Fleck 20, Geffie du Toit 17

SHARKS
(coach Kevin Putt)

lost to	Stormers at Cape Town	18–40
beat	Brumbies at Durban	25–17
lost to	Waratahs at Durban	36–49
lost to	Hurricanes at Durban	20–35
lost to	Highlanders at Durban	19–23
beat	Cats at Johannesburg	29–23
beat	Chiefs at Hamilton	31–25
lost to	Crusaders at Christchurch	18–23
lost to	Blues at Auckland	16–25
lost to	Reds at Brisbane	13–22
lost to	Bulls at Durban	16–24

Won 3, lost 8; placing: 11th
Tries scored: 26

Most tries: André Snyman 5, Brent Russell 4, Wylie Human 3
Most points: Butch James 101, Brent Russell 27

CHIEFS
(coach Kevin Greene)

lost to	Highlanders at Hamilton	16–29
lost to	Blues at Hamilton	27–30
beat	Reds at Hamilton	43–27
lost to	Crusaders at Christchurch	29–36
lost to	Hurricanes at Wellington	14–24
lost to	Brumbies at Canberra	31–55
lost to	Sharks at Hamilton	25–31
beat	Cats at Rotorua	40–9
lost to	Stormers at Cape Town	23–24
lost to	Bulls at Pretoria	26–29
lost to	Waratahs at Sydney	14–25

Won 2, lost 9; placing: 10th
Tries scored: 35

Most tries: Steven Bates 4, Keith Lowen 4, Jono Gibbes 3, Shayne Austin 3, Isaac Boss 3, Sitiveni Sivivatu 3
Most points: David Hill 72, Glenn Jackson 53

CATS
(coach Tim Lane)

lost to	Bulls at Bloemfontein	26–34
lost to	Waratahs at Bloemfontein	36–48
beat	Brumbies at Johannesburg	34–32
beat	Highlanders at Johannesburg	33–21
lost to	Hurricanes at Bloemfontein	21–28
lost to	Sharks at Johannesburg	23–29
lost to	Crusaders at Christchurch	34–65
lost to	Chiefs at Rotorua	9–40
lost to	Reds at Brisbane	13–41
lost to	Blues at Auckland	9–33
lost to	Stormers at Cape Town	21–27

Won 2, lost 9; placing: 12th
Tries scored: 24

Most tries: Juan Smith 4, André Pretorius 3, Jaque Fourie 3
Most points: André Pretorius 126, Kennedy Tsimba 30

🏉 Dropped goals were a popular scoring medium in 2003. With Koen leading the way, a total of 18 'pots' were recorded. The only individual to manage more than one, beside Koen who landed seven, was the Sharks' Butch James, with two.

2004

THE BRUMBIES CELEBRATED THEIR SECOND Super 12 triumph after a sensational victory over the Crusaders at Bruce Stadium in Canberra, but one individual who had mixed emotions about it all was their coach David Nucifora. A victim of player power, he'd been advised by the Brumbies management several weeks earlier that, regardless of the outcome of the 2004 event, they would not be reappointing him. He had effectively been sacked mid-term while his team was leading the competition. How unusual was that! Nucifora, who'd succeeded Eddie Jones in 2002 (and got his team through to the play-offs three years in a row), had obviously been at odds with several of the senior members of the team. The shock transfer of international locks Justin Harrison and Dan Vickerman to the Waratahs between seasons appeared to be a factor in the Brumbies management's decision not to renew his contract.

Nucifora made a dignified exit, expressing delight at the team's success while admitting he was disappointed he would not be involved again with Australia's outstanding Super 12 franchise. Indeed, when the 2005 season rolled around, Nucifora was back at the pit face, but as technical adviser to the Blues of Auckland.

The Brumbies, who had been eliminated in the semifinals in 2003, proved themselves the class act this time. They were undefeated in Canberra, their only losses coming in Pretoria, Christchurch and Sydney. While many expected the final to be a tense, tight affair, the Brumbies shattered the Crusaders with their explosive opening that, almost unbelievably, had them ahead by 33 points to nil after 19 minutes.

Joe Roff dotted down twice in the final, which was

Bill Young and Jeremy Paul celebrate the Brumbies' 2004 success. Fotopress

entirely appropriate because the second five-pointer pushed him past Christian Cullen as Super 12's most prolific try scorer, 57 against 56. In his final season of Super 12, the 28-year-old Roff amassed 182 points.

The two big improvers in 2004 were the Chiefs, who under Ian Foster's expert guidance, qualified for the play-offs for the first time, and the Stormers, who made it into the play-offs for only the second time. The Chiefs had finished 10th and and the Stormers ninth the previous year.

While those teams were on the up, the Hurricanes went into decline, plummeting from semifinalist in 2003 to second to bottom. At least they could rely on a South African team to secure the wooden spoon. With the Cats finishing 12th (as they had in 2003), this was the seventh season in succession a South African team had brought up the rear.

THE STARS

DAN CARTER (Crusaders)

When Christchurch's High School Old Boys coach Stephen Dods spoke meaningfully to his rookie teenage five-eighth Dan Carter back in 2001 about the need to emulate Jonny Wilkinson's preparation with his goal kicking, he little suspected that four years on they would be opposing each other in rugby's greatest showcase, the test series between the All Blacks and the British Lions.

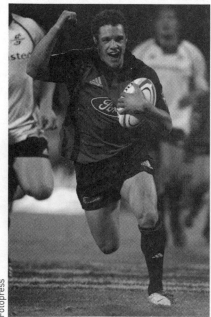

Fotopress

Dods, who recognised the immense potential in Carter, was concerned that he wasn't landing more than 50 per cent of his kicks at goal. So he called him in for a heart-to-heart. 'He was simply treating goal kicking too casually,' says Dods. 'I reminded him that Jonny Wilkinson, the best goal kicker in the world, hit 300 practice shots every week. And Grant Fox would have done the same.'

Carter never has to be told anything twice. Diligently heeding Dods' message, he too began peppering the goalposts at training. And pretty soon he was achieving a success rate comparable with Wilkinson's. If that sounds exaggerated, consider Carter's achievements as a prolific compiler of points since he first came to national prominence: 68 points in four games for New Zealand Colts in South Africa, 2002; 102 points in the six games he was the preferred goal kicker for the Crusaders in 2003; 43 points in his first three test outings in 2003; 201 points (five short of Andrew Mehrtens' record) in 12 Super 12 matches in 2004; 86 points in six All Black tests in 2004; 159 points in 11 games for the Crusaders in 2005.

The rapidity with which Carter rocketed up the New Zealand rugby ladder surprised even his most ardent fans. He advanced from club player to New Zealand Colts to Crusaders to All Blacks in just 12 months. And he made an indelible impression at each level. In his test debut, against Wales at Hamilton, operating at second-five outside Carlos Spencer, he scored 20 points, including a slashing try. He was one of the few shining lights as the All Blacks took an early exit from the World Cup.

He remained at second-five alongside Spencer throughout the Tri-nations tests in 2004, ostensibly not being risked in the No 10 jersey because he was not voluble enough. He was as quiet as Spencer and his predecessor Mehrtens were chatty. Well, he blew that theory out of the water when given his opportunity against France in Paris at season's end, turning in a 25-point blinder as New Zealand blitzed their much vaunted opponents 45–6. And he continued to thrive in the position in for the Crusaders in 2005 as they claimed their fifth Super 12 title.

Carter grew up in Leeston, south of Christchurch, to become Ellesmere College's second All Black after fellow Crusader Sam Broomhall.

GEORGE SMITH (Brumbies)

More Smiths have played rugby for Australia than players of any other name. So to be a distinguished Wallaby named Smith, you need to be an exceptional footballer. Which George most certainly is.

He aspired to the pinnacle of rugby in Australia purely on ability. He didn't have anything else going for him. Wallaby teams are studded with players who have attended private boys schools in Sydney, Brisbane and Canberra, where rugby rules. George Smith attended unfashionable Cromer High School on Sydney's North Shore, where he proved conclusively that class would always win out.

Fotopress

With seven brothers and two sisters of an Australian father and Tongan mother, Smith proudly became Cromer High's first Australian schools rugby representative and, subsequently, its first Wallaby.

He'd been identified as young as 10 as a player of exceptional talent. Thanks to enthusiastic organiser Ian MacDonald who, on Saturday mornings, used to pick up young wannabes from the Brookvale district and drop them off at the Manly and Warringah rugby clubs, Smith soon came to the attention of Manly officials, who gave him every encouragement.

In 1998 he toured the UK with the Australian schools team and the same year began playing grade rugby with Manly. In 1999, he caught the eye of Penrith premier coach Scott Johnson with his performance in an Under-19 curtainraiser. Johnson was blown away when an hour or so later the very same George Smith came on as replacement in the premier game and turned it Manly's way. 'He killed us, he ate us alive,' said Johnson.

Manly were so excited about their player they told the New South Wales union they felt they had a future Wallaby coming through. In an episode that probably explains why the Brumbies have featured in four Super 12 finals to the Waratahs' one, New South Wales told Manly they considered Smith to be only the sixth best flanker in the state.

So the Brumbies grabbed him. Smith headed south to Canberra, breaking into Eddie Jones' Super 12 team midway through the 2000 competition. He made an instant impact and scored a sensational try in the final that the Brumbies dropped agonisingly to the Crusaders, 20–19. Rod Macqueen introduced him immediately to the Wallaby squad and he made his test debut on the end-of-year tour against France in Paris.

Smith has had a remarkable effect on the game all over the world. His pace, balance and strength in both attack and defence make him an extraordinarily effective player, his trademark being his ability to steal opposition ball at breakdowns.

THE FACTS

When the Brumbies defeated the Crusaders 47–38 at Canberra, those scores became the highest winning and highest losing scores in a Super 12 final. The previous best winning score was 45 by the Blues in 1996 and previous best losing score was 21 by Natal in 1996.

When Joe Roff converted the final try (which he himself had scored) in the 2004 final at Canberra, it brought his tally of conversions for the campaign to 51, surpassing the old record held by another Brumby, Stirling Mortlock, by 12.

For the third consecutive occasion the Brumbies exceeded 60 points in their match against the Cats in Canberra. In 2000, the score was 64–nil; in 2002, it was 64–16; and in 2004, it was 68–28.

André Watson, who retired at the end of 2004, controlled his fifth Super 12 final (to go with the two World Cup finals he'd had charge of). Equally as impressive, he was refereeing a Brumbies versus Crusaders match for the seventh time.

Bulls players named Botha maintained an unusual record against the Reds. In 2002 and 2003 Ettienne Botha scored a try against them; in 2003 Bakkies Botha also scored against them; and in 2004 Gary Botha dotted down. Presumably, the Bulls' most famous Botha, Naas, was on hand to applaud each time.

When the Stormers came from 0–22 down to defeat the Highlanders, this was the seventh instance of a team conceding their opponents a 20-point start and winning in Super 12. The Stormers finished so fast they won 46–25. The biggest turnaround is claimed by the Crusaders, who came from 6–31 behind to defeat the Cats 58–38 at Nelson in 1999.

When Paddy O'Brien took control of the Hurricanes–Blues match, he was officiating in his 200th first-class match, thus becoming the first New Zealand referee to achieve this exceptional milestone.

THE FIRST SEMIFINAL

CRUSADERS 27,
STORMERS 16

AT JADE STADIUM, CHRISTCHURCH, 15 MAY

WHILE THE CRUSADERS WERE A RAGING HOT FAVOURITE to win this semifinal contest at Jade Stadium, records revealed if one South African team was capable of upsetting away from home, it was the Stormers. The South African franchises had struggled in Australia and New Zealand since the Super 12 kicked off, but the Stormers had managed to win 47 per cent of their games outside South Africa. This compared with a 33 per cent strike rate by the Sharks, while the Bulls (8.3 per cent success) and Cats (7.1 per cent success) had been perennial strugglers on tour. What made the Crusaders even more wary of the Stormers in 2004 was that they had pulverised the Blues by 51 points to 23 on Eden Park after downing the Reds in Brisbane. Plainly, they were a team to be treated with respect, even if they had lost their captain Corne Krige through suspension.

Which is why Crusaders coach Robbie Deans desperately wanted Justin Marshall fit for the play-offs. Without his masterly guidance behind the scrum, the Crusaders had taken a 37–20 drubbing from the Hurricanes in the final qualifying game, a result that would have cost a home semifinal had the Chiefs beaten the Brumbies.

Declared fit only 30 hours before kick-off, Marshall turned in an inspirational performance. In fact, it's probably not an exaggeration to say that at the final whistle he was the difference between the two teams. He stole the show, repeatedly breaking through the Stormers' well-organised defence

> 🫘 When Rupeni Caucaunibuca scored his first try against the Crusaders in round two, it brought up 3,000 points in Super 12 for the Blues, the first team to achieve this milestone. Dan Carter's try brought up 3,000 points for the Crusaders later in the same match.

and, benefiting from a lucky ricochet that saw a speculative kick bounce into Marika Vunibaka's hands, scored a crucial try. He seriously over-reacted after scoring his try but notwithstanding that, some critics were projecting him as the new All Black captain (an appointment that would eventually go to Tana Umaga).

The Crusaders trailed 12–13 at half-time, a rare experience for them, and had to dig deep in the second half to secure the victory. The home town heroes, besides Marshall, were prop Greg Somerville, who monstered Daan Human, sharp-shooting Dan Carter, who landed five penalty goals, and loose forwards Richie McCaw, Sam Broomhall and Reuben Thorne, who eventually got the better of their talented opposites Adri Badenhorst, Schalk Burger and Hendrik Gerber.

Caleb Ralph was, almost inevitably, the Crusaders' other try scorer. His five-pointer pushed him ahead of Joeli Vidiri as the second most prolific try scorer in Super 12 history.

FOR CRUSADERS: Tries by Justin Marshall and Caleb Ralph; conversion and 5 penalty goals by Dan Carter.

FOR STORMERS: Try by De Wet Barry; conversion and 3 penalty goals by Gaffie du Toit.

CRUSADERS: Ben Blair, Marika Vunibaka, Aaron Mauger, Dan Carter, Caleb Ralph, Cameron McIntyre, Justin Marshall, Sam Broomhall, Richie McCaw, Reuben Thorne (captain), Ross Filipo, Brad Thorn, Greg Somerville, Tone Kopelani, David Hewett. Replacements: Jamie Nutbrown, Corey Flynn, Chris King.

STORMERS: Werner Greeff, Tonderai Chavanga, Marius Joubert, De Wet Barry, Gus Theron, Gaffie du Toit, Bolla Conradie, Adri Badenhorst, Schalk Burger, Hendrik Gerber, Selborne Boome (captain), Quinton Davids, Eddie Andrews, Pieter Dixon, Daan Human. Replacements: Neil de Koch, Pierre Uys, Willem Stoltz, David Britz, Pat Bernard.

REFEREE: Andrew Cole

CROWD: 25,800

*When the Cats defeated the Chiefs at Ellis Park they ended a record run of 13 consecutive losses in Super 12. The Bulls had previously held that dubious record, losing 12 on the trot in 2002–03.

THE SECOND SEMIFINAL

BRUMBIES 32, CHIEFS 17

AT BRUCE STADIUM, CANBERRA, 15 MAY

BY THE TIME THE NINTH SUPER 12 swung into action only one team had failed to qualify for the semifinals, the Chiefs. Thanks to one of Waikato's favourite rugby sons, Ian Foster, all that changed in 2004. Foster's greatest claim to fame prior to taking up coaching was in scoring a try and dropping a goal at Eden Park in 1993 to allow Waikato to end Auckland's remarkable eight-year tenure of the Ranfurly Shield. He never became an All Black but he was one of the most accomplished first-fives and goal kickers in the land. He was durable, too, and still holds the Waikato record for appearances, 148 of them. His predecessors as coach of the Chiefs, Brad Meurant, Ross Cooper, John Mitchell and Kevin Greene, had all performed creditably, but in eight years none of them had got the team beyond sixth in the competition.

Given what Foster had achieved in his first two seasons in charge of Waikato, the fans (certainly those intimately involved with Waikato) had reason for optimism when the 2004 Super 12 kicked off. In 2002, Foster had guided Waikato into the final of the NPC, his team putting 59 points on Canterbury and 49 on Wellington along the way. And in 2003, the Mooloo men were back in the NPC semifinals again.

Brumbies No 8 Scott Fava attacks against the Chiefs. Fotopress

Away wins over the Blues and the Highlanders provided the Chiefs with the momentum they needed, although they still required a point from their final round-robin encounter, against the Brumbies in Hamilton, to qualify. It was a happy-sad result for Foster. In holding the Brumbies to 12–15, they created history by qualifying for the play-offs but had they won, they would have claimed second spot and secured a home semifinal (against the Crusaders).

When they pitched into Canberra for their semifinal, it was a whole new experience. The Brumbies, semifinalists in 1997, 2000, 2001, 2002 and 2003, had been there, done that many times. The Chiefs came full of hope. It was the semifinal experience factor that made the difference. The Chiefs were like cats frozen in car headlights in the opening 30 minutes. By the time they settled down and began playing their natural game, the Brumbies were out of reach.

The super-cool efficiency of players like George Gregan, Stephen Larkham, Joe Roff, George Smith, Jeremy Paul and Owen Finegan proved too much for the Chiefs. When Stirling Mortlock exited the game with medial ligament damage, Finegan assumed the captaincy and lifted his game to a new level.

The Chiefs also lost a key player, halfback Byron Kelleher, who went off after being struck in the head by Gregan's elbow.

FOR BRUMBIES: **Tries by Stirling Mortlock, Mark Gerrard, Mark Chisholm, Radike Samo and Clyde Rathbone; 2 conversions and a penalty goal by Joe Roff.**

FOR CHIEFS: **Tries by Lome Fa'atau and Steven Bates; 2 conversions and a penalty goal by Glenn Jackson.**

BRUMBIES: **Joe Roff, Clyde Rathbone, Stirling Mortlock (captain), Matt Giteau, Mark Gerrard, Stephen Larkham, George Gregan, Scott Fava, George Smith, Owen Finegan, Mark Chisholm, Radike Samo, Nic Henderson, Jeremy Paul, Bill Young.**
Replacements: **Joel Wilson, Mark Bartholomeusz, Matt Henjak, David Giffin, Jone Tawake, Guy Shepherdson, David Palavi.**

CHIEFS: **Todd Miller, Lome Fa'atau, Keith Lowen, Mark Ranby, Sitiveni Sivivatu, Glenn Jackson, Byron Kelleher, Steven Bates, Marty Holah, Wayne Ormond, Keith Robinson, Jono Gibbes (captain), Deacon Manu, Scott Linklater, Michael Collins.**
Replacements: **Adrian Cashmore, David Hill, Isaac Boss, Scott Couch, Aleki Lutui, Simms Davison.**

REFEREE: **Jonathan Kaplan (South Africa).**

CROWD: **23,191**

🏉 Brumbies halfback George Gregan became the first player to notch up 100 Super 12 appearances when he took the field against the Waratahs. He'd been a member of the team since the competition's inaugural season, 1996.

🏉 In defeating the Bulls 56–19, the Blues scored nine tries — for the third consecutive year. They'd hammered the Bulls 56–28 at Pretoria in 2003 and dealt to them 65–24 in Auckland in 2002.

THE FINAL

BRUMBIES 47,
CRUSADERS 38

AT BRUCE STADIUM, CANBERRA, 22 MAY

WHEN ANDREW MEHRTENS TOOK his place on the Crusaders reserves bench for the 2004 final at Bruce Stadium, he was anticipating a modicum of involvement later in the evening. Instead, he was rushed into action at the 20-minute mark with his team in a state of absolute crisis. The Brumbies, on fire, had established an incredible 33–nil advantage in 19 minutes through a bewildering mix of precision play by themselves and bumbling inefficiency on the part of the Crusaders.

Crusaders coach Robbie Deans, who had controversially and stubbornly declined to utilise Mehrtens' talents during the 2004 campaign, now turned to the old maestro with things going nightmarishly wrong. Mehrtens wielded such influence that the Crusaders won the balance of the game 38–14 and but for another tragic lapse immediately after half-time by fullback Ben Blair, who experienced a horror game of massive proportions, they could have gone close to pulling off the most amazing comeback victory in the history of the game.

Crusaders lock Brad Thorn up highest during the 2004 final at Canberra. Fotopress

Even with all their blunders and conceding such a whopping start, the Crusaders closed to within nine points in the final quarter, but the Brumbies, nosed out in 2003, weren't going to let this one get away. They hadn't lost at Fortress Bruce Stadium since the 2003 final and, like true champions, they were able to uncork one more try, their seventh of the evening, when it mattered most.

In the absence of injured captain Stirling Mortlock, winger Mark Gerrard (a Joe Roff lookalike) stepped up for the Brumbies, becoming the first player to score three tries in a Super 12 final. He and lock Radike Samo, who was dynamite with ball in hand, were unexpected heroes of the Brumbies' epic victory.

Joe Roff had cause for a double celebration, because when he dotted down behind the posts in the second half, he became Super 12's leading try scorer, his haul of 57 eclipsing Christian Cullen's record by one. Referee André Watson was aware of the achievement and shook Roff by the hand. 'Congratulations,' he said, 'that's the record.'

FOR BRUMBIES: Tries by Mark Gerrard 3, Joe Roff 2, Jeremy Paul and Matt Giteau; 6 conversions by Roff.

FOR CRUSADERS: Tries by Dan Carter, Brad Thorn, Aaron Mauger, Casey Laulala, Chris King and Richie McCaw; 4 conversions by Carter.

BRUMBIES: Joe Roff, Clyde Rathbone, Joel Wilson, Matt Giteau, Mark Gerrard, Stephen Larkham, George Gregan, Scott Fava, George Smith, Owen Finegan (captain), Mark Chisholm, Radike Samo, Nic Henderson, Jeremy Paul, Bill Young.
Replacements: Mark Bartholomeusz, Lenny Beckett, Matt Henjak, Jone Tawake, David Giffin, Guy Shepherdson, David Palavi.

CRUSADERS: Ben Blair, Marika Vunibaka, Aaron Mauger, Dan Carter, Caleb Ralph, Cameron McIntyre, Justin Marshall, Sam Broomhall, Richie McCaw, Reuben Thorne (captain), Chris Jack, Brad Thorn, Greg Somerville, Tone Kopelani, Dave Hewett.
Replacements: Casey Laulala, Andrew Mehrtens, Jamie Nutbrown, Corey Flynn, Chris King.

REFEREE: André Watson (South Africa)

CROWD: 28,753

The 6–5 victory recorded by the Reds against the Sharks in Durban equalled the lowest aggregate of points in a Super 12 match. The Reds were also involved in the other 11-point game, against the Hurricanes in 1999. On that occasion, the Reds won 11–nil.

THE RESULTS

BRUMBIES
(coach David Nucifora)

beat	Blues at Canberra	44–27
beat	Cats at Canberra	68–28
beat	Sharks at Canberra	23–20
lost to	Bulls at Pretoria	21–32
beat	Stormers at Cape Town	33–15
beat	Reds at Canberra	51–8
lost to	Crusaders at Christchurch	28–47
beat	Highlanders at Canberra	50–18
lost to	Waratahs at Sydney	29–37
beat	Hurricanes at Canberra	46–25
beat	Chiefs at Hamilton	15–12

Won 8, lost 3; placing: 1st
Tries scored: 55

Semifinal: beat Chiefs at Canberra   32–17

Final: beat Crusaders at Canberra   47–38

Most tries: Stirling Mortlock 10, Mark Gerrard 10, Clyde Rathbone 9, Joe Roff 7, Matt Giteau 6, Jeremy Paul 6, Mark Chisholm 6
Most points: Joe Roff 182, Stirling Mortlock 50, Mark Gerrard 50

STORMERS
(coach Gert Smal)

beat	Cats at Johannesburg	28–23
beat	Highlanders at Cape Town	46–25
lost to	Hurricanes at Cape Town	19–25
beat	Waratahs at Cape Town	27–23
lost to	Brumbies at Cape Town	15–33
beat	Bulls at Cape Town	25–11
beat	Reds at Brisbane	21–20
beat	Blues at Auckland	51–23
lost to	Chiefs at Hamilton	14–29
lost to	Crusaders at Christchurch	9–24
beat	Sharks at Durban	31–24

Won 7, lost 4; placing: 3rd
Tries scored: 37

Semifinal: lost to Crusaders at Christchurch   16–27

Most tries: Marius Joubert 5, Breyton Paulse 4, Tonderai Chavhanga 4, Adri Badenhorst 3, De Wet Barry 3, Werner Greeff 3
Most points: Chris Rossouw 77, Gaffie du Toit 45

CRUSADERS
(coach Robbie Deans)

lost to	Waratahs at Christchurch	19–43
lost to	Blues at Christchurch	29–38
beat	Reds at Brisbane	20–17
beat	Chiefs at Hamilton	36–15
beat	Highlanders at Christchurch	46–29
beat	Brumbies at Christchurch	47–28
lost to	Sharks at Durban	25–29
beat	Cats at Johannesburg	39–37
beat	Bulls at Christchurch	40–21
beat	Stormers at Christchurch	24–9
lost to	Hurricanes at Wellington	20–37

Won 7, lost 4; placing: 2nd
Tries scored: 37

Semifinal: beat Stormers at Christchurch   27–16

Final: lost to Brumbies at Canberra   38–47

Most tries: Marika Vunibaka 7, Dan Carter 6, Caleb Ralph 5, Richie McCaw 5, Aaron Mauger 4
Most points: Dan Carter 201, Marika Vunibaka 35

CHIEFS
(coach Ian Foster)

beat	Hurricanes at Hamilton	19–7
lost to	Reds at Brisbane	25–39
beat	Blues at Auckland	27–20
lost to	Crusaders at Hamilton	15–36
beat	Waratahs at Hamilton	32–17
beat	Highlanders at Dunedin	36–31
lost to	Cats at Johannesburg	21–23
beat	Sharks at Durban	34–27
beat	Stormers at Hamilton	29–14
beat	Bulls at Hamilton	24–22
lost to	Brumbies at Hamilton	12–15

Won 7, lost 4; placing: 4th
Tries scored: 28

Semifinal: lost to Brumbies at Canberra   17–32

Most tries: Lome Fa'atau 6, Sione Lauaki 5, Sitiveni Sivivatu 4, Keith Lowen 3
Most points: Glenn Jackson 77, David Hill 66

BLUES
(coach Peter Sloane)

lost to	Brumbies at Canberra	27–44
beat	Crusaders at Christchurch	38–29
lost to	Chiefs at Auckland	20–27
lost to	Reds at Brisbane	3–20
drew with	Hurricanes at Wellington	26–26
beat	Waratahs at Auckland	22–17
beat	Bulls at Auckland	56–19
lost to	Stormers at Auckland	23–51
beat	Cats at Johannesburg	35–28
beat	Sharks at Durban	37–26
beat	Highlanders at Auckland	50–22

Won 6, lost 4, drew 1; placing: 5th
Tries scored: 44

Most tries: Doug Howlett 7, Rupeni Caucaunibuca 5,
Carlos Spencer 4, Joe Rokocoko 4,
Sam Tuitupou 4
Most points: Carlos Spencer 96, Ben Atiga 36,
Doug Howlett 35

SHARKS
(coach Kevin Putt)

beat	Bulls at Pretoria	23–18
lost to	Waratahs at Sydney	14–48
lost to	Brumbies at Canberra	20–23
beat	Highlanders at Dunedin	36–35
beat	Hurricanes at New Plymouth	21–20
beat	Cats at Durban	42–28
beat	Crusaders at Durban	29–25
lost to	Chiefs at Durban	27–34
lost to	Reds at Durban	5–6
lost to	Blues at Durban	26–37
lost to	Stormers at Durban	24–31

Won 5, lost 6; placing: 7th
Tries scored: 31

Most tries: Brent Russell 7, Henno Mentz 5,
Adrian Jacobs 4, Trevor Halstead 4,
Craig Davidson 3
Most points: Butch James 118, Brent Russell 37

BULLS
(coach Rudy Joubert)

lost to	Sharks at Pretoria	18–23
beat	Hurricanes at Pretoria	40–19
drew with	Highlanders at Pretoria	16–16
beat	Brumbies at Pretoria	32–21
beat	Waratahs at Pretoria	38–27
lost to	Stormers at Cape Town	11–25
lost to	Blues at Auckland	19–56
beat	Reds at Brisbane	23–17
lost to	Crusaders at Christchurch	21–40
lost to	Chiefs at Hamilton	22–24
beat	Cats at Pretoria	62–52

Won 5, lost 5, drew 1; placing: 6th
Tries scored: 36

Most tries: Fourie du Preez 5, Frikkie Welsh 4,
Edrich Fredericks 4, Ettienne Botha 3,
Piet Krause 3, Odwa Ndungane 3
Most points: Derick Hougaard 101, Willem de Waal 31

WARATAHS
(coach Ewen McKenzie)

beat	Crusaders at Christchurch	43–19
beat	Sharks at Sydney	48–14
beat	Cats at Sydney	46–10
lost to	Stormers at Cape Town	23–27
lost to	Bulls at Pretoria	27–38
lost to	Chiefs at Hamilton	17–32
lost to	Blues at Auckland	17–22
beat	Hurricanes at Sydney	49–31
beat	Brumbies at Sydney	37–29
lost to	Highlanders at Sydney	28–29
lost to	Reds at Brisbane	7–23

Won 5, lost 6; placing: 8th
Tries scored: 40

Most tries: Lote Tuqiri 7, Mat Rogers 4, Morgan Turinui 4,
Cameron Shepherd 4
Most points: Mat Rogers 82, Matt Burke 62, Lote Tuqiri 35,
Tim Donnelly 23

✏ Matt Burke kicked six penalty goals for the Waratahs against the Brumbies for the second time. Curiously, in 10 matches over nine seasons, no Brumbies player had ever kicked more than two penalty goals in a match against the Waratahs.

HIGHLANDERS
(coach Greg Cooper)

beat	Reds at Invercargill	39–8
lost to	Stormers at Cape Town	25–46
drew with	Bulls at Pretoria	16–16
lost to	Sharks at Dunedin	35–36
beat	Cats at Dunedin	29–17
lost to	Crusaders at Christchurch	29–46
lost to	Chiefs at Dunedin	31–36
lost to	Brumbies at Canberra	18–50
beat	Hurricanes at Dunedin	26–14
beat	Waratahs at Sydney	29–28
lost to	Blues at Auckland	22–50

Won 4, lost 6, drew 1; placing: 9th
Tries scored: 36

Most tries: Nick Evans 4, Seilala Mapusua 4,
Anton Oliver 4, Matt Saunders 4
Most points: Tony Brown 104, Nick Evans 35

HURRICANES
(coach Colin Cooper)

lost to	Chiefs at Hamilton	7–19
lost to	Bulls at Pretoria	19–40
beat	Stormers at Cape Town	25–19
beat	Cats at Wellington	42–25
lost to	Sharks at New Plymouth	20–21
drew with	Blues at Wellington	26–26
beat	Reds at Wellington	29–12
lost to	Waratahs at Sydney	31–49
lost to	Highlanders at Dunedin	14–26
lost to	Brumbies at Canberra	25–46
beat	Crusaders at Wellington	37–20

Won 4, lost 6, drew 1; placing: 11th
Tries scored: 33

Most tries: Brent Ward 8, Andrew Hore 6,
Roy Kinikinilau 5, Tane Tuipolotu 3
Most points: David Holwell 90, Brent Ward 40

REDS
(coach Jeff Miller)

lost to	Highlanders at Invercargill	8–39
beat	Chiefs at Brisbane	39–25
lost to	Crusaders at Brisbane	17–20
beat	Blues at Brisbane	20–3
lost to	Brumbies at Canberra	8–51
lost to	Hurricanes at Wellington	12–29
lost to	Stormers at Brisbane	20–21
lost to	Bulls at Brisbane	17–23
beat	Sharks at Durban	6–5
beat	Cats at Bloemfontein	47–23
beat	Waratahs at Brisbane	23–7

Won 5, lost 6; placing: 10th
Tries scored: 28

Most tries: Steve Kefu 4, Wendell Sailor 4,
Chris Latham 4, John Roe 4
Most points: Elton Flatley 58, Steve Kefu 22

CATS
(coach Tim Lane, replaced by Chester Williams)

lost to	Stormers at Johannesburg	23–28
lost to	Brumbies at Canberra	28–68
lost to	Waratahs at Sydney	10–46
lost to	Hurricanes at Wellington	25–42
lost to	Highlanders at Dunedin	17–29
lost to	Sharks at Durban	28–42
beat	Chiefs at Johannesburg	23–21
lost to	Crusaders at Johannesburg	37–39
lost to	Blues at Johannesburg	28–35
lost to	Reds at Bloemfontein	23–47
lost to	Bulls at Pretoria	52–62

Won 1, lost 10; placing: 12th
Tries scored: 34

Most tries: Juan Smith 5, Jaque Fourie 4, Jorrie Muller 4,
Gerrie Britz 4, Wikus van Heerden 3
Most points: André Pretorius 102, Nel Fourie 27

🏉 The 51–23 scoreline achieved by the Stormers against the Blues at Eden Park represented their highest score in any Super 12 match and the highest score by any South African team in New Zealand, the previous highest being Free State's 49 against the Highlanders at Invercargill in 1997.

2005

AS THE CURTAIN CAME DOWN on a decade of Super 12, the Crusaders of Canterbury confirmed their status as the most consistently powerful rugby team out of New Zealand, Australia and South Africa, wrapping up their fifth title with a handsome victory over the Waratahs. Remarkably, two individuals featured in all five finals victories dating back to 1998, former captain Reuben Thorne and evergreen first-five Andrew Mehrtens.

The Crusaders' victory meant that in 10 years of intense and enthralling competition only three franchises had sampled success — the Blues (in 1996, 1997 and 2003), the Brumbies (in 2001 and 2004) and the Crusaders (in 1998, 1999, 2000, 2002 and 2005). And only six captains got to make winning speeches: Zinzan Brooke (twice) and Xavier Rush for the Blues; George Gregan for the Brumbies; and Todd Blackadder (three times), Reuben Thorne and Richie McCaw for the Crusaders.

While New Zealand and Australian franchises shared all the finals and derived handsome profits from them, sadly, the best South Africa could manage was having the Sharks participate in two finals, in 1996 and 2001.

Participating in the final in 2005 was a new experience for the Waratahs, who had set the pace throughout the competition, only to be nosed out as top qualifier when the Blues denied them a fourth (bonus point) try in the final round-robin game.

A disappointing aspect of the final Super 12 championship was the number of high-quality personalities who were making farewell appearances before heading overseas to take up presumably lucrative contracts. They

Richie McCaw after the Crusaders' handsome win in 2005. Fotopress

included former All Blacks Carlos Spencer, Justin Marshall, Andrew Mehrtens, Norm Maxwell, Dave Hewett and Xavier Rush, and former Wallabies Owen Finegan and Nathan Grey.

One individual who wasn't going anywhere, however, was the Crusaders' successful coach Robbie Deans, who'd been in charge of the team since 2001. In those five years he'd guided the team into four finals, winning two.

'We are losing several key players and a lot of intellectual property,' said Deans following the 2005 final. 'That's going to take some replacing and the challenge excites me. I always said when I left the place I wanted to pull out with the side in full running order.'

The competition welcomed in a couple of exciting newcomers, Waratahs fullback/winger Peter Hewat, who scored 173 points including 10 tries (several of them from intercepts) in a sensational debut season, and Bulls winger Bryan Habana, who also ran in 10 tries. Chasing Hewat all the way as a point scorer was Dan Carter of the Crusaders, who finished with 171 points, while Hewat and Habana finished second equal as try scorers behind the hot-shot Crusaders winger Rico Gear, who dotted down 15 tries. Gear scored a pair of tries on six occasions.

THE STARS

JUSTIN MARSHALL (Crusaders)

No individual better qualifies for recognition in this book, celebrating the first decade of SANZAR, than Justin Marshall. After featuring in the Canterbury Crusaders' first Super 12 game (against the Waikato Chiefs) in 1996, he was still wearing the No 9 jersey (with great distinction) 10 years on, one of the exclusive few to celebrate a century of Super 12 appearances. He also participated in the inaugural Tri-nations encounter at Wellington's Athletic Park in 1996, scoring a try as the All Blacks, transcending dreadful conditions, overwhelmed the Wallabies by 43 points to 6. His celebrated international career, extending to 77 tests — making him the most capped All Black — continued through into 2005.

Marshall thought his quality of play in the 2005 Super 12 merited selection for the much-hyped series against the Lions, and, being the forthright individual he is, said so. All Black coach Graham Henry agreed, starting Marshall in the first test on his home turf, Jade Stadium. It was a great way for Marshall to end his New Zealand career before heading to the UK and a fresh challenge with the Leeds club.

Until Marshall came along, the greatest claim to sporting fame for the freezing works town of Mataura in the deep south, was that it was the birth place of the first million-dollar trotter, Cardigan Bay. Marshall was to achieve greater world-wide recognition.

He broke into representative rugby with Southland and might have lingered longer there had the Southland coach of 1994 not preferred a fellow called Dave

Fotopress

Wheeley for most of the important matches. This despite the fact Marshall had already played for the New Zealand Colts. That was where he first teamed up with Andrew Mehrtens, who remembers him as being 'devastating' at age group level with 'an abrasive tough competitive attitude, that's never changed'.

Marshall was lured to Christchurch by Canterbury coach Vance Stewart, and never looked back, even though the Crusaders embarrassingly finished up with the wooden spoon in that first season of Super 12, 1996. By then, Marshall had made it into the All Blacks, winning selection in Laurie Mains' team for the end-of-year tour of Italy and France, his test debut coming in Paris where the All Blacks produced attacking rugby of divine quality.

Notwithstanding a torn Achilles tendon injury, that abruptly curtailed his Super 12 campaign in 1998, Marshall has shared in just about every rugby honour going, with the solitary exception of the World Cup. He has played his part in five Super 12 titles, four Tri-nations successes and four NPC wins and, of course, was part of the All Black team of 1996 that created history by finally winning a series on South African soil.

OWEN FINEGAN (Brumbies)

The Super 12 (or its equivalent, the Super 14) isn't going to be the same without Owen Finegan, the Brumbies' abrasive and often under-rated all-purpose forward who in 2005 headed to Newcastle in England to link up with another famous Australian player, Matt Burke. Finegan, a foundation member

of the Brumbies, exits as the competition's leading forward try scorer, having dotted down 30 times in his 92 Super 12 outings, a remarkable strike rate for a 114 kg forward who operated variously at flanker, No 8 and lock.

The Super 12 couldn't have come along at a more appropriate time for Finegan who, as a Randwick club player, had debuted for New South Wales against Southland at Invercargill in 1994 (funnily enough, scoring a hat trick of tries). He was on the fringe of state selection when rugby went professional in 1996.

The Waratahs' first coach, Chris Hawkins, obviously didn't recognise the potential in Finegan, but Rod Macqueen, who was given charge of the Brumbies, sure did. Other New South Wales spare parts that Macqueen latched on to were prop Ewen McKenzie, lock John Langford and outside back Mitch Hardy, who would all give great service to the new franchise.

Apart from the 2000 season, when he was sidelined having his shoulder reconstructed, Finegan was an integral part of the Brumbies throughout the decade, sharing in the championship victories of 2001 and 2004 and proving an often immovable obstacle for opponents. He went on to make 55 test appearances for the Wallabies, playing a significant role in the World Cup of 1999. His try in the final against France was a magical moment.

The pen portraits issued for the Wallabies in 2003 described Finegan as 'a niggler and supreme practical joker' who possessed a special try-scoring talent, his game presenting 'the perfect mix of strength and strategy'. It was often claimed that when he played well, the Wallabies played well. As a practical joker, he was described as 'relentless' and nobody, not even his captain George Gregan, was immune to his pranks. If there wasn't a practical joke to be had, he would simply indulge in verbals, reminding team-mates of some lapse or other of which they'd been guilty.

His original nickname of 'Melon' related to his physical dimensions, but those closest to him later called him 'Listo', because he would never admit to a hangover but would guzzle Listerine in a desperate bid to recover.

THE FACTS

Volunteering Anton Oliver and Carl Hoeft for the tsunami relief match in the UK meant that for the first time since 9 March 1996 the Highlanders played a match without at least one of these two great troopers in the front row, a truly amazing record. During the 2005 campaign, Oliver became the first New Zealand player to register 100 Super 12 appearances.

Three bastions fell in one weekend of Super 12 action in 2005: the Hurricanes beat the Blues for the first time (at Auckland), the Waratahs beat the Reds for the first time (at Sydney) and the only two teams that had never been involved in a draw, the Brumbies and the Chiefs, ended their game 28-all at Canberra.

When Justin Marshall scored against the Brumbies in 2005 it meant that over the course of a decade he had scored against every Super 12 opponent (that is, if you equate Transvaal, the original Johannesburg-based team, with the Cats).

When the Highlanders defeated the Sharks 43–7, it was the second time they had scored 43 points in Durban. But on the first occasion, in 1997, the opposition amassed 75!

When the Reds defeated the Chiefs 20–6 in Hamilton, they ended a six-year losing streak in New Zealand.

Niva Ta'auso from Counties Manukau distinguished himself as the only NPC second division player to appear in Super 12 in 2005.

Reuben Thorne and Andrew Mehrtens are the only individuals to feature in each of the Crusaders' seven finals appearances, which extend from 1998 to 2005. Thorne, remarkably, was on the field for every minute of those seven finals. Thorne's tally of Super 12 appearances stands at 98 (the same number as Stephen Larkham, Caleb Ralph and Carl Hoeft).

THE FIRST SEMIFINAL

CRUSADERS 47, HURRICANES 7

AT JADE STADIUM, CHRISTCHURCH, 20 MAY

THE CRUSADERS' FEISTY HALFBACK Justin Marshall dominated the news bulletins in the wake of this surprisingly one-sided semifinal, but not just for his man-of-the-match performance. A Sunday newspaper quoted Marshall as saying that, because of his impending departure for Leeds, he wasn't sure whether he would be sufficiently focused to play the test series against the British Lions and, anyway, Graham Henry had only contacted him once in six months and it didn't seem like the selectors were interested in him.

As a wave of outrage swept the country, because Marshall had been the standout halfback throughout the Super 12, the concept was promulgated that the selectors' preference for the Lions series was the slick-passing Byron Kelleher. Coach Henry declined to be drawn into the argument, although he did make a phone call to Marshall, who subsequently announced that he was still 'in consideration' for the All Blacks.

The Hurricanes found Marshall too hot to handle at Jade Stadium. His probing runs, combined with the deft ability of the Crusaders forwards, Richie McCaw in particular, to turn over possession, left the Hurricanes gasping. They trailed 18–nil at half-time and were 42–nil in arrears before Jimmy Gopperth finally managed to convert the Hurricanes' generous share of possession into a tangible reward.

Incredible as it may seem, given the scoreline, the Hurricanes broke even in both possession and territory. But they were vulnerable to the Crusaders' turnovers and slick counterattacks. The turning point — if there was such a definitive moment — came shortly before half-time, with the Crusaders ahead 11–nil. The Hurricanes put together eight or nine phases and were zeroing in

> When Marius Hurter, Naka Drotske and Os du Randt came together in the front row for the Cats in 2005 they claimed a combined age totalling 100 years! Hurter and Drotske were 34 and du Randt 32.

on the goalposts when McCaw (who else?) effected a turnover and, moments later, after a bewildering exchange of passes, Scott Hamilton scored 90 metres away.

The Hurricanes, who'd lost 40–20 to the same opponent on the same ground seven days earlier, had to operate without their classy centre Conrad Smith, out with concussion. Tane Tuipulotu came in at second-five, with captain Tana Umaga moving out to centre. The rejigging of the backline didn't work, with Tuipulotu consistently running into blind alleys.

The Crusaders' special achievers on the night were Rico Gear, whose early five-pointer allowed him to equal Joe Roff's Super 12 try-scoring record of 15 (and he set up two tries by Scott Hamilton as well), and Dan Carter, who struck some booming long-distance goals in a 22-point performance.

Many spectators believed that the Crusaders did not bother to take a conversion of the try Greg Somerville scored after the final siren. Andrew Mehrtens tells a different story. With his team-mates all clustered around, shaking hands, Mehrts couldn't be bothered summoning the kicking tee, so took a snap drop-kick . . . and missed!

FOR CRUSADERS: Tries by Scott Hamilton 3, Rico Gear, Greg Somerville and Daniel Carter; 4 conversions and 3 penalty goals by Carter.

FOR HURRICANES: Try and conversion by Jimmy Gopperth.

CRUSADERS: Leon MacDonald, Rico Gear, Caleb Ralph, Aaron Mauger, Scott Hamilton, Daniel Carter, Justin Marshall, Mose Tuiali'i, Richie McCaw (captain), Reuben Thorne, Ross Filipo, Chris Jack, Greg Somerville, Corey Flynn, Dave Hewett. Replacements: Tone Kopelani, Campbell Johnstone, Sam Broomhall, Johnny Leo'o, Jamie Nutbrown, Andrew Mehrtens, Vilimoni Delasau.

HURRICANES: Shannon Paku, Lome Fa'atau, Tane Tuipulotu, Tana Umaga (captain), Ma'a Nonu, Jimmy Gopperth, Piri Weepu, Rodney So'oialo, Chris Masoe, Jerry Collins, Luke Andrews, Ross Kennedy, Neemia Tialata, Andrew Hore, Tony Penn. Replacements: Gordon Slater, Paul Tito, Ben Herring, Hosea Gear, Brent Ward.

REFEREE: Andrew Cole (Australia)

CROWD: 29,000

The 35 points scored by Morne Steyn for the Bulls against the Stormers is the most by a player in Super 12 since Gavin Lawless scored 50 for Natal against the Highlanders in 1997.

THE SECOND SEMIFINAL

WARATAHS 23, BULLS 13

AT AUSSIE STADIUM, SYDNEY, 21 MAY

ASTUTE RUGBY COACHES WILL TELL YOU that important matches are won and lost on elementary mistakes. The Bulls, unfamiliar foe around the Super 12 play-offs, made two horrendous, basic errors at Aussie Stadium that cost them a famous victory against the Waratahs. Winger Bryan Habana, who'd so often been a Bulls hero in scoring 10 tries during the campaign, must still be cursing his decision to try to scoop up the ball 2 metres from the goalline, with his team ahead 13–6, when a controlled grubber would surely have secured him a five-pointer. The Waratahs couldn't believe their luck. They were so close to being at least a dozen points in arrears. They celebrated by kicking a penalty goal shortly after.

And then before half-time, the men from Pretoria were guilty of another clanger, this one gift-wrapped with a handsome bow on it. When Waratahs centre Morgan Turinui blasted a path through a midfield gathering of the enemy

Tryscorer Nathan Grey in possession against the Bulls. Fotopress

and hoisted a high kick towards the 22, he must have wondered whether it was even worth chasing. He'd chosen the most populated zone on the ground for the ball to come down. It was packed with Bulls defenders. Oh well, thought Turinui, I'll tackle whichever one fields the ball. Well, guess what? None of them caught it. The five defenders closest to Point X all shouted 'Yours!' Okay, they didn't actually shout 'Yours!', but that's what each of them was thinking. The ball pitched at a point equidistant from all five and sat up beautifully for Turinui, who grabbed it and, with a huge smile on his face, sprinted away to the goalposts.

Instead of a potentially substantial half-time deficit, which would have been a matter of some concern, the Waratahs were able to contemplate a 16–13 lead. Within sight of their first final, they weren't going to let this one get away. Veteran midfielder Nathan Grey, making his last Sydney appearance in a Waratah jersey, gave his team a winning break with one of his trademark bulldozing tries early in the second half. Four defenders had a go at stopping him.

However, if the Waratahs expected jetlag to slow down the Bulls in the final quarter, they were mistaken. Through forward grunt, the South Africans exerted tremendous pressure for long periods, but against resolute defence they failed to breach the goalline.

Although it wasn't one of the team's more polished performances of 2005, the Waratahs, with a reputation for choking, hung in resolutely to secure the victory, the main starring roles coming from No 8 David Lyons, openside flanker Phil Waugh, midfielder Grey and winger Lote Tuqiri.

FOR WARATAHS: Tries by Nathan Grey and Morgan Turinui; 2 conversions and 3 penalty goals by Peter Hewat.

FOR BULLS: Try by Johan Roets; conversion and 2 penalty goals by Morne Steyn.

WARATAHS: Mat Rogers, Peter Hewat, Morgan Turinui, Nathan Grey, Lote Tuqiri, Lachlan MacKay, Chris Whitaker (captain), David Lyons, Phil Waugh, Justin Harrison, Dan Vickerman, Rocky Elsom, Al Baxter, Brendan Cannon, Matt Dunning. Replacements: Cameron Shepherd, Shaun Berne, Al Kanaar, Stephen Hoiles, Adam Freier.

BULLS: Johan Roets, Akona Ndungane, J P Nel, Ettiene Botha, Bryan Habana, Morne Steyne, Fourie du Preez, Anton Leonard (captain), Pedrie Wannenburg, Jacques Cronje, Victor Matfield, Bakkies Botha, Richard Bands, Gary Botha, Kees Lensing. Replacements: Wynand Olivier, Warren Brosnihan, Danie Rossouw, Danie Coetzee, Wessel Roux.

REFEREE: Steve Walsh (New Zealand)

CROWD: 35,433

Akona Ndungane scored a try for the Bulls against the Waratahs in round five — 12 months after his twin brother Odwa had scored a try for the Bulls against the Waratahs in round five.

THE FINAL

CRUSADERS 35, WARATAHS 25

AT JADE STADIUM, CHRISTCHURCH, 28 MAY 2005

AS THE CHAMPION CRUSADERS players grouped together for photographers in the middle of Jade Stadium after their comprehensive defeat of first-time finalists the Waratahs, they chanted 'Reuben Thorne, Reuben Thorne, Reuben Thorne.' Why? He wasn't the captain, he hadn't scored a try or kicked a winning goal, and he certainly wasn't a charismatic personality in the manner of Andrew Mehrtens. No, Reuben Thorne was being championed because of his amazing achievement in featuring for 80 minutes in all five Crusaders finals victories.

Mehrtens also claimed a share of that fame, being involved, like Thorne, in the 1998, 1999, 2000, 2002 and 2005 finals, but not to the same extent, and, indeed, he featured for no more than two minutes against the Waratahs, just long enough to make one tackle.

Thorne's career endured some rocky passages after he became All Black captain, particularly when his side took an early exit from the 2003 World Cup, but he has never been a less than totally committed achiever for Canterbury and the Crusaders. Just ask Waratahs lock Justin Harrison, who had a couple of important line-out throws stolen from under his nose by Thorne in the final.

If 35–25 sounds like a thrilling contest, it wasn't. It was completely one-sided, the Crusaders breezing away to a 35–6 lead before taking their foot off the accelerator with the game secure. Coach Robbie Deans was chuffed, labelling the 2005 Crusaders team the best ever and vowing to return for another season as coach.

'What made the 2005 team superior,' said Deans, 'was the leadership. This side has so many experienced individuals who are initiating and driving the course of play on the field.' Deans was thrilled because his team had completely shut out the Waratahs. 'And that hadn't been done by any other opponent all year,' he added. Deans' team set a new Super 12 try-scoring record, the 71 touchdowns eclipsing the 70 achieved by Graham Henry's champion (and unbeaten) Blues team back in 1997.

If there was a disappointment for the Crusaders fans it was that Rico Gear missed the try that would have taken him past Joe Roff as Super 12's record

Justin Marshall, Dave Hewett and Andrew Mehrtens after the Crusaders' triumph in 2005.

Fotopress

try-getter. Not that he didn't have the opportunity. But just as he was preparing to cross the goalline for his 16th try of the series, Morgan Turinui sneakily punched the ball from his grasp. 'I pride myself on being a finisher,' said Gear later. 'Missing the record doesn't worry me, but missing the try hurt.'

The crowd gave a special farewell to three of its heroes who were overseas — halfback Justin Marshall (who was chaired around by his team-mates), prop Dave Hewett and lock Norm Maxwell (who missed the final through injury).

Strategically, the Waratahs played it all wrong, persistently kicking away possession, unsmart against an opponent so powerful on the counterattack.

FOR CRUSADERS: Tries by Scott Hamilton, Dave Hewett, Leon MacDonald and Caleb Ralph; 3 conversions and 2 penalty goals by Dan Carter; dropped goal by Aaron Mauger.

FOR WARATAHS: Tries by Mat Rogers 2 and Phil Waugh; conversion and 2 penalty goals by Peter Hewat; conversion by Rogers.

CRUSADERS: Leon MacDonald, Rico Gear, Caleb Ralph, Aaron Mauger, Scott Hamilton, Dan Carter, Justin Marshall, Mose Tuiali'i, Richie McCaw (captain), Reuben Thorne, Ross Filipo, Chris Jack, Greg Somerville, Corey Flynn, Dave Hewett.
Replacements: Casey Laulala, Sam Broomhall, Campbell Johnstone, Andrew Mehrtens.

WARATAHS: Mat Rogers, Peter Hewat, Morgan Turinui, Nathan Grey, Lote Tuqiri, Lachlan MacKay, Chris Whitaker (captain), David Lyons, Phil Waugh, Rocky Elsom, Dan Vickerman, Justin Harrison, Al Baxter, Brendan Cannon, Matt Dunning.
Replacements: Shaun Berne, Cameron Shepherd, Al Kanaar, Adam Freier, Chris O'Young, Stephen Hoiles.

REFEREE: Jonathan Kaplan (South Africa)

CROWD: 36,339

THE RESULTS

CRUSADERS
(coach Robbie Deans)

lost to	Brumbies at Canberra	21–32
beat	Chiefs at Christchurch	50–18
beat	Reds at Nelson	59–24
beat	Blues at Auckland	41–19
beat	Waratahs at Sydney	33–27
lost to	Bulls at Pretoria	20–35
beat	Stormers at Cape Town	51–23
beat	Cats at Christchurch	40–36
beat	Sharks at Christchurch	77–34
beat	Highlanders at Dunedin	27–13
beat	Hurricanes at Christchurch	40–20

Won 9, lost 2; placing: 1st
Tries scored: 61

Semifinal: beat Hurricanes at Christchurch 47–7

Final: beat Waratahs at Christchurch 35–25

Most tries: Rico Gear 15, Scott Hamilton 8, Caleb Ralph 8, Dan Carter 5, Aaron Mauger 5, Justin Marshall 4, Leon MacDonald 4
Most points: Dan Carter 171, Rico Gear 75, Andrew Mehrtens 52

BULLS
(coach Heyneke Meyer)

lost to	Cats at Johannesburg	17–23
lost to	Brumbies at Canberra	19–21
lost to	Highlanders at Dunedin	0–23
beat	Hurricanes at Wellington	21–12
lost to	Waratahs at Sydney	12–42
beat	Crusaders at Pretoria	35–20
beat	Reds at Pretoria	32–7
beat	Chiefs at Pretoria	29–26
beat	Blues at Pretoria	38–24
beat	Sharks at Durban	23–17
beat	Stormers at Pretoria	75–14

Won 7, lost 4; placing: 3rd
Tries scored: 36

Semifinal: lost to Waratahs at Sydney 13–23

Most tries: Bryan Habana 10, Akona Ndungane 6, Ettienne Botha 6, Jacques Cronje 3
Most points: Morne Steyn 110, Bryan Habana 50

WARATAHS
(coach Ewen McKenzie)

beat	Chiefs at Sydney	25–7
beat	Sharks at Durban	36–13
beat	Cats at Johannesburg	40–19
beat	Stormers at Sydney	25–10
beat	Bulls at Sydney	42–12
lost to	Crusaders at Sydney	27–33
lost to	Hurricanes at Wellington	24–26
beat	Brumbies at Canberra	10–6
beat	Highlanders at Dunedin	41–20
beat	Reds at Sydney	27–8
beat	Blues at Sydney	25–20

Won 9, lost 2; placing: 2nd
Tries scored: 38

Semifinal: beat Bulls at Sydney 23–13

Final: lost to Crusaders at Christchurch 25–35

Most tries: Peter Hewat 10, Morgan Turinui 7, Lote Tuqiri 5, Mat Rogers 4, Phil Waugh 4
Most points: Peter Hewat 173, Mat Rogers 47

HURRICANES
(coach Colin Cooper)

beat	Reds at Brisbane	24–10
beat	Cats at Johannesburg	45–32
beat	Sharks at Durban	29–23
lost to	Bulls at Wellington	12–21
beat	Stormers at Palmerston North	12–9
beat	Chiefs at Wellington	28–16
beat	Waratahs at Wellington	26–24
lost to	Highlanders at Wellington	16–26
beat	Brumbies at Wellington	49–37
beat	Blues at Auckland	22–10
lost to	Crusaders at Christchurch	20–40

Won 8, lost 3; placing: 4th
Tries scored: 31

Semifinal: lost to Crusaders at Christchurch 7–47

Most tries: Ma'a Nonu 7, Lome Fa'atau 6, Jimmy Gopperth 3
Most points: Jimmy Gopperth 139, Ma'a Nonu 35

BRUMBIES
(coach Laurie Fisher)

beat	Crusaders at Canberra	32–21
beat	Bulls at Canberra	21–19
beat	Stormers at Canberra	22–19
beat	Cats at Johannesburg	34–29
lost to	Sharks at Durban	24–36
lost to	Blues at Auckland	0–17
lost to	Highlanders at Dunedin	18–19
lost to	Waratahs at Canberra	6–10
lost to	Hurricanes at Wellington	37–49
drew with	Chiefs at Canberra	28–28
beat	Reds at Brisbane	38–21

Won 5, lost 5, drew 1; placing: 5th
Tries scored: 33

Most tries: Matt Giteau 5, Stirling Mortlock 4,
Scott Fava 3, Radike Samo 3
Most points: Matt Giteau 62, Stirling Mortlock 52

BLUES
(coach Peter Sloane)

beat	Highlanders at Dunedin	30–14
beat	Reds at Auckland	18–15
lost to	Chiefs at Hamilton	9–18
lost to	Crusaders at Auckland	19–41
beat	Brumbies at Auckland	17–0
beat	Cats at Albany	23–6
beat	Sharks at Auckland	36–13
beat	Stormers at Cape Town	37–24
lost to	Bulls at Pretoria	24–38
lost to	Hurricanes at Auckland	10–22
lost to	Waratahs at Sydney	20–25

Won 6, lost 5; placing: 7th
Tries scored: 30

Most tries: Doug Howlett 6, Joe Rokocoko 5,
Isa Nacewa 3, Mils Muliaina 3, Tasese Lavea 3
Most points: Luke McAlister 99, Doug Howlett 30

CHIEFS
(coach Ian Foster)

lost to	Waratahs at Sydney	7–25
lost to	Crusaders at Christchurch	18–50
beat	Blues at Hamilton	18–9
lost to	Reds at Hamilton	6–20
lost to	Hurricanes at Wellington	16–28
beat	Sharks at Hamilton	40–5
beat	Cats at Hamilton	45–14
lost to	Bulls at Pretoria	26–29
beat	Stormers at Cape Town	37–34
drew with	Brumbies at Canberra	28–28
beat	Highlanders at Hamilton	31–8

Won 5, lost 5, drew 1; placing: 6th
Tries scored: 33

Most tries: Sitiveni Sivivatu 8, Sosene Anesi 6,
Niva Ta'auso 4
Most points: David Hill 107, Sitiveni Sivivatu 40

HIGHLANDERS
(coach Greg Cooper)

lost to	Blues at Dunedin	14–30
drew with	Stormers at Invercargill	16–16
beat	Bulls at Dunedin	23–0
beat	Sharks at Durban	43–7
beat	Cats at Johannesburg	16–12
beat	Reds at Brisbane	23–16
beat	Brumbies at Dunedin	19–18
beat	Hurricanes at Wellington	26–16
lost to	Waratahs at Dunedin	20–41
lost to	Crusaders at Dunedin	13–27
lost to	Chiefs at Hamilton	8–31

Won 6, lost 4, drew 1; placing: 8th
Tries scored: 21

Most tries: Ben Blair 3, Craig Newby 3, Josh Blackie 3
Most points: Ben Blair 107, Nick Evans 34

⚑ The Highlanders have appeared at Ballymore in Brisbane five times, where their scores have been 23, 23, 24, 20 and 24.

⚑ The Highlanders have drawn only two matches in a decade of Super 12 action — on 5 March 2004 against the Bulls and on 5 March 2005 against the Stormers.

STORMERS
(coach Gert Smal)

beat	Sharks at Cape Town	26-12
drew with	Highlanders at Invercargill	16-16
lost to	Brumbies at Canberra	19-22
lost to	Waratahs at Sydney	10-25
lost to	Hurricanes at Palmerston North	9-12
beat	Reds at Cape Town	15-13
lost to	Crusaders at Cape Town	23-51
lost to	Blues at Cape Town	24-37
lost to	Chiefs at Cape Town	34-37
beat	Cats at Cape Town	25-20
lost to	Bulls at Pretoria	14-75

Won 3, lost 7, drew 1; placing: 9th
Tries scored: 25

Most tries: Jean de Villiers 7, Breyton Paulse 3, Tonderai Chavhana 3, Eddie Andrews 3
Most points: Gaffie du Toit 58, Jean de Villiers 35, Chris Rossouw 32

CATS
(coach Chester Williams)

beat	Bulls at Johannesburg	23-17
lost to	Hurricanes at Johannesburg	32-45
lost to	Waratahs at Johannesburg	19-40
lost to	Brumbies at Johannesburg	29-34
lost to	Highlanders at Johannesburg	12-16
lost to	Blues at Albany	6-23
lost to	Chiefs at Hamilton	14-45
lost to	Crusaders at Christchurch	36-40
lost to	Reds at Brisbane	15-21
lost to	Stormers at Cape Town	20-25
drew with	Sharks at Bloemfontein	20-20

Won 1, lost 9, drew 1; placing: 11th
Tries scored: 23

Most tries: Conrad Jantjes 5, Jaque Fourie 4, Juan Smith 3
Most points: André Pretorius 118, Conrad Jantjes 25

REDS
(coach Jeff Miller)

lost to	Hurricanes at Brisbane	10-24
lost to	Blues at Auckland	15-18
lost to	Crusaders at Nelson	24-59
beat	Chiefs at Hamilton	20-6
lost to	Highlanders at Brisbane	16-23
lost to	Stormers at Cape Town	13-15
lost to	Bulls at Pretoria	7-32
beat	Sharks at Brisbane	30-25
beat	Cats at Brisbane	21-15
lost to	Waratahs at Sydney	8-27
lost to	Brumbies at Brisbane	21-38

Won 3, lost 8; placing: 10th
Tries scored: 24

Most tries: Drew Mitchell 4, Junior Palesasa 3, Chris Latham 3
Most points: Julian Huxley 54, Elton Flatley 28

SHARKS
(coach Kevin Putt, replaced by Dick Muir)

lost to	Stormers at Cape Town	12-26
lost to	Waratahs at Durban	13-36
lost to	Hurricanes at Durban	23-29
lost to	Highlanders at Durban	7-43
beat	Brumbies at Durban	36-24
lost to	Chiefs at Hamilton	5-40
lost to	Blues at Auckland	13-36
lost to	Reds at Brisbane	25-30
lost to	Crusaders at Christchurch	34-77
lost to	Bulls at Durban	17-23
drew with	Cats at Bloemfontein	20-20

Won 1, lost 9, drew 1; placing: 12th
Tries scored: 26

Most tries: Brent Russell 4, Cedric Mkize 4, Ruan Pienaar 3
Most points: Ruan Pienaar 36, Butch James 25

🏉 The Crusaders starting fifteen against the Blues at Eden Park in March (a game they won 41–29) was comprised entirely of All Blacks. This game represented the first occasion in 10 years the Crusaders had achieved a bonus point for four tries against the Blues.

SUPER 12 STATISTICS

SUMMARY OF SUPER 12 TEAMS' FINISHING POSITIONS, 1996–2005

The finishing postions detailed in the table below reflect the final position of the team after the semifinals and finals. Semifinal losers are both credited with third place, so there is no fourth position in the statistics.

	1996	1997	1998	1999	2000	2001	2002	2003	2004	2005
Blues	1	1	2	9	6	11	6	1	5	7
Chiefs	6	11	7	6	10	6	8	10	3	6
Hurricanes	9	3	8	10	8	9	9	3	11	3
Crusaders	12	6	1	1	1	10	1	2	2	1
Highlanders	8	12	3	2	3	5	3	7	9	8
Reds	3	10	5	3	7	3	5	8	10	10
Waratahs	7	9	6	8	9	8	3	5	8	2
Brumbies	5	2	10	5	2	1	2	3	1	5
Bulls[4]	3	8	11	12	11	12	12	6	6	3
Cats[2]	10	5	12	11	3	3	11	12	12	11
Stormers[3]	11	–	9	3	5	7	7	9	3	9
Sharks[1]	2	3	3	7	12	2	10	11	7	12
Free State[5]		7								

1. The Natal-based team that became the Sharks was originally known as Natal (1996), then Natal Sharks (1997), and Coastal Sharks (1998) before adopting their final name of Sharks in 1999.
2. The Johannesburg-based team that became the Cats was originally known as Transvaal (1996), then Gauteng Lions (1997), and Golden Cats (1998) before adopting their final name of Cats in 1999.
3. The Cape Town-based team that became the Stormers was originally known as Western Province (1996) and Western Stormers (1998) before adopting their final name of Stormers in 1999.
4. The Bulls adopted their final name in 2000. Prior to that they were known as Northern Transvaal (1996), Northern Transvaal Blue Bulls (1997) and Northern Bulls (1998–99).
5. Free State only competed in the competition in 1997, having taken the place of Western Province.

Most points in a season
206	Andrew Mehrtens (Crusaders), 1998
201	Dan Carter (Crusaders), 2004
194	Stirling Mortlock (Brumbies), 2000
192	Andrew Mehrtens (Crusaders), 1999
182	Andrew Mehrtens (Crusaders), 2002
182	Joe Roff (Brumbies), 2004
180	Adrian Cashmore (Blues), 1998

Most tries in a season
15	Joe Roff (Brumbies), 1997
15	Rico Gear (Crusaders), 2005
13	James Small (Sharks), 1996
13	Andrew Walker (Brumbies), 2000
12	André Joubert (Sharks), 1996
12	Tana Umaga (Hurricanes), 1997
12	Peter Rossouw (Stormers), 2002
12	Roger Randle (Chiefs), 2002
12	Doug Howlett (Blues), 2003

Best performances in a season team by team
BLUES
Most points: 180 – Adrian Cashmore, 1998
Most tries: 12 – Doug Howlett, 2003

CHIEFS
Most points: 128 –Glenn Jackson, 2001
Most tries: 12 – Roger Randle, 2002

HURRICANES
Most points: 152 – Jon Preston, 1997
Most tries: 12 – Tana Umaga, 1997

CRUSADERS
Most points: 206 – Andrew Mehrtens, 1998
Most tries: 15 – Rico Gear, 2005

HIGHLANDERS
Most points: 150 – Tony Brown, 2000
Most tries: 10 – Jeff Wilson, 1998

REDS
Most points: 155 — John Eales, 1996
Most tries: 10 — Chris Latham, 2002

WARATAHS
Most points: 173 — Peter Hewat, 2005
Most tries: 10 — Peter Hewat, 2005

BRUMBIES
Most points: 194 — Stirling Mortlock, 2000
Most tries: 15 — Joe Roff, 1997

BULLS
Most points: 142 — Jannie Kruger, 1996
Most tries: 10 — Bryan Habana, 2005

CATS
Most points: 157 — Louis Koen, 2001
Most tries: 9 — Jannie van der Walt, 1998

STORMERS
Most points: 153 — Braam van Straaten, 2001
Most tries: 12 — Pieter Rossouw, 2002

SHARKS
Most points: 170 — Gavin Lawless, 1997
Most tries: 13 — James Small, 1996

Most points overall
990 Andrew Mehrtens (Crusaders)
959 Matt Burke (Waratahs)
817 Tony Brown (Highlanders)
699 Stirling Mortlock (Brumbies)
619 Adrian Cashmore (Blues)
608 Carlos Spencer (Blues)
602 David Holwell (Hurricanes)
579 Elton Flatley (Reds)
481 Glenn Jackson (Chiefs)
474 Dan Carter (Crusaders)
441 André Pretorius (Cats)
434 Braam van Straaten (Stormers)

Most points in a game
50 Gavin Lawless (Natal) v Highlanders, 1997
39 Jannie Kruger (Bulls) v Highlanders, 1996
35 Morne Steyn (Bulls) v Stormers, 2005
34 Peter Hewat (Waratahs) v Bulls, 2005
33 Matt Burke (Waratahs) v Northern Transvaal, 1997
32 Gavin Johnson (Cats) v Highlanders, 1997
30 David Holwell (Hurricanes) v Highlanders, 2001
29 Ben Blair (Crusaders) v Bulls, 2001
28 Braam van Straaten (Stormers) v Hurricanes, 2000
27 Adrian Cashmore (Blues) v Highlanders, 1998
26 Simon Culhane (Highlanders) v Reds, 1998
26 Elton Flatley (Reds) v Stormers, 2003
25 Stirling Mortlock (Brumbies) v Stormers, 2001
25 Joe Roff (Brumbies) v Chiefs, 2003

Most tries overall
57 Joe Roff (Brumbies)
56 Christian Cullen (Hurricanes)
52 Caleb Ralph (Chiefs, Blues, Crusaders)
49 Doug Howlett (Highlanders, Hurricanes, Blues)
43 Joeli Vidiri (Blues)
42 Tana Umaga (Hurricanes)
37 Chris Latham (Reds)
36 Stirling Mortlock (Brumbies)
35 Jeff Wilson (Highlanders)
32 Pieter Rossouw (Stormers)

Leading forward tryscorers overall
29 Owen Finegan (Brumbies)
21 Jeremy Paul (Brumbies)
16 Scott Robertson (Crusaders)
15 André Venter (Cats)
15 Isitolo Maka (Highlanders, Chiefs)
15 Richie McCaw (Crusaders)

Most tries in a game
4 Joe Roff (Brumbies) v Natal, 1996
4 Gavin Lawless (Natal) v Highlanders, 1997
4 Stefan Terblanche (Sharks) v Chiefs, 1998
4 Joeli Vidiri (Blues) v Bulls, 2000
4 Doug Howlett (Blues) v Hurricanes, 2002
4 Mils Muliaina (Blues) v Bulls, 2002
4 Caleb Ralph (Crusaders) v Waratahs, 2002

Highest team scores
96 Crusaders v Waratahs, Christchurch, 2003
77 Crusaders v Sharks, Christchurch, 2005
75 Natal v Highlanders, Durban, 1997
75 Crusaders v Bulls, Christchurch, 2000
75 Bulls v Stormers, Pretoria, 2005
74 Blues v Stormers, Auckland, 1998
73 Brumbies v Bulls, Canberra, 1999
70 Brumbies v Highlanders, Canberra, 1996

Most appearances overall
111 George Gregan (Brumbies)
108 Anton Oliver (Highlanders)
105 Justin Marshall (Crusader)
101 Tana Umaga (Hurricanes)
98 Stephen Larkham (Brumbies)
98 Reuben Thorne (Crusaders)
98 Caleb Ralph (Crusaders)
98 Carl Hoeft (Highlanders)
96 Carlos Spencer (Blues)
93 Chris Whitaker (Waratahs)
92 Jeremy Paul (Brumbies)
91 Owen Finegan (Brumbies)

Tri-nations

THE PERFECT RUGBY PRODUCT (PRP)
was hatched during a brainstorming session in Brisbane.
The desirability of this PRP (Super 12 and Tri-nations)
was that it allowed the NPC in New Zealand and
the Currie Cup in South Africa to continue in
existing form with only minor overlapping.

1996

PROFESSIONALISM ARRIVED, AN EXCITING NEW competition embracing
the SANZAR nations was introduced and fresh rules changes were implemented
as the 1996 southern hemisphere international rugby season moved into top
gear. But one thing didn't change — the All Blacks' resolution to take revenge
for their heart-breaking loss to the Springboks in extra time in the World Cup
final at Ellis Park a year earlier.

In the painful days that followed the epic World Cup showdown, the
outcome of which sent the Rainbow Nation into raptures, senior members
of the All Black squad pledged to return to the land of their defeat and prove
they were a superior team to South Africa. The record books show that the
Springboks, operating with immense courage and commitment, won the World
Cup final by 15 points to 12, and that can never be taken away from them, but
the All Blacks knew that their chances were undermined when 23 of the team
fell ill with food poisoning 45 hours before kick-off, all evidence indicating
they were deliberately poisoned.

So when the All Blacks flew into Cape Town in 1996, with the same captain,
Sean Fitzpatrick, the same 'senior pros', Zinzan Brooke, Ian Jones, Michael
Jones, Frank Bunce and Jeff Wilson, but with a new coach, John Hart, they
were grimly determined to right what they considered to be the wrongs of 1995.
It mattered not that as a consequence of their thrilling victories at Wellington,
Christchurch and Brisbane, two of them epic come-from-behind efforts, the
new, oversized Tri-nations Trophy — oversized because the manufacturers
had got the dimensions seriously wrong — was already theirs. Neither the
Springboks, who they still had to play in Cape Town, nor the Wallabies could
overtake them. Against an inconsequential opponent the All Blacks could,
therefore, have afforded to slip into cruise mode. But only one thing mattered
— defeat of the world champion South Africans.

The All Blacks duly achieved their goal at Cape Town, scoring the tries
that had eluded them in the World Cup final, defeating the Springboks 29–
18 to finish a commanding 11 points clear of South Africa and Australia in
the inaugural Tri-nations championship. The team would go on to achieve a

Sean Fitzpatrick's All Blacks acknowledge their fans after clinching the inaugural Tri-nations title.
Fotopress

historic first series victory on South African soil, but that came later. Their first assignment, wrapping up the Tri-nations satisfactorily, had been achieved.

The inaugural Tri-nations was a sensational success, with attendances at the six internationals averaging 44,000. The All Blacks were the only team to win away from home.

Interestingly, none of the World Cup coaches survived into the first year of professional rugby. Hart replaced Laurie Mains with the All Blacks, John Williams succeeded Kitch Christie with the Springboks, and Greg Smith took over from Bob Dwyer with the Wallabies.

IRB law changes had an influence on the game, lifting in line-outs being permitted for the first time. This produced quicker ball to the halfbacks and provided more open play, with defending teams often reluctant to kick into touch, knowing that the throwing-in side was virtually guaranteed possession.

1996 FINAL STANDINGS

	P	W	L	D	For	Against	Points
New Zealand	4	4	–	–	119	60	17
South Africa	4	1	3	–	70	84	6
Australia	4	1	3	–	71	116	6

Tries: New Zealand 10, South Africa 5, Australia 5; Total 20.

Penalty goals: New Zealand 19, Australia 14, South Africa 13; Total 46.

THE STAR
SEAN FITZPATRICK

Sean Fitzpatrick wasn't a player to miss an opportunity. He took maximum advantage of the two big breaks that came his way, in 1986 and 1992. His first gift from Heaven occurred as a consequence of the rebel Cavaliers tour of South Africa that brought two-match suspensions for the 30 All Blacks involved. It meant that when Brian Lochore fielded his Baby Blacks team against France at Lancaster Park, half the players were virgin internationals, Fitzpatrick among them. Fitzy made such an instant impact he would miss only two internationals over the next decade.

Likewise with the captaincy, the freakish opportunity came out of nowhere. Laurie Mains had earmarked Mike Brewer for the leadership of his new-look squad in 1992, but that came unstuck when Brewer was seriously injured in the final trial. Fitzpatrick was the next cab off the rank. He would go on to establish himself as one of New Zealand's most inspirational, dynamic and successful leaders. When his wonky knee finally forced him into retirement early in 1998, he could boast 92 test appearances, 51 of them as captain.

Fitzpatrick endured heartbreak at the 1995 Rugby World Cup when Joel Stransky's dropped goal in extra time denied the All Blacks the success most critics felt was deserved, but he exacted satisfying revenge the following year when he led New Zealand to its first series success on South African soil.

The 1996 season was Fitzpatrick's finest. At the age of 33, he shared in the Auckland Blues' Super 12 triumph, followed that as All Black captain with the series win in South Africa and twin successes with the Tri-nations and Bledisloe Cup, and on the domestic scene he was heavily involved as Auckland won the NPC title and claimed back the Ranfurly Shield. Not surprisingly, he was crowned New Zealand Rugby Player of the Year for 1996.

In 1997, his final season, Fitzpatrick shared in further Super 12 and Tri-nations glory before his knee became a source of major concern, restricting him to two appearances as a reserve on the tour of Ireland, Wales and England. The indestructible hooker finally had to cry 'enough'.

THE GAMES
NEW ZEALAND 43,
AUSTRALIA 6

AT ATHLETIC PARK, WELLINGTON, 6 JULY

THIS WAS THE FIRST OCCASION in New Zealand where sports betting operated on a rugby match. And of the $50,000 wagered on the head-to-head contest, not one person correctly selected a final score of 43–6! Which was hardly surprising. The bitingly cold southerly sweeping up from the Antarctic made conditions as miserable as they could be, which suggested a tight, low-scoring game. And in 91 years of rivalry between the trans-Tasman rivals, neither side had ever scored as many as 43 points.

No one, but no one, anticipated such overwhelming superiority by John Hart's team in this inaugural Tri-nations contest, even though the All Blacks were in rampant mood, having put 62 points on Scotland a couple of weeks earlier. The one area in which the Wallabies were plainly inferior was in terms of experience. Not only did they arrive in the capital with a rookie coach, Greg Smith, and a rookie captain, John Eales, but the All Black forwards claimed almost 200 more caps than their opponents. Smith and his fellow selectors had introduced a number of players of considerable potential, but because collectively they had not been tested under pressure, they were obviously vulnerable against a team as powerful as the All Blacks.

That vulnerability was ruthlessly exposed. To be fair to the Australians, it was a stinker of a day. Wellington in mid-winter can be as inhospitable as McMurdo Sound, and seven of the Wallabies' starting fifteen came from tropical Queensland.

The Australians, having taken first use of what most agreed was a 15-point wind, were in serious trouble after 17 minutes, by which time the All Blacks had scored three tries and led 15–3. By half-time, that had lengthened to 25–6. A shell-shocked Smith, huddling under an umbrella, told his troops at the break, to 'Start making a few tackles, display some commitment and salvage some pride.' Good advice, but things didn't get a lot better for the visitors. The rain intensified, which probably slowed down the All Blacks, who managed just two further tries in the second half. The Wallabies did display

Zinzan Brooke scores in the 43–6 demolition of Australia at Athletic Park. Fotopress

improved form, but against aggressive defence they never once breached the New Zealand goalline.

The All Black performance bordered on the unbelievable. In the entire game there were just five handling errors by Sean Fitzpatrick's men. It ranks as one of the mightiest displays ever by the men in black.

Every player contributed to this astonishing victory, but a couple who demonstrated quite extraordinary skills in the conditions were Andrew Mehrtens, who had a hand in four of the six tries, master tackler Zinzan Brooke and captain Sean Fitzpatrick, who led his side inspirationally before retiring with a shoulder injury, the first time he had been replaced in 77 tests.

FOR NEW ZEALAND: Tries by Michael Jones, Christian Cullen, Justin Marshall, Zinzan Brooke, Jeff Wilson and Jonah Lomu; 2 conversions and 3 penalty goals by Andrew Mehrtens.

FOR AUSTRALIA: 2 penalty goals by Matt Burke.

NEW ZEALAND: Christian Cullen (temporarily replaced by Eric Rush), Jeff Wilson, Frank Bunce, Walter Little, Jonah Lomu, Andrew Mehrtens, Justin Marshall, Zinzan Brooke, Josh Kronfeld, Michael Jones, Robin Brooke, Ian Jones, Olo Brown, Sean Fitzpatrick (captain, replaced by Norm Hewitt), Craig Dowd.

AUSTRALIA: Matt Burke, Ben Tune, Joe Roff, Tim Horan, David Campese, Scott Bowen, Sam Payne, Michael Brial, David Wilson, Owen Finegan, John Eales (captain), Garrick Morgan, Dan Crowley, Michael Foley, Richard Harry.

REFEREE: Ed Morrison (England)

CROWD: 39,523

AUSTRALIA 21, SOUTH AFRICA 16

AT SYDNEY FOOTBALL STADIUM, SYDNEY, 13 JULY

THE SPRINGBOKS' 15-TEST WINNING SEQUENCE came to a shuddering halt in Sydney against an Australian team that rediscovered its passion and power following the traumas of Athletic Park. Entering the contest as the world champions, unbeaten since losing to the All Blacks in Wellington in 1994, the Springboks were favoured to win. But André Markgraaf's men never reproduced the verve and skills that had carried them to the pinnacle of the rugby world. They trailed 11–3 at half-time and 21–9 with time running out before a try by winger Pieter Hendricks salvaged them a bonus point.

Markgraaf claimed afterwards his team was underprepared. 'We needed another game,' he said at the press conference. 'That was the difference against such a formidable opponent.'

Some might have argued that although the Wallabies had the benefit of that extra game, the 43–6 slaughtering they sustained in Wellington seven days earlier would have left them psychologically handicapped as they sought revenge for the shock defeat they'd taken from the Springboks in the World Cup opener 14 months earlier. However, the Australians prepared well for this game upon their return to Sydney, which included spending an hour with former league icon Wayne Pearce, who spoke to them about the benefits of offensive defence.

It was what they needed. Just how much their pride had been wounded by the All Blacks was evident as they undertook a victory lap of Sydney Stadium, to the delight of their wildly applauding fans. It seemed the demons of Athletic Park had been well and truly exorcised.

With No 8 Michael Brial the standout, the Australians recaptured their confidence and composure and took the game aggressively to their opponents. Where their defence in Wellington had been as leaky as a sieve, this time they let through just one try, in the dying moments when victory was assured. Brial was in his element. His tough, no-nonsense style (which would be even more graphically demonstrated, at Frank Bunce's expense, in Brisbane a week later) was just what the Australians needed to counter the rugged Springboks. One of his tackles, a thundering effort on Francois Pienaar five minutes into the second half, brought loud gasps from the crowd. Shortly after, Pienaar departed the field.

'I will remember that game for a long time,' said Brial afterwards. 'It was extremely physical and we had to stand up and be counted. We did and whatever they dished out, we gave back with interest.'

Brial was presented with the man-of-the-match award.

Given their status as world champions, the Springboks disappointed, with only prop Os du Randt, who made Dan Crowley's life a misery in the scrums, enhancing his reputation. Halfback Joost van der Westhuizen had probably his poorest game ever for his country, fullback André Joubert conceded the second try when his wild pass was scooped up by Tim Horan, who had an unchallenged sprint to the goalline, flyhalf Henry Honiball had scant attacking opportunities and Pienaar was a shadow of the individual who shone at the World Cup.

Australia's first try was created by Pat Howard, who had replaced Scott Bowen at flyhalf. A blindside dart where he linked with Daniel Manu, another newcomer, led to Joe Roff being driven across the goalline.

FOR AUSTRALIA: Tries by Joe Roff and Tim Horan; conversion and 3 penalty goals by Matt Burke.

FOR SOUTH AFRICA: Try by Pieter Hendriks; conversion and 2 penalty goals by Henry Honiball; penalty goal by André Joubert.

AUSTRALIA: Matt Burke, Ben Tune, Joe Roff, Tim Horan, David Campese, Pat Howard, George Gregan, Michael Brial, David Wilson, Daniel Manu (replaced by Owen Finegan), John Eales (captain), Garrick Morgan, Andrew Heath, Michael Foley, Dan Crowley (replaced by Richard Harry).

SOUTH AFRICA: André Joubert, James Small, Japie Mulder, Brendan Venter, Pieter Hendriks, Henry Honiball, Joost van der Westhuizen (replaced by Johan Roux), Gary Teichmann, Ruben Kruger, Francois Pienaar (captain, replaced by Naka Drotske), Mark Andrews, Johan Ackermann, Marius Hunter, John Allan, Os du Randt.

REFEREE: Tony Spreadbury (England)

CROWD: 41,850

NEW ZEALAND 15, SOUTH AFRICA 11

AT LANCASTER PARK, CHRISTCHURCH, 20 JULY

TWO OF NEW ZEALAND'S HEROES at the World Cup in South Africa, Andrew Mehrtens and Josh Kronfeld, had distressingly come to grief in separate incidents in October 1995. Kronfeld had contorted his ankle in the NPC final at Eden Park, and although cleared for the All Black tour of France he seriously aggravated it, tearing the lateral ligaments, while preparing for the match at Bayonne. Mehrtens, meanwhile, had torn his anterior cruciate ligament in the tour opener at Catania in Sicily and was invalided home on crutches. Both underwent reconstructive surgery, both setting their sights on being fit for the domestic internationals in 1996 and, in particular, the inaugural Tri-nations series.

Not without moments of anxiety, Mehrtens and Kronfeld returned to action in time to take possession of jerseys 10 and 7, respectively, for the crunch home encounters against Australia and South Africa. Which was as well, for Mehrtens kicked all New Zealand's points and Kronfeld made countless important tackles as the All Blacks eked out this hard-earned victory over the Springboks at Lancaster Park.

Coming after the spectacular demolition of the Wallabies in Wellington, this was almost an anticlimax. But a win is a win, and the All Blacks were more than happy to take the four points on offer against their old rivals. They had, after all, suffered more than their share of narrow, agonising losses in almost identical circumstances in South Africa.

Mehrtens won't remember this game with particular fondness, given that he twice drop-kicked out on the full and failed to put pressure on Joel Stransky, but he did land five penalty goals in a match in which Scottish referee Ray Megson's whistle played too prominent a role. Megson, plainly still in Five Nations mode, dished out 37 penalties (24 of them against the Springboks), about twice the average in internationals down under. One penalty in particular had the South Africans seething. With the All Blacks leading 12–11, and just five minutes left on the clock, Megson incredibly penalised the Springboks for ostensibly collapsing a scrum 5 metres from the New Zealand goalposts.

Springbok coach André Markgraaf was nonplussed. 'It's crazy to suggest we would collapse the scrum in those circumstances,' he said. 'We had the stronger scrum and everything to gain.'

The penalty allowed the All Blacks to clear to touch, advance into South African territory and remain there until Mehrtens landed his fifth penalty goal.

One penalty the South Africans couldn't complain about was against hooker John Allan for head-butting Sean Fitzpatrick at the first scrum, an outrageous act that cost his team three points.

It was a sobering comedown for the All Blacks after the dizzy heights of Athletic Park, where they had scored six tries and made almost no mistakes. This time, in vastly improved conditions, they scored no tries and made countless errors. With the exception of one incisive run by second-five Walter Little, whose pass to Frank Bunce was desperately knocked down by André Joubert, the All Blacks never came close to a five-pointer.

FOR NEW ZEALAND: **5 penalty goals by Andrew Mehrtens.**

FOR SOUTH AFRICA: **Try by André Joubert; 2 penalty goals by Joel Stransky.**

NEW ZEALAND: **Christian Cullen, Jeff Wilson (replaced by Eric Rush), Frank Bunce, Walter Little, Jonah Lomu, Andrew Mehrtens, Justin Marshall, Zinzan Brooke, Josh Kronfeld, Michael Jones, Robin Brooke, Ian Jones, Olo Brown, Sean Fitzpatrick (captain), Craig Dowd.**

SOUTH AFRICA: **André Joubert (replaced by Justin Swart), James Small, Japie Mulder, Brendan Venter, Pieter Hendriks, Joel Stransky, Johan Roux, Gary Teichmann, Ruben Kruger, Francois Pienaar (captain), Mark Andrews, Johan Ackermann, Marius Hurter, John Allan, Os du Randt.**

REFEREE: **Ray Megson (Scotland)**

CROWD: **39,000**

NEW ZEALAND 32, AUSTRALIA 25

AT SUNCORP STADIUM, BRISBANE, 27 JULY

WHEN YOU HAVE AN INTREPID INDIVIDUAL like Andrew Mehrtens calling the shots in the backline, anything is possible, as the All Blacks proved in executing a sensational comeback victory at Suncorp Stadium that guaranteed them the Tri-nations Trophy. Against the team they'd hammered 43–6 a fortnight earlier, the All Blacks demonstrated their greatness by rebounding from a 9–22 deficit in the second half to level at 25-all. The opportunity to claim a famous victory came when the final scrum of the game packed down near halfway, New Zealand's put-in.

Sean Fitzpatrick, playing in his 50th test, gave his backs license to go for a try. 'We never considered a dropped goal,' he admitted later, although obviously the Wallabies did, which may have helped the All Blacks create their winning try. Mehrtens didn't need any coaxing to conjure up a match-winning concept. He called the Canterbury move, one he'd borrowed from the red and blacks' bag of tricks. 'Obviously, we have a store of moves for special occasions,' he later explained, 'ones you hope the opposition don't know about, and certainly don't know the code names of!

'We felt the circumstances were ideal for us to uncork our Canterbury move. It worked a treat for Canterbury and I was confident it would come off with the All Blacks, even though we'd never attempted it in a match before. Executed at pace, it's exceedingly difficult to defend against.'

Walter Little initially confused the enemy by taking off on a dummy run while Mehrtens was working a midfield double-round with Frank Bunce. That created a gap, which Mehrtens exploded into. It was then simply a case of finishing off, because the All Blacks had the Wallaby defence seriously outnumbered. However, there was a temporary hitch when Christian Cullen backed himself to score by stepping inside George Gregan, rather than unloading to Jeff Wilson.

Wilson admitted to a sense of déjà vu as the move was unfolding, as he saw Gregan hastening across in defence. In identical circumstances at Sydney in 1994, Gregan had dislodged the ball from Wilson's grasp as he launched into what should have been a matchwinning dive.

When Cullen slipped to the turf a metre from the goalline while trying to elude Gregan, the move lost its momentum. Had the first player on the scene been a Wallaby, the try-scoring opportunity would have been lost. But first to arrive was Bunce. 'Set it, set it!' he screamed to Cullen as he bore down upon the scene. Cullen obliged and after scooping up the ball, Bunce was driven across the goalline by Josh Kronfeld to score the winning try.

Bunce thus had the last laugh on Wallaby No 8 Michael Brial, who had attacked him violently earlier in the game, being fortunate not to get his marching orders from the referee. Coach John Hart spoke out strongly against Brial's 'uncontrollable punching', saying he was surprised he escaped serious punishment.

A sensational 70-metre solo try by fullback Matt Burke highlighted Australia's play as they built their 22–9 lead. The All Blacks were headed for defeat until Fitzpatrick called for a big finish from his forwards. 'I didn't feel they had contributed a lot,' he said. 'They were needed now. Fortunately, they responded.'

FOR NEW ZEALAND: Tries by Justin Marshall and Frank Bunce; 2 conversions and 6 penalty goals by Andrew Mehrtens.

FOR AUSTRALIA: Tries by Matt Burke and George Gregan; 5 penalty goals by Burke.

NEW ZEALAND: Christian Cullen, Jeff Wilson, Frank Bunce, Walter Little, Jonah Lomu, Andrew Mehrtens, Justin Marshall, Zinzan Brooke, Josh Kronfeld, Michael Jones, Robin Brooke, Ian Jones, Olo Brown, Sean Fitzpatrick (captain), Craig Dowd.

AUSTRALIA: Matt Burke, Ben Tune, Joe Roff, Richard Tombs, David Campese, Pat Howard, George Gregan, Michael Brial, David Wilson, Daniel Manu, John Eales (captain), Garrick Morgan (replaced by Tim Gavin), Andrew Heath, Michael Foley, Richard Harry.

REFEREE: Jim Fleming (Scotland)

CROWD: 39,000

SOUTH AFRICA 25, AUSTRALIA 19

AT BLOEMFONTEIN STADIUM, BLOEMFONTEIN, 3 AUGUST

IN THE 13 MONTHS SINCE he'd sent the Rainbow Nation into raptures with the magnificent dropped goal that shattered the All Blacks' World Cup dreams at Ellis Park, the lustre had gone off Joel Stransky's play. Mediocre form in the wake of the World Cup celebrations had resulted in the Springbok test jersey being handed to Henry Honiball. The 30-year-old Stransky had the post-World Cup blues and South African fans were regarding him as yesterday's man.

He'd sat on the reserves bench for the Springboks' Tri-nations opener in Sydney, coming into the starting line-up against the All Blacks in Christchurch when Honiball was injured, where he gave a sound display without performing any miracles. He'd always been a big-occasion performer and back in the limelight in South Africa, he responded gloriously when the pressure went on against the Wallabies at Bloemfontein.

A third straight defeat would have condemned the Springboks to wooden-spoon status, an embarrassing comedown a year after stamping themselves as the best team in the world. But defeat at Bloemfontein was never a possibility, although the Wallabies did stage a stirring late comeback that had South African supporters more than a little anxious before referee Brian Stirling blew his whistle for full time.

Stransky scored all of South Africa's points, as he had in the World Cup final against the All Blacks. On that occasion his haul was 15 points (three penalty goals and two dropped goals). This time he amassed 25 points, which included his team's only try. Thanks to his deadly accurate goal kicking, the Springboks built a commanding 16–3 lead by half-time, which lengthened to 25–9, before the Wallabies, demonstrating great character, came storming back.

Victory came at a cost for the South Africans, who already had a sizeable injury list. Lock Johan Ackermann tore medial knee ligaments and prop Balie Swart was concussed, disastrous news for coach André Markgraaf ahead of four demanding tests against the All Blacks.

Markgraaf said of Ackerman, 'That kid never goes down, so when he couldn't get up, I knew the injury was serious. It is a hell of a blow for us.'

The result was hugely deflating for the Wallabies, who'd rebounded from their catastrophic start to the campaign by defeating the Springboks in Sydney and taking the All Blacks to the wire in Brisbane. They were outpassioned at Bloemfontein, their spirited revival — that included an excellent try to Ben Tune — coming too late. Forced to play catch-up rugby, they demonstrated a willingness to attack from any position on the field, which made for a highly entertaining contest.

It had been Greg Smith's first major challenge as Wallaby coach and John Eales' first as captain. In

Giant Springbok Os du Randt on the charge at Bloemfontein. Fotopress

tailing the Tri-nations field, they had little to celebrate. Smith had kept ringing the changes, to the extent that only two forwards (Eales and David Wilson) had held their positions throughout the winter. More ominously, however, Smith and Eales weren't jelling as a partnership. There would be gloomy days ahead before finally Smith was axed.

FOR SOUTH AFRICA: **Try, conversion and 6 penalty goals by Joel Stransky.**

FOR AUSTRALIA: **Try by Ben Tune; conversion and 3 penalty goals by John Eales; penalty goal by Matt Burke.**

SOUTH AFRICA: **James Small, Justin Swart, Japie Mulder, Brendan Venter, Pieter Hendriks, Joel Stransky, Johan Roux (replaced by Joost van der Westhuizen), Gary Teichmann, Ruben Kruger, Francois Pienaar (captain), Mark Andrews, Johan Ackermann, Balie Swart (replaced by Hannes Strydom), John Allan (replaced by Dawie Theron), Os du Randt.**

AUSTRALIA: **Matt Burke (replaced by Joe Roff), Ben Tune, Daniel Herbert, Pat Howard, David Campese, Scott Bowen, George Gregan, Tim Gavin, David Wilson, Michael Brial, John Eales (captain), John Welborn, Andrew Heath, Michael Foley, Dan Crowley.**

REFEREE: **Brian Stirling (Ireland)**

CROWD: **60,000**

NEW ZEALAND 29, SOUTH AFRICA 18

AT NEWLANDS, CAPE TOWN, 10 AUGUST

A COUPLE OF BLOKES NAMED OS commanded the headlines both before and after this action-packed encounter at Newlands, in which the All Blacks claimed victory by virtue of another breathtaking second-half comeback. New Zealand's 'Os', winger Glen Osborne, was in the news the moment he was selected for the game ahead of the 1995 World Cup colossus Jonah Lomu. The South Africans couldn't believe Lomu was being relegated to the reserves bench, given the impact he'd made in Cape Town 14 months earlier. But Osborne thoroughly justified his inclusion, scoring a spectacular try in the 70th minute that put the All Blacks ahead for the first time in the game.

Osborne's try actually broke an amazing try drought for the men in black, his touchdown being the first by the All Blacks against the Springboks in six and a half hours' endeavour, dating back to Wellington in 1994. From that moment the Boks had kept the All Blacks tryless at Auckland in 1994, in the World Cup final in Johannesburg in 1995, and in Christchurch in 1996.

The other 'Os' to feature was South Africa's man mountain prop, Os du Randt. He captured his share of headlines first for scoring a try but, more pertinently, for leaving the field in the second half, ostensibly because he was *gatvol* (brassed off). The comment was picked up and interpreted as du Randt capitulating, bringing scorn upon him. South Africans, like New Zealanders, understood that the only way props exited a game early was on a stretcher. Du Randt had walked off, seemingly unhurt. In fact, he had painfully damaged his jaw.

When the 'brassed off' rumour reached team management, he was severely reprimanded after an internal inquiry. Manager Morne du Plessis let it be known to du Randt that as long as a Springbok had breath in his body he should remain on the field. In an interview two years on, du Randt said because everybody kept asking him what had happened, he finally 'snapped' and said, 'I was *gatvol*, which got misinterpreted.'

There was a bizarre edge to this contest between the game's greatest rivals, because both sides could afford to lose. Neither wanted to, of course, but technically there was nothing at stake. It was the final leg of the Tri-nations championship which, following their thrilling victories at Wellington, Christchurch and Brisbane, was already wrapped up by the All Blacks. And Springbok coach, André Markgraaf, had stated, more than once, that, given those circumstances, his team's focus would be on the three-test series that was to begin in Durban the following weekend. For his team, Cape Town would be 'just a match'.

Well, 'just a match' it might have been, but what a match. There was three times the action, three times the drama and three times the excitement of the Christchurch international these sides had played three weeks earlier.

Prospering from All Black blunders, the Springboks established a commanding 18–6 advantage soon after half-time, which over the next 25 minutes Andrew Mehrtens narrowed to 18–12 through two penalty goals. With barely 10 minutes left, something special was required to salvage the game for New Zealand. The backs provided it, in stunning fashion, launching into attack from deep in their own territory. By doubling round behind replacement back Alama Ieremia, Mehrtens provided the initial impetus that Christian Cullen carried on. And when he sensed Osborne in support, a timely pass saw 'Os' cutting back to gloriously touch down between the posts.

Such was the All Black momentum, they added a further try, appropriately claimed by prop Craig Dowd, New Zealand's player of the day for the misery he inflicted on Marius Hurter at scrum time.

FOR NEW ZEALAND: Tries by Glen Osborne and Craig Dowd; 2 conversions and 5 penalty goals by Andrew Mehrtens.

FOR SOUTH AFRICA: Tries by Japie Mulder and Os du Randt; conversion and 2 penalty goals by Joel Stransky.

NEW ZEALAND: Christian Cullen, Jeff Wilson, Frank Bunce, Walter Little (replaced by Alama Ieremia), Glen Osborne, Andrew Mehrtens, Justin Marshall, Zinzan Brooke, Josh Kronfeld (replaced by Andrew Blowers), Michael Jones, Robin Brooke, Ian Jones, Olo Brown, Sean Fitzpatrick (captain), Craig Dowd.

SOUTH AFRICA: James Small, Pieter Hendriks, Japie Mulder, Hennie le Roux, Justin Swart, Joel Stransky, Joost van der Westhuizen, Gary Teichmann, Ruben Kruger, Francois Pienaar (captain, replaced by Hannes Strydom), Mark Andrews, Steve Atherton, Marius Hurter, John Allan, Os du Randt (replaced by Dawie Theron).

REFEREE: David McHugh (Ireland)

CROWD: 51,000

1997

ON THE SURFACE, the 1997 international rugby season was another one of triumph for New Zealand, with the players of Australia and South Africa unable to foot it with the men in black, who completed a second Tri-nations championship undefeated. But all that was about to change, big time. Both the Springboks and the Wallabies were in disarray in 1997, their coaches, Carel du Plessis and Greg Smith, plainly out of their depth. Administrators in both countries were about to replace them with coaches of exceptional quality.

Meanwhile, the All Blacks, seemingly unstoppable under John Hart's guidance, were approaching a critical transition stage, one that would see the team's three most experienced and influential individuals, captain Sean Fitzpatrick, Zinzan Brooke and Frank Bunce, end their illustrious international careers. It would be all downhill for Hart from that point.

Bunce, at the extreme age, for a rugby international, of 35, was the sensation as the All Blacks notched up four spectacular wins in 1997. He scored two tries as his team completed a dramatic come-from-behind win at Johannesburg, added another as the All Blacks crushed the Wallabies in front of 90,000 fans at Melbourne and taunted lightweight Percy Montgomery as the Springboks conceded 50 points for the first time, at Auckland. He notched up his 50th test appearance at Eden Park, a remarkable achievement for someone who was 30 before he pulled on the All Black jersey.

Two other backs who were sensationally effective throughout the 1997 campaign were fullback Christian Cullen, who maintained his amazing try-a-test record, and Carlos Spencer, whose goal kicking was a revelation. He averaged 18 points a test from kicks and maintained a strike rate of better than 90 per cent.

So, notwithstanding a dreadful second half against the Wallabies at Carisbrook, it was all glory for the All Blacks, who, in scoring 17 tries in four tests, remained the only Tri-nations team with the ability to win away from home.

The Wallabies and the Springboks were teams in crisis. Incredibly, South Africa had three different coaches in 1997. André Markgraaff, the incumbent,

Sean Fitzpatrick with the Tri-nations Trophy and Bledisloe Cup. Fotopress

was forced to resign after being tape recorded making crude racist comments, giving way to Carel du Plessis. Under du Plessis, the South Africans lost a home series to the British Lions 2–1 before suffering three Tri-nations defeats, losing heavily at Brisbane and Auckland. Nick Mallet would replace Du Plessis for the end-of-year tour of Italy, France, England and Scotland (when all internationals were won).

Smith steered an erratic course as coach of the Wallabies. Two further losses to the All Blacks had fans calling for his resignation. A good victory over the Springboks in Brisbane briefly restored credibility, but the humiliating 61–22 loss in Pretoria brought a conclusion to his term as coach. No one suspected that the headaches he spoke of consistently throughout the campaign were symptomatic of a brain tumour that would soon have a devastating effect on his career.

1997 FINAL STANDINGS

	P	W	L	D	For	Against	Points
New Zealand	4	4	–	–	159	109	18
South Africa	4	1	3	–	148	144	7
Australia	4	1	3	–	96	150	6

Tries: South Africa 18, New Zealand 17, Australia 13; Total 48.

Penalty goals: New Zealand 16, South Africa 8, Australia 7; Total 31.

THE GAMES

NEW ZEALAND 35, SOUTH AFRICA 32

AT ELLIS PARK, JOHANNESBURG, 19 JULY

BEFORE THIS SHOWDOWN at Ellis Park, 35-year-old Frank Bunce had played 10 tests against the Springboks without scoring a try against them. He remedied that in spectacular fashion, his two five-pointers allowing the All Blacks to retrieve an international that almost got away from them. His second score, a stunning 60-metre solo effort, ranks as one of the great individual All Black tries. Springbok captain Gary Teichmann branded it a 'soft' try because his players fell off their tackles. But the All Black management saw it as a classic example of the Bunce genius they had gambled on.

Coach John Hart admitted he had given Bunce 'favourable treatment' when he was carrying a foot injury, because he knew he needed him for this very game. Hart and his fellow selectors Ross Cooper and Gordon Hunter knew that Bunce's immense experience and cool head were qualities the team could not do without in the cauldron that is Ellis Park.

'Frank always has a calming influence on those around him,' said Hart afterwards, 'plus the ability to inspire his team-mates with a crunching tackle or a scorching break.' That he would achieve a double helping of tries was a far greater bonus than the All Black management team ever dreamed of. Even Bunce himself was surprised at what he achieved.

'The part of my game that hadn't returned following the foot injury was my sprinting,' he said. 'When the gap opened outside [Danie] van Schalkwyk, I wasn't quite prepared for the huge gulf that materialised in front of me.'

Bunce credited flanker Taine Randell with helping him create the try. 'James Small [on at fullback for Russell Bennett] hesitated because he thought I was going to pass to Taine. That opened the goalline to me, and I had just enough gas in the tank to get there.'

The Springboks made such an explosive beginning they appeared to have established a winning advantage after 30 minutes, by which stage they led 23–7, with tries to Naka Drotske and Russell Bennett and a bunch of goals to Jannie de Beer. If the All Black fans were getting anxious, skipper Sean Fitzpatrick certainly wasn't. He knew what his team was capable of. He summoned his troops together as de Beer was preparing for a kick and told them to remain calm and committed to the game plan but said it was essential they scored a try before half-time.

Fitzy's face took on a pained expression moments later when Carlos Spencer failed to send his restart 10 metres, but Jeff Wilson initiated the All Black comeback with two pieces of magic close to half-time. First, he charged down a Joost van der Westhuizen clearing kick, got a lucky bounce, and sprinted off to the goalposts. Then, capitalising on a beautiful pass from Bunce, he burst clear and delivered a perfect kick to the goalline to create another five-pointer for Spencer.

The second half was intensely exciting, with Bunce's epic try bringing the scores level at 26-all. After that, it was a goal-kicking competition between de Beer and Spencer. De Beer landed his first eight attempts, but with his team trailing 32–35 he struck the upright with an attempted penalty.

The result meant that after 60 years the All Blacks had finally headed off the Springboks in tests won. Not since the first test of the 1937 series had the All Blacks held an advantage over the Boks. This was the 48th international between the two nations, and the All Blacks had gone ahead 23–22, with three drawn. This was New Zealand's third test victory at Ellis Park and, at 35–32, equalled the biggest winning margin!

FOR NEW ZEALAND: Tries by Frank Bunce 2, Jeff Wilson and Carlos Spencer; 3 conversions and 3 penalty goals by Spencer.

FOR SOUTH AFRICA: Tries by Naka Drotske and Russell Bennett; 2 conversions, 4 penalty goals and 2 dropped goals by Jannie de Beer.

NEW ZEALAND: Christian Cullen, Jeff Wilson, Frank Bunce, Lee Stensness, Tana Umaga (replaced by Alama Ieremia), Carlos Spencer, Justin Marshall, Zinzan Brooke, Josh Kronfeld, Robin Brooke, Ian Jones, Taine Randell, Olo Brown, Sean Fitzpatrick (captain, replaced by Norm Hewitt), Craig Dowd.

SOUTH AFRICA: Russell Bennett (replaced by James Small), André Snyman, Percy Montgomery (replaced by Henry Honiball), Danie van Schalkwyk, Pieter Rossouw, Jannie de Beer, Joost van der Westhuizen, Gary Teichmann (captain), André Venter, Ruben Kruger, Mark Andrews (replaced by Fritz van Heerden), Krynauw Otto, Marius Hurter, Naka Drotske, Os du Randt (replaced by Dawie Theron).

REFEREE: Peter Marshall (Australia)

CROWD: 60,000

NEW ZEALAND 33, AUSTRALIA 18

AT MCG, MELBOURNE, 26 JULY

THE MARVEL OF THIS INTERNATIONAL was that the All Blacks were led on to the Melbourne Cricket Ground by Sean Fitzpatrick, because five days earlier a Melbourne surgeon had told him he would never play rugby again. The 34-year-old Fitzpatrick had limped out of the thriller at Ellis Park the previous weekend with his knee swollen and sore, and after an uncomfortable journey through from Johannesburg he'd hobbled off to consult the surgeon. The prognosis was grim. The surgeon observed that one leg was straight while the other bowed frighteningly to the right.

'He took one look at my legs and declared I would never play rugby again,' said Fitzpatrick. 'It wasn't what I wanted to hear, so I thanked him for his opinion and went straight back to our physiotherapist, David Abercrombie, to see what he could do.'

Abercrombie was far more optimistic. 'Sure he had a bowed knee,' he said, 'but by working on it using a mobilisation technique that stretched the joint and then taping it, it allowed Sean to run again. It was never going to be long-lasting, but it would allow him to play at Melbourne.'

Speculation had been rife all week that not only would Fitzpatrick be forced out of the Melbourne encounter, but that his retirement was imminent; indeed, coach John Hart had declared as late as the Wednesday that there was 'no show' of his captain playing. So when Fitzpatrick ran on to the MCG, for his 89th test appearance, he made sure the Wallabies and their multitude of fans knew he was there by producing a series of vigorous knee jumps.

'They were a ritual of mine,' he said. 'You could usually tell how well I was going to play depending on how bouncy I was when I ran on to the field.'

Benefiting from Fitzpatrick's inspirational leadership, the All Blacks coasted to a surprisingly comfortable victory, one Fitzy places right up among his most treasured experiences as an All Black.

Fitzpatrick was famous — perhaps that should be infamous — for baiting opponents and that night at the MCG he managed to completely ruffle his opponent, Michael Foley.

'I used to chat away to most of my opponents,' confessed Fitzpatrick later. 'Guys like Phil Kearns would listen and come back with something like, "Oh, shut up, Sean — get on with the game." But at Melbourne that night we really managed to upset Foley, especially when we pulled his headgear off. He really blew a fuse. Olo Brown and I had a good laugh about that.'

Fitzpatrick became the 'winningest' player in rugby in this game. The result represented his 72nd test win, one better than the record established by France's Philippe Sella.

The All Blacks led 17–3 after 15 minutes and were in charge at 30–6 before Greg Smith's Wallabies salvaged a little prestige with a couple of late tries. The special heroes of New Zealand's performance were 22-year-old blindside flanker Taine Randell, who won the man-of-the-match award, first-five Carlos Spencer, who landed seven goals from seven attempts, and veteran Bunce, who scored another try, his third in two outings.

The All Blacks lost Jeff Wilson in unusual circumstances at half-time. After a golden 40 minutes of action he collided with a team-mate while running grids before the resumption and retired with blurred vision.

Between 12,000 and 15,000 New Zealanders crossed the Tasman for this historic test at the MCG and countless others poured in from Sydney and beyond, boosting the Melbourne economy by an estimated A$16 million. Wallaby midfielder Paul Little commented: 'You could play the Bledisloe Cup at Alice Springs and you'd still get 50,000 Kiwis there!'

FOR NEW ZEALAND: **Tries by Frank Bunce, Jeff Wilson and Christian Cullen; 3 conversions and 4 penalty goals by Carlos Spencer.**

FOR AUSTRALIA: **Tries by George Gregan and Jason Little; conversion and 2 penalty goals by Matt Burke.**

NEW ZEALAND: **Christian Cullen, Glen Osborne, Frank Bunce, Alama Ieremia, Jeff Wilson (replaced by Adrian Cashmore), Carlos Spencer, Justin Marshall, Zinzan Brooke, Josh Kronfeld, Taine Randell, Ian Jones, Robin Brooke, Olo Brown, Sean Fitzpatrick (captain), Craig Dowd.**

AUSTRALIA: **Matt Burke (replaced by Sam Payne), Joe Roff, Jason Little, James Holbeck, Ben Tune, Tim Horan (replaced by Stephen Larkham), George Gregan, Michael Brial (replaced by Troy Coker), Brett Robinson (replaced by David Wilson), John Eales (captain), Garrick Morgan, Daniel Manu, Richard Harry, Michael Foley, Andrew Heath.**

REFEREE: **Ed Morrison (England)**

CROWD: **90,119**

AUSTRALIA 32, SOUTH AFRICA 20

AT SUNCORP STADIUM, BRISBANE, 2 AUGUST

DAVID KNOX HASTENED BACK FROM DURBAN in time to inspire a stunning turnaround in the Wallabies' fortunes at Brisbane's Suncorp Stadium and (briefly) take the pressure off the team's beleagured coach, Greg Smith. Previously spurned by the Australian selectors, who were stubbornly determined to convert Tim Horan into a flyhalf, Knox electrified the Australian backline, sparking four first-half tries and a crushing victory. The 33-year-old Knox thus preserved his remarkable record of never playing in a losing test team, and he did so in style, much to the chagrin of his new Natal captain, Gary Teichmann, the Springbok leader.

Knox had thrown his lot in with Natal after the Australian selectors had chosen to ignore his stunning Super 12 performances with the ACT Brumbies. Knox had scored 134 points as the Brumbies made it through to the final against the Auckland Blues. Greg Smith and his fellow selectors were convinced Horan, a world-class midfielder, could perform with equal panache in any position. But in five internationals in 1997 with Horan at flyhalf the Wallaby backline had failed to fire.

How different the backline looked with Knox in the No 10 jersey. Even though he'd been back in Australia for only 80 hours (flying home in style, on a first-class ticket) he combined sweetly with his Brumbies colleague George Gregan to create the attacking opportunities players like Ben Tune and Stephen Larkham had been thirsting for since the start of the international season. In the first 30 minutes, in which time Knox passed the ball 19 times and kicked it only three, the Wallabies scored three tries and established a commanding 19–3 lead.

The Wallabies, wearing black armbands as a mark of respect to the 18 people killed when an avalanche engulfed ski huts at Thredbo in New South Wales' Snowy Mountains, surged away to 32–10, exposing frailties in South Africa's inexperienced backline, before Teichmann's men picked up a couple of consolation tries.

The South Africans couldn't contain such artful dodgers as Gregan, Larkham

Rival halfbacks Joost van der Westhuizen and George Gregan tangle at Brisbane.

Fotopress

and 20-year-old Tune, who grabbed two great tries. Gregan was in sensational form, producing a succession of wondrous feats. He took out three defenders to create Tune's first try and ran giant prop Os du Randt into touch to avert a Springbok try. The Wallabies were so impressive they received a standing ovation at half-time from the delighted crowd and again at fulltime. The result meant neither South Africa nor Australia had yet managed to win a Tri-nations contest away from home, while the score of 32 was Australia's highest ever against the Springboks.

FOR AUSTRALIA: Tries by Ben Tune 2, Stephen Larkham and Daniel Manu; 3 conversions and 2 penalty goals by David Knox.

FOR SOUTH AFRICA: Tries by Os du Randt, Mark Andrews and Jannie de Beer; conversion and penalty goal by de Beer.

AUSTRALIA: Stephen Larkham, Ben Tune, Jason Little, James Holbeck, Joe Roff, David Knox, George Gregan, Troy Coker (replaced by Matt Cockbain), David Wilson, Daniel Manu (replaced by Brett Robinson), John Eales (captain), Owen Finegan, Richard Harry, Michael Foley, Andrew Blades (replaced by Andrew Heath).

SOUTH AFRICA: Russell Bennett, André Snyman (replaced by James Small), Percy Montgomery, Henry Honiball (replaced by Danie van Schalkwyk), James Small, Jannie de Beer, Joost van der Westhuizen, Gary Teichmann (captain), André Venter, Ruben Kruger, Mark Andrews, Krynauw Otto, Os du Randt (replaced by Adrian Garvey), James Dalton, Marius Hurter.

REFEREE: Colin Hawke (New Zealand)

CROWD: 36,416

NEW ZEALAND 55, SOUTH AFRICA 35

AT EDEN PARK, AUCKLAND, 9 AUGUST

FLANKER ANDRÉ VENTER BECAME THE FIRST PLAYER to be sent off in a New Zealand–South Africa test match. Despatched in the 47th minute for trampling on Sean Fitzpatrick's head, his exit had a profound influence on the outcome of the game. When Venter headed for the dressing room the All Blacks led 29–21, having at one stage trailed 11–21. Fifteen Springboks had been having enough problems containing the All Blacks. Fourteen were never going to cope. And within half an hour the score read 50–21.

In 76 years of competition between the two great rugby nations, it was the first time either side had cracked half a century of points. An embarrassing defeat of massive proportions loomed. However, South Africa's resolute captain Gary Teichmann implored his team-mates to salvage something from the wreckage. They did, scoring two late tries. It was still a loss — South Africa's third in a row — but the final scoreline of 55–35 allowed them to return home with their heads held high.

Only two Springboks had previously been sent off in internationals. James Small was despatched for verbal abuse of referee Ed Morrison during the 1993 tour of Australia and hooker James Dalton got his marching orders for fighting against Canada at the 1995 World Cup. On neither occasion was South Africa seriously inconvenienced, the send-offs coming late in each game.

Rugby's rich history is decorated with examples of teams achieving courageous victories after having players sent off, but while fighting on gallantly against the odds was manageable under the old laws, it's almost impossible for 14 men to survive for any length of time against 15 in the modern game, which is so wide-ranging and played at breakneck speed. Sadly, this Eden Park contest, which should have been a showpiece for the game, became a huge anti-climax following Venter's departure.

All Black fullback Christian Cullen, at 21 the 'baby' of the 1997 All Blacks, had a Jekyll and Hyde afternoon, conceding two tries in a nightmare opening quarter before scoring a brace of five-pointers himself.

'I wasn't feeling great when I looked at the scoreboard and saw South Africa ahead 21–11,' said Cullen. 'I thought "Fourteen of those points are because of me." I hoped I could make them up.'

They were almost freakish tries. Teichmann hoofed away a ball Cullen had placed in a tackle and, getting a lucky bounce, retrieved it to score, while Percy Montgomery regathered a soaring 'bomb' that Cullen fatefully allowed to bounce. All Black coach John Hart later exonerated Cullen. 'I'll willingly accept the odd mistake to have the flair he brings to a team,' said Hart. 'He ignites the team from fullback. I hope we don't focus on a couple of mistakes after we've scored fifty-five points against the Springboks.' Cullen's two tries brought his haul in 17 tests to 17.

Frank Bunce was playing his 50th test, a remarkable achievement considering his All Black debut came at the advanced age of 30. He was on the ground having his elbow massaged by the physiotherapist when he heard a move being called.

'Hey,' he said, 'I'm in that move.' Brushing aside the physio, and with his arm still numb, he hastened into position, just in time to take Carlos Spencer's skip pass. He fended off Montgomery and fullback Russell Bennett to send Alama Ieremia racing to the goalline.

FOR NEW ZEALAND: Tries by Christian Cullen 2, Alama Ieremia, Carlos Spencer, Justin Marshall, Taine Randell and Tana Umaga; 4 conversions and 4 penalty goals by Spencer.

FOR SOUTH AFRICA: Tries by Ruben Kruger, Gary Teichmann, Percy Montgomery, Joost van der Westhuizen and Pieter Rossouw; conversions by Jannie de Beer 3 and Henry Honiball 2.

NEW ZEALAND: Christian Cullen, Tana Umaga, Frank Bunce, Alama Ieremia, Jeff Wilson, Carlos Spencer (replaced by Andrew Mehrtens), Justin Marshall, Zinzan Brooke (temporarily replaced by Charles Riechelmann), Josh Kronfeld, Taine Randell, Ian Jones, Robin Brooke, Olo Brown, Sean Fitzpatrick (captain), Crowd Dowd (replaced by Mark Allen).

SOUTH AFRICA: Russell Bennett, André Snyman, Percy Montgomery, Henry Honiball, James Small, Jannie de Beer (replaced by Pieter Rossouw), Joost van der Westhuizen, Gary Teichmann (captain), André Venter (ordered off), Ruben Kruger (replaced by Fritz van Heerden), Mark Andrews, Krynauw Otto (replaced by Naka Drotske), Os du Randt (replaced by Dawie Theron), James Dalton, Marius Hurter.

REFEREE: Derek Bevan (Wales)

CROWD: 48,000

NEW ZEALAND 36, AUSTRALIA 24

AT CARISBROOK, DUNEDIN, 16 AUGUST

NO ONE APPRECIATED IT AT THE TIME, but this windswept international, remarkable for the fact that all 60 points were scored at the one end, represented the last occasion Sean Fitzpatrick, Zinzan Brooke and Frank Bunce would operate together for the All Blacks. Fitzy, 34, Buncey, 35, and Zinny, 32, had wielded a massive influence on New Zealand rugby after Laurie Mains used them to help rebuild the national team in 1992. They'd helped guide the team to two Tri-nations championships, a historic first series win on South African soil and a near World Cup success. While John Hart was officially the coach, there is little question that Fitzpatrick and Brooke masterminded much of the forward play, and Bunce called many of the shots out back. Their exit would result in a tragic deterioration in All Black standards in 1998.

So this Carisbrook contest was, in a sense, their last hurrah. Brooke and Bunce would play the internationals against Ireland, England and Wales on the end of year tour, but Fitzpatrick, even after corrective knee surgery, would manage no more than a couple of brief appearances as a reserve. None would feature as All Blacks in 1998. Collectively, they boasted 197 test appearances when they arrived in Dunedin, where they participated in one of the more bizarre international contests.

The All Blacks, with the Tri-nations Trophy already secured, won the first half 36–nil; the Wallabies claimed the second half 24–nil! Another mind-boggling statistic was that French referee Joel Dume awarded no fewer than 42 free kicks and penalties, believed to be a record for a test in New Zealand.

Australia's outstanding skipper John Eales was sidelined for this game with medial ligament damage, leaving flanker David Wilson to captain his country for the first time. One can only imagine how he felt as his team trooped to the changing rooms at half-time 36 points in arrears. First-time skipper or not, he elected to give his players a serious wake-up call. 'We had two options,' he said later. 'We either allowed ourselves to be totally humiliated, or we resolved to have a crack at them. We'd been pathetic throughout the first half, conceding penalties and missing tackles. We'd never got into the game.'

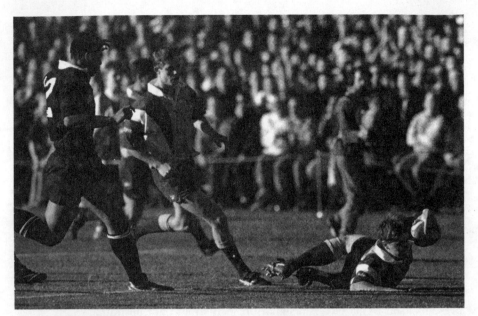

Ben Tune scores for the Wallabies in their exciting comeback at Carisbrook. Fotopress

The Wallabies had the advantage of a full-blown gale in the second half, one which swept from goalposts to goalposts. What a turnaround in Australia's fortunes. They ran in four super tries — one more than the All Blacks had managed — reducing the gap from 36 points to 12.

The highlight of New Zealand's first-half blitz was the 70-metre try scored by Christian Cullen in which he completely bamboozled the bravest of defenders, George Gregan.

FOR NEW ZEALAND: Tries by Taine Randell, Christian Cullen and Justin Marshall; 3 conversions and 5 penalty goals by Carlos Spencer.

FOR AUSTRALIA: Tries by Stephen Larkham 2, Joe Roff and Ben Tune; 2 conversions by David Knox.

NEW ZEALAND: Christian Cullen, Glen Osborne, Frank Bunce, Alama Ieremia, Jeff Wilson, Carlos Spencer, Justin Marshall (replaced by Junior Tonu'u), Zinzan Brooke, Josh Kronfeld, Taine Randell, Ian Jones (replaced by Mark Allen), Robin Brooke, Olo Brown, Sean Fitzpatrick (captain), Craig Dowd.

AUSTRALIA: Stephen Larkham, Joe Roff (replaced by Mitch Hardy), Jason Little, James Holbeck, Ben Tune, David Knox, George Gregan, Troy Coker, David Wilson (captain), Fili Finau, John Langford (replaced by Brett Robinson), Owen Finegan, Richard Harry, Michael Foley, Andrew Blades.

REFEREE: Joel Dume (France)

CROWD: 42,500

SOUTH AFRICA 61, AUSTRALIA 22

AT LOFTUS VERSFELD, PRETORIA, 23 AUGUST

THIS WAS THE RESULT that finally extinguished Greg Smith's career as coach of the Wallabies. He'd been hanging on by a thread and when the Springboks ran riot in the second spell at Loftus Versfeld Stadium, registering 60 points against an Australian team for the first time, he was doomed. As Peter FitzSimons records in John Eales' biography, within minutes of the match finishing Dick McGruther, the chairman of the Australian Rugby Union, telephoned his CEO, John O'Neill, and told him to seek Smith's resignation.

'It's time to move on,' McGruther said. 'If there is an opportunity that presents itself to get Greg's resignation, you should not hesitate.'

Smith's team was caned mercilessly in the media. Spiro Zavos wrote in the *Sydney Morning Herald* that 'the second-half performance was the most shameful 40 minutes of rugby the Wallabies have played in 93 years'.

And Greg Growden wrote: 'What a disgrace. These Wallabies are duds, but even more upsetting is that they dudded their country. They dudded their coach, Greg Smith. They dudded the Australian rugby colours. They dudded the Australian Rugby Union, who pay their way. And they dudded those countless Australian test greats who ensured that for so many years the Wallaby name typified and encouraged heroism and the ability to tackle adversity in its stride.'

Within 24 hours of returning to Sydney and after a conversation with O'Neill, Smith tendered his resignation. Within a fortnight, Rod Macqueen was installed as his successor.

In Smith's defence, the ARU didn't do him any favours by accepting a Tri-nations programme that had his team playing at high altitude in Pretoria seven days after tackling the All Blacks in Dunedin. Their schedule had them flying from Dunedin to Christchurch to Sydney (where they overnighted), then via Perth to Johannesburg and on down to Durban, where they were quartered at sea level. It was an exhausting trip. Scarcely had they got their breath back when they were journeying up to Pretoria on the eve of the match.

Having destroyed the Springboks in Brisbane, the Wallabies were quietly optimistic about their chances, even though they had to operate without their inspirational skipper John Eales, who watched the game from the grandstand with a strained medial ligament. The Wallabies trailed only 18–15 at half-time and with their scrum strong and Stephen Larkham attacking dangerously from fullback, the game still appeared winnable.

But not for long, with the next 38 minutes being won by the Springboks 41–nil! Never has a Wallaby team missed so many tackles, and once the Springboks had a sniff of glory there was no stopping them. There followed a remarkable succession of long-range tries, one from a Pieter Rossouw intercept, the others from slick counterattacks following Wallaby breakdowns. The crowd loved every minute of it, as the score surged past the half-century mark and on to the sixties.

The Springboks finished with eight tries and, thanks to a last-minute consolation touchdown by Jason Little, the Australians managed three, one too few to qualify them for the bonus point that would have allowed them to claim a share of second (which, in all honestly, they didn't deserve).

South Africa's special heroes were halfback Joost van der Westhuizen, revitalised fullback André Joubert, midfielders Percy Montgomery and Henry Honiball, and tight forwards Mark Andrews and Os du Randt.

FOR SOUTH AFRICA: Tries by Percy Montgomery 2, Johan Erasmus, James Dalton, Mark Andrews, Pieter Rossouw, Warren Brosnihan and Jannie de Beer; 6 conversions and 3 penalty goals by de Beer.

FOR AUSTRALIA: Tries by David Knox, Joe Roff and Jason Little; 2 conversions and a penalty goal by Knox.

SOUTH AFRICA: André Joubert, James Small (replaced by Werner Swanepoel), Percy Montgomery, Henry Honiball, André Snyman (replaced by Pieter Rossouw), Jannie de Beer, Joost van der Westhuizen, Gary Teichmann (replaced by Schutte Bekker), Johan Erasmus, Warren Brosnihan, Mark Andrews, Hannes Strydom (replaced by Braam Els), Marius Hurter, James Dalton, Os du Randt.

AUSTRALIA: Stephen Larkham, Ben Tune, Jason Little, James Holbeck, Joe Roff, David Knox, George Gregan, Troy Coker (replaced by Brett Robinson), David Wilson, Matt Cockbain (replaced by Toutai Kefu), John Langford, Owen Finegan, Andrew Blades, Michael Foley, Richard Harry.

REFEREE: Paddy O'Brien (New Zealand)

CROWD: 51,000

THE STAR
FRANK BUNCE

Fotopress

Frank Bunce's international career may never have got off the ground had it not been for his good friend Peter Fatialofa, who implored him to make himself available for Western Samoa. Bunce had made only a dozen appearances for Auckland over five years and at the advanced age of 29 had all but given up hope of becoming an All Black. So with the World Cup of 1991 a major attraction, Bunce finally yielded to Fatialofa's salesmanship and threw in his lot with Western Samoa. Fatialofa, who captained the side, said he knew the Samoans were going to perform strongly at the World Cup once Bunce was on board. 'I knew how good a player he was and how he could influence a whole team. He was our trump card.'

The dynamic, bruising centre, who ignited Samoa's pacy backline, caught the attention of incoming All Black coach Laurie Mains. He identified Bunce as the strong man he needed in midfield. And so when Mains launched into his international career in 1992, Bunce, then 30, became a key component; indeed, apart from the match against Japan at the 1995 World Cup, when several front-line players were rested, Bunce would feature in every test played throughout Mains' four-year reign.

Bunce survived into the John Hart era, his celebrated career extending through to the end of 1997, by which time he was eight weeks short of 36, qualifying him as the oldest back ever to represent the All Blacks (and, indeed, making him the second oldest All Black ever). He supplanted the great Bruce Robertson as New Zealand's most capped centre.

Bunce developed a lethal midfield partnership with fellow North Harbour representative Walter Little, a combination that had some classic battles with its Wallaby counterpart of Tim Horan and Jason Little.

While disappointed at missing out on World Cup glory in 1995, Bunce had plenty to celebrate the next year. He scored the matchwinning try in the Tri-nations encounter against Australia at Brisbane, and then shared in the All Blacks' famous first series triumph against the Springboks on South African soil.

1998

THE ALL BLACKS HADN'T LOST FOUR tests in succession since the calamitous 1949 season, but to the dismay of their fans they managed it in 1998 as South Africa, operating under new coach Nick Mallett, waltzed off with the Tri-nations championship for the first time. It was hard to believe these were the same three teams that had contested the championship in the first two years. Suddenly, South Africa and Australia discovered the art of winning away from home, while the All Blacks, invincible in 1996 and 1997, fell into serious decline. By taking out all four of their matches, the Springboks were a convincing winner of the competition, the Wallabies managed two victories at the All Blacks' expense and the All Blacks . . . well, for them, it was the campaign from hell.

The turnaround in fortunes for South Africa and Australia could be directly related to the appointment of new coaches, Nick Mallett and Rod Macqueen, who began achieving sporting miracles. Under Mallett, the Springboks would, incredibly, register 17 straight test victories — equalling the record the All Blacks set from 1964 to 1969 — before finally losing to England at Twickenham late in 1998, while Macqueen began constructing a team that would go through to win the World Cup in 1999.

Not altogether unpredictably, as the Springboks and Wallabies were gathering momentum the All Blacks were coming seriously unstuck, a Bledisloe Cup setback in Sydney following the Tri-nations campaign representing a fifth straight defeat. The collective departures of the great campaigners Sean Fitzpatrick, Zinzan Brooke and Frank Bunce had much to do with this, for without their input coach John Hart struggled and at season's end there were calls for him to resign. However, the NZRU, albeit narrowly, reconfirmed his appointment through to the 1999 World Cup.

Under Mallett, the Springboks were a revelation. They set themselves up for their first major title success since the 1995 World Cup by winning their away fixtures at Perth (thanks to Matt Burke missing a simple penalty attempt) and Christchurch. Gary Teichmann was an inspirational captain, who won many critics' vote as international player of the year, Joost van der Westhuizen

Percy Montgomery gets a hug from Gary Teichmann after the Springboks wrapped up the Tri-nations in 1998. Fotopress

a matchwinner at halfback, Percy Montgomery a deadly accurate goal kicker, and Bobby Skinstad a sensational newcomer.

Australian fullback Matt Burke — who was the competition's top point scorer (with 54) and leading try scorer (with three), largely thanks to his 24-point haul against the All Blacks in Melbourne — was on target to be crowned player of the series until he missed that sitter of a penalty in Perth which cost his team a one-point loss.

Tries weren't as plentiful as in 1997, when the Springboks had scored 18 and the All Blacks 17. This time, the Springboks and the Wallabies managed eight each and the All Blacks just six.

1998 FINAL STANDINGS

	P	W	L	D	For	Against	Points
South Africa	4	4	–	–	80	54	17
Australia	4	2	2	–	79	82	10
New Zealand	4	–	4	–	65	88	2

Tries: South Africa 8, Australia 8, New Zealand 6; Total 22.

Penalty goals: Australia 14, South Africa 10, New Zealand 9; Total 33.

THE STAR
JOOST van der WESTHUIZEN

Fotopress

'Joost do it' the fans' placards read around the South African rugby grounds in a paraphrase of the Nike ad. And Joost could do just about everything. The most potent weapon in the South African armoury of the 1990s, Joost van der Westhuizen simmered with an uncompromising intensity and pride of country, challenging opposing teams with his firebrand play. As Springbok scrumhalf, he roamed the field like a forward, charged at players twice his size and dazzled with his precise chip-kicking or speed from the base of a scrum. Off the field, he enjoyed nothing more than hunting on the veldt, which seemed entirely appropriate, for there was something untamed, something of the predatory hunter in his onfield presence.

Joost Heystek van der Westhuizen grew up in Pretoria, the heart of Afrikaanerdom, bringing to his game all the traditional strengths of a first-class scrumhalf, plus a few. He ran like a wing, tackled like a flanker and surged around the blind and open sides of scrums and rucks to become the most prolific test try-scoring halfback of all time. He initially struggled to establish himself as South Africa's leading halfback ahead of Johan Roux, but once he gained the selectors' confidence he entrenched himself as the No 9 of choice. He was crucial to South Africa's victory in the 1995 World Cup, tempering his natural attacking instincts by adopting the better options of strong defence and quick service from the scrum. Three years on, the Blue Bulls halfback was a major contributor as the Springboks claimed their first Tri-nations title.

During the 1990s van der Westhuizen was nominated as one of South Africa's five players of the year in six out of seven seasons, although the main award continued to elude him.

Under new national coach Nick Mallett, the 1998 season became one of van der Westhuizen's finest. First, there was the Tri-nations title, brought about by the matchwinning try he scored against the Australians in Perth, and domestically he celebated the first of his two Currie Cup triumphs with the Blue Bulls. Against northern hemisphere sides in 1998, he scored eight tries for the Springboks, including one each against Wales, Scotland and Ireland.

THE GAMES
AUSTRALIA 24,
NEW ZEALAND 16

AT MCG, MELBOURNE, 11 JULY

AUSTRALIA'S NEW COACH, ROD MACQUEEN, was proving himself wonderfully innovative as the 1998 international season unfolded. Switching Stephen Larkham to flyhalf had reaped huge rewards as the Wallabies crushed Clive Woodward's once-proud but seriously under-strength England side 76–nil. There followed two equally emphatic victories against Scotland and then Macqueen prepared his men for the most serious challenge, against the All Blacks, who had racked up seven straight victories at the Wallabies' expense.

One aspect of the New Zealanders' challenge that Macqueen was eager to negate was the haka, something his predecessor Greg Smith hadn't bothered about. Macqueen considered it gave the All Blacks a psychological advantage in the opening stanzas of the game. He bounced his plan off John Eales and when it met with the captain's approval it was announced to the team. So when the teams ran on to the Melbourne Cricket Ground the Wallabies stood and faced the haka, as they normally did, but this time they remained in their tracksuits. When the haka was finished, the Wallabies formed a tight circle and took a minute psyching themselves up for the battle. After which they removed their tracksuits and took their places for the kick-off. They had respected the haka but given themselves a buffer between it finishing and the contest beginning.

Many Australian fans believed Larkham should be wearing the fullback's No 15 jersey, but Macqueen considered his greatest worth to the Wallabies was at flyhalf. Which was as well for Australia in this contest, because the player who effectively defeated the All Blacks on his own was the player who did wear No 15, Matt Burke. They were calling him the Wizard of Oz after he'd accumulated all 24 of Australia's points to bring John Hart's team crashing down, a significant result because it represented New Zealand's first loss in three seasons of Tri-nations action. The 25-year-old Burke scored two tries, converted one and added four penalty goals. While he was coolly directing the ball between the uprights, Andrew Mehrtens and Carlos Spencer had a fearful night with their kicking, missing five reasonable kicks between them.

Australia's rock-solid defence was a major factor in the result, and here again Macqueen's inventiveness had paid dividends, for he had introduced into the mix a former league international, John Muggleton, as defensive coach. The Wallabies' concept of defensive training had never previously extended beyond the use of tackle bags. Now here was someone using videos, computers and blackboards, someone teaching them the science of defence.

Although the All Blacks led 8–nil early, Burke's genius had the Aussies ahead 15–13 by half-time and 21–13 in front going into the final quarter. The All Blacks had opportunities, but missing Sean Fitzpatrick, Zinzan Brooke and Frank Bunce, who had featured in every previous Tri-nations contest, they couldn't find any extra when it mattered. For half a dozen of the players this was their first taste of defeat as All Blacks. Among them were Taine Randell, in his 24th game, Spencer, Anton Oliver and Scott McLeod.

FOR AUSTRALIA: 2 tries by Matt Burke; conversion and 4 penalty goals by Burke.

FOR NEW ZEALAND: Tries by Josh Kronfeld and Ian Jones; penalty goals by Andrew Mehrtens and Carlos Spencer.

AUSTRALIA: Matt Burke, Ben Tune, Daniel Herbert, Tim Horan, Joe Roff, Stephen Larkham, George Gregan, Toutai Kefu (replaced by Willie Ofahengaue, replaced by Owen Finegan), David Wilson, John Eales (captain), Tom Bowman, Matt Cockbain, Richard Harry (replaced by Dan Crowley), Phil Kearns (temporarily replaced by Jeremy Paul), Andrew Blades.

NEW ZEALAND: Christian Cullen, Joeli Vidiri (replaced by Jonah Lomu), Scott McLeod, Walter Little, Jeff Wilson, Andrew Mehrtens (replaced by Carlos Spencer), Justin Marshall, Taine Randell (captain), Michael Jones (replaced by Isitolo Maka), Ian Jones, Robin Brooke, Josh Kronfeld, Olo Brown, Anton Oliver, Craig Dowd.

REFEREE: Clayton Thomas (Wales)

CROWD: 75,127

SOUTH AFRICA 14, AUSTRALIA 13

AT SUBIACO OVAL, PERTH, 18 JULY

ROD MACQUEEN'S DEBRIEFING after his Wallabies had disappointingly been edged out in the first rugby test ever staged in Perth focused on why none of his players had considered the dropped goal option in the closing stages. A solitary point in arrears, the Wallabies were perfectly positioned for a 'droppie', but none of the backs took the initiative. The obvious individual to have had a crack was flyhalf Stephen Larkham, but because he had not attempted one (let alone succeeded) since he was a schoolboy, he claimed he wasn't confident of success. And so, much to coach Macqueen's chagrin, his team let slip a golden opportunity to take a stranglehold on the competition.

When they returned to Caloundra in Queensland, where they were based while in Australia throughout the Tri-nations campaign — another of Macqueen's innovations — the backs were deployed to practise drop-kicking in case an identical scenario occurred again.

Into the third season of the Tri-nations, neither South Africa nor Australia had won beyond their own boundaries . . . until now. A mix of Joost van der Westhuizen's cheekiness, centre Pieter Muller's punishing defence and Percy Montgomery's goal kicking were factors that combined to bring the South Africans an unexpected victory. Van der Westhuizen caught the Wallabies napping when he plunged across the line from a quickly taken tap penalty; Muller put to advantage the tackling skills he'd learnt while playing a season of league in Australia with Penrith; while Montgomery's booming penalty goal from near halfway gave the South Africans their winning advantage.

Wallaby fullback Matt Burke, who a week earlier had been his team's hero, this time qualified for the dunce's cap after missing a sitter of a penalty from in front of the posts with 17 minutes to play. Burke had been on fire at Melbourne, accounting for all 24 of his team's points, but in the wind and rain at Subiaco Oval his goal kicking form deserted him. 'The ground was slippery,' he said afterwards, 'but I can't really account for all those lapses. I thought I was striking the ball well.'

Perhaps it was Burke's poor goal-kicking form that dissuaded the Wallaby backs from attempting a dropped goal. Instead, the team tried to muscle its way across for a matchwinning try, but South Africa's swarming defence held them out.

The Wallabies led 5–nil after one minute, when a classically executed backline move put Ben Tune across and 13–11 early in the second half after George Gregan finished off excellent lead-up work by the backs. But the trimmings that would normally come from Burke were despairingly missing at Subiaco Oval. He missed both conversions and a packet of penalty shots. The All Blacks, watching back in New Zealand, wouldn't have believed it was possible!

FOR SOUTH AFRICA: Try by Joost van der Westhuizen; 3 penalty goals by Percy Montgomery.

FOR AUSTRALIA: Tries by Ben Tune and George Gregan; penalty goal by Matt Burke.

SOUTH AFRICA: Percy Montgomery (temporarily replaced by Chester Williams), Stefan Terblanche, André Snyman, Pieter Muller, Pieter Rossouw, Henry Honiball, Joost van der Westhuizen, Gary Teichmann (captain), André Venter, Johan Erasmus, Mark Andrews, Krynauw Otto, Robbie Kempson (replaced by Ollie le Roux), James Dalton, Adrian Garvey.

AUSTRALIA: Matt Burke, Ben Tune (replaced by Damian Smith), Daniel Herbert, Tim Horan, Joe Roff, Stephan Larkham, George Gregan, Toutai Kefu (replaced by Willie Ofahengaue), David Wilson, Matt Cockbain (temporarily replaced by Owen Finegan), John Eales (captain), Tom Bowman, Richard Harry, Phil Kearns (temporarily replaced by Jeremy Paul), Andrew Blades.

REFEREE: Colin Hawke (New Zealand)

CROWD: 38,079

SOUTH AFRICA 13, NEW ZEALAND 3

AT ATHLETIC PARK, WELLINGTON, 25 JULY

THE SOUTH AFRICAN TEAMS may have disappointed in the 1998 Super 12 competition — the Cats, Bulls and Stormers all finishing in the bottom four — but collectively they provided ample attacking concepts for Springbok coach Nick Mallett. And one of them, a Coastal Sharks specialty, produced the try at Athletic Park that clinched the Springboks' first victory in New Zealand since 1981.

'It was a move the Sharks devised,' declared flyhalf Henry Honiball afterwards. 'We took all the moves that had worked for our Super 12 teams and integrated them into the Springbok planning.'

Executing the ploy to perfection from an attacking scrum, with the Springboks clinging to a 6–3 lead, Honiball and halfback Joost van der Westhuizen combined to deceive the All Black defence totally, allowing winger Pieter Rossouw to scythe through for a touchdown between the posts.

'I called the move because I was certain the All Blacks were expecting us to go wide,' said Honiball. 'It worked a treat. It was especially satisfying to pull such a manoeuvre against the All Blacks, who are the past masters at such things. The All Blacks have always had an impressive range of moves from attacking scrums. We've followed their lead.'

The try, 10 minutes from time, finally broke open a contest which until then had been rugby's equivalent of arm wrestling. Where the six Tri-nations contests of 1997 had averaged 67 points and eight tries a game, this one yielded a mere 16 points and Rossouw's lone five-pointer. And all this on a fine afternoon in conditions ideal for attacking rugby.

There should have been substantially more points scored, especially for the All Blacks, but coach John Hart's decision to instal Carlos Spencer as his goal kicker — after he'd publicly bagged Andrew Mehrtens for his mistakes in Melbourne — seriously backfired. Spencer, who'd been in sublime goal-kicking touch throughout 1997 but who'd yielded the role to Adrian Cashmore for the Auckland Blues in the Super 12, found Athletic Park's goalposts an elusive target. By the time he'd botched his fifth straight penalty attempt, Hart had no option but to replace him with Mehrtens, who promptly sent his first goal kick straight down the middle.

This victory, South Africa's second on the road — and their 11th straight since Mallett took over as coach — set them up for Tri-nations glory. But it was a reflection of how unsettled the Springboks had been that, of the line-up that succeeded in Wellington, only two members were from the World Cup-winning side, halfback van der Westhuizen and lock Mark Andrews. In contrast, nine members of the All Blacks who had fought out the 100-minute epic at Ellis Park in 1995 were still in action.

Mallett described his team's victory as a good thing for southern hemisphere rugby. 'Neither Rod Macqueen nor I wanted the Tri-nations to become a one-horse race again,' he said. 'For two years the All Blacks have dominated, not losing a game. That has made a lot of people in South Africa and, I expect, Australia very unhappy. While you people expect your great All Blacks to win all the time, it would be a bad thing for rugby if New Zealand always won.'

FOR SOUTH AFRICA: Try by Pieter Rossouw; conversion and 2 penalty goals by Percy Montgomery.

FOR NEW ZEALAND: Penalty goal by Andrew Mehrtens.

SOUTH AFRICA: Percy Montgomery, Stefan Terblanche, André Snyman (replaced by Franco Smith), Pieter Muller, Pieter Rossouw (temporarily replaced by Chester Williams), Henry Honiball, Joost van der Westhuizen, Gary Teichmann (captain), André Venter, Andrew Aitken (replaced by Bobby Skinstad), Mark Andrews, Krynauw Otto, Robbie Kempson (replaced by Ollie le Roux), James Dalton, Adrian Garvey.

NEW ZEALAND: Christian Cullen, Jeff Wilson, Mark Mayerhofler (replaced by Scott McLeod), Walter Little, Jonah Lomu, Carlos Spencer (replaced by Andrew Mehrtens), Justin Marshall (replaced by Junior Tonu'u), Taine Randell (captain), Josh Kronfeld, Michael Jones (replaced by Isitolo Maka), Ian Jones, Robin Brooke, Olo Brown, Anton Oliver, Craig Dowd.

REFEREE: Ed Morrison (England)

CROWD: 39,500

AUSTRALIA 27, NEW ZEALAND 23

AT JADE STADIUM, CHRISTCHURCH, 1 AUGUST

IT'S FAIR TO SAY THE WALLABIES weren't exactly relishing taking on the All Blacks in Christchurch, because they hadn't won a test match there in 40 years. The last time an Australian captain had made a victory speech at Lancaster Park (now Jade Stadium) had been in 1958, when the All Black side was captained by Wilson Whineray. The Wallaby skipper that day was Charlie Wilson. That victory represented an upset of monumental proportions, whereas the team of 1998, coming off a fine win in Melbourne, were quietly confident they could make it two in a row against John Hart's men.

They did, far more emphatically than any New Zealand fan would have considered possible, given the All Blacks' dominance against their SANZAR partners in the previous two Tri-nations campaigns. The elegant Aussies led 27–9 with 10 minutes to play, having comprehensively outsmarted their opponents, before the fresh recruits from the All Blacks reserves bench salvaged a little pride with two tries in the dying stages.

Australia's mastery was epitomised in the try Matt Burke scored shortly before half-time, after the Wallabies had eroded the All Black defence in a remarkable 18-phase sequence (lasting 3 minutes and 10 seconds). It ended in Stephen Larkham putting his fullback across the line. For the All Blacks, it was a hugely demoralising sequence of play. Hadn't they flattened the Springboks in precisely the same manner at Cape Town in 1996 to wrap up the inaugural Tri-nations series? Now here were the Wallabies doing it to them, a Wallaby team that 12 months earlier had been in crisis. The Australians pieced together four classic tries to which the All Blacks responded with two desperate efforts, when the outcome was inevitable, in the final four minutes.

Wallaby coach Rod Macqueen suggested to the media following the game that defences had become so sophisticated that teams had to create openings rather than simply try to crash through them. His men in gold had certainly created those opportunities, whereas the All Blacks, painfully missing Frank Bunce, who had left to play rugby in France, had kept running at breakneck speed into brick walls.

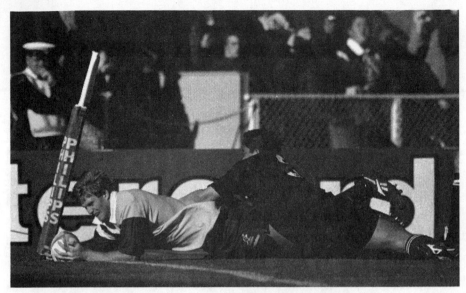

Tom Bowman beats Taine Randell to the goalline at Christchurch. Fotopress

After two Tri-nations series undefeated the All Blacks had now lost three matches in a row, prompting coach Hart to say, 'I knew this would be a difficult year, but I did not think it would be this difficult.'

The day belonged to Australia and its superstars, most notably Larkham, Jason Little, George Gregan, John Eales and David Wilson. It was Australia's first test win in New Zealand since 1990 and as the players gathered in a huddle at the finish, strains of 'Waltzing Matilda' broke out from the 400-odd Australian supporters at the southern end of the ground.

FOR AUSTRALIA: Tries by Tom Bowman, Matt Burke, Jason Little and Stephen Larkham; 2 conversions by John Eales; penalty goal by Burke.

FOR NEW ZEALAND: Tries by Christian Cullen and Jonah Lomu; 2 conversions and 3 penalty goals by Andrew Mehrtens.

AUSTRALIA: Matt Burke, Jason Little, Daniel Herbert, Tim Horan, Joe Roff, Stephen Larkham, George Gregan, Toutai Kefu (replaced by Willie Ofahengaue), David Wilson, Matt Cockbain, John Eales (captain), Tom Bowman, Dan Crowley, Phil Kearns, Andrew Blades.

NEW ZEALAND: Christian Cullen, Jeff Wilson, Mark Mayerhofler, Walter Little, Jonah Lomu, Andrew Mehrtens, Justin Marshall, Taine Randell (captain), Mark Carter (replaced by Scott Robertson), Michael Jones, Ian Jones, Robin Brooke, Olo Brown, Anton Oliver, Craig Dowd (replaced by Carl Hoeft).

REFEREE: Derek Bevan (Wales)

CROWD: 39,000

SOUTH AFRICA 24, NEW ZEALAND 23

AT KING'S PARK, DURBAN, 15 AUGUST

THE TRANSFORMATION IN THE SPRINGBOKS immediately Nick Mallett was installed as coach was truly astonishing. By the time the desperate All Blacks arrived in Durban, Mallett boasted an imposing record of 11 straight test victories and no defeats. Mallett, 41, had taken charge of the national team at the conclusion of a disastrous 1997 campaign that had seen André Markgraaff resign in disgrace (for making racist comments) and his successor Carel du Plessis sacked after losing five important internationals.

An outstanding footballer himself, talented enough to represent his country in the difficult days of the 1980s when South Africa was ostracised from the international sporting scene, Mallett launched his coaching career with the Springboks against Italy in Bologna, a game won 62–31. In rapid succession, his team swept aside France twice — the Paris test being won 52–10 — Scotland by the incredible margin of 68–10 and England. In limbering up for the 1998 Tri-nations championship, his team slaughtered Wales 96–13 at Bloemfontein and also beat England again and Ireland. Little wonder, therefore, that the Springboks took on the All Blacks and the Wallabies in the Tri-nations championship with a new-found confidence.

Their belief in themselves was never better demonstrated than at King's Park, where they found themselves 23–5 in arrears against a reconstructed All Black team with barely 15 minutes remaining. While All Black coach John Hart stubbornly declined to go to his subs bench, which included such proven internationals as Ian Jones, Craig Dowd and Carlos Spencer, Mallett injected four fresh players into the game in the second half as he sought to seize the initiative. Once the momentum changed, it became a landslide.

Tries by Joost van der Westhuizen and Bobby Skinstad positioned the Boks for a final assaul, and, from an attacking line-out, hooker James Dalton was controversially awarded a try by referee Peter Marshall, although TV replays showed he never grounded the ball, and Dalton admitted as much in an interview.

Dalton's try sent the South African fans into raptures, while All Black captain Taine Randell appeared almost in shock at the unbelievable turnaround in fortunes. 'It's hard to believe the game got away from us,' said Randell. 'We seemed to be so much in control. Sport can be so cruel.'

A year earlier the All Blacks had come from 7–23 down to win at Ellis Park. This time it was South Africa's turn to believe in fairytales.

Until Mallett's men staged their barnstorming finish, Hart and his fellow selectors were beaming. Their reconstructed pack (Isitolo Maka, Josh Kronfeld, Royce Willis and Carl Hoeft had been introduced following the loss in Christchurch) outperformed the Springboks in scrums and in driving forward play. But superbly led by Gary Teichmann, the Springboks survived the onslaught and produced a series of match-winning raids at the business end of the game.

There was something oddly symbolic about the final scoreline of 24–23. Going into the match, the All Blacks had claimed 24 test victories against their great rival, while the Springboks had won 23.

FOR SOUTH AFRICA: Tries by Stefan Terblanche, Joost van der Westhuizen, Bobby Skinstad and James Dalton; 2 conversions by Percy Montgomery.

FOR NEW ZEALAND: Tries by Justin Marshall and Taine Randell; 2 conversions and 3 penalty goals by Andrew Mehrtens.

SOUTH AFRICA: Percy Montgomery, Stefan Terblanche, André Snyman (replaced by Franco Smith), Pieter Muller, Pieter Rossouw, Henry Honiball, Joost van der Westhuizen, Gary Teichmann (captain), André Venter, Johan Erasmus (replaced by Andrew Aitken), Mark Andrews, Krynauw Otto (replaced by Bobby Skinstad), Robbie Kempson, James Dalton, Adrian Garvey (replaced by Ollie le Roux).

NEW ZEALAND: Christian Cullen, Jeff Wilson, Eroni Clarke (replaced by Norm Berryman), Mark Mayerhofler, Jonah Lomu, Andrew Mehrtens, Justin Marshall, Isitolo Maka (replaced by Scott Robertson), Josh Kronfeld, Taine Randell (captain), Robin Brooke, Royce Willis, Olo Brown, Anton Oliver, Carl Hoeft.

REFEREE: Peter Marshall (Australia)

CROWD: 52,000

SOUTH AFRICA 29, AUSTRALIA 15

AT ELLIS PARK, JOHANNESBURG, 22 AUGUST

EXPERIENCED SOUTH AFRICAN JOURNALIST Mark Keohane waxed lyrical after the Springboks had put away the Wallabies at Ellis Park, a victory that secured them the Tri-nations Trophy.

Wrote Keohane: 'Our country needs more days like this. To write of the triumph and not of the turmoil is bliss. To say South Africa is the best in the world and have New Zealand and Australia agree is bliss. To see a Springbok team happy, confident and willing to entertain, to see the winners' emotion and humility from the conquered is bliss.

'This South African team is the equal of any the game has produced in the past century. They created amazing human electricity at Ellis Park.

'The South African captain Gary Teichmann, who towered over SARU president Silas Nkanunu in receiving the Tri-nations Trophy, was humble and courageous. He complimented the Wallabies and pleaded with supporters to temper the boorish behaviour that gave South Africans a bad name. "We must stamp it out," he said. "Players' lives are endangered and it does our country no favours. We must set an example. We do not want to play tests in South Africa with a fence separating the crowd from us. And I am sure fans don't want that either."

'Saturday was bigger than the 1995 World Cup final. The crown won then can be worn with justification.'

After the dramatic comeback against New Zealand seven days earlier, victory was never in doubt in this decider. Percy Montgomery edged the Springboks ahead with a penalty goal in the first minute, and they never relinquished the lead.

An Adrian Garvey try in the sixth minute was classic Nick Mallett rugby philosophy. Mallett been working on his team to back themselves to score tries, not settle for penalty goals. So when the opportunity arose, the Boks set up an attacking lineout, Teichmann claimed the throw and a controlled drive put Garvey across for the prize.

The Australians were stunned. They kept fighting back with Matt Burke

Bobby Skinstad fends off
Tim Horan as he heads for
the goalline at Ellis Park.

Fotopress

penalty goals to trail 12–16 at half-time and 15–16 going into the final quarter
before a stunning try by replacement loosie Bobby Skinstad in the 70th minute
finally sunk the visitors. Skinstad combined speed and quick reactions to claim
a try that would have been beyond many mere mortals.

The Springboks to a man were superior. They desperately wanted to win and
prove that their World Cup success of 1995 was not a one-off performance.

FOR SOUTH AFRICA: Tries by Adrian Garvey and Bobby Skinstad; 2 conversions and
5 penalty goals by Percy Montgomery.

FOR AUSTRALIA: 5 penalty goals by Matt Burke.

SOUTH AFRICA: Percy Montgomery, Stefan Terblanche, André Snyman (replaced
by Franco Smith), Pieter Muller, Pieter Rossouw, Henry Honiball, Joost van der
Westhuizen, Gary Teichmann (captain), André Venter, Johan Erasmus (replaced by
Andrew Aitken), Mark Andrews (replaced by Bobby Skinstad), Krynauw Otto, Robbie
Kempson (replaced by Ollie le Roux), James Dalton, Adrian Garvey.

AUSTRALIA: Matt Burke, Ben Tune (replaced by Nathan Grey), Daniel Herbert
(replaced by Jason Little), Tim Horan, Joe Roff, Stephen Larkham, George Gregan,
Toutai Kefu (replaced by Willie Ofahengaue), David Wilson, Matt Cockbain (replaced
by Owen Finegan), John Eales, Tom Bowman, Dan Crowley, Phil Kearns, Andrew
Blades (replaced by Glen Panaho).

REFEREE: Jim Fleming (Scotland)

CROWD: 62,300

1999

WHAT A TOPSY-TURVY COMPETITION the Tri-nations turned out to be in 1999. The team that was invincible in 1998 finished last, while the team that was whitewashed in 1998 won it. Only the Australians were consistent, retaining their runner-up status. The All Blacks, coached for the fourth successive year by John Hart — who had been fortunate to survive given the disastrous results of 1998 — came through to claim the title for the third time. But Hart's players weren't totally convincing, suffering a 28–7 loss to the Wallabies in their final outing, an ominous outcome five weeks out from the World Cup (in which they were to come crashing down against France in the semifinals).

Neither the Australians nor the South Africans were at full strength, both sides having been ravaged with injuries. John Eales and Stephen Larkham were absentees from the Wallabies, but recovered in time to make massive contributions to their team's World Cup triumph. Nick Mallett went through a

No wonder Taine Randell looks flat. His team has just lost 28–7.

Fotopress

bucketload of centres, who kept getting injured, and had the trauma of sacking Gary Teichmann as captain and replacing him with Joost van der Westhuizen, not a decision that met with universal approval back in South Africa.

The three teams would, predictably, all qualify for the World Cup semifinals, but only Australia, astutely prepared by Macqueen, would make it through to the final. The likelihood of that happening seemed remote when the Australians crashed to a 34–15 defeat against the All Blacks at Eden Park and then were nosed out, 10–9, by the Springboks at Cape Town. But their fortunes turned around dramatically against the All Blacks in Sydney. Maybe it was the world record attendance of 107,000 at Stadium Australia that inspired them. Certainly a reinforced front row made a difference, plus the team's tenacious defence (that would be a hallmark of their World Cup performances).

It was an unfortunate aspect of the competition in 1999 that penalty goals outnumbered tries by 37 to 17. Two individuals who prospered in this respect were All Black first-five Andrew Mehrtens, who equalled the world record with nine penalty goals in the Eden Park test, then kicked another seven at Pretoria, and Matt Burke, who also banged over seven goals in Sydney.

Of the 17 tries, New Zealand and Australia accounted for seven each, with the Springboks managing a measly three.

Mehrtens was the competition's leading scorer with 70, all but five of which came from goals, followed by Burke with 54. South Africa, who used three different goal kickers — Braam van Straaten, Gaffie du Toit and Jannie de Beer — in the series failed to score a try in their two away matches.

1999 FINAL STANDINGS

	P	W	L	D	For	Against	Points
New Zealand	4	3	1	–	103	61	12
Australia	4	2	2	–	84	57	10
South Africa	4	1	3	–	34	103	4

Tries: New Zealand 7, Australia 7, South Africa 3; Total 17.

Penalty goals: New Zealand 19, Australia 13, South Africa 5; Total 37.

THE GAMES
NEW ZEALAND 28,
SOUTH AFRICA 0

AT CARISBROOK, DUNEDIN, 10 JULY

WHEN CALM RETURNED to New Zealand rugby following the disasters of 1998 and the reappointment of coach John Hart, it inevitably led to a redesigned All Black team. The most daring changes saw Jeff Wilson, a winger with astonishing try-scoring talents, switched to fullback, and Christian Cullen, who'd so consistently split open opposition defences from fullback, moved to the wing. Daryl Gibson came in at second-five, Norm Maxwell took over from Ian Jones at lock, and the all-Otago front row of Kees Meeuws, Anton Oliver and Carl Hoeft supplanted the all-Auckland front row of Olo Brown, the retired Sean Fitzpatrick and Craig Dowd.

New Zealand, the dominant side in the Tri-nations in 1996 and 1997, had come horribly unstuck in 1998. And there was only a matter of months before they were pitched into the World Cup.

Hart's revamped side enjoyed the perfect prelude to the new Tri-nations campaign, swamping France 54–7 at Athletic Park, and so there was an air of confidence about the All Blacks going into the Carisbrook opener, especially as Nick Mallett's Springboks had been ripped apart with injuries. In fact, it was hard to recognise the Springboks as the same team that had registered 17 straight test victories through to November 1998, picking up the Tri-nations title along the way. Missing were such celebrated achievers as Joost van der Westhuizen, Henry Honiball, Stefan Terblanche, Bobby Skinstad and front rowers Robbie Kempson, James Dalton and Adrian Garvey, while No 8 and captain Gary Teichmann was battling for fitness after enduring back and knee injuries.

One critical factor the All Blacks had in their favour was the venue, Carisbrook, where they had not lost a test since 1971. However, that seemed to count for little as the Springboks, just 0–6 in arrears, battered away at the All Black goalline a dozen or so minutes into the second half. The Springboks had a try declined on a hairline decision by the refere — one that in 2005 would be referred to the TMO — a definitive moment for both teams. The depleted

Springboks desperately needed a score to sustain them through to the finish. For the All Blacks, still bearing the scars of 1998, it was a lucky let-off.

When New Zealand then swept on to attack, two of their champion game-breakers stepped up to the plate: Andrew Mehrtens and Christian Cullen. The two combined exquisitely to produce the try of the afternoon. Cullen came roaring in from the right wing shouting for the ball. 'I heard him so clearly,' said Mehrtens, 'it's a wonder the Springboks didn't as well. There was no one in behind their backline, so a chip kick was the obvious play.'

Such was the precision of Mehrtens' kick that Cullen was able to gather the ball at full speed and sprint unchallenged around behind the goalposts. It was his 28th try in 32 tests, a most remarkable record.

That try represented a huge psychological blow to the Springboks. Sure, they'd fought back from 5–23 down at Durban the previous year, but on that occasion all their game-breakers had been on board. This time there were too many rookies involved, with the least experienced twosome, inside backs David von Hoesslin and Gaffie du Toit, being ruthlessly exposed.

In the final 10 minutes, with the Springboks thoroughly demoralised, the All Blacks ran in two cracking tries to create a record-winning margin of 28 points against the great old foe.

FOR NEW ZEALAND: Tries by Christian Cullen, Jeff Wilson and Justin Marshall; conversion and 3 penalty goals by Andrew Mehrtens; conversion by Tony Brown.

NEW ZEALAND: Jeff Wilson, Tana Umaga, Alama Ieremia, Daryl Gibson, Christian Cullen, Andrew Mehrtens, Justin Marshall, Taine Randell (captain), Josh Kronfeld, Andrew Blowers, Robin Brooke, Norm Maxwell, Kees Meeuws, Anton Oliver, Carl Hoeft. Replacements: Jonah Lomu, Byron Kelleher, Tony Brown, Dylan Mika, Royce Willis.

SOUTH AFRICA: Percy Montgomery, Breyton Paulse, Japie Mulder, Pieter Muller, Pieter Rossouw, Gaffie du Toit, David von Hoesslin, Gary Teichmann (captain), André Venter, Corne Krige, Mark Andrews, Krynauw Otto, Cobus Visage, Naka Drotske, Os du Randt.
Replacements: Willie Meyer, Braam van Straaten, Robbie Fleck, Selborne Boome, André Vos, Ollie le Roux.

REFEREE: Peter Marshall (Australia)

CROWD: 42,000

AUSTRALIA 32, SOUTH AFRICA 6

AT SUNCORP STADIUM, BRISBANE, 17 JULY

WHAT A DIFFERENCE A DEFEAT MAKES. Nick Mallett was everybody's hero in South Africa throughout most of 1998 when his Springboks brimmed with confidence, swept aside every opponent and broke numerous records. Then came the end-of-year tour to Europe that nobody wanted, not Mallett and not the players. Things started to fall apart. Suddenly, the team looked vulnerable and unsure. Suddenly, Mallett looked like a man in two minds.

The loss to England at Twickenham, after 16 straight victories, was Mallett's first. It shouldn't have been a traumatic occasion, but it became one because Mallett, concerned at the injuries that were troubling his great captain Gary Teichmann, began thinking about replacing him.

Rather than allow Teichmann's damaged neck and knee to mend, Mallett insisted he prove his fitness by playing the Super 12. He survived, but when the Springboks lost, for the first time ever, to Wales in Cardiff, then took a 28–nil drubbing in the Tri-nations opener in Dunedin, Mallett pulled the pin. Declaring Teichmann to be injured for this contest in Brisbane, the Springbok coach appointed Johan 'Rassie' Erasmus captain and when the team returned to South Africa he dropped Teichmann altogether. His proud reign as captain had come abruptly to an end.

Much-respected rugby correspondent Paul Dobson would later declare it 'a mistake' and said everyone knew it. He said Teichmann had earned an iconic status among the South African public . . . 'and you are not supposed to shoot icons'.

Dobson said that Teichmann's demotion 'fatally ruptured the public's trust in an outstanding coach and the anger and recriminations would resurface all the way to Mallett's own dismissal 12 months later'.

Without their trusty leader the Springboks were a dispirited, disorganised bunch who had no answer to Australia's super-slick backline, being crushed by four tries to none and returning home to South Africa without a solitary try to show for 160 minutes of onfield endeavour. One dimensional, they offered little beyond power scrummaging.

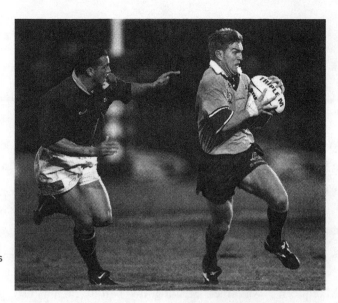

Tim Horan runs in one
of Australia's four tries
at Brisbane.
Fotopress

The match belonged to the Australian backs and in particular Matt Burke, back on the international scene after a 10-month lay-off, and flyhalf Tim Horan. Burke's performance was amazing, because he went into the game after only a handful of outings at club level and one serious trial against New Zealand A. He scored a try and landed a series of pressure goals for a 17-point haul as his team achieved its biggest winning margin against the Springboks. Having lost twice to South Africa in 1998, the result provided a major psycholocial boost to Rod Macqueen's team three months out from the World Cup.

FOR AUSTRALIA: Tries by Joe Roff 2, Tim Horan and Matt Burke; 3 conversions and 2 penalty goals by Burke.

FOR SOUTH AFRICA: 2 penalty goals by Braam van Straaten.

AUSTRALIA: Matt Burke, Joe Roff, Daniel Herbert, Nathan Grey, Ben Tune, Tim Horan, George Gregan, Toutai Kefu, David Wilson (captain), Matt Cockbain, John Welborn, David Giffin, Patricio Noriega, Jeremy Paul, Dan Crowley.
Replacements: Tiaan Strauss, Mark Connors, Glenn Panoho, Phil Kearns.

SOUTH AFRICA: Percy Montgomery, Breyton Paulse, Robbie Fleck, Pieter Muller, Stefan Terblanche, Braam van Straaten, Werner Swanepoel, Anton Leonard, André Venter, Johan Erasmus (captain), Selborne Boome, Krynauw Otto, Kobus Visage, Naka Droske, Os du Randt.
Replacements: David von Hoesslin, Deon Kayser, Pieter Rossouw, Ollie le Roux, Willie Meyer.

REFEREE: Paddy O'Brien (New Zealand)

CROWD: 31,677

NEW ZEALAND 34, AUSTRALIA 15

AT EDEN PARK, AUCKLAND, 24 JULY

WHEN ANDREW MEHRTENS READ that Keiji Hirose of Japan had landed a world record nine penalty goals against Tonga earlier in 1999 he thought it was a mark he would never match.

'It struck me it was a hell of a lot of penalty goals,' says Mehrtens. 'Frankly, I couldn't ever see me or any All Black for that matter kicking that many penalty goals. I didn't think any All Black would ever get enough chances.'

But it happened in the first night test at Eden Park at the expense of Rod Macqueen's Wallabies. Striking the ball with masterly precision, Mehrtens slotted nine penalty goals from nine attempts — two better than Grant Fox's New Zealand record set in 1993 on the same ground against Western Samoa. Afterwards, a modest Mehrtens admitted he had no idea how many goals he'd landed. While he was delighted that the All Blacks had taken revenge on the Aussies, who'd outgunned them three times in 1998, his greatest concern had been that the crowd would start to boo him.

'Spectators basically come along to watch tries being scored, not goal kickers chasing world records,' he said. 'I just hope the fans appreciated that I was instructed to take that final kick [when the All Blacks were ahead 31–15]. I wasn't volunteering. And I certainly don't like being booed.'

However, Mehrtens defends the All Blacks' decision to take all the three-pointers on offer. 'Having blown an 18-point advantage in Durban the previous year, we wanted to keep as much daylight between us and Australia as possible.'

Mehrtens emphasised that the plethora of penalty goals eventuated because of the relentless pressure his team maintained. 'We weren't awarded that many penalties in the game, but because of our huge territorial advantage, every time a penalty did come along, it was within kicking range.'

While the capacity crowd acknowledged Mehrtens' kicking skills, they would undoubtedly have preferred applauding tries. But their team managed only one, and that was a gift-wrapped present from Joe Roff, who dropped a straightforward pass from George Gregan on his own goalline, to Justin

Marshall's delight. Gregan walked across and consoled Roff, who was mortified at the mistake he'd made.

It was the All Black forwards, operating with immense energy and enthusiasm, who controlled the game. The scrum, anchored by Kees Meeuws, regularly had the Wallaby pack in reverse. Marshall, who became the All Blacks' most capped halfback (eclipsing Graeme Bachop's record of 31 test appearances) turned in one of his finest performances and combined brilliantly with Mehrtens.

Seemingly down and out at 28–3 after 50 minutes, the Wallabies showed character and resolve to score two fine tries, one of which went to centre Daniel Herbert, the game's most penetrative back. In the absence of John Eales, who was in a race against time to get fit for the World Cup, the Aussies were captained by David Wilson.

It was an occasion to cherish at Eden Park — the 50th All Black test on the ground, the inaugural night test and the opening of the magnificent new ASB Bank stand.

FOR NEW ZEALAND: Try by Justin Marshall; conversion and 9 penalty goals by Andrew Mehrtens.

FOR AUSTRALIA: Tries by George Gregan and Daniel Herbert; conversion and penalty goal by Matt Burke.

NEW ZEALAND: Jeff Wilson, Tana Umaga, Alama Ieremia, Daryl Gibson, Christian Cullen, Andrew Mehrtens, Justin Marshall, Taine Randell (captain), Josh Kronfeld, Dylan Mika, Robin Brooke, Norm Maxwell, Kees Meeuws, Anton Oliver, Carl Hoeft. Replacements: Jonah Lomu, Tony Brown, Royce Willis, Andrew Blowers, Greg Feek.

AUSTRALIA: Matt Burke, Joe Roff, Daniel Herbert, Nathan Grey, Ben Tune, Tim Horan, George Gregan, Tiaan Strauss, David Wilson (captain), Matt Cockbain, John Welborn, David Giffin, Patricio Noriega, Jeremy Paul, Glenn Panoho. Replacements: Toutai Kefu, Dan Crowley, Mark Connor.

REFEREE: Derek Bevan (Wales)

CROWD: 50,000

NEW ZEALAND 34, SOUTH AFRICA 18

AT LOFTUS VERSFELD, PRETORIA, 7 AUGUST

A CHANCE DEVELOPMENT in this Tri-nations encounter at Pretoria would have a major influence on the backline formation the All Blacks would use at the World Cup. Until Daryl Gibson exited the scene injured at Loftus Versfeld, Christian Cullen, who'd operated for three years at fullback, was firmly ensconced as a winger, a pretty effective one, who'd continued merrily on his way as a try scorer supreme. However, with Gibson's departure, the All Black backline was reshuffled, Cullen taking over at centre to allow Jonah Lomu to come off the reserves bench and operate on the wing.

Cullen on this occasion was an absolute dynamo at centre, scoring two tries that blew the Springboks out of the game. The selectors had been considering the centre option for him for some time, apparently, but critics felt he wasn't robust enough for the No 13 jersey, that he wouldn't pass and that his flair would be stultified. Well, none of those shortcomings was obvious at Pretoria. True, he didn't pass, but who needs to when you possess gazelle-like pace and the goalline beckons so tantalisingly! His tries came at the optimum moment in each half, when the All Blacks were leading 12–8 and 26–18.

The embattled Boks, under siege following their dismal showings at Dunedin and Brisbane, where they were bereft of tries, had been responding to the urgings of their newly installed captain Joost van der Westhuizen, rattling the All Blacks with ferocious forward play at the start of each half.

The All Blacks uncorked a nifty move where Justin Marshall doubled round behind Andrew Mehrtens and threw a long pass to Cullen. Had Alama Ieremia, the other midfielder, taken it, the bulkier Wellingtonian may have struggled to get past Robbie Fleck, a resolute defender. But Cullen opened up the turbo and Fleck saw only his shadow as he bolted away to the goalline. Again, in the second half, Cullen's exceptional acceleration left defenders grasping as they hung off expecting him to pass to Tana Umaga. Instead, he scythed through for another five-pointer.

While it was an improved showing by the Springboks — the teams scoring two tries apiece — they still finished 16 points in arrears, which represented

New Zealand's greatest winning margin on South African soil, and they'd been playing there for 71 years.

Van der Westhuizen made an impact in his first outing as captain and afterwards claimed his team had improved 'a hell of a lot'. But coach Nick Mallett couldn't believe his misfortune when André Snyman broke his ankle in scoring a try. He became the eighth top-flight midfielder to be seriously injured in 1999. Already on the casualty list were Pieter Muller, Franco Smith, Brendan Venter, Japie Mulder, Lourens Venter, Danie van Schalkwyk and Joe Gillingham.

No one was happier with the outcome at Pretoria than All Black captain Taine Randell, who finally got to make a test-winning speech overseas, his team having lost at Melbourne, Durban and Sydney in 1998. While Mehrtens kicked another seven penalty goals, to go with the nine he'd landed against the Wallabies, the goal that caught the imagination in Pretoria was Jeff Wilson's dropped goal, a beauty from 45 metres from a wayward clearing kick.

FOR NEW ZEALAND: 2 tries by Christian Cullen; dropped goal by Jeff Wilson; 7 penalty goals by Andrew Mehrtens.

FOR SOUTH AFRICA: Tries by André Snyman and Joost van der Westhuizen; conversion and 2 penalty goals by Gaffie du Toit.

NEW ZEALAND: Jeff Wilson, Tana Umaga, Alama Ieremia, Daryl Gibson, Christian Cullen, Andrew Mehrtens, Justin Marshall, Taine Randell (captain), Josh Kronfeld, Andrew Blowers, Norm Maxwell, Robin Brooke, Kees Meeuws, Anton Oliver, Greg Feek.
Replacements: Jonah Lomu, Royce Willis, Reuben Thorne, Mark Hammett, Craig Dowd.

SOUTH AFRICA: Percy Montgomery, Deon Kayser, André Snyman, Franco Smith, Pieter Rossouw, Gaffie du Toit, Joost van der Westhuizen (captain), Johan Erasmus, André Venter, Ruben Kruger, Albert van den Berg, Selborne Boome, Cobus Visagie, Naka Drotske, Os du Randt.
Replacements: Stefan Terblanche, Robbie Fleck, Mark Andrews, André Vos, Ollie le Roux, Chris Rossouw.

REFEREE: Ed Morrison (England)

CROWD: 51,000

SOUTH AFRICA 10,
AUSTRALIA 9

AT NEWLANDS, CAPE TOWN, 14 AUGUST

WHILE AUSTRALIAN RUGBY OFFICIALS were obviously interested in how their national team performed against the Springboks at Cape Town, knowing that a victory kept alive their prospects of winning the Tri-nations for the first time, of more immediate concern to them — because the biggest prize offering in 1999 was the World Cup — was whether John Eales and Stephen Larkham would come through an outing for the Australian Barbarians against Fiji at North Sydney Oval a few days later.

Both had undergone surgery earlier in the year, Eales for a seriously damaged shoulder, Larkham for torn medial knee ligaments. Both were crucial to Australia's World Cup bid. Both were in a race against time if they were to participate in the World Cup. Coach Rod Macqueen regarded Eales so highly that he kept him closely involved with the Wallabies throughout the year, Eales attending all the games in Australia and many of the training camps.

The thrashing by the All Blacks at Eden Park and this, albeit narrow, loss to the Springboks, highlighted just how much the Aussies needed Eales in the engine room and Larkham directing operations in the backline. As Peter FitzSimons wrote in the Eales biography, at Eden Park 'the line-out had gone to hell in a handcart, the scrum had imitated a squeaky shopping trolley on a bad day, rucking was non-existent and it looked for all the world as if the entire pack were getting bonus payments every time they wantonly turned the ball over or gave away kickable penalties'.

To the immense relief of Eales and Larkham, coach Macqueen and the entire Australian rugby fraternity, they came through their outing against Fiji unscathed. They wouldn't have pocketed man-of-the-match awards, but they were up and running again. No one was more relieved that Macqueen, who told them he would not risk them against the All Blacks in the remaining Tri-nations fixture but would effectively keep them on ice for the World Cup. Australia's subsequent success in the World Cup final at Cardiff on 6 November shows what an intelligent attitude this was.

The outcome of the Cape Town international meant more to Springbok

Springbok captain Francois Pienaar on the burst against the Wallabies in Sydney in 1996. Fotopress

Frank Bunce en route to the goalline against the Springboks at Ellis Park in 1997. Fotopress

Springbok winger Pieter Rossouw scores the match-clinching try against the All Blacks at Wellington in 1998 to the despair of Josh Kronfeld. Fotopress

Jonah Lomu's power evident against the Wallabies in Sydney in 1999. Fotopress

All Blacks Tom Willis and Justin Marshall unimpressed with the streaker at Sydney's Telstra Stadium in 2002. Fotopress

The New Zealand–South Africa match at Durban in 2002 was marred by Pieter van Zyl's attack on Irish referee David McHugh. Officials march him off after he's dislocated McHugh's shoulder. Fotopress

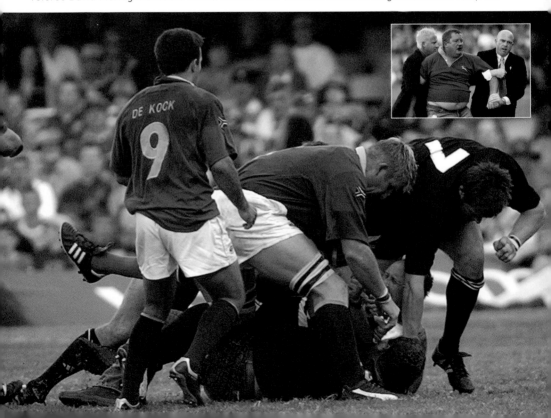

Doug Howlett is dumped by Werner Greeff at Durban in 2002. Fotopress

Above
Wallaby winger Lote Tuqiri gets his pass away under fire from Juan Smith at Brisbane in 2003. Fotopress

Opposite above
Wallabies centre Mat Rogers taken low by Richie McCaw in the 2003 Tri-nations decider at Eden Park.
Fotopress

Opposite below
IRB Player of the Year for 2004, Schalk Burger, tangles with Stephen Larkham at Durban. Fotopress

Springbok speedster Bryan Habana leaves Rocky Elsom sprawling as he heads for a try at Perth in 2005. Fotopress

coach Nick Mallett, because it ended a nightmarish losing sequence. 'I never doubted my own ability,' said Mallett. 'Public opinion was so pro-me last year. A coach gets far too much credit or too much blame.'

He said South Africa could now approach the World Cup knowing it could beat one of the top two teams in the world.

The win eased the pressure not only on Mallett but also on his fullback Percy Montgomery, who had had to endure heavy criticism from the public and media after an error-ridden performance against New Zealand. 'Percy was magnificent,' said Mallett. 'He made some mistakes, but he was under a lot of pressure. Let's take our hats off to him.'

The Wallabies had the opportunity to salvage victory with a late wide-angle penalty goal, but it wasn't a win they deserved. 'We were technically inept,' said coach Macqueen. 'The Springboks showed up deficiencies in our kicking game.'

FOR SOUTH AFRICA: Try by Robbie Fleck; conversion and penalty goal by Jannie de Beer.

FOR AUSTRALIA: 3 penalty goals by Matt Burke.

SOUTH AFRICA: Percy Montgomery, Deon Kayser, Robbie Fleck, Brendan Venter, Pieter Rossouw, Jannie de Beer, Joost van der Westhuizen (captain), Johan Erasmus, André Venter, André Vos, Albert van den Berg, Selborne Boome, Cobus Visagie, Naka Drotske, Os du Randt.
Replacements: Breyton Paulse, Ruben Kruger, Mark Andrews, Chris Rossouw, Ollie le Roux.

AUSTRALIA: Matt Burke, Ben Tune, Daniel Herbert, Nathan Grey, Joe Roff, Tim Horan, George Gregan, Toutai Kefu, David Wilson (captain), Matt Cockbain, David Giffin, Tom Bowman, Richard Harry, Phil Kearns, Andrew Blades.
Replacements: Jason Little, Tiaan Strauss, Mark Connors, Patricio Noriega.

REFEREE: Paul Honiss (New Zealand)

CROWD: 48,000

AUSTRALIA 28, NEW ZEALAND 7

AT STADIUM AUSTRALIA, SYDNEY, 28 AUGUST

YOU WOULD NEVER HAVE THOUGHT the All Blacks had lost five internationals in a row the previous year the way they marketed themselves in 1999. While a positive attitude is a commendable thing, and a hint of arrogance tolerable, the World Cup favourites seriously overplayed their hand in the shakedown to the year's big event in the UK and France. Three Tri-nations victories (against opponents missing key individuals and focusing more on the World Cup) plainly lulled the All Blacks into a false sense of security.

Prior to this Tri-nations finale in Sydney — which would be played before the biggest attendance ever at a rugby game — All Black coach John Hart declared his team would be targeting new flyhalf Rod Kafer, and Jeff Wilson was on radio describing how the backline was going to promote the expansive game. A couple of months later — and this was the NZRU's doing, not theirs — they brazenly flew into London in an Air New Zealand jumbo jet featuring giant images of front rowers Kees Meeuws, Carl Hoeft and Anton Oliver. Yes, siree, the All Blacks were all hyped up, and God help anyone who got in their way!

Well, Australians don't give a stuff about opponents who beat their own chests and market themselves as superior beings, as events at Stadium Australia (and subsequently at the Millennium Stadium in Cardiff) were to prove.

John Hart might have thought Kafer was a weak link, but Kafer thrived on the attention and was among the evening's standout performers. And while Wilson's intentions were commendable, every time the All Blacks moved the ball wide they were cut down by ferocious tackling. The Wallabies were unrecognisable from the team beaten 34–15 a month earlier and spent most of the evening going forward. The scrum that had buckled embarrassingly at Eden Park had been reinforced with an entirely new front row and now stood solid.

It was precisely the dress rehearsal for the World Cup the All Blacks didn't want. A win was preferable, a narrow defeat would have been a valuable stir-up; instead, the men in black were ruthlessly swept aside, being reduced to the ragtags of 1998.

Although the Wallabies managed only one try, their score built relentlessly through the deadly accurate goal kicking of Matt Burke, who landed seven penalty goals and the conversion to Mark Connors' try. The All Blacks trailed 22–7 at half-time and their prospects of a second-spell fightback diminished when a torrential downpour put puddles on the field and left the ball slippery.

Apart from the explosive qualities demonstrated again by Tana Umaga, operating on the wing, there was almost nothing the All Blacks could take out of this performance. But it was just the boost the Aussies needed a month out from the World Cup, especially knowing John Eales and Stephen Larkham were ready to rejoin the squad.

FOR AUSTRALIA: Try by Mark Connors; conversion and 7 penalty goals by Matt Burke.

FOR NEW ZEALAND: Try and conversion by Andrew Mehrtens.

AUSTRALIA: Matt Burke, Ben Tune, Daniel Herbert, Tim Horan, Jason Little, Rod Kafer, George Gregan, Toutai Kefu, David Wilson (captain), Matt Cockbain, David Giffin, Mark Connors, Richard Harry, Phil Kearns, Andrew Blades.
Replacements: Nathan Grey, Chris Whitaker, Owen Finegan, Tiaan Strauss, Joe Roff, Michael Foley, Patricio Noriega.

NEW ZEALAND: Jeff Wilson, Tana Umaga, Alama Ieremia, Daryl Gibson, Christian Cullen, Andrew Mehrtens, Justin Marshall, Taine Randell (captain), Josh Kronfeld, Dylan Mika, Robin Brooke, Norm Maxwell, Kees Meeuws, Anton Oliver, Carl Hoeft.
Replacements: Jonah Lomu, Tony Brown, Byron Kelleher, Craig Dowd, Royce Willis, Andrew Blowers.

REFEREE: Jim Fleming (Scotland)

CROWD: 107,042

THE STAR
JOSH KRONFELD

Fotopress

As a promising young Otago loose forward in 1995 Josh Kronfeld inherited a mighty mantle, that of replacing the great Michael Jones at No 7 for the All Blacks. 'I'd idolised Michael since I was a little kid,' confessed Kronfeld, 'and so it was quite an awesome undertaking.'

The Otago University student who hailed from Hawke's Bay had played rep rugby through the age-grades in his home province but had found it difficult to progress into representative Otago sides. That was until Otago coach Gordon Hunter watched him play club rugby one afternoon in 1992 and followed it up with a phone call, which marked the start of his Otago career that would lead on to the All Blacks.

Within a season of taking over from Jones, Kronfeld was establishing the same devoted following as his predecessor had, and, over the next five years, he became acknowledged as the finest openside flanker in the world. A fearsome tackler and scavenger for the ball and a certainty for the All Blacks when uninjured, Kronfeld, wearing always his trademark headgear, was a mighty runner and was as individual a character off the field as on.

His passion for rugby was matched only by that for surfing. He was by his own admission 'an unusual kind of bloke', typified by that jiggling of his head during the playing of the National Anthem before tests. It wasn't that he was unpatriotic, he explained to those critical of his actions. It was a ritual he'd formulated early in his career to allow him to focus on the game ahead.

Kronfeld was at his tearaway, try-scoring best on the hard surfaces of South Africa, both during the World Cup and in 1996, when his performances were also a decisive factor in New Zealand's series win over the Springboks. He experienced a crisis of confidence in 1997, due in part to differences of opinion with the All Black coach, John Hart, before storming back for the 1998 season when his outstanding form won him the coveted Kelvin Tremain Memorial Trophy as New Zealand's player of the year.

2000

PROFESSIONAL SPORT IS ALL ABOUT performing under pressure and because the Wallabies possessed individuals who remained ice cool in desperate situations, the Tri-nations Trophy went to Australia in 2000 for the first time. John Eales, the Wallabies' celebrated skipper, landed a challenging penalty goal in injury time to break New Zealand fans' hearts in Wellington, and Stirling Mortlock repeated the achievement against the Springboks in Durban, just when it seemed the All Blacks would claim another title. Those two heart-stopping victories, 24–23 and 19–18, confirmed Australia's status as the world's No 1 rugby nation. It meant they held the World Cup, the Bledisloe Cup and the Tri-nations Trophy.

While it was essentially a team effort, with Rod Macqueen the plotter and Eales the inspirational leader, the remarkable point-scoring achievements of Stirling Mortlock made the difference. He amassed a record 71 points (from four tries, six conversions and 13 penalty goals), although the solitary penalty

The Wallabies engulf John Eales after he'd won the game in Wellington.

Fotopress

kicked by Eales at Wellington, under the most intense pressure, is probably the goal that is most remembered from 2000.

The fifth Tri-nations championship produced a series of spectacular contests, none more so than the thriller between the All Blacks and Wallabies in Sydney, a game that was labelled the Match of the Century. The average attendance was an exceptional 63,600, substantially boosted by the two games at the new Olympic Stadium in Sydney, where a record 109,878 watched the opening contest, an unbelievable event in which the All Blacks led 24–nil after eight minutes, only to be pegged back to 24-all at half-time before winning 39–35. Little wonder the players received a standing ovation at half-time and fulltime.

Fresh from their triumph at the fourth World Cup, the Wallabies were eager to confirm their status as the premier team in the world, and they did, which is more than the Springboks managed in the year after the 1995 World Cup.

While the coaches who'd had charge at the 1999 World Cup prepared the Wallabies and the Springboks, the All Blacks were under new management, Wayne Smith and Tony Gilbert having supplanted John Hart. They kicked their campaign off wonderfully well in Sydney but cruelly had victory snatched from them in Wellington and after staging a dazzling comeback in Johannesburg, hitting the lead 40–39 after trailing 13–33, they succumbed to a late Springbok try. Surprisingly, that was South Africa's only win in the series, which put huge pressure back on to coach Nick Mallett, who would not see out the year.

Mortlock wasn't the only individual to rack up the points in 2000. Andrew Mehrtens collected 59 points for the All Blacks and Braam van Straaten 49 for the Springboks. The standout try scorer was Christian Cullen, the All Black fullback, who dotted down seven times in four the four tests, another Tri-nations record.

2000 FINAL STANDINGS

	P	W	L	D	For	Against	Point
Australia	4	3	1	–	104	86	14
New Zealand	4	2	2	–	127	117	11
South Africa	4	1	3	–	82	110	6

Tries: New Zealand 13, Australia 10, South Africa 6; Total 29.

Penalty goals: Australia 14, South Africa 13, New Zealand 12; Total 39.

THE STAR
JOHN EALES

Fotopress

Stone the crows, mate. You mean, he not only captains the team from lock, controls the line-outs and runs like a loose forward, he kicks the bleedin' goals as well? He's got to be Captain Fantastic. Which pretty much sums up John Eales, who led his Wallaby team to World Cup glory in 1999 and to dual Tri-nations championship successes in 2000 and 2001.

New Zealanders don't spare a lot of sympathy for Australians, but they came to admire Big John, even though he broke their hearts at Westpac Stadium, Wellington, in 2000 when he landed a challenging, wide-angled penalty goal in injury time to snatch away a test match the All Blacks appeared to have in safe keeping. Eales, an unlikely goal kicker at 2.01 metres, was delighted his team had been awarded this match-saving penalty at the death . . . until hooker Jeremy Paul pointed out that the team's goal kicker, Stirling Mortlock, had left the field with cramp. 'You're up, John,' he said. Eales had played himself to a standstill for 80 minutes without the worries of goal kicking. Now he was expected to handle the most important kick of the game. Of course, it went between the uprights. What else would you expect of Captain Fantastic?

By 2000, Eales strode the rugby scene like a colossus, having captained Australia to its World Cup win at the Millennium Stadium in Cardiff. It was his second taste of World Cup glory, having participated, as a 21-year-old rookie — precociously early for an international lock — in the success of the Nick Farr-Jones led side at Twickenham in 1991. His contribution to Australian rugby throughout the nineties and on to 2001, when he finally retired, was incomparable. For such a huge man he displayed an astonishing athleticism.

He was Mr Nice Guy, universally liked and respected, innately competitive but always courteous. He played the most matches as Australian captain, became the most capped Wallaby lock and was unrivalled in the world as a point-scoring forward.

THE GAMES
NEW ZEALAND 39,
AUSTRALIA 35

AT STADIUM AUSTRALIA, SYDNEY, 15 JULY

ALL BLACK CAPTAIN TODD BLACKADDER summed it up perfectly: 'I couldn't believe what was going on around me. After seven or eight minutes, we hadn't had a scrum or a line-out, I certainly hadn't touched the ball . . . and we were twenty-one points in front!'

In what would become known as the Match of the Century, the Wallabies incredibly pulled back a 24-point deficit to level at 24-all by half-time and go ahead in the second half, only to have victory stolen from them by that man Jonah Lomu, so often the Wallabies' *bête noire*, in the frantic final minutes. What a way for Wayne Smith and Tony Gilbert to launch their All Black coaching careers against their major southern hemisphere rivals . . . a game never to be forgotten.

Seldom has a test match opened in such explosive fashion. Three All Black tries in eight minutes should have ended Australian resistance before the players had their second wind. But the home side were not world champions for nothing and fought back with that indomitable Wallaby spirit. Little wonder the world-record crowd at one of international rugby's newest venues gave standing ovations at both half- and full-time.

Under the stars in fine conditions, there was a surreal atmosphere from the first whistle as some of the All Blacks' complex but stunningly effective back moves paid dividends. Pita Alatini, one of the visitors' best, had his finest hour in the black jersey and he was central to two of the opening salvoes, scoring one himself. The new star of Australian rugby, right wing Stirling Mortlock (fresh from a 29-point haul against the Springboks), grabbed one back for a home side that regrouped swiftly.

Those with a sense of history may have recalled the 1985 Ranfurly Shield clash between Canterbury and Auckland, which many billed 'the provincial match of the century'. Then, Auckland raced to a 24–nil lead before withstanding a marvellous fightback from the proud holders.

Here it was scarcely believable, but John Eales galvanised his troops so well

Tana Umaga try-bound
in the frenetic opening
moments at Sydney.
Fotopress

the scores were locked at 24-all after 40 minutes. Then when Jeremy Paul (New Zealand-born, in a touch of irony) crashed over in the 74th minute to put his team ahead 35–34, it seemed the Wallabies would steal a miraculous victory. But there was Jonah, latching onto a fine, lobbed pass from Taine Randell to brush off a defender and tip toe in for the try.

FOR NEW ZEALAND: Tries by Tana Umaga, Christian Cullen, Pita Alatini, Justin Marshall and Jonah Lomu; 4 conversions and 2 penalty goals by Andrew Mehrtens.

FOR AUSTRALIA: Tries by Stirling Mortlock 2, Chris Latham, Joe Roff and Jeremy Paul; 2 conversions and 2 penalty goals by Mortlock.

NEW ZEALAND: Christian Cullen, Tana Umaga, Alama Ieremia, Pita Alatini, Jonah Lomu, Andrew Mehrtens, Justin Marshall, Ron Cribb, Scott Robertson, Taine Randell, Norm Maxwell, Todd Blackadder (captain), Kees Meeuws, Anton Oliver, Carl Hoeft. Replacements: Josh Kronfeld, Troy Flavell, Tony Brown, Byron Kelleher, Mark Hammett, Craig Dowd.

AUSTRALIA: Chris Latham, Stirling Mortlock, Daniel Herbert, Jason Little, Joe Roff, Stephen Larkham, George Gregan, Jim Williams, David Wilson, Mark Connors, John Eales (captain), David Giffin, Richard Harry, Michael Foley, Fletcher Dyson. Replacements: Jeremy Paul, Toutai Kefu, Rod Kafer, Glenn Panoho, Andrew Walker, Troy Jaques.

REFEREE: André Watson (South Africa)

CROWD: 109,878

NEW ZEALAND 25,
SOUTH AFRICA 12

AT JADE STADIUM, CHRISTCHURCH, 22 JULY

AT THE AGE OF 24, the Christian Cullen of 2000 was at his peak. Incredibly, the Rolls-Royce of fullbacks would score at least one try in every test during the season. And there were seven of them. Compare that with Don Clarke, who scored two tries in 31 tests, and Fergie McCormick, no tries in 16 tests.

Cullen was the difference in this otherwise knock-'em-down-drag-'em-out All Blacks versus Springboks arm wrestle, his two tries being the only five-pointers of the torrid encounter. The first came when he latched on to an Andrew Mehrtens kick which took a wicked bounce for Springbok fullback Percy Montgomery. Not long afterwards, Mehrtens gave an accurate cut-out pass to put Cullen down the left flank and in for a record eighth try against the Springboks. That completed the try-scoring action after just 14 minutes! The fans, who had anticipated a repeat of the tryfest in Sydney, were to be disappointed.

Cullen had to be resilient to survive a pile-driving tackle from Corne Krige, similar to the one from Brian Lima that had rattled Cullen's ribcage on his test debut against Western Samoa four years earlier.

The Springboks entered this test under siege. A home defeat of Canada preceded a squared series against England and a conclusive loss to the Wallabies under the Colonial Stadium roof in Melbourne. Coach Nick Mallett was no longer enjoying the widespread support of 1998. *Au contraire*, he was now fighting to hold his position while attempting to drag South African back play into the new millennium with an expansive style. Negating this, Braam van Straaten, though reliable with the boot, was never going to spark his outsides in the manner of the All Blacks. It seemed a lifetime ago that the Springboks had beaten the All Blacks into third place at the 1999 World Cup, after which the All Black coach John Hart had tendered his resignation. Mallett knew there was very little between these two sides in Christchurch: 'It was a very tight test match and turned on the two scoring opportunities that New Zealand took through Christian Cullen. We had four opportunities ourselves, but didn't take them. Taking those little opportunities makes all the difference.'

The Jade Stadium crowd may have hoped for more pyrotechnics, but the reality was this was always going to be a far more physical, gnarly clash. Most tests between these two nations are battles of attrition. The afternoon air and brisk breeze may have given a hint of open rugby, but the All Blacks were content to grind the win. That is why they reintroduced Troy Flavell at lock (for Norm Maxwell) and openside flanker Josh Kronfeld (for Scott Robertson). The whole pack marked up, while Mehrtens and Cullen provided the X-factor in the backs, and rookie centre Mark Robinson earned a pass mark in his first big international. The Springboks were combative, but lost five line-out throws, for which hooker Charl Marais copped most of the criticism. Flighty Percy Montgomery also came under the spotlight for a fumbling display.

FOR NEW ZEALAND: Tries by Christian Cullen 2; 3 penalty goals and a dropped goal by Andrew Mehrtens; penalty goal by Tony Brown.

FOR SOUTH AFRICA: 3 penalty goals by Braam van Straaten; dropped goal by Percy Montgomery.

NEW ZEALAND: Christian Cullen, Tana Umaga, Mark Robinson, Pita Alatini, Jonah Lomu, Andrew Mehrtens, Justin Marshall, Ron Cribb, Josh Kronfeld, Taine Randell, Troy Flavell, Todd Blackadder (captain), Kees Meeuws, Anton Oliver, Carl Hoeft.
Replacements: Leon MacDonald, Norm Maxwell, Craig Dowd, Mark Hammett, Tony Brown, Scott Robertson.

SOUTH AFRICA: Percy Montgomery, Breyton Paulse, Robbie Fleck, De Wet Barry, Thinus Delport, Braam van Straaten, Werner Swanepoel, André Vos (captain), Corne Krige, Rassie Erasmus, Albert van den Berg, André Venter, Robbie Kempson, Charl Marais, Cobus Visagie.
Replacements: Warren Brosnihan, John Smit, Willie Meyer, Jannes Labuschagne, Grant Esterhuizen.

REFEREE: Chris White (England)

CROWD: 49,000

AUSTRALIA 26, SOUTH AFRICA 6

AT STADIUM AUSTRALIA, SYDNEY, 29 JULY

STIRLING MORTLOCK'S STOCKS continued to rise after this test. The 23-year-old, an unlikely looking character, had already stung the Springboks with a 29-point haul in Melbourne only weeks earlier. Here, before another massive crowd, Mortlock showed his mettle with 21 points, which included a try and six goals from six attempts. He had stepped into the injured Matt Burke's goal-kicking boots and done the job. It was a far cry from a wayward Super 12 final night at Canberra Stadium when his costly misses contrasted strongly with the sharp shooting of Andrew Mehrtens. By the end of this test he had racked up an impressive 92 points from his five caps.

Australia's league fraternity looked on in envy as their rugby counterparts prospered in the wake of the Wallabies' epic World Cup win. Huge crowds highlighted the game's growing popularity, and league types saw real attraction in the 15-man code. It would not be long before the haemorrhaging of rugby players to league would cease. The then Auckland Warriors chief executive, Trevor McKewen, warned on Australian television that New Zealand's Super 12 franchises were well placed to attract league juniors.

Rebounding from the narrow loss to the All Blacks, the Wallabies staked their claim for the Tri-nations title with a professional display, led by the old firm of George Gregan and Stephen Larkham, and some powerful work off the bench by loose forward Toutai Kefu. The occasion was an emotional send-off for veterans Richard Harry and David Wilson, both of whom were making their farewell appearances on Australian soil.

Captain John Eales used his extreme height and bounce to deflect another penalty goal attempt, this time by Braam van Straaten (the first time he pulled the stunt was off a Carlos Spencer kick in a Super 12 game at Ballymore).

The Springboks persevered with their open rugby, but missing Percy Montgomery they had even fewer resources to throw at the Wallabies. The test try drought extended to 208 minutes. Coach Nick Mallett had to cop his side's fourth loss in a row: 'Things will be hot for me when I return home. I'm sure there will be a lot of questions asked, but that is part of the job.'

Rod Macqueen urged caution, but must have privately beamed at the Wallabies' water-tight defence and clinical finishing. 'We worked very hard in defence,' he said 'but we will have to be a lot better next weekend, particularly out wide where Jonah Lomu threatens.' Mortlock was no Lomu, but he was still proving a match winner in his nascent test career.

FOR AUSTRALIA: Tries by Stirling Mortlock and Jeremy Paul; 2 conversions and 4 penalty goals by Stirling Mortlock.

FOR SOUTH AFRICA: 2 penalty goals by Braam van Straaten.

AUSTRALIA: Chris Latham, Stirling Mortlock, Daniel Herbert, Jason Little, Joe Roff, Stephen Larkham, George Gregan, Jim Williams, David Wilson, Mark Connors, John Eales (captain), David Giffin, Fletcher Dyson, Michael Foley, Richard Harry.
Replacements: Rod Kafer, Ben Tune, Toutai Kefu, Matt Cockbain, Glenn Panoho, Jeremy Paul.

SOUTH AFRICA: Thinus Delport, Breyton Paulse, Robbie Fleck, De Wet Barry, Pieter Rossouw, Braam van Straaten, Werner Swanepoel, André Vos (captain), André Venter, Corne Krige, Mark Andrews, Albert van den Berg, Cobus Visagie, Charl Marais, Robbie Kempson.
Replacements: Percy Montgomery, Joost van der Westhuizen, Warren Brosnihan, Ollie le Roux, John Smit.

REFEREE: Ed Morrison (England)

CROWD: 77,048

AUSTRALIA 24, NEW ZEALAND 23

AT WESTPAC TRUST STADIUM, WELLINGTON, 5 AUGUST

NEW ZEALAND'S ADMIRATION FOR John Eales took another huge lift after the world's best lock stepped up and coolly slotted a white-hot pressure goal to again deny the All Blacks the increasingly elusive Bledisloe Cup. In one of the last regular daytime test matches in New Zealand, the All Blacks, not for the first or last time, had victory wrenched from their grasp at the death by those darned Wallabies. This after concocting two marvellous tries, finished off in expert style by Christian Cullen, who equalled Jeff Wilson's test record of 39.

When referee Jonathan Kaplan awarded the fateful 80th-minute penalty, Eales was confident Stirling Mortlock, who'd been kicking like a champion, would be up to the challenge. All that changed when hooker Jeremy Paul approached his captain and said, 'Stirling's off. You're up, John.' Sure enough, Mortlock had exited the game a few minutes earlier with bad cramp and was marooned on the sideline.

That put a different complexion on things. It meant Eales, who'd played himself to a near standstill, had to assume responsibility for the pressure kick of all pressure kicks. As he lined up the kick, he went through the kicking mantra he had developed over the years, the one taught him by, of all people, Grant Fox: 'Head down, slow, follow through to the posts . . .'

The ball went clean over the black dot, to the exultation of Australian rugby fans in both countries. The test was won, the Bledisloe Cup secured. As he would recount in his biography: 'Outside of winning a World Cup, it just didn't get any better than this.'

The Wallabies, mindful of their sluggish start in Sydney, had broken first with a try to that man Stirling Mortlock, skidding under the posts off a Daniel Herbert break. When winger Joe Roff crossed out wide, the visitors led 12–0 and New Zealand's hold on the Tri-nations Trophy looked tenuous at best. However, All Black No 8, Ron Cribb, in shades of his superb chip and regather to split open the Super 12 final only weeks earlier, put in a deft grubber kick that Cullen latched onto to pull one back for the hosts. All Blacks coach Wayne Smith took special satisfaction from Cullen's next score, which featured some fine passing and a Lomu decoy to hold the defence. Umaga broke through and the flying Cullen did the rest.

'It's one of those moves we practised all week,' said Smith. 'When it comes off textbook in game like that, it's real pleasing.'

In training, Cullen said to Mehrtens, 'We're going to score off this move, and I'll probably end up passing you the ball.' But Umaga ended up making the break and 'gave the try to me. It's one of the best moves we've put together all year.'

At 23–21, the game was New Zealand's to lose. Veteran prop Craig Dowd, who had subbed Carl Hoeft, made the critical error in injury time. He was crestfallen. Sadly, referee Kaplan was heckled by boorish sections of the crowd and even had to avoid a projectile as he left the pitch. Norm Maxwell tried to shield him. The Bledisloe Cup was still in Australian hands, but the Tri-nations was still a possibility for the disheartened All Blacks.

FOR AUSTRALIA: Tries by Stirling Mortlock and Joe Roff; conversion and 3 penalty goals by Mortlock, penalty goal by John Eales.

FOR NEW ZEALAND: Tries by Christian Cullen 2; 2 conversions and 3 penalty goals by Andrew Mehrtens.

AUSTRALIA: Chris Latham, Stirling Mortlock, Daniel Herbert, Jason Little, Joe Roff, Stephen Larkham, George Gregan, Jim Williams, David Wilson, Toutai Kefu, John Eales (captain), David Giffin, Richard Harry, Michael Foley, Fletcher Dyson.
Replacements: Jeremy Paul, Ben Tune, Matt Connors.

NEW ZEALAND: Christian Cullen, Tana Umaga, Alama Ieremia, Pita Alatini, Jonah Lomu, Andrew Mehrtens, Justin Marshall, Ron Cribb, Josh Kronfeld, Taine Randell, Norm Maxwell, Todd Blackadder (captain), Kees Meeuws, Anton Oliver, Carl Hoeft.
Replacements: Reuben Thorne, Tony Brown, Byron Kelleher, Craig Dowd, Mark Hammett.

REFEREE: Jonathan Kaplan (South Africa)

CROWD: 36,500

SOUTH AFRICA 46, NEW ZEALAND 40

AT ELLIS PARK, JOHANNESBURG, 19 AUGUST

NO VENUE SEEMS TO PSYCHE OUT the All Blacks more than Ellis Park. Although they'd been successful there twice in the nineties, the ground had proved a graveyard for the teams of 1949, 1960, 1970, 1976, 1995 and 1996. And again in 2000, although the Springboks were winless in the Tri-nations going into this contest against the competition front runners, they had Fortress Ellis Park on their side. And it counted, as the Springboks, laden with Cats players who had reached the Super 12 semifinals under Laurie Mains, raced away to a 33–13 advantage before half-time.

Springbok centre Grant Esterhuizen afterwards reckoned Ellis Park was worth 10 points to the Springboks. 'I think it's a psychological thing as much as anything,' he said. 'Our opponents are always wary of the place, while it seems to bring out the best in our players. It doesn't matter whether it's the Lions, the Cats or the Springboks, playing at Ellis Park is a huge advantage.'

Pre-match talk surrounded the need for the All Blacks to not only win but to secure a bonus point. Well, they appeared to be leaving the defensive side of the game for another day in their pursuit of tries. Gaping holes opened as loose forwards André Vos and Johan Erasmus helped bash a path for new talents such as Tinus Delport and Robbie Fleck. Such was the severity of the Springbok assault, as they galloped to a 33–13 lead in 33 minutes, that the humiliating prospect of conceding a half-century of points confronted the All Blacks.

Just when it appeared the record books would be rewritten, the All Blacks awoke from their slumber and tries by Christian Cullen and Tana Umaga before half-time meant Tri-nations fans were in for another thriller. The All Blacks came back so resolutely in the second spell that they hit the front at 40–39 with 15 minutes to play, before halfback Werner Swanepoel, enjoying his best game in Springbok colours, grabbed his second try.

Although there were several near misses in the final moments, the Springboks held on for a thrilling victory, much to the relief of Bok coach Nick Mallett, who was battling to keep his job. Names such as André Markgraaf, Harry Viljoen and even Francois Pienaar were being bandied about as possible replacements should South Africa finish winless in the Tri-nations.

Christian Cullen's two tries gave him seven for the series, an amazing strike rate, but he would willingly have traded a five-pointer or two for an All Black victory. As it was, the defeat meant the outcome of the Tri-nations was now out of their hands. They'd opened the gate for the Wallabies.

FOR SOUTH AFRICA: Tries by Robbie Fleck 2, Werner Swanepoel 2, Tinus Delport and Chester Williams; 5 conversions and 2 penalty goals by Braam van Straaten.

FOR NEW ZEALAND: Tries by Christian Cullen 2 and Tana Umaga 2; 4 conversions, 3 penalty goals and a dropped goal by Andrew Mehrtens.

SOUTH AFRICA: Tinus Delport, Breyton Paulse, Grant Esterhuizen, Robbie Fleck, Chester Williams, Braam van Straaten, Werner Swanepoel, André Vos (captain), Corne Krige, Johan Erasmus, Mark Andrews, André Venter, Piet Visagie, Charl Marais, Ollie le Roux.
Replacements: John Smit, Albert van den Berg, Warren Brosnihan, Willie Meyer, Jaco van der Westhuyzen.

NEW ZEALAND: Christian Cullen, Tana Umaga, Alama Ieremia, Pita Alatini, Jonah Lomu, Andrew Mehrtens, Justin Marshall, Ron Cribb, Josh Kronfeld, Taine Randell, Norm Maxwell, Todd Blackadder (captain), Kees Meeuws, Anton Oliver, Carl Hoeft.
Replacements: Troy Flavell, Greg Somerville, Mark Hammett, Leon MacDonald, Scott Robertson.

REFEREE: Andrew Cole (Australia)

CROWD: 57,250

AUSTRALIA 19, SOUTH AFRICA 18

AT ABSA STADIUM, DURBAN, 26 AUGUST

WHEN THE WALLABIES WERE AWARDED their fateful last-second penalty in Wellington, goal kicker Stirling Mortlock was on the sideline being treated for cramp and skipper John Eales had to do the business. On this occasion, when New Zealand referee Paul Honiss antagonised an entire nation by penalising the Springboks at the last ruck, Mortlock was ready, willing and able. He went straight up to his captain and said, 'Ealsy, it's my kick.'

Mortlock admitted later he had a good feeling about the kick, that was as wide-angled and challenging as Eales' had been in Wellington. 'All I was saying to myself was, "You've got to get this, you've got to get this."'

And he did, to the delight of his team-mates, who were becoming accustomed to their side snatching dramatic last-minute victories. The goal hoisted Australia from 16–18 to 19–18 and secured for them, for the first time, the Tri-nations Trophy. Had Mortlock's kick missed, New Zealand would have retained the trophy.

Another turbulent week in South African rugby preceded this decider, with allegations of phone tapping by former South African rugby boss Louis Luyt. Coach Nick Mallett desperately needed another (home) victory to secure his position, but it wasn't to be; his team, fresh from the try-fest against the All Blacks, failing to secure a five-pointer, managing just six penalty goals by Braam van Straaten.

Macqueen dearly wanted a victory as a fitting farewell to three of his great achievers, Jason Little, David Wilson and Richard Harry, who were either retiring or heading to the UK. The Wallabies had played smart, resourceful rugby since winning the World Cup and Macqueen had moulded a squad that knew how to win in tight situations.

Fullback Chris Latham scored the game's only try in a rare Australian foray into Springbok territory in the first half. Mark Andrews was the dominating individual in the line-outs and the Springbok pack as a whole was thoroughly efficient, but the backs were again disappointing in their option taking, leaving it to van Straaten's goal kicking to keep them in the game.

Daniel Herbert finds progress difficult in the decider at Durban. Fotopress

The Wallabies proved the old adage about a good team being one that can win when not playing especially well.

'It was not the way we would have liked to have won,' said Macqueen. 'We turned over a lot of ball, which is uncharacteristic of this side, but South Africa's defence was excellent. They'd obviously done their homework on us.'

FOR AUSTRALIA: Try by Chris Latham; conversion and 4 penalty goals by Stirling Mortlock.

FOR SOUTH AFRICA: 6 penalty goals by Braam van Straaten.

AUSTRALIA: Chris Latham, Stirling Mortlock, Daniel Herbert, Jason Little, Joe Roff, Stephen Larkham, George Gregan, Jim Williams, David Wilson, Mark Connors, John Eales (captain), David Giffin, Fletcher Dyson, Michael Foley, Richard Harry.
Replacements: Ben Tune, Matt Cockbain, Toutai Kefu, Jeremy Paul, Glen Panoho, Rod Kafer.

SOUTH AFRICA: Tinus Delport, Chester Williams, Grant Esterhuizen, Robbie Fleck, Breyton Paulse, Braam van Straaten, Werner Swanepoel, André Vos (captain), Corne Krige, Johan Erasmus, Mark Andrews, André Venter, Cobus Visagie, Charl Marais, Robbie Kempson.
Replacements: Warren Brosnihan, Albert van den Berg, John Smit, Ollie le Roux.

REFEREE: Paul Honiss (New Zealand)

CROWD: 52,000

2001

IT'S GOT TO BE A VINTAGE Tri-nations championship when the title is decided by a try in the final minute of the final contest. That's how it was in 2001, with Toutai Kefu's epic plunge for the goalline, in front of almost 91,000 fans in Sydney, providing the perfect send-off for Australia's already legendary captain, John Eales. Kefu's try was to have massive consequences. Immediately, it meant the Australian Rugby Union's trophy cabinet boasted a full set of silverware, with the Tri-nations Trophy taking its place alongside the World Cup and the Bledisloe Cup. The outcome was the perfect result for Australia's new coach Eddie Jones, who'd taken over the national team after Rod Macqueen had a little surprisingly announced his retirement following the thrilling series victory over the British and Irish Lions.

If life was suddenly a bunch of roses for Eddie Jones, across the Tasman it was all doom and gloom for All Black coaches Wayne Smith and Tony Gilbert. The previous winter they'd suffered the agony of watching Eales land an injury-time penalty goal at Wellington to deny them the Bledisloe Cup and, subsequently, the Tri-nations Trophy; now Kefu had plunged the nation's legion of rugby followers into despair once again. Line-out malfunctions contributed significantly to both defeats.

The Sydney result left Smith so stunned he was unable to supply convincing answers when questioned back home about whether he wanted to remain head coach of the All Blacks. As a consequence, the NZRU decided to advertise the coach's position. Smith was welcome to apply, and did, but he'd effectively shot himself in the foot. John Mitchell was appointed and took the team to the UK two months later.

Coaches were in the news all round. Harry Viljoen had taken over the Springboks from Nick Mallett late in 2000, with the 2001 Tri-nations becoming his first major challenge. After a damp squib opening against the All Blacks in Cape Town, Viljoen's team scored a handsome victory over the Wallabies in Pretoria and then drew with them in Perth.

It was a weird competition in many ways. As champions, the Wallabies couldn't beat the Springboks, home or away. The All Blacks comfortably

John Eales all smiles after his Wallaby team retained the Tri-nations Trophy, just. Fotopress

disposed of the Springboks twice, but couldn't get past the Wallabies in Dunedin (which is really saying something, for Australia had been unsuccessful on its 11 previous visits there!). And so it all came down to the Sydney classic which, to the absolute delight of their fans, the Wallabies won.

Sadly, penalty goals outnumbered tries 43 to 13 in the 2001 series; indeed, not since 1997 had tries been more plentiful than penalty goals. The Springboks found tries hard to come by, managing just two to go alongside the 14 penalty goals kicked by Braam van Straaten.

2001 FINAL STANDINGS

	P	W	L	D	For	Againts	Points
Australia	4	2	1	1	81	75	11
New Zealand	4	2	2	–	79	70	9
South Africa	4	1	2	1	52	67	6

Tries: New Zealand 6, Australia 5, South Africa 2; Total 13.

Penalty goals: Australia 16, South Africa 14, New Zealand 13; Total 43.

THE GAMES

NEW ZEALAND 12, SOUTH AFRICA 3

AT NEWLANDS, CAPE TOWN, 21 JULY

As was often the case prior to the Tri-nations, the Springbok build-up was racked by infighting and dubious form. The calls for coach Harry Viljoen's head were growing after a bad loss and a win over France before Italy was cast aside. In a bold move, Viljoen installed No 8 Bobby Skinstad as skipper.

The All Blacks, also under a new captain, Anton Oliver, were rather more accurate, first dealing to Samoa and Argentina and then subduing France. But these tests were played against the backdrop of a compelling Wallabies–Lions series, in which the northern tourists were squeezed out 2–1.

The new positional move of playing Tana Umaga at centre was starting to show promise as the All Blacks went to Cape Town in search of another away win to kick off the competition. In slippery conditions, which did not aid the visitors' intentions to spread good ball to their dangerous wingers, Doug Howlett and Jonah Lomu, the two old foes contested their first non-try test match since the infamous World Cup final of 1995. All the scoring took place in the first half, as Tony Brown slotted four penalty goals from four attempts. The Otago pivot was a model of efficiency with the boot and potency on the tackle. His goal-kicking counterpart Percy Montgomery was a polar opposite, missing a handful of gettable kicks to allow the All Blacks to retain the initiative.

Marshalled brilliantly by the resourceful Taine Randell at No 7, the All Black pack committed to the breakdown, though they were beaten at set-piece time. That determined defensive attitude rubbed off on some of the backs. Lomu, not always noted for his defensive qualities, made two bone-shuddering tackles on hapless Springbok attackers. One on lock Mark Andrews, just off the All Black line, was especially memorable, for it saved a certain five points.

Springbok debutant Marius Joubert, who would become a thorn in All Black sides in future years, was outpointed by his opposite Umaga, but in truth there were precious few opportunities for the outsides to shine, with the ball resembling the proverbial cake of soap.

Tony Brown's kick
is charged down
by Joost van der
Westhuizen at
Cape Town.
Fotopress

All Black skipper Oliver was his usual pragmatic self after an encounter in which his side's character may have been the most pleasing aspect: 'We've won one game. Let's not kiss ourselves good night. It has brought us a bit of time and we can go home on the long flight with sweet dreams.'

Notwithstanding the home defeat, the Springboks were upbeat, having absorbed important lessons, the most obvious of which was that you should never go into a test of this magnitude without a specialist goal kicker.

FOR NEW ZEALAND: **4 penalty goals by Tony Brown.**

FOR SOUTH AFRICA: **Penalty goal by Percy Montgomery.**

NEW ZEALAND: **Jeff Wilson, Doug Howlett, Tana Umaga, Pita Alatini, Jonah Lomu, Tony Brown, Justin Marshall, Ron Cribb, Taine Randell, Reuben Thorne, Troy Flavell, Norm Maxwell, Greg Somerville, Anton Oliver (captain), Carl Hoeft.**
Replacements: Leon MacDonald, Chris Jack, Marty Holah.

SOUTH AFRICA: **Percy Montgomery, Breyton Paulse, Marius Joubert, Robbie Fleck, Dean Hall, Butch James, Joost van der Westhuizen, Bobby Skinstad (captain), André Venter, André Vos, Mark Andrews, Victor Matfield, Cobus Visagie, Lukas van Biljon, Robbie Kempson.**
Replacements: Deon Kayser, Johan Ackerman, Ollie le Roux, John Smit, Joe van Niekerk.

REFEREE: **Scott Young (Australia)**

CROWD: **50,000**

SOUTH AFRICA 20, AUSTRALIA 15

AT LOFTUS VERSFELD, PRETORIA, 28 JULY

NEWLY APPOINTED AUSTRALIAN COACH Eddie Jones made an inauspicious entry into the Tri-nations scene, his team crashing to defeat against a revitalised Springbok team on the high veldt at Pretoria. The Wallabies, as defending champions, were coming off a thrilling series victory over the British and Irish Lions, and went to Pretoria chock-full of confidence although missing their gifted flyhalf Stephen Larkham, who was injured.

Well, Jones' men suffered more than just the pain of defeat at the Loftus fortress. They lost lock David Giffin for three weeks, the first Tri-nations player to be suspended by an independent citing commissioner. Giffin was outed for striking the head of Springbok centre Robbie Fleck. Wallaby coach Eddie Jones was disappointed, but knew it would give a chance to 27-year-old newcomer Justin Harrison in the matches ahead.

A desperate Springbok side knew another loss would effectively end their Tri-nations hopes. Up stepped No 8 and skipper Bobby Skinstad, who blew the match open with a superbly taken solo try on the stroke of half-time. Skinstad had so often failed to deliver on his undoubted potential, but on this occasion he produced a true captain's performance.

There was again turmoil in South African rugby leading up to this match, with former Springbok coach Nick Mallett accused of spying for France, a charge he strongly denied. Debate swirled over the merits of second-five Braam van Straaten's inclusion. His general play stifled the Bok backline, but his metronomic goal kicking was crucial in the wash-up.

Although the Wallabies were the pre-match favourites, it was the Springbok pack, with only one change following the loss at Newlands (Johan Ackerman in for Victor Matfield), that lifted its game, exerting pressure on the Wallaby scrum and line-out. The Wallabies were architects of their own demise, taking poor options and missing the guiding hand and boot of Larkham. Even more galling was seeing the expertise of one of their own — former Kangaroo league rep Les Kiss — work against them. Kiss, who'd earlier assisted the 2005

Waratahs, was used by Harry Viljoen as their defence coach. Kiss soon had the Springboks running smoothly in the defence area.

Adding to the visitors' woes were some perceived ambiguities from Irish referee David McHugh. Wallaby hooker Michael Foley was especially outspoken: 'You've got a referee penalising you for what he calls a swinging strike, something I've never heard of or encountered in any rugby rule book. Certainly, I've never been pinged for a swinging strike in 24 years of playing rugby, so there's obviously going to be questions asked.'

For South Africa, who had not beaten the world champions in five tests since 1999, the Pretoria result provided a massive boost to their self-belief.

FOR SOUTH AFRICA: **Try by Bobby Skinstad; 5 penalty goals by Braam van Straaten.**

FOR AUSTRALIA: **4 penalty goals by Matt Burke, penalty goal by Manny Edmonds.**

SOUTH AFRICA: **Conrad Jantjes, Breyton Paulse, Robbie Fleck, Braam van Straaten, Dean Hall, Butch James, Joost van der Westhuizen, Bobby Skinstad (captain), André Venter, André Vos, Mark Andrews, Johan Ackerman, Cobus Visagie, Lukas van Biljon, Robbie Kempson.**
Replacements: **Corne Krige, Ollie le Roux, John Smit, Joe van Niekerk.**

AUSTRALIA: **Matt Burke, Andrew Walker, Daniel Herbert, Nathan Grey, Joe Roff, Elton Flatley, George Gregan, Toutai Kefu, George Smith, Owen Finegan, John Eales (captain), David Giffin, Rod Moore, Michael Foley, Nick Stiles.**
Replacements: **Matt Cockbain, Ben Darwin, Manny Edmonds, David Lyons, Chris Latham.**

REFEREE: **David McHugh (Ireland)**

CROWD: **37,500**

AUSTRALIA 23, NEW ZEALAND 15

AT CARISBROOK, DUNEDIN, 11 AUGUST

EVERYTHING POINTED TO an All Black victory at the House of Pain. The Wallabies were licking their wounds after their Pretoria nightmare, the All Blacks were refreshed after a rare three weeks off, and Mehrtens and Lomu were both raising their half centuries of test appearances. Oh yes, and the Wallabies had never won in 11 test visits to Carisbrook.

It was a brilliantly sunny mid-winter Saturday afternoon in the south as the scarfies and like-minded rugby folk crammed expectantly into the 'brook. Such was the influx of visitors, some had to fly in on the day from Christchurch or further north as there weren't enough beds to accommodate them in Dunedin. But the pubs and retail outlets weren't complaining: the test weekend was estimated to have added $17 million to the city's economy!

The Wallabies seemed more focused from the get-go. Perhaps it was the poor rendition of 'Advance Australia Fair', but after conceding a try to Lomu (his 31st) off a deft Tana Umaga grubber in the first minute, the Wallabies seized the initiative, and never relinquished it. George Smith was all over the tackled ball area like a rash, and the All Blacks were filled with lassitude and were inaccurate. In the 16th minute, Wallaby fullback Matt Burke scored a staggering third long-range solo try against the All Blacks (to rank with those of Brisbane in 1996 and Melbourne in 1998). But it was not until the 62nd minute that the Wallabies pulled clear with a Joe Roff penalty try, the first ever conceded by the All Blacks in a test.

The All Blacks rallied late, with the admirable Lomu creating Jeff Wilson's last test try with seven minutes to play. Captain Anton Oliver turned down the opportunity to shoot for a penalty goal and a bonus point. It was a naïve piece of captaincy, if understandable given how the hooker plays the game.

Again the refereeing of the tackled ball situation was an issue. Andrew Mehrtens, who entered the fray late, put in his two cents' worth. 'I'm not going to suggest anything,' he said, 'but if players are allowed to keep their hands on the ball when they are getting up then you have to think that the administrators of the game must look at the rules.'

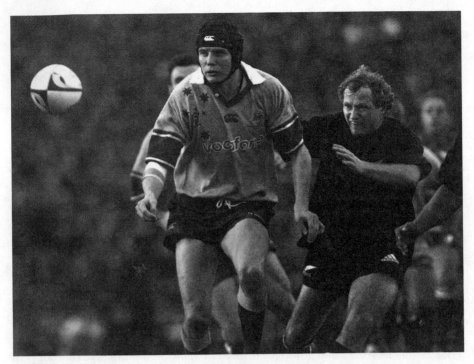

Stephen Larkham passes at Carisbrook under pressure from Tony Brown. Fotopress

FOR AUSTRALIA: Tries by Matt Burke and Joe Roff (penalty try); 2 conversions and 3 penalty goals by Burke.

FOR NEW ZEALAND: Tries by Jonah Lomu and Jeff Wilson; conversion by Andrew Mehrtens; penalty goal by Tony Brown.

AUSTRALIA: Matt Burke, Andrew Walker, Daniel Herbert, Nathan Grey, Joe Roff, Stephen Larkham, George Gregan, Toutai Kefu, George Smith, Owen Finegan, Justin Harrison, John Eales (captain), Rod Moore, Michael Foley, Nick Stiles.
Replacements: Ben Darwin, Matt Cockbain, Phil Waugh, Chris Latham, Elton Flatley.

NEW ZEALAND: Jeff Wilson, Doug Howlett, Tana Umaga, Pita Alatini, Jonah Lomu, Tony Brown, Justin Marshall, Ron Cribb, Taine Randell, Reuben Thorne, Troy Flavell, Norm Maxwell, Greg Somerville, Anton Oliver (captain), Carl Hoeft.
Replacements: Mark Cooksley, Carl Hayman, Leon MacDonald, Byron Kelleher, Andrew Mehrtens, Marty Holah.

REFEREE: Steve Lander (England)

CROWD: 37,500

AUSTRALIA 14, SOUTH AFRICA 14

AT SUBIACO OVAL, PERTH, 18 AUGUST

This stalemate in Australia's Wild West left the Tri-nations race wide open. It meant Australia and South Africa were three and two points, respectively, ahead of New Zealand, who had a game in hand. Australia had dropped winger Andrew Walker for this international after he had left the squad without permission in what may have been an alcohol-related issue. It was not the last time Walker's professionalism would come under the spotlight in a brilliant, but often fractured, career in both rugby and league. Meanwhile, the Springboks were preoccupied with a spy drama, after a pundit apparently filmed one of their trainings.

Perth is an ideal location for a Wallaby–Springbok international, with its large population of ex-pat South Africans. The visitors responded to that support with another staunch defensive effort in their 100th test since readmission to international rugby in 1992. New Zealand referee Steve Walsh was not able to allow a free-flowing affair, blowing 35 penalties, two to one against the Boks.

South Africa's cause was not helped by the loss of centre and vice-captain Robbie Fleck and the sinbinnings of flyhalf Butch James and captain Bobby Skinstad, which meant they played out 60 minutes of the game with 14 men. The physical James was binned for 'repeated tackling infringements', but coach Harry Viljoen claimed his pivot was unfairly targeted by referee Walsh.

Mark Andrews' record 12th test try just prior to the break came about through a superb counterattack by the Boks. André Venter and Conrad Jantjes handled before the veteran lock crashed over for an 8–3 advantage at half-time.

The Wallabies could not answer until the 72nd minute when second-five Nathan Grey muscled over, the first try South Africa had conceded in 232 minutes of Tri-nations action in 2001. The normally reliable Matt Burke missed a relatively straightforward conversion attempt, and both he and Braam van Straaten traded penalties before Walsh blew fulltime.

The Springboks had good reason to feel more satisfied given their penalty count and loss of personnel. But Viljoen was not in a charitable mood after the match, contending his side was robbed. Skinstad also gave officials a spray for their perceived focus on James' tackling.

Eddie Jones, still seeking his first Tri-nations win, conceded South Africa was the better team, but felt the messy tackled ball area gave rise to a clash that resembled a 'dockyard brawl'. 'All in all, though, we didn't play well,' said Jones. 'Our skills let us down. The Boks attacked us well in the scrums and line-outs and defended very well. I will not take that away from them.'

FOR AUSTRALIA: Try by Nathan Grey; 3 penalty goals by Matt Burke.

FOR SOUTH AFRICA: Try by Mark Andrews; 3 penalty goals by Braam van Straaten.

AUSTRALIA: Matt Burke, Chris Latham, Daniel Herbert, Nathan Grey, Joe Roff, Stephen Larkham, George Gregan, Toutai Kefu, George Smith, Owen Finegan, John Eales (captain), Justin Harrison, Rod Moore, Michael Foley, Nick Stiles.
Replacements: Phil Waugh, Ben Darwin, Matt Cockbain, Graeme Bond.

SOUTH AFRICA: Conrad Jantjes, Breyton Paulse, Robbie Fleck, Braam van Straaten, Dean Hall, Butch James, Joost van der Westhuizen, Bobby Skinstad (captain), André Venter, André Vos, Mark Andrews, Victor Matfield, Cobus Visagie, Lukas van Biljon, Robbie Kempson.
Replacements: Deon Kayser, Ollie le Roux, Albert van den Berg, John Smit.

REFEREE: Steve Walsh (New Zealand)

CROWD: 42,650

NEW ZEALAND 26, SOUTH AFRICA 15

AT EDEN PARK, AUCKLAND, 25 AUGUST

EDEN PARK IS SO OFTEN the catalyst for character-filled All Black displays. And this was another one. Lambasted for a fortnight by their home press in the wake of the pain at Carisbrook, the All Blacks seized this encounter by the scruff, two tyros earning their spurs in slippery, challenging conditions on a wet Auckland night. Byron Kelleher, in his 15th cap at halfback (the bulk of which had been as a substitute), had never played better in the black jersey, while Chris Jack gave a commanding performance in his first test start at lock.

It was later revealed that the Springboks had drama aplenty in the days leading up to the test, with coach Harry Viljoen claiming that star backs Joost van der Westhuizen and Conrad Jantjes were food poisoned, though unlike the days before the 1995 World Cup final (in which the All Blacks suffered) there was no suggestion of skullduggery. Viljoen did not use it as an excuse for his team's lack of cutting edge. His magnanimity extended to the comment that the penalty try awarded when Lukas van Biljon took down Leon MacDonald was fair.

Kelleher combined well with the veteran Andrew Mehrtens to control All Black field position, but the foundation, as ever, was laid by a vigorous pack display. Mehrtens' unerring boot and pinpoint passes had the Springboks on the back pedal for most of the match, and outside him Pita Alatini thrived. The second-five scored after only eight minutes, receiving a fine in-pass after a Kelleher snipe. The All Blacks led 13–9 at the break and surged on, with MacDonald's penalty try effectively ending the Boks' resistance. All the visitors could come up with were penalty goals from Braam van Straaten.

The 22-year-old Chris Jack may have felt he was entering the lions' den when he fronted Mark Andrews and Victor Matfield, but he responded with calmness and accuracy under real pressure. It mirrored the debut of another young lock — Gary Whetton against the same foe 20 years earlier on an afternoon when flour bombs rained down on to Eden Park. Captain Oliver was mightily impressed, but he wasn't going to prematurely wax lyrical on Jack. 'He just got swept up in the focus the forward pack had,' he said. 'In many ways, it was really easy for him, because he just had to do his own job and that was made pretty succinct — it was just cleaning out at ruck time, making tackles and controlling the air. They're the three things a lock must do, and he did them well.'

Coach Wayne Smith knew his side had not clinically seized all their opportunities, but he was more than satisfied with the style and commitment. The Springboks had again held up the Tri-nations ladder. The All Blacks knew the title was in their grasp. All they needed to do was lower the Wallabies in Sydney. Pretty straightforward, really!

FOR NEW ZEALAND: Tries by Pita Alatini and Leon MacDonald (penalty try); 2 conversions and 4 penalty goals by Andrew Mehrtens.

FOR SOUTH AFRICA: 5 penalty goals by Braam van Straaten.

NEW ZEALAND: Leon MacDonald, Jeff Wilson, Tana Umaga, Pita Alatini, Jonah Lomu, Andrew Mehrtens, Byron Kelleher, Ron Cribb, Taine Randell, Troy Flavell, Chris Jack, Norm Maxwell, Greg Somerville, Anton Oliver (captain), Carl Hoeft.
Replacements: Mark Cooksley, Marty Holah, Carl Hayman.

SOUTH AFRICA: Conrad Jantjes, Breyton Paulse, André Snyman, Braam van Straaten, Dean Hall, Butch James, Joost van der Westhuizen, Bobby Skinstad (captain), André Venter, André Vos, Mark Andrews, Victor Matfield, Cobus Visagie, Lukas van Biljon, Robbie Kempson.
Replacements: Joe van Niekerk, John Smit, Ollie le Roux, Albert van den Berg, Deon Kayser.

REFEREE: Peter Marshall (Australia)

CROWD: 45,000

AUSTRALIA 29,
NEW ZEALAND 26

AT STADIUM AUSTRALIA, SYDNEY, 1 SEPTEMBER

WHAT STARTED OUT AS A WEEK so full of promise for All Black coach Wayne Smith and his assistant Tony Gilbert was to end in such disappointment that they would never prepare the national team again. Conversely, John Eales, making his 82nd and final appearance for the Wallabies, bowed out of international rugby on a perfect note. A wonderful servant of the game, at the start of the season Eales had won every honour the game offered except for a Super 12 title. He never did achieve that, but, thanks to Toutai Kefu's dramatic 80th-minute try at Stadium Australia, he could retire utterly content.

Eales told Kefu afterwards that Kefu would not have to buy him a drink again as long as he drew breath. 'Usually,' said Eales, 'you brood over a loss for a week, or perhaps through a whole summer, but I had my whole life to think about this one if we'd lost!'

There's something about Stadium Australia that brings out the best in trans-Tasman rugby contests. Twelve months earlier the All Blacks and Wallabies had played out the match of the century, with the Aussies hitting back from 0–24 to level at 24-all before losing 35–39. Now here was another epic. Initially, it seemed the Wallabies were going to romp away to victory as they constructed a 19–6 half-time lead, the sinbinning of Norm Maxwell (for retaliation following a Michael Foley punch) and the erratic line-out throwing of Anton Oliver contributing substantially to this state of affairs. But the All Blacks were unrecognisable after the interval. With the penetrative Pita Alatini in explosive form, they took charge, establishing a 26–22 advantage well into the final quarter. The stage was set for Bledisloe redemption after four years of All Black heartache and heartbreak.

All week the talk had been of John Eales and how marvellous and appropriate it would be for him to bow out on a triumphant note. Now Eales was calling on his players' resolve during the desperate final stages of the game. While Eales was heroic in those final clinches, his rival Oliver endured excruciating agony, losing all confidence in his ability to throw to the line-out, an unbelievable nine Oliver throws being pilfered by Eales and co.

The line-out disasters notwithstanding, the All Blacks hung on by their fingernails as the clock ticked towards full time. Inside the two-minute mark, with fatigue setting in, they opted to find touch from an indirect penalty, rather than seek to retain possession. It provided Eales' men with the opportunity they needed, and from a perfectly executed line-out and drive the powerful Kefu launched himself into a desperate surge at the goalline that the All Blacks were unable to contain.

The All Blacks were crestfallen, none more so than coach Smith, who eventually lost his job after publicly expressing doubt over whether he still wanted the head coach's role. He admitted that the Australians were superior at reacting well under pressure. Eales was ecstatic, of course, as was every Wallaby fan in the house. 'We kept our heads and kept the pressure on,' he said. 'With that bit of good fortune at the end, we got away with it.'

FOR AUSTRALIA: Tries by Chris Latham and Toutai Kefu; conversions by Matt Burke and Elton Flatley; 4 penalty goals by Burke; penalty goal by Andrew Walker.

FOR NEW ZEALAND: Tries by Doug Howlett and Pita Alatini; 2 conversions and 4 penalty goals by Andrew Mehrtens.

AUSTRALIA: Matt Burke, Chris Latham, Daniel Herbert, Nathan Grey, Joe Roff, Stephen Larkham, George Gregan, Toutai Kefu, George Smith, Owen Finegan, David Giffin, John Eales (captain), Rod Moore, Michael Foley, Nick Stiles.
Replacements: Phil Waugh, Ben Darwin, Andrew Walker, Matt Cockbain, Elton Flatley.

NEW ZEALAND: Leon MacDonald, Doug Howlett, Tana Umaga, Pita Alatini, Jonah Lomu, Andrew Mehrtens, Byron Kelleher, Ron Cribb, Taine Randell, Troy Flavell, Chris Jack, Norm Maxwell, Greg Somerville, Anton Oliver (captain), Carl Hoeft.
Replacements: Marty Holah, Christian Cullen, Justin Marshall, Carl Hayman.

REFEREE: Tappe Henning (South Africa)

CROWD: 90, 978

THE STAR
GEORGE GREGAN

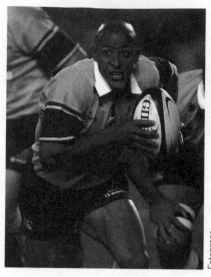

Fotopress

The year was 1994, the occasion the one-off Bledisloe Cup contest at the Sydney Football Stadium. The All Blacks were trailing 16–20 and their star winger Jeff Wilson was launching himself into a dive for the goalline that would make it game, set and match for Laurie Mains' team. Then from nowhere, it seemed, Wilson was struck amidships by Australia's aggressive 21-year-old scrumhalf, George Gregan, who generated such power in the tackle that the ball was knocked from Wilson's grasp. The Wallabies, unbelievably, held on to win the game.

Who was this George Gregan? The question rang around the rugby world. Out flew the CVs. He'd been born in Zambia and migrated to Australia with his parents when he was one, was educated at St Edmund's College in Canberra, had broken into rugby with ACT (who in those days were the Kookaburras, not the Brumbies), been a member of the Australian sevens team that lost narrowly to New Zealand in the final of the Hong Kong tournament, and made his test debut earlier in 1994 against Italy at Ballymore.

Gregan had burst on to the international scene, famous not just for that monster tackle on Wilson, but also for his explosive and aggressive presence around the field. From that occasion on he would become an integral member of the Wallaby team and, before long, be dubbed the world's leading scrumhalf.

Gregan was no respecter of size. He weighed only 80 kg, but that proved no deterrent when lowering much larger opponents with his trademark tackles.

He formed a lethal partnership with Stephen Larkham for both the Brumbies and the Wallabies; indeed, rugby has known few more effective combinations. When they were operating together alarm bells consistently rang among opposition defences. They were a potent factor in Australia's World Cup win of 1999, the dual Tri-nations successes of 2000 and 2001, and the Brumbies' breakthrough Super 12 victory in 2001.

When John Eales, Australia's great leader, announced his retirement in September 2001, Gregan was his natural successor.

2002

THE SECRET TO ACHIEVING Tri-nations glory is to win away from home. That the All Blacks were the only team to achieve that in 2002 meant they managed to prise the trophy away from the Wallabies in another closely contested competition. The Wallabies had come out on top in 2000 by winning at Wellington and Durban and they'd succeeded again in 2001 by virtue of an unexpected victory at Carisbrook. This time, it was the turn of the All Blacks to defy jetlag (and humidity) to put away the Springboks at Durban.

The occasion proved too much for ardent Springbok supporter Pieter van Zyl, however. He perceived that a disproportionate share of referee David McHugh's rulings were going against his beloved countrymen. So he decided to vent his anger on the said referee. Despite the presence of more than 400 security guards, van Zyl managed to make his way out into the middle of ABSA Stadium where, to the astonishment of the players, he attacked McHugh, dislocating the referee's shoulder. His actions were reprehensible, but to the dismay of sportsmen worldwide, several writers and commentators attempted to justify his private crusade, promoting the argument that 'referees like McHugh deserve everything they get'. Yeah, right! Fortunately, van Zyl got what he deserved: a lifetime ban from all rugby matches in South Africa.

New Zealand referee Paddy O'Brien, who had watched the Durban shenanigans with horror from a hotel in Johannesburg, was given a personal guard for the next week, until he flew back home. Although he tempted fate by issuing a red card to a Springbok in the final Tri-nations encounter, he was forgiven when the Boks came through to score a sensational last-minute victory over the Wallabies. Had the Wallabies won at Ellis Park and taken a bonus point, they would have completed a hat trick of Tri-nations victories, albeit on differential. They neither won nor scored four tries, leaving the All Blacks secure atop the championship ladder.

The 2002 matches were played in vastly contrasting conditions. For the opening game in Christchurch, between New Zealand and Australia, a bitingly cold southerly blew in straight from Antarctica, while for the final two games at Durban and Johannesburg, temperatures were in the high 20s.

Mark Hammett hugs Daryl Gibson after the All Blacks edged out the Springboks in Durban.
Fotopress

Unusually, the bottom team, South Africa, scored the most tries, 13, three more than New Zealand and four better than Australia. However, the South Africans conceded 16, 10 more than New Zealand.

Among the individual point scorers, Andrew Mehrtens, with 47, headed off his old mate Matt Burke, with 40. They were well clear of Werner Greeff, 20. Wallaby fullback Chris Latham was the leading try scorer with three, ahead of a bunch of players who managed two each.

2002 FINAL STANDINGS

	P	W	L	D	For	Against	Points
New Zealand	4	3	1	–	97	65	15
Australia	4	2	2	–	91	86	11
South Africa	4	–	4	–	103	140	2

Tries: South Africa 13, New Zealand 10, Australia 9; Total 32.

Penalty goals: New Zealand 12, Australia 11, South Africa 4; Total 27.

THE STAR
TANA UMAGA

Fotopress

New Zealand rugby should be eternally grateful to Tana Umaga's mother Tauesa and brother Mike for luring him away from league and encouraging him to play the game at which he has become a national icon. Until 1992, the focus for Tana Jonathan Falefasa Umaga was league. It was a game he was damned good at. He represented the Junior Kiwis two years in a row. But at the beginning of 1993, Umaga suddenly decided he wanted to play rugby. His mother had been openly hostile towards league and whenever he sustained an injury she would say, 'That's what you get, playing that stupid game.'

Finally, he listened to her, and also he had a desire to play alongside older brother Mike, who was making his mark with Wellington and Western Samoa. It was Mike who took him along to the Petone club, where he introduced him to senior coach Frank Walker. Initially, Walker was taken aback. 'He looked like something the cat had dragged in,' he said. 'He was wearing ear muffs and scruffy jeans and seemed totally unenthusiastic about playing rugby.'

Admitting that it took 'a wee while to sort Tana the person out', Walker says that the moment he first received the ball in senior club play, it was apparent he was something special. 'He brought his tackling skills from league and every time he got the ball he achieved something.'

Within a year he was playing for the New Zealand Colts (he and Jonah Lomu being equal top try scorers on the tour of Australia) and Wellington. And when rugby became professional in 1996, Umaga starred for the Hurricanes in the very first Super 12 game.

With Lomu struck down with a kidney disease in 1997, Umaga took his place on the wing, making his test debut against Fiji at Albany, launching an international career that has reached stellar heights. He was New Zealand's Player of the Year in 2000, after which he relocated himself at centre and has since operated equally effectively at second-five.

THE GAMES
NEW ZEALAND 12,
AUSTRALIA 6

AT JADE STADIUM, CHRISTCHURCH, 13 JULY

THIS CLASH, IN FILTHY CONDITIONS and arctic temperatures, reignited the growing debate on the wisdom of night tests in the middle of New Zealand's winter. It was the first tryless encounter between these traditional rivals since the Eden Park test of 1991, also blighted by a wet ball and surface.

Both nations entered this competition on the back of thorough preparation, the All Blacks having disposed of Italy and Fiji comfortably (though at some cost, with a bad injury to Leon MacDonald) and Ireland, not without some angst. The Wallabies had fought off stern and stirring challenges from New Zealand Maori and France.

Much of the talk surrounding the All Blacks squad was the plethora of Crusaders in the starting fifteen, 12 for this match, but there were 14 for the Ireland test at Carisbrook. Such a massive representation was deemed worthy due to the Crusaders' amazing 13 victories on the bounce as they annexed another Super 12 crown. Certainly, the All Blacks put on a defensive display reminiscent of that champion outfit. Their forwards, led by the tireless loose trio of Scott Robertson, Richie McCaw and Reuben Thorne, muscled up and denied Australia any opportunity to expand their game or exert pressure. Andrew Mehrtens, who also kicked the goals that mattered, drove the Wallabies deep back into their half, though careful to keep the ball in play and allow the visitors to make errors or force line-outs. The tactics worked a treat, if not making for a dynamic spectacle.

The Wallabies did in fact have the wood on the All Blacks in the line-outs, helped by some expert pilfering by Justin Harrison and some wayward throwing by Mark Hammett. No fewer than six throws were lost by the All Blacks.

Referee Jonathan Kaplan was again under the Bledisloe Cup spotlight when he sinbinned centre Mark Robinson for holding back Wallaby No 12 Dan Herbert. Kaplan did not take the drastic step of awarding a penalty try (although many Australia supporters argued he should have), but the 14-man All Blacks had to show composure and character for the final eight minutes.

While the Wallabies used five substitutions, All Black coach John Mitchell decided against going to his bench, which was probably smart because they all looked frozen solid on the sideline. Conditions wouldn't have been much worse if they'd been playing at McMurdo Sound!

Mitchell was full of praise for his team's tackling and determination. 'The effort was huge and our defensive line was a bit like a rock tonight,' he said, along with a parting shot at the timing of the match kickoff. 'Considering the quality of players in both teams, and their ambitions to play attacking football, I question playing test rugby in the evening, especially in New Zealand at this time of year. I'm sure people come out of Super 12 with high expectation for ball movement and you don't get it mid-winter here.'

FOR NEW ZEALAND: **4 penalty goals by Andrew Mehrtens.**

FOR AUSTRALIA: **2 penalty goals by Matt Burke.**

NEW ZEALAND: **Christian Cullen, Doug Howlett, Mark Robinson, Aaron Mauger, Caleb Ralph, Andrew Mehrtens, Justin Marshall, Scott Robertson, Richie McCaw, Reuben Thorne (captain), Simon Maling, Chris Jack, Greg Somerville, Mark Hammett, Dave Hewett.**

AUSTRALIA: **Chris Latham, Stirling Mortlock, Matt Burke, Dan Herbert, Ben Tune, Stephen Larkham, George Gregan (captain), Toutai Kefu, George Smith, Owen Finegan, Justin Harrison, Nathan Sharpe, Patricio Noriega, Jeremy Paul, Bill Young.**
Replacements: Mat Rogers, Matt Cockbain, David Lyons, Elton Flatley, Ben Darwin.

REFEREE: **Jonathan Kaplan (South Africa)**

CROWD: **36,500**

NEW ZEALAND 41, SOUTH AFRICA 20

AT WESTPAC TRUST STADIUM, WELLINGTON, 20 JULY

LEADING UP TO THE 2002 Tri-nations competition there was talk of South Africa pulling out and switching its allegiance to the northern hemisphere's Six Nations event. Those thoughts may have solidified after the Springboks were on the receiving end of a sterling All Black display at the capital's Cake Tin.

John Mitchell kept faith with the fifteen who had responded for him in diabolical conditions at Jade Stadium the week before, and the dry conditions were more conducive to his desired expansive style. It was Scott Robertson who delivered the command performance from No 8, cleaning out rucks, hurting the Springboks with some powerful tackling and having a hand in three of the All Blacks' five tries, while also scoring one himself.

Hooker Mark Hammett's try, where Robertson fed him from a line-out move, was highly dubious as the ball did not travel the requisite 5 metres and the hooker's foot was plainly over the touchline. This try broke a 13-all deadlock, after the Springboks had started with serious intent. They threw everything at the All Blacks in the opening 20 minutes, stinging the home side through a fine solo try to impressive fullback Werner Greeff, who stepped past three hapless All Black defenders. While Greeff was the pick of the Boks, there were valuable contributions by tearaway openside flanker Joe van Niekerk and halfback Bolla Conradie, and the potential of rookie flyhalf André Pretorius was evident.

The All Blacks slowly took control, leading 21–13 at half-time and giving voice to the capacity, mostly blacked-out, crowd. They scored some excellent second-half tries as Mitchell finally called up some reinforcements, among them Jonah Lomu and Tana Umaga. Typically for this traditional rugby rivalry, it was a willing battle, with several skirmishes. Springbok centre Marius Joubert was sinbinned for punching Umaga.

Other than the ebullient Robertson, All Blacks to impress were Justin Marshall and his old sparring partner Andrew Mehrtens, who scored 16 points, and the outside backs Christian Cullen and Doug Howlett. Prop Greg Somerville led a sound pack effort. Sam Broomhall entered the fray for his test debut.

Referee Stuart
Dickinson shows
Marius Joubert
the yellow card
at Wellington.

Fotopress

Springbok coach Rudolf Straeuli was far from despondent: 'I thought it came down to a couple of marginal decisions,' he said, 'but we can take plenty from this game. We had a lot of possession and we carried the ball well, but we let in two soft tries.'

At the end of the game the All Blacks sat atop the Tri-nations table with an eight-point advantage over the Wallabies, who had a game in hand.

FOR NEW ZEALAND: Tries by Doug Howlett, Mark Hammett, Reuben Thorne, Justin Marshall and Scott Robertson; 2 conversions, 3 penalty goals and a dropped goal by Andrew Mehrtens.

FOR SOUTH AFRICA: Tries by Werner Greeff and Marius Joubert; 2 conversions and a penalty goal by André Pretorius; dropped goal by Greeff.

NEW ZEALAND: Christian Cullen, Doug Howlett, Mark Robinson, Aaron Mauger, Caleb Ralph, Andrew Mehrtens, Justin Marshall, Scott Robertson, Richie McCaw, Reuben Thorne (captain), Simon Maling, Chris Jack, Greg Somerville, Mark Hammett, Dave Hewett.
Replacements: Tana Umaga, Tom Willis, Jonah Lomu, Royce Willis, Sam Broomhall, Byron Kelleher, Joe McDonnell.

SOUTH AFRICA: Werner Greeff, Stefan Terblanche, Marius Joubert, De Wet Barry, Dean Hall, André Pretorius, Bolla Conradie, Bobby Skinstad, Joe van Niekerk, Corne Krige (captain), Jannes Labuschagne, Victor Matfield, Willie Meyer, James Dalton, Lawrence Sephaka.
Replacements: Ollie le Roux, Adrian Jacobs, Faan Rautenbach, A J Venter, Neil de Kock.

REFEREE: Stuart Dickinson (Australia)

CROWD: 37,700

AUSTRALIA 38, SOUTH AFRICA 27

AT THE 'GABBA, BRISBANE, 27 JULY

THE 'GABBA HAS SEEN SOME of Australia's greatest triumphs — mostly from men in white sporting baggy green caps — but the Wallabies had never won in five internationals at the home of Queensland cricket. You could have been forgiven for thinking a cricket score was on the cards when the Wallabies sprinted out of the blocks for a 24–3 lead before the half-hour mark, putting on a display of skilful, direct attacking football. But then an all-in brawl seemed to stimulate the Springboks, who lifted their game, not before English referee Steve Lander had shown yellow cards to Wallabies Jeremy Paul and Justin Harrison and Bok fullback Werner Greeff. Some of the Wallabies may have taken exception to pre-match comments by Rudolf Straeuli that the Australians were soft.

Greeff's illegal tackle on his opposite, Chris Latham, was perhaps the catalyst for the mêlée. The spiteful antics did not end there. South African flanker Corne Krige suffered damage to his cornea after a punch from Wallaby winger Ben Tune. Krige left the field late in the first half with blood streaming from his face.

Krige's side profited from the extra man to post 10 points. Centre Marius Joubert scored the first of a well-merited double when he stood up Latham. The Boks then nailed two breakout tries, the first to Bobby Skinstad off some nice De Wet Barry work. Brent Russell showed his startling pace with a 60-metre burst for the second.

George Gregan's late gamble to go for the bonus point in spurning a penalty shot at goal paid off when Latham scored his second to deny the visitors that same extra point. The Springboks had no real cause for complaint, given they were on the end of a 22–10 penalty count.

Outstanding for the Wallabies were Latham, flanker George Smith and lock Nathan Sharpe, while Joubert and Skinstad were strong for the Boks.

The Tri-nations had sparked into try-scoring life after a lean 2001 and a penalty-goal dominated opener in Christchurch. Fifteen tries at the halfway mark were in stark contrast to the 13 five-pointers for the whole of the 2001 competition.

Tune, who scored one of the Australian tries, was back in the news off the field. The IRB wanted the Australian Rugby Union (ARU) to provide a chronology of events surrounding the prescription of a banned substance (probenecid) to Tune the previous year as part of treatment for an infected knee. The winger was due to front a disciplinary tribunal in August to decide his fate after the ARU was originally accused of a cover-up.

FOR AUSTRALIA: Tries by Chris Latham 2, Ben Tune and Stirling Mortlock; 3 conversions and 3 penalty goals by Matt Burke, penalty goal by Mortlock.

FOR SOUTH AFRICA: Tries by Marius Joubert 2, Bobby Skinstad and Brent Russell; 2 conversions and a penalty goal by André Pretorius.

AUSTRALIA: Chris Latham, Stirling Mortlock, Matt Burke, Dan Herbert, Ben Tune, Stephen Larkham, George Gregan (captain), Toutai Kefu, George Smith, Owen Finegan, Nathan Sharpe, Justin Harrison, Patricio Noriega, Jeremy Paul, Bill Young.
Replacements: Brendan Cannon, David Lyons, Mat Rogers, Matt Cockbain, Ben Darwin, Elton Flatley.

SOUTH AFRICA: Werner Greeff, Breyton Paulse, Marius Joubert, De Wet Barry, Stefan Terblanche, André Pretorius, Bolla Conradie, Bobby Skinstad, Joe van Niekerk, Corne Krige (captain), Jannes Labuschagne, Victor Matfield, Lawrence Sephaka, James Dalton, Willie Meyer.
Replacements: Hendro Scholtz, Ollie le Roux, Delarey du Preez, Brent Russell, Adrian Jacobs.

REFEREE: Steve Lander (England)

CROWD: 37,250

AUSTRALIA 16, NEW ZEALAND 14

AT TELSTRA STADIUM, SYDNEY, 3 AUGUST

IT WAS A SCENARIO all too agonisingly familiar to New Zealand rugby fans. With time running out and the Bledisloe Cup within their grasp, the All Blacks again came crashing down in flames against the Wallabies. In 2000, John Eales had ruined the All Black party, coolly slotting a challenging penalty goal after the final siren in Wellington, and in 2001 Toutai Kefu had penetrated the All Black defences to land the matchwinning try a minute from time in Sydney.

It surely couldn't happen again, New Zealand fans were telling themselves, as they saw a handy 14–8 advantage trimmed to 14–13 well inside the final quarter. Matt Burke had missed the opportunity to give his team the lead by striking the uprights with his conversion of Mat Rogers' late try. But, next thing, he was lining up a penalty goal with only a couple of minutes remaining.

'Knock it over and you're the hero, miss it and you're the villain,' Burke, ever the professional, said to himself as he was lining up the kick. Although a massive point scorer for the Wallabies, Burke had been known to miss kicks from close range, but rarely when crucial encounters like this hung on it. 'It was a case of head down, follow through and hopefully guide the ball between the uprights.'

Which was precisely what Burke managed, to the dismay, yet again, of the All Blacks, who'd been hoping to make it a blue-riband weekend for New Zealand rugby following the New Zealand sevens team's success at the Kuala Lumpur Commonwealth Games.

The Wallabies, convinced they would triumph given decent playing conditions, bounded out to an early advantage when Nathan Sharpe scored, but the All Blacks stayed within striking range and hit the front early in the second half when Richie McCaw stole a wayward Jeremy Paul line-out throw to score his first test try. An Andrew Mehrtens penalty goal in the 57th minute had the visitors ahead by 14 points to 8.

However, the Wallabies gathered momentum as the game wore on. Rogers botched a try but made amends just three minutes later. Burke missing the conversion meant the 80,000 fans packed into Telstra Stadium were on the edge of their seats for the remainder of the game, until Burke produced his moment of heroism.

All Black coaches John Mitchell and Robbie Deans were making no excuses after the match, nor were they commenting on referee André Watson's decision to award Australia a critical penalty at the death, against Leon MacDonald for handling in a ruck. 'Everyone will learn a lot about themselves today,' said Mitchell. 'It's a hiccup in our journey ['journey' being a favourite word of his at the time] but we're still in the competition and we can still win.'

Wallaby coach Eddie Jones paid tribute to his players who, he said, once again demonstrated coolness under pressure. They had launched wave after wave of multi-phase raids at the opposition until finally the All Blacks had cracked.

It was the third successive thriller New Zealand and Australia had fought out at what was now called Telstra Stadium. The first had gone to the All Blacks, the other two to the Wallabies.

FOR AUSTRALIA: Tries by Nathan Sharpe and Mat Rogers; 2 penalty goals by Matt Burke.

FOR NEW ZEALAND: Try by Richie McCaw; 3 penalty goals by Andrew Mehrtens.

AUSTRALIA: Chris Latham, Stirling Mortlock, Matt Burke, Dan Herbert, Ben Tune, Stephen Larkham, George Gregan (captain), Toutai Kefu, George Smith, Owen Finegan, Justin Harrison, Nathan Sharpe, Patricio Noriega, Jeremy Paul, Bill Young.
Replacements: Elton Flatley, David Lyons, Mat Rogers, Matt Cockbain, Ben Darwin.

NEW ZEALAND: Christian Cullen, Doug Howlett, Tana Umaga, Aaron Mauger, Caleb Ralph, Andrew Mehrtens, Justin Marshall, Scott Robertson, Richie McCaw, Reuben Thorne (captain), Simon Maling, Chris Jack, Greg Somerville, Tom Willis, Dave Hewett.
Replacements: Marty Holah, Joe McDonnell, Daryl Gibson, Leon MacDonald.

REFEREE: André Watson (South Africa)

CROWD: 79,543

NEW ZEALAND 30, SOUTH AFRICA 23

AT ABSA STADIUM, DURBAN, 10 AUGUST

YEARS FROM NOW this contest will not be recalled for the stirring battle it was, but as the match in which a laager lout raced onto the pitch to attack the referee. The match itself had drama aplenty even before the unwelcome intrusion of Pieter van Zyl, who attempted to inflict some grievous bodily harm on Ireland's David McHugh for his perceived biased refereeing. Admittedly, a couple of dubious calls went the All Blacks' way, but that did not excuse van Zyl's actions. In fact, pitch invasions were a Tri-nations hot topic even before his antics. In Sydney, two men had made their mark with some shameless advertising on their naked torsos for a mobile phone company.

Van Zyl's entry came with the score at 17-all. McHugh dislocated his shoulder as van Zyl drove him to the ground, but Richie McCaw and AJ Venter acted quickly to prevent further damage. Van Zyl was escorted off the field by two of the 419 security people he managed to evade. McHugh had to be replaced by England's Chris White.

Notwithstanding the van Zyl sensation, the game produced some outstanding rugby, and was played at a frenetic pace. The All Blacks opened with real purpose under the Durban sun on a hard ground, but that was after conceding a stunning 70-metre score to halfback Neil de Kock from tremendous lead-up work. Leon MacDonald struck back with a try for the visitors, before McHugh awarded a penalty try to Tana Umaga after a high tackle by De Wet Barry.

James Dalton had a try controversially disallowed for obstruction, but shortly thereafter Springbok flyhalf André Pretorius showed his wares with a superb solo try. During the game, the Cats pivot scored in all four ways.

Tana Umaga put Doug Howlett over just before the break to tie up the scores prior to the van Zyl saga. The All Blacks withstood some prolonged assaults on their line in the second half, but delivered the knock-out blow with a nicely taken try to Aaron Mauger that secured the bonus point.

John Mitchell often spoke of character, and this All Black side had plenty of it. 'We have made a lot of progress and got a lot of systems and patterns of play in place,' he said, 'and it has been a really good foundation for us.'

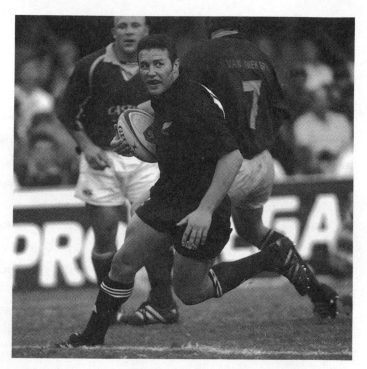

Aaron Mauger across for the deciding try at Durban.

Fotopress

The All Blacks would have to wait a week before having their Tri-nations fate determined. The five-point advantage they held could be wiped out if the Wallabies demolished the Springboks at Ellis Park. The All Blacks flew home reasonably smug, knowing not many teams ever managed that.

FOR NEW ZEALAND: Tries by Leon MacDonald, Tana Umaga, Doug Howlett and Aaron Mauger; 2 conversions and 2 penalty goals by Andrew Mehrtens.

FOR SOUTH AFRICA: Tries by Neil de Kock and André Pretorius; 2 conversions, 2 penalty goals and a dropped goal by Pretorius.

NEW ZEALAND: Leon MacDonald, Doug Howlett, Tana Umaga, Aaron Mauger, Caleb Ralph, Andrew Mehrtens, Justin Marshall, Scott Robertson, Richie McCaw, Reuben Thorne (captain), Simon Maling, Chris Jack, Greg Somerville, Tom Willis, Dave Hewett. Replacements: Mark Hammett, Sam Broomhall, Daryl Gibson, Byron Kelleher.

SOUTH AFRICA: Werner Greeff, Breyton Paulse, Marius Joubert, De Wet Barry, Dean Hall, André Pretorius, Neil de Kock, Bobby Skinstad, Joe van Niekerk, Corne Krige (captain), Jannes Labuschagne, A J Venter, Willie Meyer, James Dalton, Lawrence Sephaka. Replacements: Brent Russell, Bolla Conradie, Ollie le Roux, Faan Rautenbach, Victor Matfield, Hendro Scholtz.

REFEREE: David McHugh (Ireland), replaced by Chris White (England)

CROWD: 52,000

SOUTH AFRICA 33, AUSTRALIA 31

AT ELLIS PARK, JOHANNESBURG, 17 AUGUST

A NUMBER OF THE ALL BLACKS stayed up till the early hours of the morning to see confirmation of their Tri-nations title. They would have seen a stirring game of topsy-turvy rugby between two bitter rivals that was again decided after the final hooter.

All the talk in the republic during the week centred around ground security following the van Zyl saga and how far (or otherwise) the Springboks had come under Rudolf Straueli. Fortunately, talk of rugby, and not politics or pitch invasions, held sway after these 80 minutes.

The Springboks gained the initiative in the opening exchanges, with Jannes Labuschagne, Lawrence Sephaka, AJ Venter, Joe van Niekerk and Bobby Skinstad in dominant mood. Skinstad, no longer skipper but still a talismanic presence, showed his skill with a round-the-corner pass to send van Niekerk to the goalline. Behind the pack, new flyhalf Brent Russell and winger Breyton Paulse were constant threats to the Wallabies' defensive alignment. Paulse's work rate was rewarded with two tries.

The Wallabies sprung out to an 'against the run of play' 9–0 lead through the boot of Matt Burke before the Springbok pack took over. Then Paddy O'Brien made big calls to send off De Wet Barry for a punch on Chris Latham (not the first time the Queensland fullback had copped an illegal South African fist or tackle) and yellow-carded Marius Joubert for repeated high tackling.

It was to Australia's credit that they made a late rally, scoring three tries and troubling the hitherto accurate home side. Replacement forwards Brendan Cannon and David Lyons were combative and penetrative, while Mat Rogers was at his elusive best. George Gregan said afterwards he felt the Wallabies had pulled off a miraculous victory with the score reading 31–26, but he did not reckon on Werner Greeff. The Springbok fullback had already scored one solo try in Wellington. He somehow conjured up another he had no right to score, shrugging off his despairing Wallaby foes to dot down on fulltime. He then calmly slotted the conversion to spark scenes of unbridled joy and jubilation at Ellis Park.

Unsurprisingly, Corne Krige paid tribute to Paddy O'Brien's refereeing display, which he said was 'unbelievable'. The Australians now knew how the New Zealanders felt.

In an ironic twist, the Springboks, who scored the most tries in 2002 (13), placed last in the Tri-nations, while the winning All Blacks conceded the least (six). Ultimately, the New Zealanders deserved the trophy as they were the only side to win away from home.

FOR SOUTH AFRICA: Tries by Breyton Paulse 2, Brent Russell, Joe van Niekerk and Werner Greeff; 4 conversions by Greeff.

FOR AUSTRALIA: Tries by Mat Rogers, Toutai Kefu and Brendan Cannon; 2 conversions and 3 penalty goals by Matt Burke; dropped goal by George Gregan.

SOUTH AFRICA: Werner Greeff, Breyton Paulse, Marius Joubert, De Wet Barry, Dean Hall, Brent Russell, Neil de Kock, Bobby Skinstad, Joe van Niekerk, Corne Krige (captain), Jannes Labuschagne, A J Venter, Willie Meyer, James Dalton, Lawrence Sephaka.
Replacements: Hendro Scholtz, Faan Rautenbach, Ollie le Roux, Bolla Conradie, Stefan Terblanche.

AUSTRALIA: Chris Latham, Stirling Mortlock, Matt Burke, Dan Herbert, Ben Tune, Stephen Larkham, George Gregan (captain), Toutai Kefu, George Smith, Owen Finegan, Justin Harrison, Nathan Sharpe, Ben Darwin, Jeremy Paul, Bill Young.
Replacements: David Lyons, Matt Cockbain, Mat Rogers, Brendan Cannon, Rod Moore.

REFEREE: Paddy O'Brien (New Zealand)

CROWD: 63,000

2003

AS A POINTER TO the World Cup, the Tri-nations championship of 2003 was worthless, but it did produce an exciting footballer who instantly became a star on the world stage, Joe Rokocoko. Just turned 20, Fijian-born but Auckland-educated, Rokocoko stamped himself as a try-scorer extraordinaire, running in 11 tries in his first seven internationals, six of them in Tri-nations matches, including a hat trick against the Wallabies in Sydney.

Whether or not it was Rokocoko's exploits on the wing that distracted them, both the Springboks and the Wallabies collapsed in a heap against the All Blacks at what had previously been regarded as favourite home patches, Pretoria and Sydney. The All Blacks, in a rich vein of form, hit the half-century mark at both venues, shattering records in the process. Such was their dazzling form, they were naturally promoted as the southern hemisphere team most likely to challenge Clive Woodward's Englishmen for the World Cup crown come October and November.

Tragically for the All Blacks, they would not be able to recreate their Tri-nations form at Telstra Stadium during the World Cup. The Wallabies, with essentially the same backline but a reshaped pack, erased memories of their 21–50 humiliation in July with a 22–10 victory that propelled them into the final against England. Plainly, Australian coach Eddie Jones had targeted the World Cup, not the Tri-nations. Conversely, John Mitchell's All Blacks had obviously peaked in July and couldn't recreate that form when it counted most in mid-November.

The Springboks, again captained by Corne Krige, began the Tri-nations campaign encouragingly with a good win over the Wallabies in Cape Town, but then went into rapid decline and retained the wooden spoon. They scored only four tries, although they did play with commitment against the All Blacks in Dunedin.

Given their scoring sprees at Pretoria and Sydney, it wasn't surprising the All Blacks dominated the point-scoring and try-scorer charts. Their 18 tries completely overshadowed Australia's six and South Africa's four. Rokocoko

Dave Hewett and Reuben Thorne with the trophies following the All Blacks' win at Eden Park.
Fotopress

was the individual star with six tries, although Doug Howlett enjoyed a vintage campaign also, dotting down five times.

Carlos Spencer, who would surprisingly yield the goal-kicking duties to Leon MacDonald for the crunch matches at the World Cup, was the leading point scorer with 60, well clear of South Africa's Louis Koen, 42, and Australia's Elton Flatley, 31, who shared the kicking duties with Matt Burke.

2003 FINAL STANDINGS

	P	W	L	D	For	Against	Points
New Zealand	4	4	–	–	142	65	18
Australia	4	1	3	–	89	106	6
South Africa	4	1	3	–	62	122	4

Tries: New Zealand 17, Australia 9, South Africa 4; Total 30.

Penalty goals: New Zealand 13, Australia 11, South Africa 11; Total 35.

THE GAMES
SOUTH AFRICA 26, AUSTRALIA 22

AT NEWLANDS, CAPE TOWN, 12 JULY

HISTORY HAS PROVEN that a wounded Springbok is a dangerous animal. The Wallabies, who four months later would reach the final of the World Cup, certainly appreciated that after being dealt to in the competition opener at Newlands. After feeble warm-up performances against Scotland and Argentina, few people had rated the Springboks but they made all the running and won convincingly. Their hero was a pint-sized fullback who started the day on the reserves bench, getting involved only when Jaco van der Westhuyzen sustained a serious knee injury. Brent Russell descended on the game like a mini tornado, electrifying the South African backline and scoring one of the most spectacular tries of the competition, a 70-metre effort that left the Australians gasping. He instigated another try, finished off by Victor Matfield, before the interval, allowing the Springboks to take a commanding 20–10 advantage into the break, and in the second half he brought off a courageous tackle on Wallaby No 8 Toutai Kefu, who was in full flight.

Russell's dynamic display proved that size isn't everything in international rugby. About the size of your average halfback, he demonstrated that whippy, diminutive backs can make just as much impact as big, powerful three-quarters.

There were plenty of headline-grabbing developments in the run-in to the 2003 Tri-nations. England had sounded an ominous World Cup warning by defeating both the Wallabies and the All Blacks, the former in fine style, prompting coach Eddie Jones to drop Nathan Grey and Jeremy Paul.

Then there was a lot of talk about the progress (or lack of it) made by Springbok coach Rudolf Straeuli, and about an unsavoury spat in Australian rugby over the players' World Cup agreements, while in New Zealand there was shock at the sudden axing of hooker Anton Oliver.

After Matt Burke had opened the account with a fine dropped goal, the Springboks ripped into their work, Russell almost instantly made his presence felt with a jaunty try. Matfield's superb team try just before the break could be

Captains Corne Krige
and George Gregan
eyeball-to-eyeball at
Cape Town.
Fotopress

attributed to the brilliance of Russell, who started the movement that swept through several hands.

De Wet Barry harried and hammered in the midfield (though he did spent 10 minutes in the bin for a professional foul) while his forward pack won the breakdown battle and gained parity in the set pieces. George Smith was sorely missed by the visitors for his foraging skills. Louis Koen's boot was again decisive. Though they were outscored three tries to two, the home side was well worth its victory after such an unpromising start to the international season.

FOR SOUTH AFRICA: Tries by Brent Russell and Victor Matfield; 2 conversions and 4 penalty goals by Louis Koen.

FOR AUSTRALIA: Tries by Wendell Sailor, Phil Waugh and Joe Roff; 2 conversions and a dropped goal by Matt Burke.

SOUTH AFRICA: Jaco van der Westhuyzen, Stefan Terblanche, Marius Joubert, De Wet Barry, Thinus Delport, Louis Koen, Joost van der Westhuizen, Juan Smith, Wikus van Heerden, Corne Krige (captain), Victor Matfield, Bakkies Botha, Richard Bands, Danie Coetzee, Lawrence Sephaka.
Replacements: Brent Russell, Gcobani Bobo, Pedrie Wannenburg, Robbie Kempson, Dale Santon, Selborne Boome.

AUSTRALIA: Matt Burke, Wendell Sailor, Mat Rogers, Steve Kefu, Joe Roff, Elton Flatley, George Gregan (captain), Toutai Kefu, Phil Waugh, David Lyons, David Giffin, Dan Vickerman, Patricio Noriega, Brendan Cannon, Bill Young.
Replacements: Nathan Sharpe, Owen Finegan, Ben Darwin, Steve Larkham, Lote Tuqiri, Adam Freier.

REFEREE: Steve Walsh (New Zealand)

CROWD: 49,000

NEW ZEALAND 52, SOUTH AFRICA 16

AT LOFTUS VERSFELD, PRETORIA, 19 JULY

NOT EVEN JOHN MITCHELL'S most ardent supporter could have dreamt up this score-line. The wonder is that it was played out against a backdrop of All Black player unrest over World Cup bonus payments that threatened to derail not just this match but the whole campaign.

New Zealand rugby has known some golden moments in South Africa. Loftus Versfeld was the scene for one of the All Blacks greatest triumphs — when they beat the Springboks in a series in the republic for the first time in 1996. But that was a brave display hewn on commitment, doggedness and the brilliance of Jeff Wilson.

The 80 minutes of this game were a dynamic showcase of 15-man running rugby on a hard field under a hot South African sun. It was a performance that coaches John Mitchell and Robbie Deans had been hinting at and building towards. Dave Hewett was a late change for Carl Hoeft at loosehead prop, but this was a minor blip on the All Blacks' preparation.

Though Carlos Spencer opened with an early try, the All Blacks did not break free of the shackles until the 23rd minute, when Doug Howlett crossed for the first of two scores. That sparked a three-try blitzkrieg, which exposed Brent Russell's flimsy defence and had the Springboks reeling. Only rookie winger Ashwin Willemse seemed to have the stomach for the fight, and he was rewarded with a fine 71st-minute try.

The All Blacks scarcely missed a beat, even when Kees Meeuws, just after extending his props' try-scoring record, was sinbinned for elbowing Robbie Kempson. They scored twice more before Meeuws re-entered the battle, with second-five Aaron Mauger pushing them over the 50 mark.

All Black captain Reuben Thorne was gracious in victory. 'I don't think they were weak at all. It was just one of those days for us. We managed to find the space out wide and were then able to finish it off. It was still extremely tough up front, though.'

In contrast, Springbok skipper Corne Krige was not quite as humble, though he felt the score-line did not reflect the combative forward battle. He had overseen two 50-point thrashings inflicted on his team in eight months, his team having lost to England, 53–3 at Twickenham. 'I must admit, there was a sense of déjà vu when I was standing behind the poles today. But this game was different, because it was on a knife's edge for a while.'

A whole stack of All Black v. Springbok records were lowered, chief among them the highest winning margin. It was not a test for the 83-times capped Joost van der Westhuizen to recall with any fondness.

FOR NEW ZEALAND: Tries by Doug Howlett 2, Joe Rokocoko 2, Carlos Spencer, Kees Meeuws and Aaron Mauger; 4 conversions and 3 penalty goals by Spencer.

FOR SOUTH AFRICA: try by Ashwin Willemse; conversion, 2 penalty goals and a dropped goal by Louis Koen.

NEW ZEALAND: Mils Muliaina, Doug Howlett, Tana Umaga, Aaron Mauger, Joe Rokocoko, Carlos Spencer, Steve Devine, Jerry Collins, Richie McCaw, Reuben Thorne (captain), Ali Williams, Chris Jack, Greg Somerville, Keven Mealamu, Dave Hewett. Replacements: Brad Thorn, Kees Meeuws, Mark Hammett, Justin Marshall, Rodney So'oialo.

SOUTH AFRICA: Brent Russell, Stefan Terblanche, André Snyman, De Wet Barry, Ashwin Willemse, Louis Koen, Joost van der Westhuizen, Juan Smith, Wikus van Heerden, Corne Krige (captain), Victor Matfield, Bakkies Botha, Richard Bands, Danie Coetzee, Lawrence Sephaka. Replacements: Robbie Kempson, André Pretorius, Dale Santon, Craig Davidson, Pedrie Wannenburg, Selborne Boome.

REFEREE: Alain Rolland (Ireland)

CROWD: 50,008

NEW ZEALAND 50, AUSTRALIA 21

AT TELSTRA STADIUM, SYDNEY, 26 JULY

THE ALL BLACKS AGAIN SENT Geoff Miller and other stats gurus scurrying for their record books as they scored a point for every one of Tana Umaga's tests. The Wallabies had every reason to be fearful of the All Blacks' strike power after the demolition in Pretoria a week earlier. However, the All Blacks were still in turmoil off the field, with little chance of an agreement in sight between the Players Association and the NZRU, with the All Blacks demanding a bonus of $120,000 each if the Webb Ellis Cup was won, while the NZRU was holding fast on $50,000 a man. Good thing then that the All Blacks appeased the growing disquiet among their fans with as exhilarating a display of running rugby as they had shown in eight seasons of Tri-nations play.

Yet it was the Wallabies who started with more purpose, Matt Burke scoring another solo try against New Zealand and Mat Rogers and Lote Tuqiri proving dangerous on the break. The All Blacks hit back with three beautiful tries to lead 23–11 at half-time before cutting loose in a second half in which Wendell Sailor's marvellous score was the only bright spot for the home town fans.

There were few All Blacks who did not outplay their opposite, though Keven Mealamu had problems throwing in to the line-out. Greg Somerville, Jerry Collins and Chris Jack were the picks of a dominant forward effort. In the back division, the All Blacks were rampant, and none shone brighter than Joe Rokocoko. The 20-year-old winger nailed a hat trick, embarrassing the bigger Wendell Sailor with some exquisite moves and sheer pace. Rokocoko's try tally after this match stood at 10 from just five tests.

Mils Muliaina was nigh on faultless from the back, while second-five Aaron Mauger again showed his qualities when fully fit. He had shrugged off injury concerns to the benefit of the All Blacks' direction. Dan Carter made a seamless transition when he subbed on for Spencer for the last half hour, scoring a try and directing traffic.

The fine night conditions in Sydney clearly met with winger Doug Howlett's approval: 'A dry ball on a dry field really helps. We didn't really have any favourable conditions back in New Zealand before we arrived in South Africa

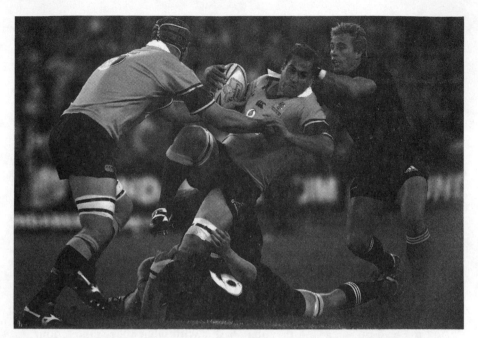

George Smith ambushed by All Blacks at Sydney where his team conceded 50 points. Fotopress

for the first Tri-nations game, so we're looking forward to a bit more of it later this year.' Alas, it was not to be. But the All Black back three of Muliaina, Howlett and Rokocoko was now the most feared in world rugby.

FOR NEW ZEALAND: Tries by Joe Rokocoko 3, Doug Howlett, Tana Umaga, Dan Carter and Aaron Mauger; 2 conversions and 3 penalty goals by Carlos Spencer, conversion by Carter.

FOR AUSTRALIA: Tries by Matt Burke, Wendell Sailor and Mat Rogers; 2 penalty goals by Burke.

NEW ZEALAND: Mils Muliaina, Doug Howlett, Tana Umaga, Aaron Mauger, Joe Rokocoko, Carlos Spencer, Justin Marshall, Jerry Collins, Richie McCaw, Reuben Thorne (captain), Ali Williams, Chris Jack, Greg Somerville, Keven Mealamu, Dave Hewett.
Replacements: Dan Carter, Kees Meeuws, Brad Thorn, Marty Holah, Mark Hammett, Caleb Ralph, Steve Devine.

AUSTRALIA: Matt Burke, Wendell Sailor, Mat Rogers, Elton Flatley, Lote Tuqiri, Stephen Larkham, George Gregan (captain), Toutai Kefu, Phil Waugh, George Smith, David Giffin, Dan Vickerman, Patricio Noriega, Brendan Cannon, Bill Young.
Replacements: Ben Darwin, Chris Latham, Nathan Sharpe, Adam Freier, Owen Finegan, Steve Kefu.

REFEREE: Tony Spreadbury (England)

CROWD: 82,096

AUSTRALIA 29,
SOUTH AFRICA 9

AT SUNCORP STADIUM, BRISBANE, 2 AUGUST

FOR TWO TEAMS coming off 50-point batterings, a victory was more than desirable at Suncorp Stadium. It was imperative. Unfortunately, Rudolf Straeuli's Springboks would not only crash (heavily) to defeat again, they would stand accused of foul play. Straeuli was feeling the heat at the end of this spiteful encounter and it was not just his side's disappointing onfield display that was under the spotlight. His Wallaby counterpart Eddie Jones did not hold back at the press conference, condemning what he felt were deliberate foul play tactics by the South Africans.

'It was a disgrace for international rugby,' said Jones. 'The intent was there during the lead-up week and they matched it with what they spoke about [in pre-game interviews],' Jones said. 'I won't go into specifics, but certainly there was a case where a player's eye was gouged, there was spitting on the field and obviously the cheap shot on Kefu.'

Springbok skipper Corne Krige came under the cosh for his role in the perceived illegalities. But he was vehement in his denial of dirty play. 'If you try and play like that in this era of world rugby, you're crazy,' he said. 'If there were one or two incidents, then steps will be taken. But we don't plan that as a team. We came here to play positively, and that's what I thought happened. It's really frustrating. We've paid a lot of attention to our discipline. We've got a referee on board full time. Every time we get penalised, he checks it out and works with the players.'

There was at least a grain of truth in Jones' assertion, given referee Paddy O'Brien sinbinned Danie Coetzee and Robbie Kempson either side of half-time. Kempson was suspended for four weeks for a late, high tackle, while lock Bakkies Botha, cited, was given an eight-week 'holiday' for recklessly attacking the face of an opponent.

Suncorp Stadium's record crowd for a rugby test could have expected more from an international involving two of the world's heavyweights. The Wallabies made hard work of their task when they weren't caught up in the niggle. After the scores were locked at 6-all after 40 minutes, centre Mat Rogers broke the game wide open with a try from a loose Louis Koen pass. But they had to wait until the final two minutes for Phil Waugh's score to drive the nail home. It was after Kefu had delivered the last pass that he was felled by Kempson with a swinging arm that left him in a neck brace and feeling pins and needles.

Happily for the Wallabies' back three, after the nightmare at Sydney, they made all 19 of their tackles to shut out the Springboks. They had 'stayed tight under pressure', according to skipper George Gregan, and the 100 per cent goal kicking of Elton Flatley helped immeasurably.

Strong performers included Waugh, Tuqiri, Rogers — growing into the midfield role — and hooker Brendan Cannon. The Wallabies were under no illusions about the task ahead of them in Auckland, while the limited Springboks accepted they would be massive underdogs in Dunedin.

FOR AUSTRALIA: Tries by Mat Rogers and Phil Waugh; 2 conversions and 5 penalty goals by Elton Flatley.

FOR SOUTH AFRICA: 3 penalty goals by Louis Koen.

AUSTRALIA: Chris Latham, Wendell Sailor, Mat Rogers, Elton Flatley, Lote Tuqiri, Stephen Larkham, George Gregan (captain), Toutai Kefu, Phil Waugh, George Smith, David Giffin, Dan Vickerman, Patricio Noriega, Brendan Cannon, Bill Young.
Replacements: Jeremy Paul, Nathan Sharpe, Glenn Panoho, Owen Finegan, Chris Whitaker, Matt Burke, Matt Giteau.

SOUTH AFRICA: André Pretorius, Stefan Terblanche, Jorrie Muller, De Wet Barry, Ashwin Willemse, Louis Koen, Craig Davidson, Juan Smith, Joe van Niekerk, Corne Krige (captain), Victor Matfield, Selborne Boome, Richard Bands, Danie Coetzee, Robbie Kempson.
Replacements: Wikus van Heerden, Dale Santon, Joost van der Westhuizen, Bakkies Botha, Brent Russell, Lawrence Sephaka.

REFEREE: Paddy O'Brien (New Zealand)

CROWD: 51,188

NEW ZEALAND 19, SOUTH AFRICA 11

AT CARISBROOK, DUNEDIN, 9 AUGUST

THOUGH THE MEDIA AND PUBLIC may have expected another hefty All Blacks win — perhaps even a third 50-pointer — the reality was this was always going to be a tight affair given the cold night conditions and Springbok pride. The Springboks badly needed a boost after a woeful pair of results since upsetting Australia in the first match. The likes of Joost van der Westhuizen were still smarting after the hiding in Pretoria.

Much of the talk surrounding the test was on the vexed issue of night rugby, especially in the South Island mid-winter. It levelled the playing field for the Boks, but the All Blacks did not play with anywhere near the same accuracy and dynamism as in their away triumphs.

Critical changes in the pack saw Marty Holah and Brad Thorn replace Richie McCaw and Chris Jack. Both newcomers had torrid battles, with the Springboks scrapping hard for possession.

The All Blacks started ominously, an Aaron Mauger grubber pounced on by the prolific Joe Rokocoko to open the scoring after just five minutes. However, less than 10 minutes later South African prop Richard Bands scored what many claim is the finest try by a front rower in international rugby history. He took a short pass close to the ruck from van der Westhuizen 50 metres out from the chalk. Bursting through the gap, he then showed such acceleration no All Blacks defenders could reel him in. Carlos Spencer was swatted aside in ignominious fashion as Bands dived over at the corner to strike a blow for the front row club. International rugby's most prolific try-scoring prop, Kees Meeuws, wearing the No 3 black jersey, must have suppressed a wry smile.

Incredibly, that completed the five-point action. First-fives Louis Koen and Carlos Spencer traded penalties thereafter. Spencer's five-from-five kicking record in this match gave cause to wonder why he was not used as goal kicker in the World Cup a few months later.

The All Black forwards were as committed as ever, but they lost crucial line-out throws and their backline was not given the same platform as in the two previous tests. Having said that, the back division did not help itself, with some pushed passes and questionable depth.

Ali Williams took a senior role in the absence of Jack and gave a fine display, though he had some stiff competition from Springbok ace Victor Matfield. All Black coach John Mitchell felt the 80 minutes was Williams' finest for his country. But Mitchell was also more than happy to have a vigorous arm wrestle just before the Bledisloe Cup decider.

For the All Blacks, there was satisfaction at retaining the Tri-nations Trophy, the first time since 1997 they had successfully defended the title. But they knew a tougher quest awaited them at Eden Park in seven days' time. The Bledisloe Cup was still in the Australian trophy cabinet, as it had been for five years. The All Blacks sought its return at any cost. They weren't even worried the game would again be at night, though that was the major topic in the post-mortems.

FOR NEW ZEALAND: Try by Joe Rokocoko; conversion and 4 penalty goals by Carlos Spencer.

FOR SOUTH AFRICA: Try by Richard Bands; 2 penalty goals by Louis Koen.

NEW ZEALAND: Mils Muliaina, Doug Howlett, Tana Umaga, Aaron Mauger, Joe Rokocoko, Carlos Spencer, Justin Marshall, Jerry Collins, Marty Holah, Reuben Thorne (captain), Ali Williams, Brad Thorn, Kees Meeuws, Mark Hammett, Dave Hewett. Replacements: Chris Jack, Greg Somerville, Keven Mealamu.

SOUTH AFRICA: Thinus Delport, Stefan Terblanche, Jorrie Muller, Gcobani Bobo, Ashwin Willemse, Louis Koen, Joost van der Westhuizen, Juan Smith, Joe van Niekerk, Corne Krige (captain), Victor Matfield, Geo Cronje, Richard Bands, Danie Coetzee, Lawrence Sephaka.

Replacements: Chris Bezuidenhout, Lukas van Biljon, Selborne Boome.

REFEREE: Peter Marshall (Australia)

CROWD: 37,000

NEW ZEALAND 21, AUSTRALIA 17

AT EDEN PARK, AUCKLAND, 16 AUGUST

AFTER THIS DESPERATELY hard-fought encounter in wet, challenging conditions at Eden Park, the All Blacks were in possession of both the Bledisloe Cup (a trophy they hadn't possessed since 1998) and the Tri-nations Trophy. All that was missing was the World Cup, but the campaign to secure that much-prized trophy, just six weeks away, would go horrendously wrong for Mitchell's men.

It was defence that won this encounter for the All Blacks. It was the mantra of the fine Crusaders Super 12 side that won the 2000 final in Canberra with very little ball. At Eden Park, All Black assistant coach Robbie Deans, who oversaw that win, had impressed upon the flamboyant Blacks that this would be a grind.

This encounter overshadowed the first round of the NPC, which had kicked off the previous night. Indeed, much hype centred on it being 100 years since the All Blacks' first test (in Sydney back in 1903). It was also the 100th contest for the Bledisloe Cup.

From the get-go, in heavy showers and with a dewy surface, the All Blacks hammered into their work, driving the Wallabies back with some jarring tackles. One special by Joe Rokocoko on his opposite Wendell Sailor stood out.

The All Blacks were swift in retaliation for Flatley's early penalty goal, Howlett scoring off a superb Keven Mealamu pass after the hooker had made inroads into a hole in the Wallaby defensive line. Carlos Spencer and Jerry Collins assisted in Howlett's second try, which brought the capacity crowd (and press box) to its feet. A TMO decision ruled out a third try just before the break, but the All Blacks led 15–9 and clung to the initiative.

The Wallabies characteristically did not buckle under the heavy All Black defence, but kept probing for holes. They were eventually rewarded with a try to flanker George Smith after a turnover by Spencer. Then the All Blacks had to withstand the pressure, and did so with the captain Reuben Thorne playing the knock, calling three important line-out throws to himself. It must be said the

All Blacks were again not always accurate in this facet, but this was the only stain on Mealamu's performance.

As the final whistle blew, it was evident how much the Bledisloe Cup meant to the New Zealanders. Dave Hewett's face, in particular, was beaming with joy as the All Blacks embraced. They had shown they could win when under the cosh, demonstrating they were not simply the entertainers of the Tri-nations, with 17 tries and 53 more points than the Wallabies in their four games.

John Mitchell nearly allowed himself the luxury of a smile: 'The defence was outstanding tonight,' he said. 'What Australia threw at us around the 55 to 60 minute mark… it shows the trust the players have in each other.'

FOR NEW ZEALAND: 2 tries by Doug Howlett; conversion and 3 penalty goals by Carlos Spencer.

FOR AUSTRALIA: Try by George Smith; 4 penalty goals by Elton Flatley.

NEW ZEALAND: Mils Muliaina, Doug Howlett, Tana Umaga, Aaron Mauger, Joe Rokocoko, Carlos Spencer, Justin Marshall, Jerry Collins, Richie McCaw, Reuben Thorne (captain), Ali Williams, Chris Jack, Greg Somerville, Keven Mealamu, Dave Hewett.
Replacement: Leon MacDonald.

AUSTRALIA: Chris Latham, Wendell Sailor, Mat Rogers, Elton Flatley, Lote Tuqiri, Stephen Larkham, George Gregan (captain), Toutai Kefu, Phil Waugh, George Smith, David Giffin, Dan Vickerman, Glenn Panoho, Brendan Cannon, Bill Young.
Replacements: Al Baxter, Matt Burke, Nathan Sharpe, Owen Finegan, Jeremy Paul, Matt Giteau.

REFEREE: Jonathan Kaplan (South Africa)

CROWD: 46,000

THE STAR
RICHIE McCAW

It's hard to say which ranks as the more impressive — the speed with which Richie McCaw swoops on breakdowns to secure possession for his team or the speed with which he burst on to the national scene in 2001. Some astute rugby judges had seen him coming. He hadn't captained the Otago Boys High School First XV for nothing and both New Zealand Colts coach Peter Sloane and Canterbury coach Robbie Deans had hastened him into their teams as a 19-year-old in 2000. However, one appearance for each of those sides — for the Colts against Samoa and as a substitute for Canterbury against North Harbour — hardly suggested the farmer boy from Hakataramea, studying for a Bachelor of Agricultural Science degree at Lincoln University, was going to take the rugby world by storm when the new season rolled around.

But he did, and then some. In rapid succession he bounded from bench player for the Crusaders to captain of the New Zealand Colts to openside flanker for the championship-winning Canterbury NPC team to the All Blacks, making such a smash hit on the end-of-year tour he was named player of the match against Ireland and included in several experts' world fifteens.

Although he'd demonstrated leadership qualities and exciting skills in leading the New Zealand Colts to tournament glory against Australia in Sydney, the performance that made Kiwi fans suddenly sit up and take notice was when he scored three tries before half-time in the NPC game against Otago at Jade Stadium.

Josh Kronfeld was regarded as the finest modern-day exponent in New Zealand at securing possession for his team at breakdowns. Now here was a young kid demonstrating precisely those same qualities. And he could match Kronfeld as a tackler.

McCaw had a huge year in 2003, for the Crusaders and the All Blacks, at the conclusion of which he became the recipient of the Kel Tremain Memorial Trophy as New Zealand's player of the year.

2004

BOTH THE SPRINGBOKS AND THE ALL BLACKS went into the 2004 Tri-nations championship with new coaches, and it was Jake White and not, as many people anticipated, Graham Henry who came up with the major prize. After snaring vital bonus points in their away fixtures at Christchurch and Perth, the Springboks produced two quality performances back home in South Africa to finish atop the Tri-nations ladder for only the second time in nine years.

The competition went right to the wire, not being decided until referee Paddy O'Brien blew fulltime in the final encounter, involving the Wallabies, at Durban. With all six matches being won by the home team, bonus points decided the outcome. South Africa claimed three, Australia two and New Zealand one.

The Springboks were a deserving winner, because they scored 13 tries against the Wallabies' nine and the All Blacks' measly four. It certainly wasn't the outcome Graham Henry was looking for, although he made significant changes for the end-of-year trek to Europe, finally getting his combinations right, in spectacular fashion, against France in Paris.

The South Africans played an attractive, expansive game, which the outside backs appreciated, in particular winger Jean de Villiers, one of the stars of the campaign, and centre Marius Joubert, although the individual who would make the greatest impact, going on to win the IRB's Player of the Year award, was the dashing openside flanker Schalk Burger.

The Wallabies remained invincible at home but again struggled to win on the road, although they were only four points short of glory in the decider at Durban (outscoring the Springboks four tries to three). Landing the wooden spoon was a huge disappointment for the All Blacks, who were seeking to complete a hat trick of Tri-nations successes and, more importantly, to rebound positively from their disastrous World Cup campaign.

Three players topped the try-scoring chart, with three each — Springboks Joubert (who scored all his in one match, against the All Blacks at Johannesburg) and de Villiers, and Wallaby Lote Tuqiri. Springbok fullback Percy Montgomery

After a six-year absence, the Tri-nations Trophy returns to South Africa. Skipper John Smit shows it off. Fotopress

was the most prolific point scorer with 45, ahead of New Zealand's Dan Carter, 38 (who had to share the goal-kicking duties with Andrew Mehrtens and Carlos Spencer), and Australia's Matt Giteau, 26.

2004 FINAL STANDINGS

	P	W	L	D	For	Against	Points
South Africa	4	2	2	–	110	98	11
Australia	4	2	2	–	79	83	10
New Zealand	4	2	2	–	83	91	9

Tries: South Africa 13, Australia 9, New Zealand 4; Total 26.

Penalty goals: New Zealand 19, South Africa 9, Australia 8; Total 36.

THE STAR
SCHALK BURGER

Schalk Burger burst on to the South African rugby scene in 2004, the most spectacular newcomer for many a year. His arrival was so good for rugby — the great personality who played with all the energy of a young, energetic, fearless, loyal amateur. He made more tackles than anybody else, contested every tackle and charged with reckless intent. The IRB voted him Player of the Year, Young Player of the Year and Players' Player of the

Fotopress

Year. Awards in South Africa mirrored those. And he only turned 21 in April 2004. He was in just his second year of provincial rugby for Western Province and his first season of Super 12 for the Stormers.

There is pedigree. Schalk Willem Petrus Burger was born in Port Elizabeth because his father was playing for Eastern Province at the time. His father — who played lock for the Springboks in the eighties — is Schalk Willem Petrus Burger. His grandfather was Schalk Willem Petrus Burger. It is, you may say, a family name. In fact, Schalk, the present Springbok, is the ninth Schalk Willem Petrus Burger in his line.

Like his father, little Schalk went to Paarl Gymnasium. Little? When his father played lock for South Africa he stood 1.95 metres and weighed 97 kg. 'Little' Schalk stands 1.93 metres and weighs 110 kg. There are differences. The father was saturninely dark, the son flamboyantly blond.

The Irish journeyed to South Africa in 2004 expecting to win both tests. They won neither and said it was Schalk Burger who 'hurt' them most.

It is frightening to think that Schalk was nearly lost to rugby, because as a schoolboy he also achieved great success at cricket. While in his school's First XI he played first league men's cricket for Wellington (SA), a batsman who could bowl. In one remarkable week in 2001 he participated in Craven Week, the big annual tournament for provincial school rugby teams, and at the same time took part in the South African Under-19 cricket trials.

THE GAMES
NEW ZEALAND 16,
AUSTRALIA 7

AT WESTPAC STADIUM, WELLINGTON, 17 JULY

WELLINGTONIANS WERE GETTING READY to honour George Gregan's 100th test appearance, a remarkable rugby milestone attained by only three other players (David Campese, Philippe Sella and Jason Leonard), but a shoulder injury forced him out of the Tri-nations opener in the wet and windy capital. Wearing the No 9 jersey for the Wallabies instead was perennial benchwarmer Chris Whitaker.

Graham Henry wasn't too concerned who operated at halfback for Australia. Preparing the All Blacks for a Tri-nations campaign for the first time, all he wanted was a victory. His team had delivered some mixed lead-up work — fine wins against England were clouded by some loose play in nevertheless comfortable victories over Argentina and the Pacific Islanders. The Wallabies arrived in Wellington also boasting four wins from four. They would look to the 51–15 hiding dished out to England as their benchmark.

Henry resisted the urge to pluck powerful loose forward Sione Lauaki from the Pacific Islanders team (for which Lauaki gave a series of sensational performances) even though he was still without Richie McCaw, who was troubled by headaches after concussion. The Wallabies strangely opted to start with George Smith on the bench. Other match-ups, including the tyro second-fives — Dan Carter and Matt Giteau — were rendered irrelevant due to the driving rain that hit the capital.

The All Black pack took control early, with Carl Hayman putting the squeeze on Bill Young, and Chris Jack ruling the air. But such was the slippery ball they could not convert their dominance into tries.

It was Doug Howlett who eventually cracked the Wallaby defence in the 62nd minute, his 33rd test try taking the All Blacks out to a seemingly unassailable 13–0 lead. Were it not for a spilled bomb by Joe Rokocoko that gifted a try to Stirling Mortlock, the margin would have looked more convincing.

Justin Marshall gave a typically assertive performance from the scrum base and the conditions were tailor-made for the nine-man rugby he plays so well.

The All Black pack stood tall, and the evening gave special satisfaction to No 8 Xavier Rush, who had waited six years to gain revenge on the Australians after a difficult and losing test debut in Sydney.

Graham Henry was satisfied that many of the questions posed of his pack were answered, and of course that the Bledisloe Cup was retained. 'We had a lot more chances than they did,' he said, 'but we won the game and won it convincingly in territory and possession.'

His counterpart, Eddie Jones, attempted to put a dampener on the celebrations, suggesting the All Blacks had used illegal tactics at the breakdown and someone should have been suspended after the Brendan Cannon–Keven Mealamu fracas, which left both men in the sinbin and Mealamu sporting a nasty cut from a well-aimed punch by the aptly named hooker. Cannon subsequently received a two-week ban after an IRB judicial hearing.

FOR NEW ZEALAND: Try by Doug Howlett; conversion and 3 penalty goals by Dan Carter.

FOR AUSTRALIA: Try by Stirling Mortlock; conversion by Matt Giteau.

NEW ZEALAND: Mils Muliaina, Doug Howlett, Tana Umaga (captain), Dan Carter, Joe Rokocoko, Carlos Spencer, Justin Marshall, Xavier Rush, Marty Holah, Jono Gibbes, Simon Maling, Chris Jack, Carl Hayman, Keven Mealamu, Kees Meeuws. Replacements: Jerry Collins, Andrew Hore.

AUSTRALIA: Chris Latham, Clyde Rathbone, Stirling Mortlock, Matt Giteau, Lote Tuqiri, Stephen Larkham, Chris Whitaker, David Lyons, Phil Waugh, Radike Samo, Nathan Sharpe (captain), Justin Harrison, Al Baxter, Brendan Cannon, Bill Young. Replacements: Jeremy Paul, Wendell Sailor, Dan Vickerman, Matt Dunning, Matt Henjak.

REFEREE: Alain Rolland (Ireland)

CROWD: 37,500

NEW ZEALAND 23, SOUTH AFRICA 21

AT JADE STADIUM, CHRISTCHURCH, 24 JULY

THE ALL BLACKS WOULD HAVE EXPECTED to make good strides after their brave first-up effort in challenging conditions in Wellington. Instead, they regressed against a determined Springbok outfit that, under new coach Jake White, came within a whisker of its first test victory in Christchurch since 1965, and indeed its first Tri-nations win in New Zealand since 1998.

The Jade faithful barely had time to settle in their seats when the Springboks shocked all with a try inside 25 seconds. It went to versatile winger Jean de Villiers off a turnover. Though the metronomic Dan Carter then slotted three goals, two heady pieces of Fourie du Preez play wrested the initiative back from the All Blacks. His clean break and link with AJ Venter led to Jacques Cronje's try and not long after he scored in the corner himself to give the visitors a 21–12 lead at halftime.

It fell to Doug Howlett in the 79th minute to push the All Blacks into the lead. But he could thank Xavier Rush, Carlos Spencer and Mils Muliaina for creating space as he skidded across out wide. It was thought to be the first try scored by the All Blacks this late to win a test match from behind.

Schalk Burger was the most impressive of the Springboks. Before the year was out he would be named IRB Player of the Year and this display was up there with his best. He combined nicely with AJ Venter in the two-flanker game the Springboks use to good effect. He tackled with accuracy and hurt, and was invariably a nuisance for the All Blacks at the breakdown, where Marty Holah had his work cut out.

All Black captain Tana Umaga was full of respect for the Springbok effort, though he admitted he did not admire them in the heat of battle.

'They scored some great tries,' he said. 'They were a very passionate side. They are going through a lot of troubles back home in South Africa and I think them getting away for two or three weeks has pulled them close together.'

A major talking point was the lack of fluency in the All Black backline, at the time attributed to the 'flat backline' formation adopted. In reality, the recycling of the ball was too slow in cool conditions for any panache to surface.

Coach Graham Henry, however, said it was not the time to discard his strategy of a flatter alignment. 'We have just got to get better at it. Rome was not built in a day. We're trying to introduce new ideas and you need to practise them until you perfect them . . . I don't think we need to panic on that.'

FOR NEW ZEALAND: Try by Doug Howlett; penalty goals by Dan Carter 5 and Carlos Spencer.

FOR SOUTH AFRICA: Tries by Jean de Villiers, Jacques Cronje and Fourie du Preez; 3 conversions by Percy Montgomery.

NEW ZEALAND: Mils Muliaina, Doug Howlett, Tana Umaga (captain), Dan Carter, Joe Rokocoko, Carlos Spencer, Justin Marshall, Xavier Rush, Marty Holah, Jerry Collins, Simon Maling, Chris Jack, Greg Somerville, Keven Mealamu, Kees Meeuws.
Replacements: Ali Williams, Byron Kelleher, Sam Tuitupou.

SOUTH AFRICA: Percy Montgomery, Breyton Paulse, Marius Joubert, De Wet Barry, Jean de Villiers, Jaco van der Westhuyzen, Fourie du Preez, Jacques Cronje, Schalk Burger, A J Venter, Albert van den Berg, Bakkies Botha, Eddie Andrews, John Smit (captain), Os du Randt.
Replacements: Faan Rautenbach, Joe van Niekerk, Quinton Davids, Brent Russell.

REFEREE: Andrew Cole (Australia)

CROWD: 36,000

AUSTRALIA 30,
SOUTH AFRICA 26

AT SUBIACO OVAL, PERTH, 31 JULY

AND SO IT CAME TO PASS that George Gregan, Australia's talismanic skipper, joined the exclusive club of test match centurions, a club previously comprising just one Wallaby (David Campese), one Frenchman (Philippe Sella), one Englishman (Jason Leonard) and no All Blacks or Springboks. The Zambian-born scrumhalf could lay claim to the tag of world's best halfback over several years.

Gregan's milestone provided ample motivation for the Australians, who were desperate for a victory after the disappointment of losing in Wellington. Although technically Perth represents a home game for the Wallabies, there are so many South Africans now living in Western Australia, the Springboks certainly don't feel disadvantaged playing there; indeed, they have an excellent record in internationals played in Perth.

Fortunately for the fans (more than 42,000 of whom crammed into Subiaco Oval), the teams did not serve up the ill-tempered slugfest of Brisbane 2003. They exploded into this clash with positive attitudes, intent on victory *and* the bonus point. Lote Tuqiri got the ball rolling early, plucking a pinpoint Matt Giteau 'bomb' out of the air to score the opening try. South Africa was not fazed, and produced two fine tries, to Jaco van der Westhuyzen and an intercept by winger Jean de Villiers. The Wallabies still had the Steve Larkham ace up their sleeve, and the elusive pivot, coupled with the boot of Giteau, saw Australia close to within one point by half-time.

Though mercurial replacement Gaffie du Toit dotted down to keep the scoreboard ticking over for the Boks, Chris Latham and winger Clyde Rathbone also crossed the chalk to give the Wallabies the money. It was especially galling for the Springboks to see one of their own (Rathbone, a former Springbok Under-21 representative) win the game for Australia, and was further excuse, if any was needed, as to why the Brumbies flyer meets such antipathy in the land of his birth.

Starting in the No 6 jersey for the Wallabies after prolonged bouts of benchwarming, George Smith showed he was back on his game, outshining

Wallaby wing Clyde Rathbone across for the decider against his fellow countrymen at Perth.
Fotopress

Schalk Burger and invariably arriving first at the breakdown. John Hart had claimed Jonah Lomu could best regain his hunger from the bench in the lead-up to World Cup in 1999. Perhaps Eddie Jones felt the same . . . it worked, anyway.

Gregan wasn't the only individual celebrating a notable milestone for the Wallabies. New Zealand-born hooker Jeremy Paul was participating in his 50th test.

FOR AUSTRALIA: Tries by Lote Tuqiri, Stephen Larkham, Chris Latham and Clyde Rathbone; conversions by Matt Giteau and Matt Burke; 2 penalty goals by Giteau.

FOR SOUTH AFRICA: Tries by Jaco van der Westhuyzen, Jean de Villiers and Gaffie du Toit; conversions and 3 penalty goals by Percy Montgomery.

AUSTRALIA: Chris Latham, Clyde Rathbone, Stirling Mortlock, Matt Giteau, Lote Tuqiri, Stephen Larkham, George Gregan (captain), David Lyons, Phil Waugh, George Smith, Nathan Sharpe, Justin Harrison, Al Baxter, Jeremy Paul, Bill Young.
Replacements: John Roe, Dan Vickerman, Matt Burke, Matt Dunning.

SOUTH AFRICA: Percy Montgomery, Breyton Paulse, Marius Joubert, De Wet Barry, Jean de Villiers, Jaco van der Westhuyzen, Fourie du Preez, Jacques Cronje, Schalk Burger, A J Venter, Gerrie Britz, Bakkies Botha, Eddie Andrews, John Smit (captain), Os du Randt.
Replacements: Joe van Niekerk, Gaffie du Toit, CJ van der Linde.

REFEREE: Chris White (England)

CROWD: 42,107

AUSTRALIA 23, NEW ZEALAND 18

AT TELSTRA STADIUM, SYDNEY, 7 AUGUST

THE ALL BLACKS NEEDED LITTLE REMINDER of what transpired the last time they faced the Wallabies in Sydney. Hot favourites then, they crashed out of the World Cup at the semi-final stage, out-thought and comprehensively outplayed by a less athletically gifted, but more mature side prepared by the canny Eddie Jones.

Much the same could be said of this game. The All Blacks knew a rare Sydney win would give them one hand on the Tri-nations Trophy for an unprecedented third year on the trot. But they were lacking confidence within their talented back division, and their forwards, so forceful in the Wellington wet, had not marked up in Christchurch. There was to be none of the rampant All Blacks play of a year earlier when Joe Rokocoko made Wendell Sailor's life a misery as he ran in a hat trick of tries.

Pre-match there was drama of sorts when All Black management told the players a suspected terror attack had been planned for their test a week hence at Ellis Park. Andrew Mehrtens played down any talk of a possible return home or any impact on concentration levels for the Wallaby test.

'It was important we decided we weren't going over there with anything in the back of our minds or any worries at all,' said Mehrtens. 'Everyone had to be comfortable with it . . . and the guys came pretty quickly to the conclusion we wanted to get over there and get stuck into the game.'

They got stuck into this game, hitting rucks with venom and stretching the Wallabies' defence to the limit. The penalty count went in the All Blacks' favour, and they led 9–0 before a quarter of the match had expired.

But the Justin Marshall–Carlos Spencer axis was not firing as it should have been, and the All Blacks were starting to raise the ire of referee Kaplan. The 12-all deadlock looked tenuous when Ali Williams was sent to the bin and George Smith's hegemony at the breakdown started to wear down the nous and energy of the All Blacks, who reverted to using one-out runners in preference to pick and go.

Lote Tuqiri's try, seven minutes after the resumption, was decisive and the dynamic George Smith was appropriately the man to deliver the final pass (after No 8 David Lyons had ignored an overlap not long before).

The All Blacks saw enough possession late in the match to post a try, but their workmanlike pack and impatient backs were not good enough to deliver in the face of typically staunch Wallaby tackling. Eddie Jones charitably remarked that the All Blacks were on the right track with their flatter backline alignment. He predicted they would cut loose in Johannesburg.

Interestingly, there were five goal kickers used in this encounter, Dan Carter, Carlos Spencer and Andrew Mehrtens for the All Blacks and Matt Burke and Matt Giteau for the Wallabies, all of whom raised the flags at various stages.

FOR AUSTRALIA: Try by Lote Tuqiri; 4 penalty goals by Matt Giteau, 2 penalty goals by Matt Burke.

FOR NEW ZEALAND: 4 penalty goals by Dan Carter; penalty goals by Carlos Spencer and Andrew Mehrtens.

AUSTRALIA: Chris Latham, Clyde Rathbone, Stirling Mortlock, Matt Giteau, Lote Tuqiri, Stephen Larkham, George Gregan (captain), David Lyons, Phil Waugh, George Smith, Nathan Sharpe, Justin Harrison, Al Baxter, Brendan Cannon, Bill Young. Replacements: Matt Dunning, Matt Burke, Jeremy Paul, Dan Vickerman, John Roe, Wendell Sailor.

NEW ZEALAND: Mils Muliaina, Doug Howlett, Tana Umaga (captain), Dan Carter, Joe Rokocoko, Carlos Spencer, Justin Marshall, Xavier Rush, Marty Holah, Jono Gibbes, Ali Williams, Chris Jack, Carl Hayman, Keven Mealamu, Kees Meeuws. Replacements: Sam Tuitupou, Andrew Mehrtens, Mose Tuiali'i, Greg Somerville.

REFEREE: Jonathan Kaplan (South Africa)

CROWD: 83,147

SOUTH AFRICA 40, NEW ZEALAND 26

AT ELLIS PARK, JOHANNESBURG, 14 AUGUST

IT WAS 24 YEARS SINCE a Springbok had scored a hat trick of tries against the All Blacks, but Marius Joubert managed it in glorious fashion as the searing sun beat down on Ellis Park. Not everyone was as certain as Springbok coach Jake White that Joubert was the ideal player to partner De Wet Barry in midfield, having been sent off against Australia in 2002 and been found guilty, at one stage of his career, of making racist comments. But this was Joubert's day, two of his tries coming in the first spell, after the All Blacks had established an early 10–nil advantage, the other just before full time.

'It's a fairytale,' he told the media afterwards. 'Never in my wildest dreams could I have imagined myself scoring three tries against the All Blacks. I wouldn't have scored one, let alone three, had it not been for the remarkable spirit within the team. We have a Springbok team for the future here.'

The Springboks, who'd positioned themselves well in the competition by taking bonus points from their matches in Christchurch and Perth, were strengthened by the return of lock Victor Matfield and loose forward Joe van Niekerk. Matfield had managed only 20 minutes of Currie Cup action, but coach White was keen to get him involved, and he responded with a huge performance.

The All Blacks arrived battered and bruised from their game in Sydney. Dan Carter was forced out with injury and although Sam Tuitupou was carrying bruised ribs, he was included on the strength of his 38-minute performance (as a substitute) against Australia.

The All Blacks led 10–nil early through a brilliantly taken try by fullback Mils Muliaina, but from then on the Springboks were in charge, even though a Joe Rokocoko try in the 53rd minute and an Andrew Mehrtens penalty goal in the 64th minute had the All Blacks in front 23–22 and then 26–25. But the Springboks finished over the top of the visitors, tries by Jean de Villiers and Joubert giving them a handsome victory.

Although Mehrtens made little impact as a first-five, he kicked well, in the process becoming the first player in the history of the game to land 50 penalty goals against a single opponent. His 209 points against South Africa was also a record for one player.

The result meant the Springboks could advance to Durban with an excellent chance of claiming their first Tri-nations title since 1998.

Interestingly, only two of the All Black forwards who played in this game (Chris Jack and Carl Hayman) would appear in the starting line-up against France in Paris three months later.

FOR SOUTH AFRICA: Tries by Marius Joubert 3, Breyton Paulse and Jean de Villiers; 3 conversions and 3 penalty goals by Percy Montgomery.

FOR NEW ZEALAND: Tries by Mils Muliaina and Joe Rokocoko; 2 conversions and 4 penalty goals by Andrew Mehrtens.

SOUTH AFRICA: Percy Montgomery, Breyton Paulse, Marius Joubert, De Wet Barry, Jean de Villiers, Jaco van der Westhuyzen, Bolla Conradie, Joe van Niekerk, Schalk Burger, Gerrie Britz, Victor Matfield, Bakkies Botha, Eddie Andrews, John Smit (captain), Os du Randt.
Replacements: C J van der Linde, Fourie du Preez, A J Venter, Jacques Cronje, Hanyani Shimange.

NEW ZEALAND: Mils Muliaina, Doug Howlett, Tana Umaga (captain), Sam Tuitupou, Joe Rokocoko, Andrew Mehrtens, Justin Marshall, Xavier Rush, Marty Holah, Jono Gibbes, Simon Maling, Chris Jack, Carl Hayman, Keven Mealamu, Kees Meeuws.
Replacements: Craig Newby, Mose Tuiali'i, Greg Somerville, Byron Kelleher, Aaron Mauger.

REFEREE: Nigel Williams (Wales)

CROWD: 68,000

SOUTH AFRICA 23, AUSTRALIA 19

AT ABSA STADIUM, DURBAN, 21 AUGUST

JAKE WHITE HAD ASSURED his captain John Smit that he would be holding the Tri-nations Trophy aloft at Durban, and so it came to pass after the Springboks overwhelmed the Wallabies in the second spell of the decider at ABSA Stadium. From 0–7 behind moments before the interval, the Springboks didn't let up until they had established a commanding, and ultimately winning, lead of 23–7. Although the Wallabies uncorked a rousing finish, it was too little too late, allowing the Springboks to claim the Tri-nations for only the second time in nine years.

No one was more delighted at the outcome than Smit, who, some critics claimed, was not the best hooker in South Africa. Those critics didn't have much credibility after this game, in which Smit turned in a massive performance.

Afterwards, he lauded coach White. 'Jake has created an unbelievable environment,' he said. 'He has been consistent in selections and honest from day one. He coached a lot of these guys from under-21 level, and it's showing.'

Fifty-two thousand crammed into the ground, in perfect conditions, and looked on patiently while the teams effectively arm-wrestled each other throughout the opening spell. A Lote Tuqiri try, converted, was responded to on the tick of half-time by a Percy Montgomery penalty goal.

The third quarter was all South Africa's. Victor Matfield, who has scored a surprising number of test tries for a lock, and fellow forward Joe van Niekerk scored tries and with a succession of conversions and penalty goals from Percy Montgomery the Springboks appeared to be home and hosed at 23–7.

However, Montgomery's temporary banishment by referee Paddy O'Brien for persistent infringing allowed the Wallabies to stem the tide and launch a late revival. But there was only a minute remaining after George Smith's try, and the Springboks weren't going to let this one get away.

Wallaby coach Eddie Jones took the loss on the chin. 'The better team won, without doubt,' he conceded. 'I will not retract my comment that this is the best Tri-nations competition we have been involved in.'

Marius Joubert shows his delight after the victory over Australia in Durban. Fotopress

FOR SOUTH AFRICA: Tries by Victor Matfield and Joe van Niekerk; 2 conversions and 3 penalty goals by Percy Montgomery.

FOR AUSTRALIA: Tries by Lote Tuqiri, Stirling Mortlock and George Smith; 2 conversions by Matt Giteau.

SOUTH AFRICA: Percy Montgomery, Breyton Paulse, Marius Joubert, De Wet Barry, Jean de Villiers, Jaco van der Westhuyzen, Bolla Conradie, Joe van Niekerk, Schalk Burger, A J Venter, Victor Matfield, Bakkies Botha, Eddie Andrews, John Smit (captain), Os du Randt.
Replacements: Jacques Cronje, Fourie du Preez, Gerrie Britz, C J van der Linde, Hanyani Shimange.

AUSTRALIA: Chris Latham, Clyde Rathbone, Stirling Mortlock, Matt Giteau, Lote Tuqiri, Stephen Larkham, George Gregan (captain), David Lyons, Phil Waugh, George Smith, Nathan Sharpe, Justin Harrison, Al Baxter, Brendan Cannon, Bill Young.
Replacements: John Roe, Dan Vickerman, Jeremy Paul, Wendell Sailor, Matt Dunning, Matt Burke.

REFEREE: Paddy O'Brien (New Zealand)

CROWD: 52,000

2005

ALL BLACK COACH GRAHAM HENRY branded the Tri-nations the toughest competition in the world after his team had survived a brazen comeback by the Wallabies at Eden Park to clinch their sixth title in 10 years.

Henry, whose team had bowed to the Jake White-prepared Springboks in 2004, claimed the quality of rugby produced in the Tri-nations was greater than in the British Lions series that had preceded it. And he branded the Springboks and the Wallabies better teams than the Lions. 'New Zealand, Australia and South Africa are the three best teams in the world,' he said. 'The Tri-nations is a marvellous series and it's a huge thrill to win it.'

The All Blacks rebounded from a loss to the Springboks in Cape Town to finish with three wins, edging out the Springboks on bonus points.

Eddie Jones's Wallabies finished winless — indeed, their loss in the final encounter at Eden Park meant they had endured five successive test defeats for the first time since 1969 — but, man, did they threaten the All Blacks in the finale at Eden Park. Rebounding from 20–nil, they closed to 19–20 at one stage of the second half. A Wallaby win would have gifted the Tri-nations Trophy to South Africa again, but the All Blacks managed to wrap it up with a Doug Howlett try eight minutes from time.

The Springboks finished with more wins and more championship points than in 2004 but had to settle for second placing this time. They scored victories at Pretoria, Cape Town and Perth, in the process stamping themselves as champion burglars of tries. They created just one themselves in the entire series but were sensationally efficient at converting opponents' mistakes into five-pointers.

Wingers were the standout players in 2005: newcomer Bryan Habana for the Springboks, who specialised in length-of-the-field tries; Joe Rokocoko and Doug Howlett, who scored three tries each for the All Blacks; and, in the enthralling final game at Eden Park, Mark Gerrard for the Wallabies.

While Henry and White were lauded for their achievements as coaches, Eddie Jones, Australia's mentor, came in for harsh criticism from both media

Keven Mealamu, Mils Muliaina, Joe Rokocoko and the newest All Black, halfback Kevin Senio, celebrate New Zealand's 2005 Tri-nations victory. Fotopress

and public, as his team stumbled from loss to loss. Many were also calling for the head of skipper George Gregan, who saved his best performance for Eden Park where he equalled Englishman Jason Leonard's record of 114 test appearances.

Springbok fullback Percy Montgomery emerged as the leading individual scorer with 52 points. All Black flyhalf Dan Carter, who might have challenged him, dropped out after breaking his leg at Sydney.

2005 FINAL STANDINGS

	P	W	L	D	For	Against	Points
New Zealand	4	3	I	–	III	86	15
South Africa	4	3	I	–	93	82	13
Australia	4	–	4	–	72	108	2

Tries: New Zealand 12, South Africa 7, Australia 7; Total 26.

Penalty goals: South Africa 12, New Zealand 11, Australia 9; Total 32.

THE GAMES
SOUTH AFRICA 22, AUSTRALIA 16

AT LOFTUS VERSFELD, PRETORIA, 30 JULY

IT WASN'T THE ONFIELD ACHIEVEMENTS but the nocturnal antics of several members of the Australian team for which the opening encounter of the 2005 Tri-nations will be remembered. Staggeringly, a group of Wallabies were still at a nightclub in Cape Town around 4 a.m. two days before their international against the Springboks. This inappropriate behaviour came to the sporting world's attention because Brumbies halfback Matt Henjak became embroiled in an altercation with team-mate Lote Tuqiri and threw ice at him, having earlier been reprimanded by nightclub staff for causing a disturbance.

It turned out that Henjak had quite a history of outrageous behaviour in similar circumstances. The Wallabies management were not impressed and dealt him the ultimate penalty — sending him home — Henjak thus becoming the first Australian rugby player to suffer this indignity since Ross Cullen was despatched from the 1966–67 tour of the UK for biting the ear of an opponent. Tuqiri and Wendell Sailor were each fined $500 and given suspended sentences for their part in the affair.

Following the team's heavy defeat in the Nelson Mandela Trophy match a few days earlier at Ellis Park, the Cape Town incident left the Wallabies a maligned, desperate team. Few people gave them much hope of success in the Tri-nations opener.

But Australian coach Eddie Jones is a shrewd tactician and he devised a game plan based around an aerial bombardment of the Springbok back three that almost brought about a stunning victory. The Wallabies were ahead 13–6 at half-time and 16–13 entering the final quarter, but the Springboks were able to lift the intensity and secure the win courtesy of Percy Montgomery's deadly accurate boot, with André Pretorius adding a last-minute dropped goal.

Australia's aerial assault unsettled Montgomery and allowed the Wallabies to create the situations from which Matt Giteau could land penalty goals and flanker George Smith could crash over from an attacking scrum.

Breyton Paulse celebrates his matchwinning try at Pretoria with a somersault. Fotopress

And so the Wallabies have still never won a test in Pretoria and nor have they won a game at any South African venue with Eddie Jones as coach.

FOR SOUTH AFRICA: **Try by Breyton Paulse; conversion, 3 penalty goals and a dropped goal by Percy Montgomery; dropped goal by André Pretorius.**

FOR AUSTRALIA: **Try by George Smith; conversion and 3 penalty goals by Matt Giteau.**

SOUTH AFRICA: **Percy Montgomery, Breyton Paulse, Jaque Fourie, Jean de Villiers, Bryan Habana, André Pretorius, Fourie du Preez, Jacques Cronje, Juan Smith, Joe van Niekerk, Victor Matfield, Bakkies Botha, C J van der Linde, John Smit (captain), Gurthro Steenkamp.**
Replacements: Wayne Julies, Ricky Januarie, Schalk Burger, Albert van den Berg, Gary Botha.

AUSTRALIA: **Chris Latham, Wendell Sailor, Morgan Turinui, Matt Giteau, Lote Tuqiri, Stephen Larkham, George Gregan (captain), John Roe, George Smith, Phil Waugh, Dan Vickerman, Nathan Sharpe, Matt Dunning, Jeremy Paul, Bill Young.**
Replacements: Drew Mitchell, Stirling Mortlock, Rocky Elsom, Mark Chisholm, Al Baxter, Stephen Moore.

REFEREE: **Paul Honiss (New Zealand)**

CROWD: **50,000**

SOUTH AFRICA 22, NEW ZEALAND 16

AT NEWLANDS, CAPE TOWN, 6 AUGUST

WERE THE BRITISH LIONS A FEEBLE OPPONENT, or were the 2005 All Blacks truly awesome? The result of this bruising contest at Cape Town seemed to provide the answer — and it wasn't one Sir Clive Woodward would have appreciated.

The power of the Springbok forwards and the ferocity of the team's tackling so unsettled the All Blacks that Graham Henry's men only intermittently reproduced the quality touches that had swept aside the best of British.

Winning in South Africa is never easy, but, on the strength of their demolition of the Lions, the All Blacks went into the game a warm favourite. However, they seldom gave their supporters much cause for cheer. They were down 0–13 in double-quick time and, although they clawed back to 13-all, the Springboks again opened up a nine-point advantage and, in the finish, the All Blacks were probably fortunate to secure the loser's bonus point.

All Blacks don't intimidate easily, certainly not when someone as courageous as Tana Umaga is captaining the side, but Jake White's Springboks certainly ruffled the visitors, by fair means and foul. Lock Victor Matfield put Byron Kelleher out of the game in the 11th minute with a marginally late, dangerous-looking slam-dunk tackle that despatched the halfback into cuckoo land.

That tackle — which incurred a citing but no suspension — had a profound influence on the outcome of the game, for while Kelleher was battling on, not knowing whether he was at Cape Town or Carisbrook, he gave away a 75-metre intercept try to Jean de Villiers. Given that six points separated the teams at fulltime, it was a definitive moment in the game.

Having to co-exist with a fresh halfback, combined with the Springboks' menacing tackling, resulted in All Black first-five Dan Carter coming seriously back to earth (after scoring a perfect 10 against the Lions in Wellington). Although his goal kicking was again impeccable, he dropped a straightforward pass in front of his goalposts and his tactical kicking in the second half became erratic.

While the All Blacks probably played more rugby than the Springboks, they also made a lot more mistakes, under pressure from the Boks, particularly the dominant loose forwards, among whom Schalk Burger and Juan Smith were outstanding. Flanker Richie McCaw (below his best, following a bout of mumps) declared at the conclusion — speaking on behalf of his captain, Umaga, who was being treated for strained ankle ligaments — "At this level you get only so many scoring opportunities in a game, and you've got to take them. We didn't."

The best of a disappointing All Black team, on a day when a swirling wind made conditions challenging, were elusive winger Rico Gear and replacement halfback Piri Weepu.

FOR SOUTH AFRICA: Try by Jean de Villiers; conversion and 4 penalty goals by Percy Montgomery; dropped goal by André Pretorius.

FOR NEW ZEALAND: Try by Rico Gear; conversion and 3 penalty goals by Dan Carter.

SOUTH AFRICA: Percy Montgomery, Breyton Paulse, Jaque Fourie, Jean de Villiers, Bryan Habana, André Pretorius, Ricky Januarie, Joe van Niekerk, Juan Smith, Schalk Burger, Victor Matfield, Bakkies Botha, C J van der Linde, John Smit (captain), Os du Randt.
Replacements: Fourie du Preez, Gurthro Steenkamp.

NEW ZEALAND: Leon MacDonald, Rico Gear, Tana Umaga (captain), Aaron Mauger, Mils Muliaina, Dan Carter, Byron Kelleher, Rodney So'oialo, Richie McCaw, Jerry Collins, Ali Williams, Chris Jack, Carl Hayman, Keven Mealamu, Tony Woodcock.
Replacements: Joe Rokocoko, Piri Weepu, Greg Somerville, Derren Witcombe.

REFEREE: Andrew Cole (Australia)

CROWD: 49,118

NEW ZEALAND 30, AUSTRALIA 13

AT TELSTRA DOME, SYDNEY, 13 AUGUST

JOE ROKOCOKO HAVING SCORED 27 TRIES IN 23 TESTS, there was general astonishment throughout the rugby world when he failed to win selection in the All Black squad for the British Lions series.

What those outside New Zealand did not appreciate was that by the conclusion of the 2005 Super 12 series, Rokocoko was seriously lacking in form and confidence. And so, with a wealth of talent in the wing position, the All Black selectors consigned him to New Zealand sevens duties, knowing that Gordon Tietjens would sharpen him up. Intriguingly, the player who replaced him against the Lions was his Fijian-born cousin Sitiveni Sivivatu.

Rokocoko recaptured his confidence in Tietjens' capable care and was reintroduced to the All Blacks for the Tri-nations series. He came off the bench at Cape Town, where he looked good, and was handed back the No 11 jersey for Sydney. Eddie Jones' Wallabies must be wishing he'd stayed out of the frame, for he emerged as the most dangerous attacking individual in this crucial encounter that neither side could afford to lose.

After the All Blacks had endured a nightmarish replay of events at Cape Town, again finding themselves 13–nil down in 13 minutes, Rokocoko, adopting a more physical attitude, brilliantly set up a try for halfback Piri Weepu and, in the final moments, uncorked a spectacular 80-metre chip-and-retrieve five-pointer for himself.

The All Blacks won the second phase of this game 30–nil, overcoming the Telstra Dome bogey through the power of their scrum, the quality of their defence (particularly in the second half when the Wallabies came at them in waves), and through the genius of individuals like Rokocoko, Richie McCaw and Aaron Mauger.

The previous 11 Tri-nations fixtures had been won by the home team, so the All Blacks' victory was as exceptional as it was decisive. And it was achieved without first-choice halfback Byron Kelleher who was concussed. Weepu, his replacement, gave a most accomplished performance.

The turning point came in the 66th minute when McCaw tapped a penalty 5 metres out and then drove through George Gregan and several colleagues to plant the ball across the line.

English referee Tony Spreadbury came in for widespread criticism for many of his rulings, particularly at the scrum where Australia struggled. As former All Black prop John Drake put it, 'It was a disgrace that such power and technique [from the All Blacks] should be punished when the jellyfish survived.'

It was a bruising match. The All Blacks lost Dan Carter with a broken leg, while the Wallabies had to replace four injured players (Matt Giteau, Elton Flatley, Morgan Turinui and Jeremy Paul).

FOR NEW ZEALAND: Tries by Piri Weepu, Richie McCaw and Joe Rokocoko; 2 conversions and 3 penalty goals by Dan Carter; conversion by Luke McAlister.

FOR AUSTRALIA: Try by Drew Mitchell; conversion and 2 penalty goals by Matt Giteau.

AUSTRALIA: Drew Mitchell, Mark Gerrard, Stirling Mortlock, Morgan Turinui, Lote Tuqiri, Matt Giteau, George Gregan (captain), David Lyons, George Smith, John Roe, Nathan Sharpe, Dan Vickerman, Al Baxter, Jeremy Paul, Bill Young.
Replacements: Clyde Rathbone, Elton Flatley, Chris Whitaker, Phil Waugh, Mark Chisholm, Matt Dunning, Brendan Cannon.

NEW ZEALAND: Mils Muliaina, Rico Gear, Tana Umaga, Aaron Mauger, Joe Rokocoko, Dan Carter, Piri Weepu, Rodney So'oialo, Richie McCaw, Jerry Collins, Ali Williams, Chris Jack, Carl Hayman, Keven Mealamu, Tony Woodcock.
Replacements: Luke McAlister, Greg Somerville, Derren Witcombe.

REFEREE: Tony Spreadbury (England)

CROWD: 82,309

SOUTH AFRICA 22, AUSTRALIA 19

AT SUBIACO OVAL, PERTH, 20 AUGUST

FLYING WINGER BRYAN HABANA was the toast of South Africa after two length-of-the-field tries at Subiaco Oval allowed the Springboks to finally break through for a win outside South Africa.

Not since 1998, when they enjoyed double successes at Perth and Wellington, had the South Africans managed to win a Tri-nations fixture on the road. And it seemed nothing was going to change when they trailed 19–22 and were being subjected to intense pressure from the depleted, beleaguered Wallabies.

But suddenly, after seven or eight phases deep inside the Springbok 22, Wallaby winger Mat Rogers spilled the ball forward, presenting Percy Montgomery with a golden opportunity for a counterattack. The ball was expedited through replacement flyhalf Jaco van der Westhuyzen and Jaque Fourie to Habana whose blistering pace was too much for the Australian cover defence. In almost identical circumstances, Habana had scored another 90-metre try in the second minute of the game after Schalk Burger had cleverly scooped up a loose ball inches from his own goalline.

The 21-year-old Habana, who had made his test debut against England at Twickenham in November 2004 (scoring a try, of course), has rapidly become one of the game's leading celebrities. Nicknamed 'Brock', his try at Perth gave him 12 tries from 11 test appearances. He's not only sensationally fast, he's also an integral part of the Springboks' hugely effective aggressive defence that once again restricted the Wallabies to one try.

Eddie Jones' Wallabies were surprisingly competitive for a team ravaged by injury. It was bad enough that Stephen Larkham, Wendell Sailor, Chris Latham and Stirling Mortlock could not be considered for selection, but Elton Flatley compounded matters by withdrawing 10 minutes before kick-off suffering from blurred vision. Flatley, who has a history of concussions, had taken a bump to the head during the team's warm-up.

So just moments before the team ran onto Subiaco Oval, Jones had to switch Matt Giteau to flyhalf and bring Clyde Rathbone off the bench into centre. There wasn't time for them to change jerseys, so Giteau operated in No 12 and Rathbone in No 22.

The most surprised individual of all was Brumbies utility back Adam Ashley-Cooper, who'd been called in to train with the team. He was about to buy a pie and take a seat in the grandstand when Jones told him he was a reserve. With no number on his jersey at all, he replaced Rathbone for the final four minutes of the game.

Although Montgomery's goal kicking was erratic, three penalty goals and a dropped goal allowed his team to build a 17–9 lead by the 50th minute before a storming burst by Morgan Turinui gave Rathbone a try and brought Australia up to 16–17. When Rogers added a penalty goal in the 60th minute, it seemed the Wallabies might, against the odds, pull off a famous victory. But Habana was to have the last say.

FOR SOUTH AFRICA: 2 tries by Bryan Habana; 3 penalty goals and a dropped goal by Percy Montgomery.

FOR AUSTRALIA: Try by Clyde Rathbone; conversion and 3 penalty goals by Mat Rogers; penalty goal by Matt Giteau.

AUSTRALIA: Drew Mitchell, Mat Rogers, Clyde Rathbone, Morgan Turinui, Lote Tuqiri, Matt Giteau, George Gregan (captain), David Lyons, Phil Waugh, Rocky Elsom, Nathan Sharpe, Dan Vickerman, Al Baxter, Brendan Cannon, Bill Young.
Replacements: Chris Whitaker, John Roe, George Smith, Matt Dunning, Adam Ashley-Cooper.

SOUTH AFRICA: Percy Montgomery, Breyton Paulse, Jaque Fourie, Jean de Villiers, Bryan Habana, André Pretorius, Ricky Januarie, Joe van Niekerk, Schalk Burger, Juan Smith, Victor Matfield, Bakkies Botha, C J van der Linde, John Smit (captain), Os du Randt.
Replacements: Jaco van der Westhuyzen, Fourie du Preez, Albert van den Berg, Gurthro Steemkamp.

REFEREE: Alain Rolland (Ireland)

CROWD: 43,278

NEW ZEALAND 31, SOUTH AFRICA 27

AT CARISBROOK, DUNEDIN, 27 AUGUST

CARISBROOK REMAINS THE HOUSE OF PAIN for the Springboks. Unsuccessful at the venue in 84 years of trying, they had their breakthrough victory wrenched away from them by Keven Mealamu in the dying minutes of this pulsating international.

With the Wallabies out of the reckoning, the two great rivals knew the importance of winning this encounter, and so they gave it everything they had. The All Blacks constructed tries, the Springboks burgled them. But they all counted, and when the Springboks went ahead 27–24 inside the final quarter the challenge was laid down to Graham Henry's men. They had destroyed the Lions, they were ranked No 1 in the rugby world and they had enthralled their fans with a wonderful new haka. All that mattered now, however, was whether they could conjure up a try that would end South Africa's unbeaten run in the 2005 competition and prove they were a genuinely quality side.

Intelligent use of the reserves bench played an important part in the All Blacks' success. Leon Macdonald, who had performed outstandingly at first-five in the absence of injured Daniel Carter, gave way to Luke McAlister, who turned in a brilliant cameo performance. He twice probed South Africa's tiring defence and then placed an inch-perfect kick through that set the All Blacks up for their winning assault.

After a couple of near misses, South Africa's fate was sealed when the All Blacks drove with precision off an Ali Williams line-out take. They succeeded in splintering the Springbok forwards, creating a vast gulf through which Mealamu burst for the winning try. Four minutes remained as McAlister slotted the wide-angle conversion. It wasn't enough time for the South Africans to steal another try.

Mealamu and winger Joe Rokocoko were New Zealand's special heroes. Mealamu set up a try for Macdonald and scored the matchwinner himself, while Rokocoko completed two sensational opportunist tries in the opening spell, beating five South African defenders for the second.

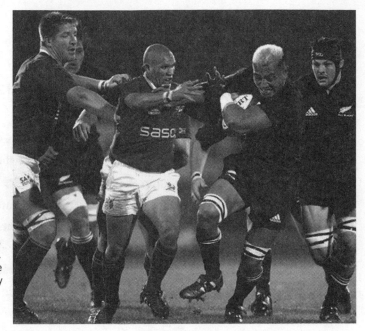

Jerry Collins powers ahead at Carisbrook. Others, from left, are Bakkies Botha, Ricky Januarie and Richie McCaw.

Fotopress

The All Blacks had a distinct edge in the scrums and held steady in the line-outs. They negated South Africa's awesome midfield defence by probing in close to the rucks and scrums through Piri Weepu and Macdonald.

Springbok coach Jake White took the setback philosophically. 'We've come from ranking sixth in the world to second in 12 months,' he said. 'That is something to be proud of.'

FOR NEW ZEALAND: Tries by Joe Rokocoko 2, Leon Macdonald and Keven Mealamu; 3 conversions and a penalty goal by Leon Macdonald; conversion by Luke McAlister.

FOR SOUTH AFRICA: Tries by Bryan Habana, Ricky Januarie and Jacques Fourie; 3 conversions and 2 penalty goals by Percy Montgomery.

NEW ZEALAND: Mils Muliaina, Rico Gear, Tana Umaga (captain), Aaron Mauger, Joe Rokocoko, Leon Macdonald, Piri Weepu, Rodney So'oialo, Richie McCaw, Jerry Collins, Ali Williams, Chris Jack, Carl Hayman, Keven Mealamu, Tony Woodcock. Replacements: Luke McAlister, James Ryan, Greg Somerville.

SOUTH AFRICA: Percy Montgomery, Bryan Habana, Jaque Fourie, De Wet Barry, Jean de Villiers, André Pretorius, Ricky Januarie, Joe van Niekerk, Juan Smith, Schalk Burger, Victor Matfield, Bakkies Botha, C J van der Linde, John Smit (captain), Os du Randt. Replacements: Jaco van der Westhuyzen, Jacques Cronje, Eddie Andrews.

REFEREE: Joel Jutge (France).

CROWD: 29,500.

NEW ZEALAND 34, AUSTRALIA 24

AT EDEN PARK, AUCKLAND, 3 SEPTEMBER

THE TRY-SCORING BRILLIANCE OF RECALLED WINGER Doug Howlett and the golden boot of young Luke McAlister rescued the All Blacks just when it seemed the impossible was going to happen at Eden Park. The beleaguered Wallabies were close to ruining the All Blacks' Tri-nations party.

The injury-ravaged Australians, without a win in the competition, were seemingly down and out when the scoreboard read 20–nil to Tana Umaga's men after 28 minutes. But they struck back so courageously they silenced the Eden Park faithful as they closed to 19–20 and 24–29 in a desperate second spell.

It took a sweet try in the 72nd minute by Howlett, who'd been on the outer since the first Lions test, to finally repel the Wallabies' brave challenge. Howlett, who gave an impeccable performance, became the first All Black to achieve a hat-trick of tries against the Wallabies on Eden Park.

One of those tries was created for him by towering lock Ali Williams, who, after tapping a penalty, nudged a beautifully judged crosskick out to the winger. It's a ploy inside backs use often, but this was undoubtedly a famous first for a 2.02-metre lock.

All Black coach Graham Henry said he made a rude comment regarding the kick because he didn't see Howlett out wide calling for the ball. 'It's great for players to express themselves,' he admitted later.

Henry was all smiles at the final whistle. 'We've won three trophies, so we're delighted,' he said. 'We've come back from difficult situations, we've won games from behind. We got ourselves into a bit of trouble tonight but we dug ourselves out of it. It's been the biggest season in All Black history with the Lions and the Tri-nations.'

It was always going to be a tough night for the Wallabies. Missing Stephen Larkham, Matt Giteau and Elton Flatley, three of 17 players on the injury list, they installed Mat Rogers at flyhalf. He responded well, growing in confidence and having a major hand in the team's second-half fightback. Australia's standout player, however, was winger Mark Gerrard, who created his team's first try for lock Mark Chisholm before scoring a beauty himself.

The 22-year-old McAlister again proved himself an ideal impact player when he landed three penalty goals in 10 minutes after coming off the bench to replace Leon Macdonald (who'd been cleared to play only on the morning of the match). The same couldn't be said for Australia's tubby prop Matt Dunning, who conceded the first two of those penalties within four minutes of joining the action.

Wallaby skipper George Gregan was so focused on the encounter, in which he equalled Jason Leonard's world record of 114 test appearances, that he ran on to Eden Park without his jersey on. It wasn't until he began to unzip his tracksuit top following the anthems and the All Black haka that he realised his blunder. 'It's the first time I've ever made that mistake,' he confessed later.

The loss was Australia's fifth in succession, the first time that had occurred since 1969. Coach Eddie Jones, who'd been under pressure from his media, took this latest reversal on the chin. 'We could take some promising things out of this performance,' he said, 'but I don't take much solace from the result. The All Blacks' composure under pressure won the night. They had it, we didn't.'

FOR NEW ZEALAND: Tries by Doug Howlett 3 and Richie McCaw; conversion by Leon Macdonald; penalty goals by Luke McAlister 3 and Macdonald.

FOR AUSTRALIA: Tries by Mark Chisholm, Mark Gerrard, Lote Tuqiri and Lloyd Johansson; 2 conversions by Mat Rogers.

NEW ZEALAND: Mils Muliaina, Doug Howlett, Tana Umaga (captain), Aaron Mauger, Joe Rokocoko, Leon Macdonald, Piri Weepu, Rodney So'oialo, Richie McCaw, Sione Lauaki, Ali Williams, Chris Jack, Carl Hayman, Keven Mealamu, Tony Woodcock. Replacements: Luke McAlister, Kevin Senio, James Ryan, Greg Somerville.

AUSTRALIA: Drew Mitchell, Mark Gerrard, Clyde Rathbone, Morgan Turinui, Lote Tuqiri, Mat Rogers, George Gregan (captain), George Smith, Phil Waugh, Rocky Elsom, Nathan Sharpe, Mark Chisholm, Al Baxter, Brendan Cannon, Bill Young. Replacements: Lloyd Johansson, Chris Whitaker, Alex Kanaar, Mat Dunning.

REFEREE: Chris White (England)

CROWD: 45,000

THE STAR
KEVEN MEALAMU

Fotopress

It wasn't that Keven Mealamu did not enjoy operating as a loose forward — he'd been good enough to win selection for New Zealand schools and New Zealand under-16 in the position: the decision in 1998 to switch to hooker was about being realistic.

A coaching colleague had convinced him he would not progress much further towards the All Blacks as a flanker because he was a runt. As a hooker, however, he had a lot more going for him. Mealamu agreed to make the switch on his own terms. He accepted he was never going to be tall or possess mega power, so he would emphasise the qualities with which he had been blessed: speed and a low centre of gravity.

Almost from the moment he donned the No 2 jersey his career took off, spectacularly, except when the Auckland Blues overlooked him, resulting in him playing the 2001 Super 12 campaign for the Chiefs. He made such an impact that within 12 months he was an All Black.

Mealamu would diligently remain behind after representative trainings, practising running in and scooping up the ball, until he had perfected the move. It is one of his trademarks now. Another is his exceptional ability to step through tackles because he is built so low to the ground.

Born in 1979 and educated at Aorere College, with a brother who has represented Samoa, Mealamu is disarmingly nice, a charming family man whose presence in the forward cauldron that is test rugby seems almost incongruous.

Benefiting from the serious injury that sidelined Anton Oliver for the 2005 international programme, Mealamu became a national hero with his match (and Tri-nations) winning try in the dying stages of the epic encounter against the Springboks at Carisbrook. His being a lightweight (at 105kg) by modern test standards did not stop the All Black scrum outgunning the Boks. 'Scrummaging is about technique, not size,' said Mealamu afterwards. He should know!

TRI-NATIONS STATISTICS

SUMMARY OF TRI-NATIONS FINISHING POSITIONS, 1996–2005

	1996	1997	1998	1999	2000	2001	2002	2003	2004	2005
New Zealand	1	1	3	1	2	2	1	1	3	1
Australia	3	3	2	2	1	1	2	2	2	3
South Africa	2	2	1	3	3	3	3	3	1	2

Most points
328 Andrew Mehrtens (New Zealand)
271 Matt Burke (Australia)
158 Percy Montgomery (South Africa)
153 Carlos Spencer (New Zealand)
94 Braam van Straaten (South Africa)
89 Stirling Mortlock (Australia)
80 Christian Cullen (New Zealand)

Most tries
16 Christian Cullen (New Zealand)
13 Doug Howlett (New Zealand)
10 Joe Rokocoko (New Zealand)
9 Joe Roff (Australia)

9 Justin Marshall (New Zealand)
7 Matt Burke (Australia)
7 Stirling Mortlock (Australia)
6 Ben Tune (Australia)
6 Chris Latham (Australia)
6 Tana Umaga (New Zealand)
5 Jeff Wilson (New Zealand)
5 Stephen Larkham (Australia)
5 Marius Joubert (South Africa)

Total tries scored, 1996–2005
New Zealand 102
Australia 82
South Africa 79